# THE CHRONICLE OF AN ANONYMOUS ROMAN

# THE CHRONICLE OF AN ANONYMOUS ROMAN

ROME, ITALY, AND LATIN CHRISTENDOM, C.1325–1360

✻

TRANSLATED,
WITH AN INTRODUCTION,
BY
JAMES A. PALMER

ITALICA PRESS
NEW YORK & BRISTOL
2021

COPYRIGHT © 2021 BY JAMES A. PALMER
ITALICA PRESS, INC.
99 WALL STREET, NEW YORK, NY 10005

Italica Press Medieval & Renaissance Texts Series

All rights reserved. No part of this publication may be reproduced, stored in a retrieval system, or transmitted, in any form or by any means, electronic, mechanical, photocopying, recording, or otherwise, without prior permission of Italica Press. It may not be used in a course-pack or any other collection without prior permission of Italica Press. Please contact inquiries@italicapress.com.

**Library of Congress Cataloging-in-Publication Data**
Names: Palmer, James A. (James Allen), 1977- editor, translator, writer of introduction.
Title: The chronicle of an anonymous Roman : Rome, Italy, and Latin Christendom, c.1325-1360 / translated, with an introduction by James A. Palmer.
Other titles: Vita di Cola di Rienzo. English.
Description: New York ; Bristol : Italica Press, Inc., 2021. | Series: Italica Press medieval & Renaissance texts | Includes bibliographical references and index. | Summary: ""The Chronicle of an Anonymous Roman" offers the first complete English translation of the Anonimo Romano's "Cronica." Includes an introduction to the text and its author, as well as an introduction to its fourteenth-century world"-- Provided by publisher.
Identifiers: LCCN 2021020506 (print) | LCCN 2021020507 (ebook) | ISBN 9781599103846 (hardcover) | ISBN 9781599103853 (trade paperback) | ISBN
  9781599103860 (kindle edition) | ISBN 9781599104140 (pdf)
Subjects: LCSH: Rienzo, Cola di, -1354. | Rome (Italy)--History--476-1420. | Revolutionaries--Italy--Rome--Biography. | Rome (Italy)--Biography.
Classification: LCC DG811.6 .V6513 2021 (print) | LCC DG811.6 (ebook)
  DDC 945.6/3205092 [B]--dc23
LC record available at https://lccn.loc.gov/2021020506
LC ebook record available at https://lccn.loc.gov/2021020507

Cover image: Paolino Minorita da Venezia, Map of Rome, from *Chronologia Magna*. c. 1325. Venice, Bibl. Marciana, MS. Lat. Z 399 [=1600], fol. 98. Wikimedia. Detail showing the medieval *abitato*, with the Capitoline Hill.

For a complete list of titles in Medieval & Renaissance Texts, visit our website at: http://www.italicapress.com/index003.html.

# CONTENTS

| | |
|---|---|
| LIST OF MAPS | VIII |
| PREFACE & ACKNOWLEDGMENTS | IX |
| INTRODUCTION | I |
| CHAPTER ONE: PROLOGUE | 59 |

### CHAPTER TWO
The people drive Senator Giacomo Savelli from the Campidoglio. The knighting of Messer Stefano Colonna and Messer Napoleone Orsini    64

### CHAPTER THREE
The prince of Morea is defeated at the Porta Castel Sant'Angelo. The origins of the Guelfs and Ghibellines. The character of Dante and how he died    67

### CHAPTER FOUR
Pope John and the coming of the Bavarian to Rome, his departure, and the antipope that he created    74

### CHAPTER FIVE
The monster born in Rome. The papal legate is slain in Bologna    75

### CHAPTER SIX
Fra Venturino comes to Rome with the Doves. The bell tower of St. Peter's is burned    79

### CHAPTER SEVEN
Pope Benedict and the roof of St. Peter's in Rome, which was rebuilt    82

### CHAPTER EIGHT
The comet that appeared in parts of Lombardy. The defeat of the tyrant Messer Mastino by the Venetians    87

### CHAPTER NINE
A very cruel famine. The battle of Parabiago in Lombardy. Various new fashions    97

## CHAPTER TEN
The death of King Robert and the coming of the queen of
Hungary to Rome     110

## CHAPTER ELEVEN
The battle for Spain, the destruction of Algeciras, and the siege
of Gibraltar     117

## CHAPTER TWELVE
The duke of Athens is driven from Florence.
Pope Benedict dies. Pope Clement is elected     135

## CHAPTER THIRTEEN
The crusade carried out at Smyrna in Turkey     146

## CHAPTER FOURTEEN
The battle for France, in which the king of Bohemia dies and
the king of England defeats the king of France     161

## CHAPTER FIFTEEN
A great flood and the extent of the waters     175

## CHAPTER SIXTEEN
A ship run aground and robbed on the Roman coast     179

## CHAPTER SEVENTEEN
Leonardo of Orvieto is captured by Rome     182

## CHAPTER EIGHTEEN
The great deeds of Cola di Rienzo, august tribune of Rome     183

## CHAPTER NINETEEN
The death of Andrew, king of Puglia, by hanging.
How justice followed after this death     244

## CHAPTER TWENTY
The king of Hungary enters Italy.
The death of the duke of Durazzo, who is beheaded     244

## CHAPTER TWENTY-ONE
The cruel mortality that afflicted the whole world.
The steps of Sta. Maria in Aracoeli     244

## CHAPTER TWENTY-TWO
The earthquake in Italy 245

## CHAPTER TWENTY-THREE
The fifty-year Jubilee in Rome.
The king of Hungary's return to Rome and Puglia 246

## CHAPTER TWENTY-FOUR
The Perugians lay siege to Bettona, raze that place to its foundations, and behead the traitor, Messer Crispolto 254

## CHAPTER TWENTY-FIVE
The bell tower of St. Peter's in Rome burns.
The pope loses control of the Senate. Pope Clement dies. 255

## CHAPTER TWENTY-SIX
A senator is stoned by the Romans.
The magnificent deeds of Messer Egidio Conchese of Spain, cardinal legate, to retake the Patrimony, the March of Ancona, and Romagna 256

## CHAPTER TWENTY-SEVEN
Messer Cola di Rienzo returns to Rome and reassumes power amid much rejoicing.
He is cruelly slain by the people of Rome 271

## CHAPTER TWENTY-EIGHT
Emperor Charles comes to Rome.
His coronation and his departure for Germany 300

## BIBLIOGRAPHY 301

## INDEX 315

# MAPS

1. Rome in the fourteenth century, showing gates, *rioni*, and major baronial families. Copyright Italica Press.　　XI
2. Central Italy in the fourteenth century. Copyright Italica Press.　　XII
3. Battle of Rio Salado, 1340. From Joseph F. O'Callaghan, *The Gibraltar Crusade: Castile and the Battle for the Strait* (Philadelphia: University of Pennsylvania Press, 2011).　　XIII
4. T-O Map. 12th century. British Library, MS Royal 12 F. IV, fol. 135v. Wikimedia Commons.　　XIII
5. The Aegean Sea. Cartographic Laboratory, University of Wisconsin, Madison.　　XIV
6. The Crécy campaign, from the landing at Saint-Vaast-la-Hougue to the siege of Calais. From *The Battle of Crécy: A Casebook,* Michael Livingston and Kelly DeVries, ed. (Liverpool: Liverpool University Press, 2016).　　XIV

# PREFACE & ACKNOWLEDGEMENTS

I FIRST BEGAN WORKING with the Anonimo Romano in 2010 at Washington University in St. Louis, where I was a graduate student preparing to undertake dissertation research. From my first encounter with the text, I was utterly enamored with the Anonimo's unusual, vivid style and daydreamed about publishing a translation. While in Rome undertaking dissertation research in 2011-2012, I was struck by how little of the Anonimo's city remained, with so much either buried by layers of successive modernities or scraped away to reveal the bones of the classical past. Appreciating the Anonimo's chronicle as a beguiling remnant of a lost world led me to treasure it all the more.

By the time my dissertation was written and defended in 2015, my translation daydreams had evolved into firm intentions, but intentions necessarily delayed. I was extremely fortunate to be offered a tenure-track job in an age of ever leaner employment prospects, which meant that earning tenure immediately became my primary concern. Over the years, many senior scholars had cautioned me that, despite their essential role in teaching and growing the discipline, history departments simply did not value translations highly, tending to prize monographs above all else. So, for several years, my ambition to publish a translation of the Anonimo was put on hold as I worked toward the publication of my "tenure book."

Only in 2018, once that book was out of my hands and into those of the press, was I able at long last to sink happily into the Anonimo's pages and begin work on this translation. Perhaps fittingly for a fourteenth-century text, the introduction and finishing touches were completed during the Covid-19 pandemic of 2020-2021. The work was often done at odd hours as I struggled to balance it and the joyful task of helping to care for a new baby daughter, Charlotte (another pleasure too long delayed by the demands of academia). This translation, then, has been a labor of love, and it is truly a joy to have completed it. Inevitably, I have incurred many debts along the way, the most important of which I now wish to acknowledge.

First, I am indebted to my advisor, Daniel Bornstein, whose own experience as a translator of a medieval chronicle made him an invaluable source of advice from the nascence of the project all the way through to its completion. Heartfelt thanks are also owed to Michael Sherberg, who patiently worked with me during my days as a graduate student struggling to come to grips with fourteenth-century Romanesco. He spent many hours patiently reading through this text with me in his office, and was the first to introduce me to the Italian scholarship on the Anonimo. I am both indebted and extremely grateful to him for his time and guidance.

Time to do one's work is always in short supply, so I must also thank Grinnell College for the time I spent there as a visiting scholar during the 2018–2019 academic year. That year gave me two of the things a scholar values most: time and access to a library. The vast majority of the translation and most of the notes were completed during those months.

I would like to offer special thanks to Ronald G. Musto and Eileen Gardiner at Italica Press. I was delighted and relieved when they, very early on, expressed interest in publishing this translation. Knowing that my work would have a home encouraged me to begin the project in earnest. Working with them has been a pleasure and a boon. Above all, Musto's extensive knowledge of the Anonimo, Rome, and late medieval Italian historical writing have helped me clarify and enrich the introduction and notes beyond what would have been possible otherwise. I will be ever grateful to him and Eileen for helping me bring this project to fruition.

Finally, I dedicate this book to my wife, Weiwei Luo. For her committed partnership in the difficult task of being a "two-body" academic family, and in overcoming the many related challenges that coincided with my work on this book, I will be forever grateful.

James A. Palmer
Florida State University
May 2021

# MAPS

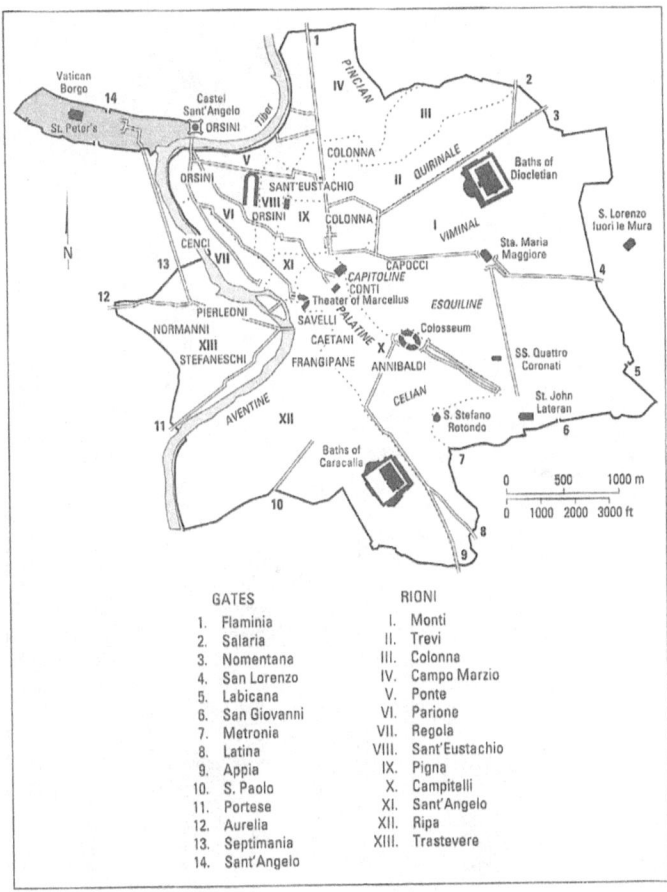

Map. 1. *Rome in the fourteenth century, showing gates,* rioni, *and major baronial families. Italica Press.*

# CHRONICLE OF AN ANONYMOUS ROMAN

*Map 2. Central Italy in the fourteenth century. Italica Press.*

✼ MAPS

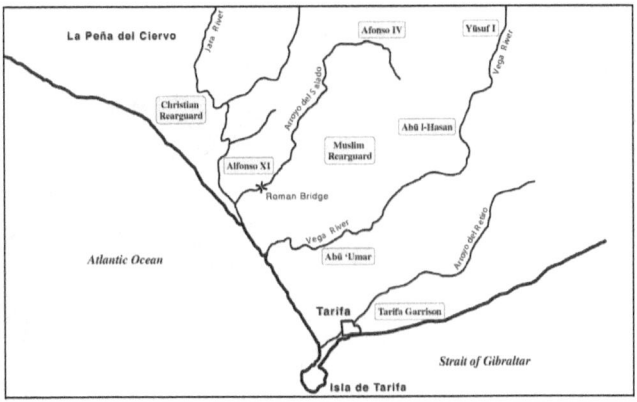

*Map 3 (above). Battle of Rio Salado, 1340. From Joseph F. O'Callaghan,* The Gibraltar Crusade: Castile and the Battle for the Strait *(Philadelphia: University of Pennsylvania Press, 2011).*
*Map. 4 (below). T-O Map. 12th century. British Library, MS Royal 12 F. IV, fol.135v. Wikimedia Commons.*

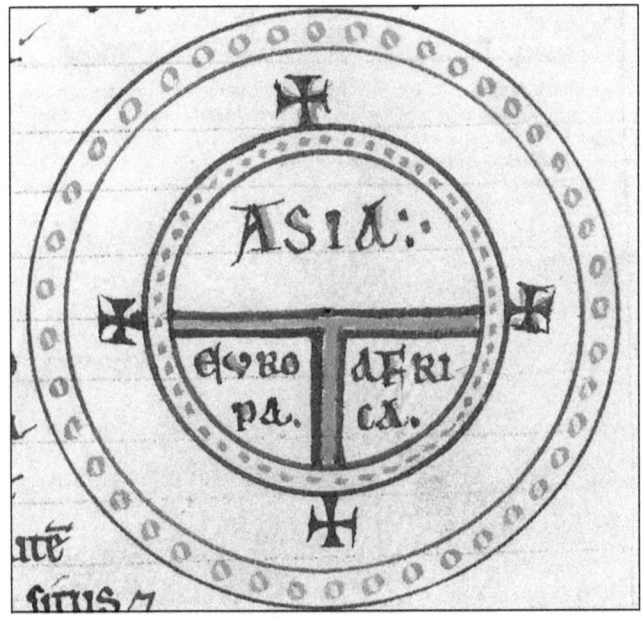

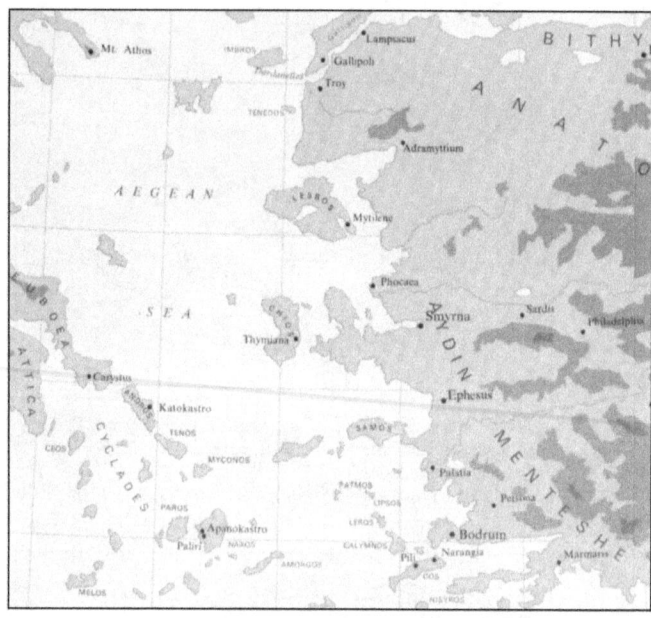

Map. 5. The Aegean Sea. Cartographic Laboratory, University of Wisconsion, Madison.
Map. 6. The Crécy campaign, from the landing at Saint-Vaast-la-Hougue to the siege of Calais. From The Battle of Crécy: A Casebook, Michael Livingston and Kelly DeVries, ed. (Liverpool: Liverpool University Press, 2016).

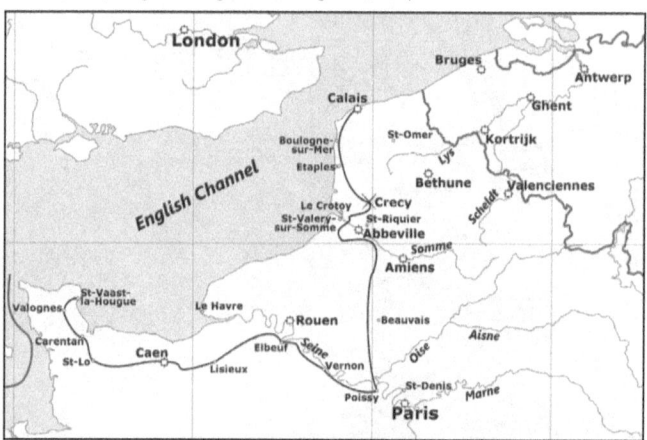

# INTRODUCTION

## THE CHRONICLE OF THE ANONIMO ROMANO

This work, a chronicle written by an unknown fourteenth-century Roman and therefore commonly known as the *Cronica* of the Anonimo Romano, is a treasure. It offers a detailed glimpse of late medieval Rome during the age of the Avignon papacy, situating that city in a broadly Mediterranean and European context, to which many of its pages are dedicated, and providing our most detailed account of the late medieval Rome's most famous son, Cola di Rienzo. The author deserves our gratitude for his vivid depiction of Cola, a charismatic and wildly eccentric man of humble birth but astonishing talent who rose to dominate Rome not once but twice. Yet this marvelous work, which provides insights and information we can find nowhere else, very nearly did not survive. Furthermore, from the time it was written it has all too often tended to be read in a piecemeal, selective manner. It was long neglected by modern scholars unsure of how to categorize it and, until recently, not particularly interested in the fourteenth-century Roman world about which it is so informative. Only gradually have scholars come to cherish this chronicle both as a literary product and as a rich source of historical data about the late medieval world from which it comes.

Above all, the chronicle shows us Cola di Rienzo's Rome, on which the majority of it is focused, and in the local vernacular of which it was written [Map 1]. But the chronicle also offers glimpses of other Italian locales, as well as of Iberia, the eastern Mediterranean, France, and, fleetingly, Hungary. The chapters relating to non-Roman matters are read all too infrequently. Yet without an understanding of the chronicle's non-Roman material as both historical and thematic context for the Roman chapters, those latter chapters are likely to be misunderstood. Such selective reading disrupts the thematic unity of the text and makes it far easier to read into it whatever one wishes to see. As a result, Roman realities and events risk becoming caricatures of themselves.[1] This translation is intended to address these problems by offering Anglophone readers, for the first time, the opportunity

---

1. For a detailed discussion of how and why fourteenth-century Rome tends to be caricatured, see James A. Palmer, "Medieval and Renaissance Rome: Mending the Divide," *History Compass* 15.11 (2017): DOI: 10.1111/hic3.12424.

to easily read the text as a whole.[2] In what follows, readers will find an introduction to the text and its mysterious author, consideration of the chronicle's style, a primer on the fourteenth-century world from which it comes, and an exploration of the lessons that, it is argued here, the author was trying to teach his intended audience.

PRESERVATION, PUBLICATION, AND STUDY OF THE TEXT

This chronicle very nearly did not survive, and one might reasonably wonder how a work now so widely recognized ever risked oblivion.[3] Its author set out to write it in the 1350s as a mature thinker at the peak of his abilities. He composed the earliest version in Latin before deciding to render it more fully in the contemporary vernacular dialect of Rome, so that it might be appreciated by a larger audience. He opened with prefatory comments and a table of contents, offered a few chapters on Roman matters, and then widened his gaze to take in events from across the Latin Christian world. Around the midpoint of the chronicle he declared, "Now is a good time to go back home" to Italy and to Rome.[4] The remainder of the text deals overwhelmingly with Cola di Rienzo's life and career, on which more will be said below, and with events in or pertaining to Rome during the years when he was out of power. The Anonimo continued to tinker with his chronicle for some time, adding Latin notes in the margins or between the lines of his vernacular account, with the probable intention of integrating these amendments in future revisions.

Unfortunately, the Anonimo died while still in his middle years, his work incomplete. Whether our Roman author was struck down by plague, like the contemporary chronicler Giovanni Villani, or died as a result of some other twist of fate we cannot know.

---

2. The only previous English translation was John Wright, *The Life of Cola di Rienzo* (Toronto: Pontifical Institute of Mediaeval Studies, 1975), but that translation followed a tradition of presenting only selected chapters, on which see more below.

3. For much of what follows, Anglophone readers may refer to Maurizio Campanelli, "The Preface of the Anonimo Romano's *Cronica*: Writing History and Proving Truthfulness in Fourteenth-Century Rome," *The Medieval Journal* 3.1 (2013): 83–101, at 84–87.

4. See below, p. 177.

Clearly, though, his chronicle very nearly died with him. No trace of either his Latin original or his vernacular manuscript has survived. Fortunately, however, sometime after his death, a late fourteenth-century copy of the text was made by a scribe who decided to integrate the author's Latin notes into the otherwise vernacular work, a sometimes confusing distortion of their relationship to the text that has continued ever after.[5] This scribe's copy of the chronicle has also been lost. The earliest surviving manuscript copy of this work, in fact, dates from the mid-sixteenth century, nearly two hundred years after its original composition, making clear how fortunate we are to have it at all.

This near-death experience perhaps paved the way for the chronicle's unfortunate reception by many of those who eventually took interest in it. By the seventeenth century at the latest, the trend of excerpting only select chapters had begun. The chronicle's earliest publishers seem to have assumed that local Roman audiences would be primarily interested to hear about Roman matters. Above all, they would be intrigued by the magnetic figure of Cola di Rienzo, a local man of humble origins who had famously risen to dominate the city in the mid-fourteenth century, before — as they assumed — falling prey to his own vices.[6] The rest of the text publishers deemed far less marketable, with the result that the chapters on Cola's Rome were printed alone with the title *Vita di Cola di Rienzo tribuno del popolo romano*. As will be made clear below, the decision to excise these chapters from the chronicle as a whole fundamentally distorts them. Nevertheless, the same choice has been made repeatedly for much the same reason, including in the modern era.[7] Presenting the

5. Maurizio Campanelli, "'Benché io l'aia ià fatta per lettera': Gli inserti Latini nella *Cronica* dell'Anonimo romano," *Filologica & Critica* 37 (2012): 3–29.

6. For recent studies of Cola, see Ronald G. Musto, *Apocalypse in Rome: Cola di Rienzo and the Politics of the New Age* (Berkeley: University of California Press, 2003); and Amanda Collins, *Greater than Emperor: Cola di Rienzo (ca. 1313–1354) and the World of Fourteenth-Century Rome* (Ann Arbor: University of Michigan Press, 2002). For most recent bibliography, see Ronald G. Musto, "Cola di Rienzo," *Oxford Bibliographies Online* (New York: Oxford University Press, 2020), at DOI: 10.1093/OBO/9780195399301-0122.

7. The first example is Pompilio Toti, *Vita di Cola di Rienzo tribuno del popolo romano* (Rome: Andrea Fei, 1624), with a second edition in 1631. Modern

3

chronicle in this way does the reader no favors, as will be shown, but early on it also posed a threat to the very survival of the text. As a result of publication strategies that fundamentally misunderstood it, much of the chronicle risked being lost by shear neglect, and it is perhaps due only Ludovico Muratori's inclusion of it in his monumental eighteenth-century collection of medieval sources that the full version survived to be handed down to later generations.[8]

Muratori's version of the Anonimo has the virtue of presenting it in its entirety, and it includes a Latin translation in addition to the original Romanesco, or Roman dialect. His preservation of the chronicle probably ensured its posterity, but it did nothing to change the fact that scholars for the most part continued to focus solely on the chapters dedicated to Cola just as their forebears had done. In fact, it was hardly guaranteed that they read it at all. Well into the twentieth century, literary scholars focused preferentially on a long-established canon of works including the likes of Dante and Petrarch and neglected those that, like this one, were deemed secondary.[9] Even in the late nineteenth and early twentieth century, as Italy became the focus of new historical arguments about the birth of modernity associated with the idea of the Renaissance, neglect of the this chronicle continued to be the norm.[10] Historians looking

---

replications of this partial publication of the chronicle include Zeferino Re, ed., *Vita di Cola di Rienzo* (Florence: Le Monnier, 1828), which was unfortunately translated into Tuscan and followed by an enlarged version in 1854; Alberto Maria Ghisalberti, ed., *La vita di Cola di Rienzo* (Rome: L.S. Olschki, 1928); Arsenio Frugoni, ed., *Vita di Cola di Rienzo* (Florence: Le Monnier, 1957); and Wright, *Life of Cola di Rienzo*.

8. Ludovico Antonio Muratori, ed., "Historiae Romanae fragmenta ab anno 1327 usque ad 1354," in *Antiquitates italicae Medii Aevi*, 6 vols. (Milan: Muratori, 1738–42), 3:247–548.

9. Giuseppe Billanovich, "Come nacque un capolavoro: La 'Cronica' del non più Anonimo Romano. Il vescovo Ildebrandino Conti, Francesco Petrarca, e Bartolomeo di Iacovo da Valmontone," *Rendiconti. Atti della Accademia Nazionale dei Lincei* Ser. 9, 6.1 (1995): 195–212, at 198.

10. Classically, of course, Jacob Burckhardt's great work of 1860, *The Civilization of the Renaissance in Italy* (London: Penguin, 1990). This argument has had a particularly lasting impact on Anglophone historiographies, with significant effects on interest in fourteenth-century Rome (and as a result in

for the roots of Italian national identity, which some perceived in the ostensibly pan-Italian political project of Cola di Rienzo, were disappointed by the chronicler's apparent failure to appreciate it.[11] All these prejudices and predilections served to divert readers from the chronicle presented here. Ultimately, this valuable source would have to wait until the mid-twentieth century before really beginning to have its moment.

It must further be noted that no early version of the chronicle, not even Muratori's, included a reliable edition of the text, of which multiple variants survive. No modern critical edition would appear until one was provoked by a new surge of interest in the chronicle of the Anonimo Romano that came only in the mid-twentieth century. This modern study of the work really began in the 1940s, with Gianfranco Contini's declaration that this little-read Roman chronicle, theretofore considered to be of minor importance, should be recognized as a true masterpiece of Italian literature. Contini called attention to the text's poetic sensibility, to its value as a rich example of a scarcely preserved medieval Roman vernacular, and rather more problematically to what he considered to be its staunchly secular, even atheistic disposition and its echoes of Petrarchan humanism.[12] Contini's advocacy secured this under-appreciated Roman text a more prominent place in the annals of Italian literature and resulted in a new generation of scholarship. That scholarship culminated in

---

this chronicle). On this, Palmer, "Medieval and Renaissance Rome: Mending the Divide."

11. For this critique, see Konrad Burdach and Paul Piur, *Briefwechsel des Cola di Rienzo 2. Kritische Darstellung der Quellen zur Geschichte Rienzos* (Weidmann: Berlin, 1928); and Paul Piur, *Cola di Rienzo: Darstellung seines Lebens und seines Geistes* (Vienna: L.W. Seidel, 1931), 223. For a convincing rebuttal of this critique, see Gustav Seibt, *Anonimo romano: Scrivere la storia alle soglie del Rinascimento* (Rome: Viella, 2000), 129–92.

12. Gianfranco Contini, "Invito a un capolavoro," *Letteratura: Rivista trimestrale di letteratura contemporanea* 4.4 (1940): 3–14. The association of Cola and Petrarch was already, of course, well known. See, for example, Mario E. Cosenza, *Francesco Petrarca and the Revolution of Cola di Rienzo* (Chicago: University of Chicago Press, 1913); revised, 3rd edition with new notes and updated bibliography, as *The Revolution of Cola di Rienzo*, Ronald G. Musto, ed. (New York: Italica Press, 1996).

Giuseppe Porta's 1979 publication, at long last, of a modern critical edition, on which most subsequent work, including this translation, rests.[13] Another wave of studies followed, especially by scholars interested in the chronicle's philological and linguistic aspects but also by those keen to reimagine the political and social world of late medieval Rome.[14] From that time onward, the chronicle of the Anonimo Romano has been consistently studied, although still primarily by Italian and other Continental scholars.

Happily, then, there is now a rich tradition of research on this chronicle by Continental scholars; but something must be said, in the introduction to its first full English translation, about its fate in Anglophone circles. Anglophone interest in fourteenth-century Italy, including Rome, has been largely inseparable from the idea of the Italian Renaissance and the birth of the cultural trend known as Renaissance humanism.[15] Until the turn of the twenty-first century, this was commonly understood to have been an intellectual

13. Anonimo Romano, *Cronica*, Giuseppe Porta, ed. (Milan: Adelphi, 1979).

14. For the language and manuscript tradition of the chronicle, see the works of Vittorio Formentin: "Proposte di restauro per la 'Cronica' d'Anonimo romano (con una nota etimologica)," *Medioevo romanzo* 14 (1989): 112–25; "Tra storia della lingua e filologia: Note sulla sintassi della 'Cronica' d'Anonimo romano," *Lingua e Stile* 37 (2002): 203–50; "Nuovi rilievi sul testo della 'Cronica' d'Anonimo romano," *Contributi di filologia dell'Italia mediana* 16 (2002): 23–47; "Schede lessicali e grammaticali per la 'Cronica' d'Anonimo romano," *La lingua italiana* 4 (2008): 25–43; "Approssimazioni al testo e alla lingua della 'Cronica' d'Anonimo Romano," in *Leggere gli apparati (testi e testimoni dei classici italiani)*, G. Raboni, ed. (Milan: Unicopli, 2012), 27–71; and "Il volto dell'Anonimo," *Filologia & Critica* 37.1 (2012): 130–49. A few other representative historical analyses of the text include Gian Mario Anselmi, "La Cronica dell'Anonimo romano: Problemi di inquadramento culturale e storiografico," *Bullettino dell'Istituto storico italiano per il Medio Evo e Archivio Muratoriano* 91 (1984): 423–40; Massimo Miglio, "Anonimo romano," in *Il senso della storia nella cultura medievale italiana (1100–1350): Atti del quattordicesimo Convegno di studi del Centro italiano di studi di storia e d'arte di Pistoia* (Pistoia: Centro italiano di studi di storia e d'arte di Pistoia, 1995), 175–87; and Anna Modigliani, "Signori e tiranni nella Cronica dell'Anonimo romano, *Rivista storica italiana* 110 (1998): 357–410.

15. For Rome's place in Anglophone historiography, see Palmer, "Medieval and Renaissance Rome."

movement ushered in by the genius of Petrarch, a Tuscan poet enamored by the memory of antiquity and keen to present himself as uniquely suited to instruct his contemporaries in the famous virtue of their ancient ancestors. Petrarch was long hailed as the father of Renaissance humanism, an intellectual movement rooted in the *studia humanitatis*, the study of grammar, rhetoric, poetry, history, and moral philosophy as found in the works of Greek and Roman antiquity. Despite Petrarch's rightful displacement as the founding figure of the movement in recent years, humanism was and has remained central to much scholarship on fourteenth- and fifteenth-century Italy, and this fact continues to shape perceptions of many things, including Rome, Cola, and our chronicle.[16]

Petrarch was fascinated with Cola di Rienzo's effort to resuscitate the greatness of antiquity in fourteenth-century Rome, and his interest has guaranteed the city at least a small place in Anglophone treatments of Italy in this period, even if subsequent humanist authors tended to speak disparagingly of fourteenth-century Rome as a ruined backwater. But the magnetic appeal of Petrarch, along with the dominance of humanism as an object of historical inquiry in Anglophone scholarship, means that his perspective, and that of later generations of humanists, is commonly privileged, while the Rome that emerges in the pages of this chronicle has tended to appear fleetingly if at all.[17] Only in works focused on Cola himself, or on the decades immediately following Cola's fall, has this chronicle been more carefully scrutinized and contextualized by scholars writing in English.[18] Furthermore, the habit of reading only select chapters of the chronicle, first established centuries ago, is still all too

16. For the current sense of Petrarch's place in this tradition, see Ronald G. Witt, *In the Footsteps of the Ancients: The Origins of Humanism from Lovato to Bruni* (Leiden: Brill, 2000); and Christopher S. Celenza, *The Intellectual World of the Italian Renaissance: Language, Philosophy, and the Search for Meaning* (Cambridge: Cambridge University Press, 2018).

17. See, for example, Cosenza, *Revolution of Cola di Rienzo*; Witt, *In the Footsteps of the Ancients*; and James Hankins, *Virtue Politics: Soulcraft and Statecraft in Renaissance Italy* (Cambridge: Harvard University Press, 2019), 7, 14–15, 120, 164–67.

18. Collins, *Greater than Emperor*; Musto, *Apocalypse in Rome*; and James A. Palmer, *The Virtues of Economy: Governance, Power, and Piety in Late Medieval Rome* (Ithaca: Cornell University Press, 2019).

common. The only English translation to-date, in fact, replicated the decision of seventeenth-century publishers by including only the chapters focused on Cola.[19] Indeed, despite a now decades-long surge in scholarly interest, the talent of the chronicle's author as a writer of history, and his precise place among other late medieval writers of history have only recently begun to receive the attention they deserve.[20]

ANONYMOUS BUT NOT UNKNOWN

The reader will perhaps by now have noted the elephant in the room, the fact that the author of this chronicle has yet barely been discussed. There is a certain irony to this, given the emphasis so far on the quality and value of his work. While it has been discussed, the author has been left to one side. In this, we have actually been reproducing something that happens all too often. Just as the Rome depicted in this chronicle has largely been displaced by Petrarchan and humanist imaginings of the city, so too does its author seem at times to be pushed aside by his own virtuosic presentation of the charismatic, domineering figure of Cola di Rienzo. The reason for this is simple; we do not know who he was.

There have been a few efforts to identify the chronicle's author over the years. The 1905 edition of the *Life*, for example, suggested that he be identified with one Tommaso Fortifocca, a claim that was already largely rejected by Contini's day.[21] More recently, Giuseppe Billanovich

---

19. Wright, *Life of Cola di Rienzo*. Wright's translation predated the appearance of Porta's edition and was based instead primarily on Ghisalberti's 1928 version of the Cola chapters, which led him to include some material that Porta omitted. See below, pp. 58, 285–86.

20. For this, see especially Seibt, *Anonimo romano;* as well as Maurizio Campanelli, "Benché io l'aia ià fatta per lettera"; "The Preface of the Anonimo Romano's *Cronica*"; and Campanelli, "The Anonimo Romano at his Desk: Recounting the Battle of Crécy in Fourteenth-Century Italy," in *The Medieval Chronicle*, Erik Kooper and Sjoerd Levelt, ed. (Leiden: Brill, 2014), 33–78; Dario Internullo, *Ai margini dei giganti: La vita intelletuale dei romani nel trecento, 1305–1367* (Rome: Viella, 2016), 184–92; Ronald G. Musto, *Writing Southern Italy before the Renaissance: Trecento Historians of the Mezzogiorno* (New York: Routledge, 2019), 19–20.

21. Contini, "Invito a un capolavoro," 4.

has argued that he should be identified as Bartolomeo di Iacovo da Valmontone, a successful clergyman who eventually became a bishop and was tied to the Conti, a powerful Roman baronial family.[22] As proof, Billanovich suggested that the tendency of the chronicle to move back and forth from Rome, to northern Italy in the vicinity of Bologna and Padua, and then back to Rome again, along with its focus on major developments abroad, reflect the curriculum vitae and professional interests of this energetic clergyman and diplomat. There is much to recommend this interpretation. The Anonimo does seem better informed of events in the north during precisely the years that we can verify Bartolomeo's presence there. Conversely, his account seems less coherent when it considers periods during which we known Bartolomeo's career had taken him elsewhere. It is certainly compelling to note that the earliest manuscript of the chronicle was found in Valmontone in the sixteenth century, carried there, Billanovich suggests, along with Bartolomeo's other possessions after his death. Despite this, however, Billanovich's identification of the chronicle's author has not been widely accepted. His identity remains uncertain, and for that reason this translation will continue the tradition of referring to him simply as the Anonimo Romano.

That we do not know the Anonimo Romano's name is not to say that we know nothing about him at all.[23] He was probably born sometime around the year 1320, making him roughly of an age with Cola di Rienzo. We know this because early in the chronicle he describes an event that transpired in 1325, saying that he remembered it "as if from a dream," because, he tells us, "though I was alive, I was still very young."[24] Like Cola, the Anonimo was of non-noble stock, coming from that stratum of Roman society, sometimes called the *popolo*, that was powerfully associated with the city's trade guilds. Cola was the son of an innkeeper and had studied to be a notary. We do not know the Anonimo's parentage but demonstrations of expertise within the chronicle strongly indicate that he was an educated man.

22. Billanovich, "Come nacque un capolavoro." On the barons, see below, 36–38.
23. For the most recent summary of what we know, see Musto, *Writing Southern Italy*, 19–20, et passim.
24. See below, chapter 2, p. 66.

Unlike Cola di Rienzo, the Anonimo's education does not seem to have been that of a notary; but he was familiar with and fond of famous literary works, as well as with scripture and materials common to anyone with a university education at the time. Rather than having a legal or notarial education, he is commonly believed to have studied medicine at Bologna. He refers repeatedly to texts associated with the medical arts, and often digresses at some length on medical topics. The clearest example of this comes in chapter seven, when the Anonimo pauses his discussion of repairs to St. Peter's and describes the near-death experience of its head architect, Nicola di Agniletto of Vetralla.[25] After nearly falling to his death from a height, half of Nicola's beard is said to have turned white, and the Anonimo draws on Avicenna's medical writings to explain the phenomenon whereby such a seemingly incredible thing could actually happen. We see similar digressions on the topic of prophetic dreams in chapter eighteen, where the Anonimo draws medicalized explanations from Aristotle, while also reflecting on other writings[26] He reports in detail the dietary regimen imposed by doctors on the papal legate Annibaldo da Ceccano.[27] The Anonimo also signals his ties to the medical faculty of Bologna when, in chapter eleven, the Anonimo reports that he took some of his information about King Alfonso's arguments with the pope about his mistress from news heard in the home of Bologna's rector of medicine.[28] Finally, Gustav Seibt has pointed out convincingly that the Anonimo's gaze is often that of a doctor, especially in his description of wounds, mutilation, and the bodies of the dead.[29] Evidence like this suggests clearly that the Anonimo's university education was in the medical field, while his awareness of and seeming access to the details of the communal government's internal workings, as Dario Internullo has aptly pointed out, suggests that he possibly practiced his medical arts on behalf of Rome's communal government, granting him an insider's access.[30]

25. See below, pp. 85–87.
26. See below, pp. 209–12.
27. See below, p. 252.
28. See below, p. 134.
29. See Seibt, *Anonimo romano*, 256–58.
30. Internullo, *Ai margini*, 186–89 suggests a strong relationship between the Anonimo's style as an historian and his training as a doctor.

✳ INTRODUCTION

Like his professional formation as a doctor, the Anonimo's political views can be discerned in the text, and although they are not identical with Cola's, they often find common ground with him when it comes to the basic values of the Roman *popolo*. Certainly, as we shall see below, the Anonimo was invested in the project of the Roman popular commune. He was also, however, extremely sympathetic to the papacy and its political priorities, perhaps to such an extent that he could reasonably be considered a Guelf. Enemies of the church do not fare well here. Francesco Ordelaffi, a Romagnol lord and Ghibelline, is caricatured as a murderous, atheistic heretic.[31] Lewis of Bavaria, the enemy of John XXII and Benedict XII and supporter of papal critics like the Spiritual Franciscans and Marsiglio of Padua, is presented in chapter eighteen as secretly desperate to avoid dying as an excommunicate.[32] Any problems with papal political action in Italy are attributed not to the papacy but to morally flawed legates like Annibaldo da Ceccano, who is presented as disastrously arrogant, unjust in his persecution of Cola di Rienzo, and ultimately killed by his own gluttony.[33] Most tellingly of all, the Anonimo's positive evaluation of Cola di Rienzo tends to correspond to periods when he was in the papacy's good graces, and his downfall similarly corresponds to his break with the papacy. Taken together, this evidence of the Anonimo's political views makes clear that being a supporter of the popular commune did not necessarily mean being opposed to the papacy, a fact that contemporary archival evidence also makes clear.[34]

31. See below, pp. 264–65. Rendering enemies of the papacy as heretics was an increasingly common papal strategy, one the Anonimo seems to embrace when it suits him. See Janine Larmon Peterson, *Suspect Saints and Holy Heretics: Disputed Sanctity and Communal Identity in Late Medieval Italy* (Ithaca: Cornell University Press, 2019), 171–75.

32. See below, p. 217.

33. See below, pp. 249–56.

34. It was long typical to characterize late medieval Roman politics as having three foci: the commune, the papacy, and the empire, with the papacy and the empire in conflict and the commune keen to avoid domination by either of them. A classic example is Eugenio Duprè Theseider, *Roma dal comune di popolo alla signoria Pontificia, 1252–1377* (Bologna: Capelli, 1952). However, by the late fourteenth century the empire was not really a meaningful factor in Roman politics, and many Romans pinned great hopes on a possible return

Finally, despite Billanovich's claim that the Anonimo was an ecclesiastic, it is more commonly held that he was a layperson. This is not to say that he was as secular (or quasi-atheistic) as Contini claimed.[35] Rather, the Anonimo is highly representative of the lay piety of the Italian communes, a world in which politics, nature, and all the ebbs and flows of a life were inseparably bound up with a sacred cosmology about which one might not always think but the truth of which no one could deny.[36]

The Anonimo's account is, then, one that offers a glimpse into the mindset of a politically important stratum of Roman society, one that otherwise rarely reveals itself to us except through the surviving records of their quotidian affairs: contracts, court cases, last wills and testaments, and other documents preserved in the notebooks of the city's notaries.[37] As a narrative of astonishing dynamism and detail, the chronicle is unique among surviving sources generated by the late medieval Roman *popolo*. This alone makes it worthy of study. But there is a twofold reason for understanding it to be even more valuable still, each of which will be explored in the remainder of this introduction. First, when considered within the historiographical tradition of its day, the Anonimo's account shines with unique brilliance, a purpose-driven narrative crafted in a unique style and demonstrating considerable literary talent that remains evident (one hopes) even in translation. Second, the account of Rome that the Anonimo provides, situated within a wider sense of the Latin Christian world, provides insights into the nature of Roman society that can be found nowhere else, shedding light on a scantily

from Avignon by the papacy, in one case even going so far as to leave testamentary bequests for bells to be made and rung in honor of the occasion. See Palmer, *Virtues of Economy*, 154.

35. The tendency to emphasize the secularity of the Anonimo's account, as Contini did, is still sometimes encountered. See, for example, Giovanni Spani, "Anonimo Romano," in *Encyclopedia of the Medieval Chronicle,* Graeme Dunphy and Christian Bratu, ed. (Leiden: Brill, 2016) at: http://dx.doi.org/10.1163/2213-2219_emc_SIM_00197.

36. On this, see Augustine Thompson, *Cities of God: The Religion of the Italian Communes, 1125–1325* (University Park: Pennsylvania State University Press, 2005).

37. On the source situation in Rome, see Palmer, *Virtues of Economy*, 4–5.

documented but historically pivotal period in Roman history. This insight comes not simply in the form of obvious facts and details about specific people and events. Rather, by getting at what the Anonimo wanted to say to his Roman audience, we glimpse the values and concerns that were shaping late fourteenth-century Rome. In short, the Anonimo's chronicle is among our best tools for understanding Rome as the Romans of his day would have. It frees us from dependence on the perspective of outsiders like Petrarch, for whom Rome tended to act as a foil, important only because of what it had once been rather than for what it was.

## THE ANONIMO ROMANO AND HISTORY WRITING

As a good *popolano* and possibly an employee of the Roman commune, we might expect the Anonimo Romano to have written a history akin to those written in and about other Italian communes. To some extent, that is what he did. Like Giovanni and Matteo Villani, who are among the most famous authors in this genre, the Anonimo included plenty of material about the wider world. Despite this, we can hardly doubt that the Anonimo's home city was the real focus of his work, just as Florence was the heart of the Villani chronicle. But the Anonimo's style of writing is dramatically different from that of the two Villani, and from that of other writers of communal chronicles.[38] As will be discussed in more detail below, the Anonimo was focused on the recent history of his commune, and he gave particular attention to questions pressing to its governing class both in the chapters pertaining to Rome and to those focused on other places.

Like many chroniclers, the Anonimo drew on classical examples of history writing in crafting his chronicle. He frequently used classical references and figures to underscore moral issues.[39] This reflected both the elementary education typical in fourteenth-century Rome, which taught grammar and rhetoric by reading excerpts focused on questions of virtue and vice and drawn from classical and Christian sources, and

---

38. As an illustration in the different styles of the two chronicles, Seibt offers a striking comparison of the Anonimo and Matteo Villani's treatment of the stoning of a Roman senator. See his *Anonimo romano*, 9–21. For more on their narrative styles and structures, see Musto, *Writing Southern Italy*.

39. Musto, *Writing Southern Italy*, 45–46.

the work of contemporary and near contemporary Roman writers like Giovanni Cavallini, Giacomo di Pietro Stefaneschi, and Landolfo and Giovanni Colonna.[40] Above all, he drew on classical depictions of human psychology in order to explore the inner worlds of his actors.[41] A case in point is his clear dependence on Sallust's portrait of Cataline for his own portrayal of Cola di Rienzo's ostensible intemperance and instability toward the end of his life. Sallust tells us that Cataline's mind was restless because he was plagued with guilt, his skin pale, his eyes bloodshot, and his gait irregular so that he seemed like a madman.[42] In chapter 27, the late Cola is described by the Anonimo similarly, with rapidly shifting facial expressions, red eyes, and an inconstant mind.[43] Another example juxtaposes Cola's panicked attempt to flee in disguise in the moments before his death with the far more admirable stoic virtue of the ancients, drawing on Livy to describe the way Rome's senators died at the hands of the Gauls while deliberately dressed in a manner that proclaimed their office.[44] The Anonimo had no way to know the state of Cola's mind in his final hour, but he invented it by drawing upon classical sources in order to drive home his overall evaluation of Cola's character, a topic we will revisit below.

Of course, the Anonimo also knew and drew upon medieval sources. Among the medieval sources of particular importance to him we can include Gregory the Great, Isidore of Seville, the chronicle of Martin of Poland, the *Liber ystoriarum Romanorum*, the *Mirabilia*, and perhaps Dante and *l'Aquila* (a medieval compilation of historical information about ancient Rome).[45] Although some, like Gregory and Isidore, would have been part of a standard elementary education, the vast majority of these medieval sources were of interest to the Anonimo precisely because of their own focus on

40. Internullo, *Ai margini,* 58–59, 310, 314.

41. Musto, *Writing Southern Italy,* 49.

42. Sallust, *Bellum Catalinae,* 15:3–5.

43. See below, p. 281.

44. Livy, *Ab urbe condita libri,* V.41. For the Anonimo's discussion, see below, pp. 301–2. On the Anonimo's use of Livy here, see too Musto, *Writing Southern Italy,* 46.

45. Internullo, *Ai margini,* 314; on *l'Aquila*, see 304–7. Also on the medieval sources, see Seibt, *Anonimo romano,* 23–24, 73–86.

Rome and their use of classical sources. The Anonimo's use of the Dominican author Martin of Poland, also known as Martin of Troppau, is an example of this. Martin was a chronicler who wrote in a fairly streamlined manner, presenting simple facts without much embellishment or effort at synthesis. The Anonimo's writing could not be more different. But Martin knew his classical literature, and the Anonimo drew from him, for example, the useful story of emperor Marcian's prophetic dream, which he juxtaposed with one of Cola's.[46] Overall, the Anonimo did not call out his use of medieval sources in the same way he did classical ones. Instead, he tended to weave them into his own account in ways that hint at his use of them without being explicit enough to verify.[47]

The Anonimo's use of classical sources therefore shows him to be a product of the learned culture we now know to have been typical of fourteenth-century Rome, and his apparent interest in medieval sources suggests his appetite for works focused on Roman matters. But despite his stylistic borrowings from classical and medieval sources alike, the Anonimo imitated the style of neither slavishly. Instead, as we shall see shortly, he drew on his own intellectual formation as a doctor, producing a kind of history that marks him out as unique among his peers. Doing so would have been at least somewhat natural to him, though it also seems to have presented a challenge.

So far as we can tell, the Anonimo worked on his chronicle until the end of his life, and it is clear from his efforts that he believed himself to have something to say that his Roman contemporaries needed to hear. His decision to write in the local vernacular, Romanesco, the dialect of fourteenth-century Romans, is clear evidence of this. Tragically, however, the Anonimo never completed his chronicle.[48] In saying this, it must be noted that the fourteenth

---

46. Seibt, *Anonimo romano*, 74–75; for the prophetic dream, see below, pp. 209–10.

47. See Musto, *Writing Southern Italy*, 50–51.

48. There is some debate over just how finished the surviving version of the chronicle is. Seibt, *Anonimo romano*, 27–29 argues that the chronicle's missing chapters were never written, though he admits that this is debatable. Campanelli, "'Benché io l'aia fatta per lettera,'" 3–6; and "The Preface of the Anonimo Romano's *Cronica*," 86–87, argues otherwise.

century did not have the same notions of textual production that we do, and the idea of "completing" a work was not present in the same way prior to (or even after) the advent of print.[49] But even with this in mind, the Anonimo's chronicle is strikingly incomplete. Whole sections remain unwritten and others lack the signs of final revision, so that they stand out from the work's more finished pages. This is particularly true of the longest and most famous chapters, those devoted to the deeds of Cola di Rienzo. Here there seems to have been so much to say that the chronicler struggled to put order to his account.[50] In the end, no matter how complete the chronicle was or was not, it is clear that the Anonimo labored assiduously over his task, that he saw it as unfinished, and that he apparently felt it important enough to have continued to work at it until the end of his life. Given his dedication to this task, we should reflect on what it was he probably understood himself to be doing.

SITUATING THE CHRONICLE

At first glance, the Anonimo seems to have written for reasons similar to those of other chroniclers of his day. This is not, however, precisely true, a fact that we can only appreciate if we consider contemporary trends in the genre. Rather than becoming sidetracked by the broader historiographical tradition of Europe, or the details of its earlier monastic annals and other such texts, we can simply point out that in Italy, as elsewhere, one of the dominant modes of early historical writing was the universal chronicle, which situated events within a narrative scheme that encompassed the entirety of human history beginning with God's creation of the world. In Italy, however, a distinct mode of history writing emerged alongside the early city communes (on which we will say more

---

49. For a detailed account of the evolution of modern ideas about publication and the finished state of published works, see David McKitterick, *Print, Manuscript, and the Search for Order: 1450–1830* (Cambridge: Cambridge University Press, 2003).

50. Seibt offers details arguments about which portions of the chronicle are more or less finished in various parts of his *Anonimo romano*. See, for example, pp. 27–29, on its missing chapters in general, and 176–81, on the Anonimo's struggle with the Cola chapters. Formentin has called for a new edition that would revisit these questions. See his "Approssimazioni al testo e alla lingua della 'Cronica' d'Anonimo Romano," 36–44.

below). These communal chronicles generally reflected an emerging sense of citizenship and a need to analyze and mediate the political conflicts endemic to the communes. The method of communal chronicles bore some relationship to, and perhaps emerged from, the established courtroom process of arriving at the truth of things via the testimony of witnesses.[51] Gradually, a more robust tradition of communal historiography took shape, incorporating ever more detail and synthesizing it through the application of increasingly coherent ideological schemes.

By the late thirteenth and fourteenth centuries, interest in the historical past, and in modern political and legal matters, began to be increasingly linked to interest in and conscious emulation of classical Roman texts. This was the central characteristic of an emerging humanist tradition that began, as Ronald Witt has argued, not with Petrarch but with the likes of Lovato Lovati in the late 1200s.[52] Of course, humanist historiography was no more homogenous in its motivations or thematic interests than was earlier communal historiography, but it can safely be said to have been particularly concerned in its early days with questions of political order, virtue, and an increasing historicity, which is to say a sense of the crucial importance of context for understanding a past increasingly recognized as being quite different from the present. By the early fifteenth century, humanist historiography's potential was

51. David Foote, "How the Past Becomes a Rumor: The Notarialization of Historical Consciousness in Medieval Orvieto," *Speculum* 75.4 (2000): 794–815; Enrico Faini, "Alle origini della memoria communale: Prime richerche," *Quellen und Forschungen aus italienischen Archiven und Bibliotheken* 88 (2008): 61–81; Chris Wickham, "The Sense of the Past in Italian Communal Narratives," in *The Perception of the Past in Twelfth-Century Europe*, Paul Magdalino, ed. (London: Hambledon Press, 1992), 173–90. On the Anonimo's own efforts to convert eye-witness testimony into a literary form, see Seibt, *Anonimo romano;* and Campanelli, "The Preface of the Anonimo Romano's *Cronica.*" On these deliberative and forensic rhetorical styles and courtroom traditions in medieval historiography, see as well, Matthew Kempshall, *Rhetoric and the Writing of History, 400–1500* (Manchester: Manchester University Press, 2011). On eyewitness, and various rhetorical modes deployed by the Anonimo and other historians, see Musto, *Writing Southern Italy,* 50–51, 64–68.

52. Witt, *In the Footsteps of the Ancients,* 1–30, 81–116.

increasingly harnessed in service to particular political regimes, as in the famous case of Leonardo Bruni's *History of Florence*.[53]

The Anonimo shares with most early humanist writers a clear interest in and inspiration by classical sources; a concern with virtue, good government, and other common themes; and a healthy interest in the active life of public affairs. In many respects, the Anonimo demonstrates a classicism typical of the thirteenth- and fourteenth-century *popolo*. He clearly saw classical texts as a source of valuable lessons for how one ought to live, rule, and navigate trying circumstances, drawing for example on Livy, Lucan, and Sallust.[54] We see this in his aside on the failure of Hannibal to follow up on his victories over the Romans.[55] Dropped in the midst of a long chapter on the life of Cola di Rienzo, this tale drawn from Livy emphasizes that he was making the same mistake Hannibal had. Yet, although the Anonimo clearly shared humanist interest in such texts, small details demonstrate that he was not a thoroughgoing philologist in the manner typical of later humanists. For example, he drops the diphthong in Aemelius Paulus in a manner typical of his era, and he seems to understand references to the Roman plebians as directly comparable to the *popolo* of his own day. Above all, the Anonimo can be seen to depart from Livy in numerous ways, creating a sense of immediacy by shifting from indirect to direct speech when describing Hannibal's conversation with his cavalry commander, Maharbal, which he also makes longer and more explicit.[56] One might argue, then, that the Anonimo is at best a kind of pre- or proto-humanist, but the utility of these categories is questionable. Indeed, Dario Internullo has suggested that such efforts at intellectual taxonomy are not much help in understanding fourteenth-century Roman culture, serving to erase a complex, dynamic culture by reducing it to a precursor to or incomplete

---

53. For current work on fifteenth-century humanism, see also Celenza, *The Intellectual World of the Italian Renaissance;* and Hankins, *Virtue Politics*.

54. For the Anonimo's relatively loose relationship with the models he encountered in Livy, Lucan, and Sallust, see Seibt, *Anonimo romano*, 87–93.

55. See below, pp. 236–39.

56. For a detailed comparison of this passage in Livy and the Anonimo, see Seibt, *Anonimo romano*, 88–90.

expression of something that came later.⁵⁷ It is clear, then, that the Anonimo, though clearly interested in the classics, is not usefully thought of as a humanist, a fact that has complicated his reception by modern scholars.

The fact that the Anonimo does not fit neatly into the developmental trajectory of Renaissance humanism is one reason that he has not garnered the same kind of attention as some other fourteenth-century authors. Generally speaking, the study of medieval Italian chronicles and histories, whether focused on communal or humanist examples, has tended to partake in the common trend of privileging authors from and writings about northern or central Italian affairs.⁵⁸ The fact that the Anonimo was not a humanist, then, has resulted in his marginalization, as has the fact that he focused especially on Rome, a city that has long suffered from an exaggerated sense of difference from its northern peer polities. We are justified, then, in wondering how the evolving historiographical conventions of northern writers compare to the impulses that drove him.

In comparison to most of his contemporaries, the Anonimo Romano was unusually thoughtful and explicit about his motives for writing. He listed five, emphasizing the utility of his work for both reader and writer alike. The first three pertain to the memorialization of noteworthy events. First, he hopes to make it possible for his readers to see that occurrences in their own times and places often resemble those of the past and are not, in fact, as unique and novel as they might seem. Exposure to many such examples, he asserted, not only frees us from the prison of limited personal perspective, it also provides us with examples of both virtuous behavior, which was to be embraced, and the errors and vices that were to be avoided.⁵⁹ Finally, for the Anonimo, the fact that true novelty is rare means that

---

57. Internullo, *Ai margini*, 355–57.

58. For an effort to remedy this, see Musto, *Writing Southern Italy*.

59. In listing these as his motives, the Anonimo echoes the preface to Titus Livy's classic history of Rome, *Ab Urbe Condita*, a text that both he and Cola di Rienzo seem to have treasured. On the reception of classical sources by the Anonimo and his contemporaries, see Internullo, *Ai margini*, 7, 356–57.

when it occurs it is worthy of memorialization simply because it is so astonishing. These are fairly straightforward points.

Somewhat more unusually, the Anonimo then turns to personal motives. He tells the reader that he writes to satisfy a two-fold personal impulse. First, the Anonimo states that he is driven by urgent inspiration, such that his mind cannot rest if he does not write. Secondly, he admits that this inspiration stems in part from the fact that his times are greatly troubled and in writing he finds solace, a temporary escape from contemporary chaos, as well as an outlet for the strong feelings it stirs up within him.[60] His chronicle, in short, does a service for both its author and its audience. The reader will gain both discernment and sharpened acumen, the ability to recognize and embrace virtue, avoid vice, and appreciate the value of the truly unique and astonishing when they encounter it. The writer gains peace of mind and a sense of responding actively to his world rather than sitting helplessly as it is inflicted upon him. Perhaps the Anonimo even meant his reader to share in the solace he took from writing, but he does not say. Nor is that the only thing he left unsaid.

How the Anonimo Wrote

The Anonimo's reasons for writing are eloquently stated but not entirely satisfying because they do not explain his unusual style. Certainly, the personal motivations of historical actors are not easy for us to judge, and there is therefore a temptation to accept the Anonimo's explicitly stated motives, which are clear enough. But the urge to memorialize and teach moral lessons is not a self-evident one, especially for a man who was not a writer by trade. On its own, this urge does not adequately explain why, or more importantly how the Anonimo wrote. After all, chroniclers commonly suggested that

60. This personal touch is unusual in the annals of medieval history writing, in which it was far more common to claim one was attempting to write for the pleasure of the reader, rather than oneself. The Anonimo takes from Livy the idea that he should write about beautiful and novel things but tweaks Livy's position by emphasizing that doing so soothes his own soul. See Maurizio Campanelli, "The Preface of the Anonimo Romano's *Cronica*," 93–94. On the importance of prefatory statements like the Anonimo's among fourteenth-century writers seeking to signal their place in wider textual communities, see Musto, *Writing Southern Italy*, 83–84.

memorialization and edification were their goals. Giovanni Villani, too, argued that he was writing to create a memorial to Florentine greatness and to help teach people to practice virtue and shun vice.[61] One might reasonably suspect that such claims were simple boilerplate, a kind of explanatory trope that justified the whole endeavor. But it seems that the Anonimo really did set out to memorialize and instruct. What was unusual about him was his method of pursuing these goals, a fact that becomes clear when more attention is given to his style and its under-appreciated relationship to his medical training.

In order to achieve his didactic goals, the Anonimo needed his readers to accept what he was telling them, he needed for them to trust him and his account enough that they would, in essence, suspend their disbelief. He declared in his preface that he would focus primarily on events he had witnessed himself or for which he had been able to obtain multiple eye-witness accounts. "What I write is absolutely true," he declared of the things related in the chronicle, "As God is my witness… I saw and heard them. This is the case above all with things that took place in my own land and were noted by trustworthy people, whose account corroborated one another."[62] In this, the Anonimo followed the standard tendency of medieval chroniclers, who commonly understood first-hand information to be best. He further reinforced the credibility of his account by supplementing eye-witness accounts with comparative examples drawn from ancient history or by juxtaposing them with expert knowledge derived from his own medical training. For example, he assured his reader that the seemingly unusual story of one Visconti lord's trained dogs was actually not so different from ancient examples familiar from Valerius Maximus. Similarly, the idea that a man's beard might turn white with fear, the Anonimo explains, was actually readily verifiable by recourse to Avicenna's instruction on the matter, which any educated physician would have known.[63] As a doctor, it would have been easier, and probably more

61. Giovanni Villani, *Cronica nuova*, I.1.

62. See below, chapter 1, p. 61.

63. Campanelli, "The Preface of the Anonimo Romano's *Cronica*," 94–101, explores these examples and the Anonimo's ways of signaling the truthfulness of his account. For the passages in question, see below chapter 7, pp. 85–86; chapter 9, p. 105.

natural, to write in the Latin of an educated man, but his choice not to do so is relevant to his need for a trusting, open audience. "I undertake this vernacular work for the common good and for common enjoyment," he wrote.[64] Perhaps so, but, for a Roman reader, presentation in the local vernacular also served to further enable immersion, putting them at their ease with the text by making it familiar.[65]

The Anonimo's style is striking and unusual, but rather than being the product of mere idiosyncrasy, it was shaped by his didactic goals and his intellectual training as a doctor. His chronicle is not organized chronologically but rather thematically and, from the very beginning, one is struck by his narrative mode.[66] He recounts events with an evocative mixture of fine detail and impressionistic color. What results is the alternation of a straightforward account with something more like a collage of images and instances that segue from one to the next in a manner resembling the unfolding of a partially remembered dream, sometimes racing tumultuously forward and other times fixed on a single crystalline instant. We might take from this simply that the Anonimo was an idiosyncratic writer, one operating outside his normal milieu as a medical professional. There is some truth to that. But the Anonimo was not simply trapped in his own unconscious authorial tics: he chose to write this way. As a doctor, he would have understood memory to be one of the five internal senses and to be constituted of images derived from sensory impressions. Human memory might be more

64. See below, chapter 1, p. 61.

65. Internullo, *Ai margini*, 367–68 argues that during the period of the Avignon papacy, the vernacular became increasingly respectable in Rome, having already enjoyed a long period of regular use in a little studied Roman vernacular literary culture associated above all with the *popolo*. In his view, the Anonimo's work represents the apex of this development. Vittorio Formentin, "Frustoli di romanesco antico in lodi arbitrali dei secoli XIV e XV," *Lingua e Stile* 43 (2008): 21–99, has also called attention to the vernacular's use in practical texts, especially those related to peacemaking. See James A. Palmer, "Piety and Social Distinction in Late Medieval Roman Peacemaking," *Speculum* 89.4 (2014): 974–1004.

66. See Musto, *Writing Southern Italy*, chapter 4 on narrative strategies and modes.

or less accurate, based on factors like the balance of humors within individuals or the passage of time, but its fundamental mechanism relied on the impression of sensory experience.[67]

The Anonimo's style demonstrates that he was eloquently aware that memory itself can range from crystal clear to scattered, fragmentary, and impressionistic. His account of his own childhood memories, which he admitted were at best dream-like, confirms this. Describing the 1325 uprising of Stefano Colonna and Poncello Orsini against Giacomo Savelli, Rome's senator or executive official, the Anonimo says:

> All of Rome armed itself. I remember the sound well. I was standing in Santa Maria in Publicolis and I saw the train of armed knights pass by, summoned to the Campidoglio. So proudly they went! There were many of them, well mounted and armed. The last of these, if I recall rightly, wore a coat of red silk and a silken yellow headdress, with a horseman's mace in his hand. They passed directly down the street, past the fish-market, where the blacksmiths are found, alongside the house of Paolo Giovinale. The train was long. The bell was ringing.[68]

---

67. On the use of mnemonics from antiquity into the early modern period, see Frances Yates, *The Art of Memory* (Chicago: University of Chicago Press, 1966). On memory in the medieval world in particular, see Mary Carruthers, *The Book of Memory: A Study of Memory in Medieval Culture* (Cambridge: Cambridge University Press, 2008). On the theory of the five internal senses, including memory, see Simon Kemp and Garth J.O. Fletcher, "The Medieval Theory of the Inner Senses," *The American Journal of Psychology* 106.4 (1993): 559–76; as well as Jörn Müller, "Memory in Medieval Philosophy," in *Memory: A History*, Dmitri Nikulin, ed. (Oxford: Oxford University Press, 2015), 93–125. One might reasonably object that these theories were primarily the domain of philosophers, but Müller points out that the medical tradition undergirded both in its Arabic origins and its transmission to Latin readers. The primary source was Avicenna, with whose other writings the Anonimo, like any educated doctor, was well familiar.

68. See below, p. 64. On Italian communal sonic landscapes, see now Niall Atkinson, *The Noisy Renaissance: Sound, Architecture, and Florentine Urban Life* (University Park: The Pennsylvania State University Press, 2016).

We can see the signs of memory at work here. As an adult, looking back, the Anonimo knew more about what had been happening than he had as a child, and he worked to place his own memory within a grid of facts. He situated the memory in time and provided key details about the involved parties. He placed himself geographically near a well-known church and the home of an equally well-known fellow Roman. But the core of the memory is the proud train of knights that had passed before his impressionable eyes as the bells of Rome rang. Above all, he remembered the last of them, whose colorful clothes and threatening mace lingered in the mind of the boy who had seen them decades before. That man, those colors, and the sound of the bell are the heart of this memory. For the Anonimo, writing really was an act of memory and memorialization. But his concern with memory was no mere trope; he was sensitively aware of the way sensory information could impress itself upon a person in a lasting manner.

We gain further insight on the Anonimo's chosen style if we note that in the same preface in which he listed his reasons for writing, he also alluded to the origins of the art he was practicing. The opening lines of the chronicle offer a quick history of the art of history writing that the Anonimo took from Isidore of Seville's *Etymologies*, an encyclopedic early medieval text that was a standard part of a good education. Isidore indicated that the goal of history writing, from its ostensible beginnings among the Greeks, was in fact memorialization, a tradition that the Anonimo clearly understood himself to be carrying on. But, as Gustav Seibt has convincingly shown, this is not the limit of the Anonimo's debt to the *Etymologies*. Crucially, Isidore also observes that the term "history" derived from the ancient Greek *istor*, or "witness," and *istorein*, meaning "to see" but also "to know."[69] What the historian captures, then, is a sensual experience, the experience of knowing truth by witnessing. As a witness, one sees what is present (*praesens*) before oneself, in the sense that it unfolds before one's senses (*prae sensibus*). As already mentioned, communal historiographical traditions emerged, at least in part, from the tradition of synthesizing a sense of the truth out of

69. Isidore of Seville, *Etymologies*, I.41. See too, Jacques Le Goff, *History and Memory*, Steven Rendall and Elizabeth Claman, trans. (New York: Columbia University Press, 1992), 101–2.

courtroom testimony (*dicta testium*), and out of records of testimony and other evidence compiled in notarial documents.⁷⁰ This fact puts a special emphasis on the relationship of the legal profession to the new historical consciousness emerging in late medieval Italy. But while the Anonimo shares Isidore's sense of history, and his own recollections show his talent for recounting events as they passed before one's senses, his is not the perspective of a jurist.

As noted above, the Anonimo was not a lawyer but a doctor. He was, therefore, no stranger to either human cognition or the imperfections and impact of our sense perceptions. Seibt has pointed out some of the ways that his medical training inflects his text, emphasizing the Anonimo's focus on physical details, on corpses, and on the ways that external symptoms could reflect internal disorder.⁷¹ We should not be surprised, then, that the Anonimo wrote his history in the mode not of an all-seeing observer of the past, but rather from the potent if impressionistic perspective of a true witness. As he did when describing the knights he saw as a boy, the Anonimo consistently provided various crucial details to set the stage for his presentation of a decisive event. But he then shifts gears and plunges into the rush of the action. His description of the Battle of Rio Salado, an event that took place in Iberia in 1340, is a typical example. He provides various details about troop numbers and deployment, setting the stage. Then the action starts, and the reader is suddenly in the thick of the battle itself.

> Trumpets and other instruments sounded. Each side could hear the noise of the other. The shrieking was so loud it seemed no human voice could have produced it. The terrible sound echoed off the mountainside. It could be heard ten miles away. One heard shouts and cries. They crashed together, body upon body. They were hand-to-hand. Some gave ground and some pushed forward. One heard cries of "Come on! Let's go!" Other cries were silenced by powerful blows upon armored heads. Lances

---

70. Faini, "Alle origini della memoria communale," 74. For a thorough examination of judicial or forensic rhetoric, which essentially deployed evidence as if to prosecute or defend individuals in a court of law, see Kempshall, *Rhetoric and the Writing of History*, 171–229; as well as Musto, *Writing Southern Italy*, 107–8.

71. Seibt, *Anonimo romano*, 256–59.

were seen thrown, swords raised, and arrows loosed. Stones, splashing into the river, slapped down like snow.[72]

In this passage, the Anonimo's reader is granted the perspective of one standing surrounded by the swirl of events rather than coolly observing them from an artificial analytical remove. One is awash in sounds and sensations, the chaos of the moment driven home by the terrifying details of the air thick with arrows and the stones raining down all around. The Anonimo is not memorializing in any modern sense so much as giving the gift of living memory so that his audience can not only know but essentially recall events as if they had been there themselves.[73] That is why he writes the way that he does. Rather than a lawyer synthesizing the testimony of witnesses into a master account, the Anonimo is a doctor writing a history that, through its stimulation of the senses, is quite literally designed to impress itself upon the reader. It will etch itself in their memory, becoming the basis for considered action in the future.

In the chronicle of the Anonimo Romano, then, we are given the impression of an educated author who, though learned in the medical arts, was not by trade a writer of history or literature. Indeed, the Anonimo serves as a reminder that we err if we ascribe to late medieval genres or professional backgrounds the kind of firm distinctions that we, as modern observers, might expect them to have.[74] In him, we see a man that was driven to write, at least in part as a form of personal therapy, a doctor who wrote in a way profoundly shaped by his own professional formation, and a historian who justified his endeavor by appealing to its general

---

72. See below, chapter 11, p. 124.

73. On this Isidorean character of the Anonimo's style, see Seibt, *Anonimo romano*, 57–59. This dovetails well with contemporary medico-philosophical ideas about memory. Müller points out that noted Latin transmitters of the Arabic tradition, like Albert the Great and Aquinas, understood that violent or moving images (*imagines agentes*) were particularly useful for creating strong links of association between various memories.

74. On this point, see Internullo, *Ai margini*, 374–82 and 473–74, who emphasizes both the degree to which Roman literary production transcended differences of social or professional status, and the intertextual and vernacular character of Roman learned culture and literary production.

utility. The Anonimo maximized that utility by writing in the everyday language of his late medieval Roman home. By doing so he made his account more effective, using familiar language to prepare the mind of his readers for the gift of new memory. The Anonimo believed that there was wisdom to be gained from knowing the truth about noteworthy things, and he understood this truth to be best derived from first-hand knowledge. His way of presenting truth, however, was more medical than juridical, shaped by the relationship of sense and memory. Having explored how the Anonimo wrote and why, we can now consider how he chose his themes and why they mattered to him. The answer to that question, appropriately, lies in the context.

## THE ANONIMO, ROME, AND LATIN CHRISTENDOM

The Anonimo's choice of themes was informed by what he believed contemporary Roman governing elites needed to know. Although he made explicit claims about how he selected what to write about, much as he did about his motives for writing at all, the Anonimo was not as explicit about his didactic enterprise. Instead, he simply claimed that he left mundane things unexamined and focused instead on events that he considered truly significant and astonishing. This is, like his discussion of his motives, reasonable enough, but it leaves much unsaid about his criteria for selecting material. If we consider the actual contents of the chronicle, we find that easily half of it is devoted to war and military matters. Other major themes include the violence of politics and of natural catastrophes.[75] A third or more of the text concerns the unique figure of Cola di Rienzo and events in Rome relating to him. In all these cases, he tends to move between set pieces, instances of battlefield action, moments of high ceremony, or instances of famine or flood. If we take him at his word, it seems that the Anonimo's decision to stick to the truly novel has resulted in a lot of jumping about. But while the

---

75. The Anonimo's focus on war, political violence, and natural catastrophe mirrors that of many of his contemporaries, see Musto, *Writing Southern Italy*, xxvi-xxvii. Regarding warfare in particular, Musto points to Froissart's *Chroniques*, of course, as particularly focused on military detail but also signals a similar emphasis on military matters in Italian sources like the *Chronicon Suessanum*, the *Chronicon Siculum*, as well as some of the letters of Petrarch, see Musto, pp. 16, 33, 94, 246.

chronicle's thematic organization does make it rather episodic, it is not a hodgepodge miscellany of random episodes. Something more specific drove his choices of what to write about. Like his stated motives for writing, then, it appears that the Anonimo's stated criteria for determining what to include in his account were simple, uncontroversial, and incomplete.

Closer scrutiny demonstrates that the Anonimo selected what to write about in a way that tied the entirety of his chronicle together, linking the Roman and non-Roman chapters. His choices of what to write and how to present his material were both motivated by his unspoken didactic mission and his sense of his own audience. A middling *popolano* with ties to the popular communal government, the Anonimo seems to have understood himself to be writing to a widely literate Roman audience accustomed to the kind of vernacular literature that his chronicle represents, and more specifically perhaps to the elite *popolani* who were the commune's governing elite. He had a sincere interest in providing his fellow Romans, humble and elite alike, with the stuff of wisdom: the knowledge of human virtues and vices, and of their outcomes. But this was a task he had to undertake with care. In his discussion of those criteria, just as in his discussion of his own motivations, the Anonimo avoided being too heavy-handed with his audience. If he was planning to offer his contemporaries much needed instruction, he was not going to risk alienating them by beating them over the head with that fact. Given that the Anonimo seems to have been writing not only to his peers but also to his own commune's ruling class, men who were his social superiors, we might understand this as simple tact. But there is still more to it than that. The Anonimo's tact and his didactic undertaking in general were shaped by the moment in which he wrote, reflecting its particular sensitivities and exigencies. If we want to understand the selection of material that the Anonimo made for didactic purposes, we need to understand, as he did, the realities of Roman life in the late fourteenth century.

ROME AND RELIGION

Late medieval Rome was one of the great spiritual centers of Latin Christendom, a city that even more than its peer polities was defined by its churches, monasteries, chapels, and hospitals. To understand the city, we do well to begin with this most familiar of its aspects. It is crucial to be attentive to how Christianity and piety actually looked in fourteenth-century Rome, and how it worked in the Anonimo's account, rather than being distracted by what one might assume one knows about Rome. No reader would be surprised to hear that the city was one of the greatest centers of Latin Christendom in the fourteenth century. But they might be surprised to learn that the papacy was absent for much of the century, having left the city in favor of Avignon not long after Pope Boniface VIII's glorious jubilee and subsequent humiliation and death.[76] Yet, despite of the papacy's departure, pilgrims continued to visit Rome's many holy sites. Nor, in fact, was the papacy totally absent. Popes routinely delegated various aspects of their power and authority to legates during the Middle Ages, and the Anonimo depicts several of these taking a direct hand in Italian and Roman affairs. Furthermore, the papacy's absence hardly meant the absence of Christianity, or of clerical authority. Given the economic value of pilgrim traffic, the Romans were keen for the pope to declare new jubilee years, during which the volume of pilgrims would greatly increase due to the enhanced spiritual rewards on offer. Pope or no pope, Rome remained a city of churches and monasteries, saints and martyrs.[77] The Romans were well aware of this fact, and it had real impact on their lives. If the city's spiritual topography appears only fleetingly throughout the Anonimo's account, that is precisely because it was such a familiar aspect of Roman life as to require little explanation for a Roman audience.

The Anonimo's Rome is a place where God intervened on a regular basis, something the Anonimo demonstrates more or less

---

76. On the Avignon papacy, see Joëlle Rollo-Koster, *Avignon and its Papacy, 1309–1417: Popes, Institutions, Society* (Lanham, MD: Rowman and Littlefield, 2015); and Unn Falkeid, *The Avignon Papacy Contested: An Intellectual History from Dante to Catherine of Siena* (Cambridge, MA: Harvard University Press, 2017).

77. A sense of Rome's character as a pilgrimage destination can be found in Eileen Gardiner, ed., *The Marvels of Rome: Mirabilia Urbis Romae*, 2nd edition, Francis Morgan Nichols, trans. (New York: Italica Press, 1986). See also Debra J. Birch, *Pilgrimage to Rome in the Middle Ages* (Woodbridge, Suffolk: Boydell Press, 2000); and Herbert L. Kessler and Johanna Zacharias, *Rome 1300: The Path of the Pilgrim* (New Haven: Yale University Press, 2000).

explicitly throughout his Roman chapters. In his account of the flooding of the city in 1345/46, the Anonimo describes the many catastrophic effects of the event but does so mostly in general terms. When he pauses to tell the story of a specific Roman, it is that of a butcher who lost all his livestock to the rising waters. The butcher's nickname, the Anonimo notes in passing, was Pisciainsanti, "pisses on the saints." God, it seems, didn't miss a thing when it came to Roman irreverence. But God was not solely punitive; He also rewarded Roman piety. When famine afflicted the city in 1338, another butcher, a landowner named Ianni Macellaro, attracted divine rewards by being willing to feed the city's starving from his own crops rather than hoarding what he had for himself. Already known as a charitable man during good times, Ianni cemented his reputation as such in a moment of crisis. In response, God miraculously caused his fields to abound. Clearly, the Anonimo understands God's will to be at work in the world, and to be most visible in moments of high drama.[78]

Ultimately, then, what the Anonimo helps us see is not Rome's religious identity in the abstract, as it would have figured in the political or theological theories of ecclesiastical elites, but rather the religion of the Romans themselves. Like all residents of Italy's city communes, their lives were constantly inflected by the sacred calendar of Latin Christianity and by the patterns and rhythms of piety. Roman lay piety was characterized by a robust spiritual economy that was both typical and exceptional. Rome's special character as one of Christendom's great pilgrimage destinations played a role, but so did acts of charity like those seen in communities all over Italy and beyond. Just as was the case with the city's spiritual topography, the fact that the Anonimo mentions this only here and there simply indicates how obvious this would have been to Roman readers. He alludes, in his discussion of Ianni Macellaro, to the tendency of virtuous Romans to give charity to great ecclesiastical institutions like the Hospital of Santo Spirito. Some of these gifts were given as charity during life but other evidence shows that similar bequests were made in the last wills and testaments of Romans from across the social spectrum.[79] In addition,

78. For these two examples, see below, pp. 99–101, 178.
79. For Roman testamentary culture, see Palmer, *Virtues of Economy*, 71–101.

while the city was home to a great many clergy, it also hosted holy figures of another sort. Lay penitents, who at times enjoyed a kind of charismatic authority, were common.[80] Just how common is revealed in the Anonimo's description of a moment when Stefano Colonna insulted Cola di Rienzo's penchant for fine clothes. In what we can imagine was a voice dripping with sarcasm, Colonna plucked at Rienzo's fancy garb and said, "It would better suit you, Tribune, to wear the honorable garb of a holy man than these pompous things." The term the Anonimo puts in Stefano's mouth is "*vizuoco*," a masculine variant of the term *bizocca*, the common word for a lay holy woman. Once again, the Anonimo does not explain this because for a Roman it would have been easy to envision just the sort of shabbily dressed holy man Stefano had in mind.

Clearly, then, Rome was a place where religion mattered, and where Christianity was at the core of the city's very identity, but in ways more complex than a modern reader might assume. The Romans may have had an unusually high degree of familiarity with the worldly aspect of the Church, and this may at times have rendered them a bit skeptical, but the Anonimo reveals them to have been at once practical and pious. They understood the economic benefit of pilgrimage to their city, but they were not cynics. They were aware that God really did work in the world, meting out rewards to the just and punishments to the unjust. Modern readers might sense a tension between Roman economic interests in pilgrimage and their acts of piety, but to the Romans themselves there was nothing unusual in the juxtaposition.

A CITY OF RUINS BUT NOT IN RUINS

Romans lived with far more explicit contrasts in the very landscape and fabric of their city. The ruined remnants of the city's ancient imperial past lay all around them, often woven into the structures of their daily lives. Late medieval Rome was, as it remains today, famous as a former seat of empire, and for the remains of that ancient splendor. Yet, as we saw with the city's religious character, for many Romans these ancient remnants were simply an unremarkable fact of life. Unlike Cola di Rienzo, most Romans could not really read

80. For an introduction to the lay holy person, see Mary Harvey Doyno, *The Lay Saint: Charity and Charismatic Authority in Medieval Italy, 1150–1350* (Ithaca: Cornell University Press, 2019).

surviving ancient inscriptions. The workaday structures of Roman life were routinely built on, in, or of the remains of ancient edifices.[81] Throughout the medieval period, ancient remains, when they were not simply torn down for building materials, were incorporated into contemporary structures. The fish sellers who operated outside the church of Sant'Angelo in Pescheria (or "in the fish market") plied their wares on large marble slabs of antique origin, and the church itself incorporated into itself the remains of the famous Portica of Octavia. This was unremarkable. The Colosseum and the Theater of Marcellus were both fortified compounds. The Pantheon was, as it is today, the church of Santa Maria Rotonda. This, too, would have seemed perfectly normal to most Romans. Although the Anonimo presents Cola di Rienzo as unusual in both the degree of his interest in these ancient remains and his capacity to analyze and understand them, it is clear that this was an interest that the Anonimo seems to have both recognized and shared. And recent scholarship suggests that he was far from alone in this.[82] By deemphasizing Rome's rich literary culture in favor of a portrayal of Cola as uniquely curious and gifted, the Anonimo presents us with a sense of Roman degradation that cannot be entirely trusted.

Rome is rightly famous as a city of ruins, but in the minds of many it is also infamous for having been a ruin itself during the late medieval period. Drawing on a tradition as least as old as Petrarch, fifteenth-century humanists would remark, as Anonimo tells us Cola did, on the city's fall from ancient glory. Hungry for employment at the papal court, such humanists tended to suggest that it took the return of the papacy to revivify Rome.[83] Cola's depiction of

81. For an introduction to the physical fabric of the city, see Richard Krautheimer, *Rome: Profile of a City, 312–1308* (Princeton: Princeton University Press, 1980). For more recent work, see Maria Andaloro and Serena Romano, ed., *Arte e iconografia a Rome: Da Costantino a Cola di Rienzo* (Milan: Jaca Book, 2018).

82. As noted above, pp. 13–14, crucial here is Internullo, *Ai margini*.

83. For these curial humanists, see Elizabeth McCahill, *Reviving the Eternal City: Rome and the Papal Court, 1420–1447* (Cambridge, MA: Harvard University Press, 2013); and Christopher S. Celenza, *Renaissance Humanism and the Papal Curia: Lapo da Castiglionchio the Younger's* De curiae commodis (Ann Arbor: University of Michigan Press, 1999). For their impact on our sense of fourteenth-century Rome, see Palmer, "Medieval and Renaissance Rome."

Rome served his political goals, while those of the humanists served their professional goals. Indeed, the caricatures of the city produced by Cola and the humanists from Petrarch on tell us more about their authors, and their interests, than they do about Rome. Late medieval Rome couldn't hold a candle to the city at the height of its imperial grandeur. Let there be no doubt about that. Its ancient walls, built to contain a million inhabitants, contained only around thirty thousand late medieval residents. Much of the space inside those crumbling walls had become uninhabited and ruralized. But the simple fact of the medieval city's existence within the remains of a very different ancient one did not make late medieval Rome itself a wreck.

As has become increasingly clear in recent years, Rome was actually fairly typical of Italian cities of its age and size.[84] Its economic structures were akin to those of other such cities. It had a fairly typical communal government and was moving along a political trajectory resembling that of other such polities. More exceptional, perhaps, was Rome's population, which included a remarkably large Jewish community and a great many foreigners.[85] But in the end Rome had a dynamic political, social, and economic life that resembled that of its peer polities. That Rome was a sleeping ruin, trapped outside time and awaiting the dawn of the Renaissance is, simply put, a myth perpetrated by fifteenth-century writers and repeated by modern scholars despite ample evidence to the contrary.

84. On Rome's place in the history of the communes, see Jean-Claude Maire Vigueur, *L'altra Roma: Una storia dei romani all'epoca dei comuni (secoli XII–XIV)* (Turin: Einaudi, 2011); Chris Wickham, *Medieval Rome: Stability and Crisis of a City, 900–1150* (Oxford: Oxford University Press, 2015); his *Sleepwalking into a New World: The Emergence of the Italian City Communes in the Twelfth Century* (Princeton: Princeton University Press, 2015); and Palmer, *Virtues of Economy*, pp. 2–3, 20, 24, 200–201.

85. On Rome diverse population, see Palmer, *Virtues of Economy*, passim.; on Jews and other minorities, Anna Esposito, *Un'altra Roma: Minoranze nazionali e comunità ebraiche tra Medioevo e Rinascimento* (Rome: Il Calamo, 1995); for one example of a foreign population, see Margaret Harvey, *The English in Rome, 1362–1420: Portrait of an Expatriate Community* (Cambridge: Cambridge University Press, 1999).

THE POLITICS OF THE ROMAN COMMUNE

Rome was a city commune like many others. To understand this, we should begin by reflecting on the first part of that term. Rome was similar to most Italian cities, a center of trade and administration, as well as a magnet for immigrants from the local countryside and further afield. As was the case with all medieval cities, it was a characteristic of Rome that while it had its share of landowners and agricultural laborers, a substantial number of its inhabitants made their living in non-agricultural fields. As elsewhere, these were often organized into guilds. Some guildsmen owned a single humble shop, while others were the wealthy overseers of multiple concerns.[86] Keeping all these city dwellers fed required a steady supply of victuals from the countryside, which made control over that countryside paramount.[87] It is not accidental that the Anonimo is attentive to the dangers of famine, the importance of maintaining a moral economy of grain, the centrality of agricultural entrepreneurs in Roman life, and the tie between political stability and food. Nor is it by chance that he looks with favor on Cola di Rienzo's efforts to secure the countryside and eliminate violent, disruptive influences like the acquisitive baron and plunderer of ships, Martino del Porto.[88] But we must not lose sight of the fact that although the Anonimo speaks at length about famines and problems with unruly rural magnates, these were problems that faced every Italian city.

"City commune" is, of course, a compound noun of which the city and its material structures were only one part. The term "commune" refers to the manner in which the city was governed, i.e., by a communal government, and could also refer to the politically enfranchised population. Italy's communes, including Rome's, emerged in the eleventh and twelfth century.[89] They

86. On Rome's artisans and their guilds, see Isa Lori Sanfilippo, *Roma dei Romani: Arti, mestieri, e professioni nella Roma del trecento* (Rome: Istituto Storico per il Medio Evo, 2001).

87. On grain and the Roman port, see Luciano Palermo, *Mercati del grano a Roma tra Medioevo e Rinascimento* (Rome: Il Centro di Ricerca, 1990); and his *Il porto di Roma nel XIV e XV secolo: Strutture socio-economiche e statute* (Rome: Istituto di studi romani, 1979).

88. For Martino, see below, pp. 37, 48, 180, 201–2.

89. Wickham, *Sleepwalking into a New World*.

generally involved some kind of executive official or officials, one or more consultative assemblies, and increasingly refined jurisdictional claims instantiated in communal courts that were overseen by communal judges and notaries. We should not overstate the seemingly democratizing effect of quasi-republican institutions and ideas. Communal governments were the product of medieval political realities, just as were all the novel forms of political life that flourished in late medieval Europe.[90] Communal governments, including Rome's, reflected the inequities common to the worlds that birthed them. They incorporated a notion of citizenship; but that franchise did not extend very far, generally being denied to the urban poor, rural dependents, foreigners, non-Christians and, to a varying extent, women.

Political power in the communes was continuously shifting. Throughout much of Italy, the thirteenth and fourteenth centuries saw both the ascendancy of new political elites and the gradual displacement of communal governments by one-man rule. This is a trajectory Rome shared with its peer polities. The Florentine chronicler, Giovanni Villani, scoffed at Rome's decline in comparison to the glorious ascendancy of Florence.[91] But the two cities actually had a lot in common. Both were scarred by a lengthy conflict between an old aristocratic elite and political newcomers commonly associated with the guilds. And in both cases this conflict ended only with the ascendancy of a single ruler who would systematically appropriate the institutional apparatus of the commune. Cosimo de'Medici effectively captured Florence in 1434.[92] The Romans ceded sovereignty of their commune to the papacy in 1398. But both cities were simply arriving late to the one-man rule that had already supplanted Italy's other city communes and largely obviated the longstanding disputes of old and new elites. The ubiquity of this conflict in communal Italy makes it easy to slip into generalization. As we shall see, however, the Anonimo both

90. Susan Reynolds, *Kingdoms and Communities in Western Europe, 900–1300* (Oxford: Clarendon Press, 1997).

91. Giovanni Villani, *Cronica nuova*, VIII.36.

92. For an overview of Florentine history in this era, see John Najemy, *A History of Florence, 1200–1575* (Oxford: Blackwell, 2008).

recognizes the central role of elite conflict and avoids the temptation to treat it in a facile or reductive way.

In the Roman case, the old elite against whom political newcomers were forced to contend are particularly notorious. These are the so-called Roman barons, members of powerful families that had emerged from the urban nobility in the twelfth and thirteenth centuries, became closely tied to the College of Cardinals, and then used that position to amass tremendous wealth and power.[93] The reputation of these medieval barons was, and remains, one of violence, self-interest, and an unstinting hunger for power. The notoriety of the barons derives primarily from the vociferous criticism to which they were subjected by voices long privileged by historians. Cola di Rienzo himself emerges as perhaps their foremost critic, both in his own correspondence and in the telling of the Anonimo. Cola — like Petrarch — ostensibly saw the barons as responsible for the inversion of every good thing in Rome. By their influence, he said, "Justice was punished, all peace driven out, all liberty prostrate, all security snatched away, all charity damned, and all truth oppressed, and mercy and devotion profaned."[94] The contemporary jurist, Bartolo da Sassoferrato, referred to the government of Rome as a many-headed hydra, of which the various heads were constantly at war with one another and no one head was ever strong enough to prevail. This was a monstrous form of government, in his mind, a perversion that resulted from the barons' self-interested meddling.[95]

93. On the Roman barons, see Sandro Carocci, *Baroni di Roma: Dominazioni signorili e lignaggi aristocratici nel duecento e trecento* (Rome: Istituto storico italiano per il Medioevo, 1993). The two greatest families in this era were the Orsini and the Colonna. For the former, see Franca Allegrezza, *Organizzazione del potere e dinamiche familiari: Gli Orsini dal Duecento agli inizi del Quattrocento* (Rome: Istituto storico per il Medioevo, 1998). For the latter, see Andreas Rehberg, *Kirche und Macht im römischen Trecento: Die Colonna und ihre Klientel auf dem kurialen Pfründenmarkt (1278–1378)* (Tübingen: Neimeyer, 1999). For an overview of the barons' changing place in late fourteenth-century Rome, see Palmer, *Virtues of Economy*, 41–68.

94. Konrad Burdach and Paul Piur, *Briefwechsel des Cola di Rienzo*, in *Vom Mittelater zur Reformation*, vol. 2.1–5 (Berlin: Weidmann, 1912–29), 2:37.

95. Bartolo de Sassoferrato, "De regimine civitatis," in *Politica e diritto nel trecento italiano*, Diego Quaglione, ed. (Florence: Olschki, 1983), 59.

If we read only the chapters on Cola, dominated as they are by the tribune's own propaganda, we might think the Anonimo agreed wholeheartedly with his condemnation of Rome's barons. But this would be a misunderstanding. Although the barons have long served as a useful foil for all that is good in accounts of Roman history, for the Anonimo reality was far more complex. The Anonimo clearly saw some barons as villains. Martino del Porto is depicted as a moral monster, and Stefano il Vecchio Colonna figures as a traitor to the city and the arch-nemesis of Cola di Rienzo. But the Anonimo notes that Cola had baronial allies as well, and sometimes presents barons as admirable. Stefano Colonna's own brother, Sciarra, appears as Rome's savior when he marshalled the city's defense in alliance with Emperor Lewis IV and against the combined armies of a papal legate, his own brother Stefano, and the brother of King Robert of Naples. Sciarra, the Anonimo declares, was "a most virtuous baron... one of the most experienced and skilled men in the arts of war then living."[96] He organized the defense, entrusting it to his fellow Romans in a manner that the Anonimo hails as both laudable and highly competent. Nor is he the only baron so acclaimed in this moment. The Anonimo describes the death of Cola de Madonna Martomea, a member of the baronial Annibaldi family, in the ensuing battle. "How great was Rome's sadness at the loss of this famous baron," he laments.[97] For Romans, then, there was potentially plenty to admire about these supposed monsters. Throughout the chronicle, the presence of barons signals splendor and prestige, and they themselves are sometimes examples of proper virtue. King Alfonso of Castile appears accompanied in the field by his barons, who scold him for inaction against an invading Muslim host.[98] Furthermore, barons could easily fall prey to the foibles of their class without necessarily becoming cartoon villains. The baronial leadership of the Smyrna Crusade brought about their own deaths by charging into battle in an unplanned and overeager way. But the Anonimo assures us that in doing so they "received holy martyrdom and were made knights of Christ." Barons, in other words, were human beings, and the Anonimo understands them to be capable of villainy, heroism,

96. See below, p. 68.
97. See chapter 3, p. 71.
98. See chapter 11, p. 122.

or foolishness. Cola di Rienzo's anti-baronial critique, necessarily a prominent part of the chapters devoted to him, are not the whole story. The same is true of the traditional enemies of the barons, a group that included both Cola and the Anonimo himself.

For much of the late thirteenth and fourteenth centuries, the enemies of the old elite were that rising political group known as the *popolo*, who famously established what historians tend to call "popular regimes" in the communes of Italy.[99] The term *popolo* and the derived category of "popular" readily evoke a more democratic vision of society; but this should not be overstated. In Rome as elsewhere, the *popolo* were a diverse bunch, reflecting the social strata of guild society. That is not to say, however, that they lacked a coherent political vision. The communal ideology of the *popolo* commonly emphasized justice and the right ordering of things; and it associated this order with peace and stability. As we have seen, these were precisely the elements of Cola's vision that appealed to his fellow Romans. For the advocates of the popular commune, peace was desirable both as a kind of pious goal and because stability was good for trade, on which the political power of the *popolo* was based. But the stable world this imagined was still one marked by dramatic inequities and limited access to real political power. Popular communal ideology, then, hinged on the idea of the city commune as a collective ordered hierarchically, as all things were, but in such a way as to sustain justice, peace, and prosperity.

Real power in most popular regimes was held by the elite of the guild community, men whose wealth at times rivaled that of the old nobility. One can reasonably surmise that the Anonimo, like Cola di Rienzo, was of humbler stock. Both men were educated *popolani* but not among the truly elite. It is perhaps for this reason that the Anonimo excelled at seeing through the mystique of popular ideals. Just as the Anonimo saw the fundamental humanity of the barons, so too does he see the human flaws of his peers among the *popolo*. But, in yet another demonstration of tact, he most often uses Cola as his primary example of this rather than calling out the men who probably comprised his target audience. As already noted,

99. For an introduction to the *popolo*, see Andrea Zorzi, "The popolo," in *Italy in the Age of the Renaissance, 1300–1550*, John Najemy, ed. (Oxford: Oxford University Press, 2004), 145–64.

the Anonimo presents Cola's early reforms as the embodiment of "popular" communal ideology, oriented around justice and peace. But he also portrays a steady deterioration of Cola's character as his power grew. "At first," he says, "Cola led a very temperate life. Then his vices began to multiply." This is a clear warning of the dangers of power. Indeed, things only worsened as time went on. Cola, the Anonimo almost sighs, "had formerly been sober, temperate, and abstinent." But then he became "an excessive drinker, utterly given over to wine."[100] We cannot actually say for sure whether or not Cola was actually afflicted by these vices to the extent that the Anonimo claims. It is clear that the Anonimo deploys these tropes, which resonate strongly with both contemporary and classical sources, in order to build arguments about governance that were rooted in meditation on virtue and vice. As the Anonimo portrays Cola, his gluttony in drink resonated with his other great vice, greed for money and a general inability to manage it well. The risk of moral failure and the limits of competence were dangers familiar to the governors of all communes, for whom power might inevitably become intoxicating, and the fiscal demands of government presented a constant challenge in the fourteenth century. In other words, the Anonimo recognized that his own social stratum was no less corruptible than the barons. They might espouse lofty ideals of justice and peace, but their love of wealth could lead to intemperance, poor stewardship, and destruction. The Anonimo's portrayal of Cola's moral character thus speaks directly to the specific moment within which he was writing, one in which Roman elites were forced to reflect on long generations of communal political struggle in light of the recent rise and fall of Cola di Rienzo, and of their own part in it.

COLA DI RIENZO AND HIS AFTERMATH

The Anonimo Romano lived in a tumultuous age. As already noted, during the long decades of papal absence, power in Rome was contested between the city's most powerful elites — baronial families who enjoyed close ties to the papal court — and a mixed group of less wealthy urban nobility and non-noble guildsmen known as the *popolo*. These struggles, which resembled those between old elites and new men in many Italian communes, at times resulted

---

100. See below, p. 281.

in factional violence.[101] It was in this context that the Anonimo was born, and that his contemporary, Cola di Rienzo, the son of an innkeeper and a notary by profession, rose to prominence.[102] Though the Anonimo is vague on the details, he reports that Cola's brother was slain in what seems to have been an act of private, perhaps factional violence, and that this murder sparked something in his fellow Roman. "He thought long about how to avenge the blood of his brother," the Anonimo observes. "He pondered at length about how to reform misguided Rome."[103] That Cola began to move into public life in response to this is made clear by the fact that he appears in the chronicle first as part of an embassy to the pope in Avignon, serving at the behest of one of Rome's non-baronial regimes. When he returned to Rome, he did so as a papal agent, busying himself with laying the groundwork of a successful and surprisingly bloodless coup.

In addition to relying on papal support, Cola built a local following among the *popolo*'s governing elite by emphasizing the need for and possibility of administrative, financial, and legal reforms and tying said reforms to a high-minded appeal to the traditional communal ideals of justice, peace, and prosperity. Once in power, Cola granted himself the classicizing title of Tribune, an indication of his inspiration by the ancient republican past that would have resonated with a general tendency among popular regimes to associate themselves with it. According to the Anonimo, due at least in part to the slip from good virtuous governance into self-serving vice already mentioned, Cola's support from papacy and *popolo* alike gradually waned.[104] When that

101. On the problem of violence in the Italian cities, see Andrea Zorzi, ed., *Conflitti, paci e vendette nell'Italia comunale* (Florence: Firenze University Press, 2009).

102. For what follows relating to Cola's life, see Musto, *Apocalypse in Rome*, 23–82.

103. See below, chapter 18, p. 183.

104. Musto, *Apocalypse in Rome*, 230–55, demonstrates clearly that the Anonimo's sense of Cola's political trajectory was shaped by his apparent ignorance of certain facets of this complex political moment, especially his seeming unawareness of evidence pointing to the papacy's explicit effort to undermine Cola's government by cutting off trade and threatening to cancel the imminent jubilee year — which was of great economic importance to the Romans — and placing the city under papal interdict.

happened, his position in Rome became unsustainable. He fled the city, living first in hiding and then as a prisoner of first Emperor Charles IV and then of Pope Clement VI. After Clement's death, Cola was freed by his successor, Innocent VI, returning to Italy and eventually to Rome as papally appointed Senator, which he again ruled for a brief period that ended with his death at the hands of a Roman mob, and arranged by his enemies the Colonna. All of this, the Anonimo dutifully reports.

During the very years that the Anonimo was writing, the precise lessons of Cola di Rienzo's rise to power and his catastrophic fall were still being absorbed by contemporaries.[105] They were a particularly pressing concern for the city's communal elite, many of whom had supported Cola and now needed to distance themselves from the memory of his spectacular failures.[106] The Anonimo is ever tactful in how he presents this audience with their past selves. From the beginning, he says, Cola had brought together "many Roman *popolani*, good and wise men." These included "knights and those of good lineage" as well as "many wise and wealthy merchants."[107] Why would they not listen to someone who promised to reform the management of their city and to work for peace and justice? Furthermore, Cola had promised them powerful help. "My Lords," he had assured them before his bloodless coup, "do not believe that this is without the license and support of the pope."[108]

The Anonimo constructs a narrative to suggest that despite the communal elite's initial optimism about Cola, a measure of skepticism remained and slowly grew. He begins with hints, very early on, about how Cola's love of luxury and tendency to aggrandize himself began to be clear. "When Cola di Rienzo wrote," the Anonimo

---

105. On this point, see Palmer, *The Virtues of Economy*, 32–40.

106. On the various ways the Roman ruling elite responded to this moment, see Alizah Holstein, "Rome During Avignon: Myth, Memory, and Civic Identity in Fourteenth-Century Roman Politics," (Ph.D. diss. Cornell University, 2006). Holstein notes that following Cola's fall, Roman elites deliberately sought to forget aspects of their own recent past. See especially pp. 200–210.

107. See below, p. 191.

108. See below, p. 192.

observes, "he did not use a goose quill. Rather, he used one of fine silver. He said that such was the nobility of his office that the pen should be silver."[109] According to the Anonimo, Cola's personal vices were increasingly exacerbated by what the writer presents as political missteps, suggesting that his audience also recognized them as such. As the chronicle progresses, Cola comes across in the Anonimo's telling as increasingly deluded, debauched, and unreliable.

Rome's governing class, meanwhile, is presented in a manner probably reflective of the Anonimo's own experience. Some of the details of this will be provided below. For now, let it suffice to point out that while the Anonimo suggests to his readers that the "discreet men" of Rome — the city's guildsmen, notaries, and other elite *popolani* — may have erred in supporting Cola, they did so for good reasons: the pursuit of peace, justice, and good governance. Not only that, but they were never fully taken in and they wisely abandoned Cola when things went too far.

The Anonimo's account is therefore rather flattering to the elite governing class he was trying to reach but naive of papal politics and policies that were intended to destabilize Cola's regime and force his resignation. Specifically, the archival record clearly shows that the pope had instructed his legate, Cardinal Bertrand du Déaulx, to promote key destabilizing measures: to disrupt the city's food supply, to begin a disinformation campaign against Rienzo, to stir up dissension and active opposition in alliance with the barons, to move to declare Rienzo a heretic, and finally to cancel the jubilee and to place Rome under papal interdict, so striking at the heart of its economic vitality and spiritual and political authority.[110] The Anonimo's seemingly complete picture of events, despite his ignorance of these details, serves as a reminder that his depiction of Roman events was a construct that must always be balanced against other evidence.

PUTTING ROMAN POLITICS IN CONTEXT

We might be forgiven for thinking that the Anonimo Romano was horrified by the condition of his city. Certainly the didactic undertaking attributed to him here suggests that, like Cola di Rienzo, the Anonimo thought Rome was in serious need of being set straight. Furthermore, the Anonimo's account of Roman

109. See below, p. 187.

110. For these documents, see Musto, *Apocalypse in Rome*, 230–55, esp. 236–39.

violence at first seems to accord with longstanding notions of the fourteenth-century city as a shamble. But the Anonimo had not given up on the Roman commune, nor did he think Cola's failure necessarily doomed it. He was a proponent of communal ideology and its emphasis on justice, just as Cola di Rienzo ostensibly was, but we should not be fooled into thinking that the Anonimo wholeheartedly accepted Cola's critique of his city. Cola emphasized Rome's fallen state under the barons, and the Anonimo dutifully reports this. But the Anonimo no more caricatures Rome than he does the barons or the *popolani* who fought over its political fate.

The Anonimo's focus on violence and chaos in Rome is, in fact, entirely typical of his approach to the history of other parts of Italy and of the wider Christian world. There too, the Anonimo is interested primarily in the things we find in his Roman chapters: political tumult, war, and natural disaster. When he looks further afield, beyond Italy, his attention is captured mostly by battles: the Battle of Rio Salado in Iberia, the Smyrna Crusades of the eastern Mediterranean, and the Battle of Crécy in France. But the Anonimo was no mere voyeur with a taste for chaos. In every case, the Anonimo's interest was not in the events themselves but in the lessons they could teach the local Roman readership that was his intended audience. Like his classical sources, throughout the chronicle he preferentially examines key actors in moments of decisive choice, considering them as examples of virtue and vice and explaining their influence on the flow of events. What may appear as Roman exceptionalism, when read in isolation, becomes typical of the human experience when read in the context of the chronicle as a whole.

For the Anonimo, chaotic moments of battle and crisis were instances when the truth of human nature could be witnessed and evaluated both in terms of its power to shape history and in terms of its relationship to the will of God. This was true not only of his reflections on events in Iberia, France, Milan, or Bologna but also his prolonged meditation on recent Roman history, for which all the rest served as a kind of preparatory context. As his approach to Roman events makes clear, the Anonimo's sense of history, and of the actors that drove it along, was one that acknowledged this complexity. If we look only at the chapters on Cola, we risk allowing the Anonimo's account of Cola di Rienzo's political propaganda to drown out the Anonimo's more nuanced thought. Considering his treatment of Rome alongside his discussion of other places makes clear that just as the Anonimo saw two Colas — one to be admired and emulated and the other to be condemned — he saw two Romes as well. One Rome was afflicted by its own vices, to be sure, but the other was endowed with a canny governing class that both had a clear sense of justice and recognized the limits of the tribune's grandiose vision, even if Cola himself did not. This was an audience capable of learning from the lessons the Anonimo hoped to teach, lessons in which the non-Roman chapters of his work played an important contextual role. This is something we are now in a position to understand.

## THE ANONIMO'S LESSONS FOR ROME

As we have seen, the Anonimo Romano was concerned, like so many of his age, to teach his readers about virtue and vice, so that they might embrace the former and eschew the latter. This would help his target audience, Rome's governing elite, to govern virtuously, which is to say effectively, so that Rome might know the stability that all societies craved. He was determined to offer Rome these lessons because he knew that its governing elite were struggling, in the wake of Cola di Rienzo's tumultuous career and catastrophic fall, to process what they had been through. The life of Cola di Rienzo, therefore, occupied a central place in his thinking as it inevitably did for his contemporaries. But to understand the lessons the Anonimo drew from Cola's example, we need to situate them in the context of his work as a whole rather than focusing solely on the chapters dedicated to Rienzo. Given the Anonimo's nuanced understanding of all aspects of Roman political life, we cannot assume these lessons to be simple or obvious.

Furthermore, we must never lose sight of the fact that in reading the Anonimo's account, we are encountering a reality of his own creation. In part due to his didactic goals and in part due to the fact that his notions of truth and accuracy were simply different than ours, the Anonimo cannot be expected to provide us a clear window on the past "as it really was." As has already been discussed, the Anonimo at times played fast and loose with sequence and chronology, preferring to build his account around thematic units.

He took inspiration from classical models when he needed to evoke the inner workings of his actors' minds. Yet, he also insisted that everything he said was true, and made much of his dependence on eyewitness accounts. For the Anonimo, there was no inherent tension between these things. For him, a relentless positivism was not necessary for accuracy or truth-telling. One could drift away from the specifics and the sequence of events, one could even supply invented or imagined elements, and still tell the truth. If the Anonimo's lessons are not always so simple, neither is his relationship to the evidence from which he has constructed them.

Ultimately, the Anonimo's refusal to think in reductive ideological schemes led him to recognize that good governance required the balancing of a wide range of complicated challenges and tensions. On a practical level, anyone who would govern well had to balance the need for money against the universal antipathy for taxation of any kind. On a slightly more abstract level, they had to balance the importance of justice against the value of Christian mercy. Socially, they had to maintain the distinction that undergirded their power without jeopardizing their relationships with others. They had to depend on others, in fact, but also take care not to give power or privilege where it might not be appropriate. Once we examine each of these necessities in turn, we shall find that that the Anonimo understood all these complicated yet obligatory burdens to ultimately be facets of a single fundamental rule. If anyone wished to govern well and virtuously, they had to maintain a clear-eyed sense of themselves, to remember who, what, and where they were. This would ensure that they were ever aware that whatever power they had in one moment might be lost in the next, due to both their own mistakes and to divine disapproval.

### The Financial and Moral Challenges of Good Governance

One of the inevitable challenges of governance is finance, and all of Italy's communal governments, including Rome's, struggled with it. One of Cola di Rienzo's greatest missteps was the fact, or perhaps simply the appearance of the fact, that his tax policies devolved over the course of his career from examples of good governance into manifestations of personal greed. He showed an impressive competence early on, revealing to his fellow conspirators how to maximize the commune's incomes from a hearth tax, a salt tax, taxes on ports and fortresses, on livestock, and from the collection of criminal fines. "Have no concerns about money," Cola assured his fellow-conspirators as they planned for his bloodless coup, "for the Camera of Rome has inestimable sources of income."[111] Yet, from a man who understood how to use his administrative savvy to maximize communal incomes early in his reforming career, Cola became something far less laudable. Late in his career "Cola made many excuses," the Anonimo wrote, but he asserted that Rienzo had degenerated into a drunkard with a taste for fine clothes who could not manage to pay his own troops. In the Anonimo's dramatic arc, the same man who had so clearly understood the mechanisms of good governance early in his career had now become profligate and parasitical.

When we examine this theme's appearances throughout the chronicle, such characterizations — whether based on fact on not — make clear that the Anonimo is teaching a political lesson here, rather than merely telling some kind of political morality tale about Cola. In chapter 12, we find that the duke of Athens turned his Florentine allies against him by squeezing them for money with the aid of an official that the Anonimo characterizes as "diabolical."[112] In chapter 13, according to the Anonimo, the Smyrna Crusades were sparked by predatory taxation too, as Morbasciano, the Turkish lord of Smyrna, angered the Venetians and other merchants by extorting all who passed through his domain.[113] In a subtly different tale recounted in chapter 5, the papal legate who ruled in Bologna had been driven from power because his military failures had led him to raise taxes, exciting the ire of the Bolognese populace. For the Anonimo, the legate may not have been personally greedy, but he was a proud and haughty man. Such flaws in his character meant that his new taxes gave the impression of being driven by arrogance and avarice rather than being accepted as necessary.[114] These interpretive nuances put the Anonimo's discussion of Cola in a new light.

---

111. See below, p. 192.
112. See below, p. 141.
113. See below, pp. 148–49.
114. See below, p. 77.

If we read Cola's life alone, we might think that the Anonimo simply believed that responsible financial management was a virtue, with gross hedonism as its wicked opposite. But contextualizing Cola's life shows a more complex lesson. For the governor of a polity, greed and the mere appearance of greed had the same result. Just as it did the merchants of Florence under the duke of Athens, a man they had been instrumental in bringing to power, the avarice of the powerful could make even their most ardent supporters feel betrayed. Cola was right, the Anonimo informed his readers, when he noted that Rome could be financially solvent without the need to risk popular anger through the imposition of novel exactions. But this would only be true if they governed well in other areas and did not face unusual challenges. As a reformer, this is not the reality Cola faced. During his first period in power, he was forced into repeated military clashes with his enemies. The novelty of his situation required him to sustain a highly rhetorical and performative public display — not unusual for Italian communes at the time — in an attempt to both legitimize his position and to beguile the Romans into accepting his *buono stato*. But no matter how necessary this was, it was still expensive and gave the appearance, to the outsider, of profligacy. The Anonimo convinces us that Cola had an immoderate liking for the finer things in life, and that this vice undermined his ability to do what was necessary to forge the Rome he envisioned. Good governance meant facing financial challenges, but surmounting them required one to face moral challenges as well. Giving way to greed, or even allowing the mere appearance of greed, could ruin everything.

### Cruel Justice and Foolish Mercy

We have seen that the notion of justice was fundamental to the ideology underpinning all popular communes. Really this was true of all claims to legitimate authority and power in the medieval world. In an abstract sense, the just society was the rightly ordered society. It was rewarded with God's favor just as the unjust, wrongly ordered society might suffer divine wrath. At the level of governance, the wielder of power had to perform an analogous task by dealing punitive or "retributive" justice to malefactors of all kinds. This retributive justice could be harsh, but it was also necessary to obtain peace and prosperity. The Anonimo consistently admires examples of justice in its more abstract form as moral rectitude and right order. He recognizes the value of retributive justice as well. True to his characteristic sense of nuance, however, the Anonimo does not simply recommend that governors exercise justice with an iron hand. This is easy to miss if one examines only Cola's life.

The reader of the chapters on Cola finds yet another example of the Anonimo's account of his decline from virtue to vice. Early in his career Cola reformed the Roman courts, making them more expeditious, and created new communal institutions for the ending of private disputes. He went so far as to have violent, plundering barons like Martino del Porto executed. "In those days," the Anonimo says wistfully, "terrible fear afflicted the hearts of thieves, murderers, evildoers, adulterers, and every person of bad repute."[115] The result was that farmers worked the fields, travelers passed through the forests, and pilgrims made their way to the holy places in peace and security. But then, according to the Anonimo, Cola began to go too far. He began to hang members of baronial households, claiming that they were all thieves. He fined everyone who had held the executive office of Senator. "For no apparent reason" he beheaded a prominent Roman that the Anonimo describes as having been a virtuous man. Eventually, the Romans "began to fear the Tribune as if he were some kind of demon."[116] In what the Anonimo relates as resembling fits of escalating emotional instability, Cola "took to arresting people. He arrested this one and that, holding them for ransom."[117]

Even when Cola exercised restraint, the Anonimo suggests that his actions were cause for worry because they seemed simply foolish, calling his overall competence into question. After managing to capture several of his baronial enemies and preparing to execute them, Cola abruptly released them instead, with a grand show of mercy. Rather than being seen merciful, however, the Anonimo reports that the deed worried Cola's supporters. "This fellow has lit a fire and flame that he will not be able to put out," the Anonimo reports them to have muttered.[118] The Anonimo's ironic

---

115. See below, p. 199.
116. See below, p. 292.
117. See below, p. 292.
118. See below, p. 227.

staging of one of Cola's last acts before his death suggests that he learned the wrong lesson from this. When his mercenaries turned on him because he failed to pay them, Cola imprisoned Messers Arimbaldo and Bettrone, the two men who led them. Along with them he seized Fra Morreale, the great mercenary captain who was their brother and supporter. Morreale was executed and, though Cola eventually released Arimbaldo, he kept Bettrone imprisoned until the very end. But, the Anonimo writes, he was troubled by the presence of his prisoner. As the Romans stormed his palace, Cola attempted to flee. The Anonimo portrays him as fearing all the while that Bettrone was somehow communicating with the mob from his prison. In reality, Bettrone was the least of Cola's problems at this point, and he was betrayed by someone else entirely: his own kinsman, Locciolo Pellicciaro.[119] Ultimately, then, the Anonimo presents Cola as incompetent in handling political prisoners, and inconsistent when it came to balancing justice and mercy.[120]

Consideration of the chronicle as a whole reveals that the problem that the Anonimo saw with Cola's justice was not simply that it became erratic, or that it afflicted the innocent and the guilty alike. These were real problems, but the Anonimo understood the heart of the matter to be deeper still; simply put, it was not easy to discern when justice ceased to be justice and became tyranny. Lucchino Visconti of Milan is hailed by the Anonimo as a man thoroughly committed to justice and so successful in this that one could travel about his realm with money in one's pocket and fear nothing. Lucchino was even willing to threaten his own son with stern justice if he betrayed his obligation to mete out justice by taking bribes to reduce the sentences of the elite. In the Anonimo's account, he thus appears to be a man of principle. But Visconti is also depicted as frightening and savage, surrounded by terrifying hounds that protected him from all comers. When the son of one of

119. Given that Cola is described as being almost entirely alone in an empty palace, the Anonimo's portrayal of his thoughts and fears is most likely an invention. Evoking Cola's fears about Bettrone perhaps served to drive home the shock of his actual betrayal by Locciolo, a member of his own family.

120. Musto, *Writing Southern Italy*, 219–20 points out that the Anonimo was likely drawing on biblical sources in his discussion of Arimbaldo, Bettrone, and Morreale's imprisonment, using scripture to craft a kind of political *exemplum*.

his best retainers dared to chastise one of the beasts for barking, the Anonimo relates that Visconti fed the boy to the hound in question. In response to pleading by the boy's father, he exercised the very obduracy that he recommended to his son, for neither begging nor offers of money saved the boy's life.[121] As the Anonimo sees it, Lucchino Visconti did not understand the line between justice and cruelty. The Anonimo used a story about King Robert of Naples to teach a similar lesson. Faced with his own son's demand for capital punishment for a noble murderer, Robert relented but urged the young man to consider that "justice that is too harsh, where no mercy is to be found, is the worst kind of cruelty." Tellingly, the Anonimo emphasizes that Robert would have preferred to commute the execution to a fine, serving the financial needs of his government and showing mercy in a single act of good governance.[122]

As was the case with finances and greed, considering the Anonimo's discussions of justice outside the chapters on Cola reveals important details about how the Anonimo's discussion of Roman affairs should be understood. Cola was deeply concerned with justice, as all communal theorists were, but he did not have a fine understanding of it. From the Anonimo's account we gather that Rienzo's penchant for the dramatic seems to have overpowered his good sense. It was one thing to set up a House of Justice and Peace in which highly public and ritualistic ceremonies of reconciliation might take place between feuding parties; such things had their place in Rome, as elsewhere throughout the Peninsula. But it was another when Cola's rituals obscured poor decisions, like freeing his baronial enemies. In the Anonimo's account, the performance of justice or mercy did not suffice in itself. Like King Robert of Anjou, the wise ruler needed to know the proper time and place for each. According to the Anonimo, Cola's problem was, therefore, not only that his justice became increasingly arbitrary, driven by his need for money, but also that he was bad at both justice and mercy, unable to discern when to exercise one versus the other and wracked by anxiety as a result. In these matters, the Anonimo clearly relates, it was imperative that any who aspired to good governance demonstrate greater acumen and make better choices.

121. See below, p. 105.
122. See below, p. 112.

## INTRODUCTION

### THE SOCIAL NATURE OF POWER AND MORALITY

The creation and maintenance of power was a social endeavor, one that required a measure of splendor because power was reinforced not only through brute force but through performance, ritual, and display.[123] The Anonimo Romano clearly admires Cola di Rienzo's talent for this, despite his indication of reservations about things like Cola's silver quill. He describes in great detail Cola's elaborate costumes, banner-filled processions, and works of political public art. In the Anonimo's treatment, by presenting himself effectively, Cola swayed Roman crowds and cowed papal legates. His effectiveness won him support. But his public ritual had the opposite effect when it began to appear ill-considered and self-serving. In a pivotal example, marking the shift from praise to blame in the Anonimo's account, Cola had himself knighted in a public ceremony followed by a tremendous celebration. Shockingly for both the Anonimo and his contemporaries, he had himself bathed in the baptismal font of Constantine. "When word got out," the Anonimo wrote, "there were some who saw it as audacious but others who said he was delusional and insane."[124] The Anonimo described the celebration that followed in great detail. Wine poured from the nostrils of specially designed statuary. Men pranced about dressed as bulls. "Whoever wished to attend was there. There was no order at all."[125] In his description of this affair, the Anonimo draws a clear contrast to earlier civic celebrations such as that in honor of the knighting of Stefano Colonna and Napoleone Orsini. That event is described as a chivalric festival with pavilions, jousting, and music.[126] Roman festivals of this sort were often organized according to social hierarchy.[127] Even as he emphasizes the relative chaos of

---

123. For the most recent research on Roman ritual and ceremony, which puts Cola di Rienzo at the center of new Renaissance civic display, see Anna Modigliani, "Antichità e paganesimo nelle feste e nelle ceremonie romane del Rinascimento," in *Vivere la città: Roma nel Rinascimento*, Ivana Ait and Anna Esposito, ed. (Rome: Viella, 2020), 247–62.

124. See below, p. 223.

125. See below, pp. 223–24.

126. See below, p. 65.

127. The best example of the usual order in Roman civic celebration is the annual games that took place in Monte Testaccio and in the region now

Cola's celebration, the Anonimo signals that the same discreet men who doubted Cola's ill-considered mercy were troubled by what appeared to be his audacity and madness. We seem, once again, to be presented with a simple story of hubristic overreach common to trecento historical writing.

Once again, however, examination of the chronicle's wider context reveals this not to be the case. The Anonimo recognized that public ceremony mattered, but he sees the danger not in too much grandeur but rather in a kind of inconsistency between moments of ceremony and the comportment of the powerful in other moments. The importance of grandeur as a political tool is indicated by the figure of Mastino della Scala of Verona, who was notable for the luxurious court he maintained, replete with the trappings of power and luxury. No mere hedonist, Mastino used his court as a tool by which he might control conquered lands by drawing the local nobility to his grandeur and magnificence. The Anonimo clearly admires this clear example of political acumen. But he also calls attention to the fact that Mastino was intemperate. He began to ruin churches for his own gain, to slander his fellow rulers, to indulge in public luxury by having a rich crown fashioned for himself.[128]

Another example is to be found in the Anonimo's account of King Alfonso of Castile. The Anonimo portrays him as a good and successful king overall, but he stresses that the king's personal comportment made him vulnerable precisely because it offended those that mattered most. The Anonimo emphasizes, in fact, that the invading Muslims had only been able to penetrate Alfonso's kingdom because they had the help of one of his barons, one Don Ianni Manuelle, who the Anonimo asserts was disgusted by his king's libidinous penchant for adultery. Alfonso, the Anonimo recounts, "did not love his queen and did not wish to stay by her side despite the fact that they had a son. Instead, he maintained a relationship with a concubine — Donna Leonora by name —whom he loved over all other things." Not even the pope could make him give up his lover. The resulting public spectacle of sin at the highest

known as the Piazza Navona. This included ritual combat with animals, with the knights battling a bull and lesser men fighting pigs. See Palmer, *Virtues of Economy*, 167.

128. See below, pp. 88–89.

level, the Anonimo asserts, provoked Don Ianni's betrayal, even if he subsequently helped Alfonso win the decisive battle at the Rio Salado. The Anonimo was more than a little confused on the details of this event, but that makes his point no less clear. Perhaps too accustomed to the privileges of being king, the Anonimo implies, Alfonso failed to maintain a proper public majesty, alienated key followers, and compromised the social ties that undergirded his power.[129] Thinking about Cola di Rienzo, the Roman reader would surely have nodded in rueful recognition of this important truth.

The social nature of power, furthermore, underscored the fact that one also had to worry about the comportment of those who acted in one's stead as well. This meant policing one's own and being judicious in those one elevated. Mastino della Scala is again an example. In the Anonimo's account, not only did he become gluttonous and corrupt, he became blind to the vices of others. He put his equally degenerate brother, Alberto, in a position to alienate key elites. Before long, one of the very men meant to be placated by the trappings of della Scala's power could take no more of Alberto's ceaseless abuse and turned on him, betraying Alberto and Mastino to the Venetians and bringing about their downfall. The key mistake Mastino made, in the Anonimo's telling, seems to have been that he became too invested in the trapping and image of power, forgetting that the performance and reality of majesty were not the same thing, and that power could be lost. It wasn't enough to draw the local elites into his court, he had to manage his relationships with them well, or their proximity to him would be his undoing.

All of this draws our eyes to key details in the Anonimo's depiction of Cola, details that can now be seen in a new light. Early in his career, in the Anonimo's dramatic arc, Cola used grandeur well and was wise in his choice of whom to honor. When he marched to seize the Campidoglio on the day of his coup he did so in a procession that included symbolic banners that were born by prominent members of the Roman *popolo*. He also relied on baronial support, putting Orsini men in positions of military leadership. He policed his own well, having one of his own couriers branded for illicitly taking money while on an official mission. But then, according to the Anonimo, he failed to sustain his social

---

129. See below, p. 134.

savvy. He stopped paying the militia, made up largely of his own supporters. When some among the Orsini became rebellious, he had humiliating, inverted public images of them painted, a standard practice used to defame traitors.[130] Furthermore, Cola, like Mastino, was inclined to aggrandize his own family. His wife began to carry on like a noblewoman, and he made his uncle into a powerful lord. That uncle, and other relations as well, took to swanning through the streets of Rome with troops of armed men. At his knighting feast, his wife dined with her ladies in the papal palace, taking part in a meal that included "less water than wine."[131] As the Anonimo relates it, to the shock of his constables in the wake of an unexpected victory over the Colonna at the city's Porta San Lorenzo, Cola declared that his son would now be called the Knight of Victory, anointing him with bloody, muddy water from a puddle in which a slain Colonna lay. The Anonimo emphasizes the shock of Cola's companions at this behavior.

Seen through the Anonimo's account, Cola di Rienzo is depicted as having a talent for political symbol and ritual, a key element in the social production and reproduction of power, but this could only take him so far. The Anonimo portrays Cola's public behavior as inconsistent, marked by an increasing dissonance between performance and reality that he failed to control. At the same time, the Anonimo reports, he began to betray and humiliate those who served him well, while also elevating the undeserving. The Anonimo's message, taken in the context of the chronicle as a whole, is clear. The social nature of power required the same canny judiciousness, the same virtue, as did financial management and the performance of justice and mercy. Any Roman who aspired to good governance had to heed this or risk the same fate as Cola di Rienzo.

LEARNING FROM COLA DI RIENZO

In the Anonimo's chronicle Cola di Rienzo appears alongside a diverse array of contemporary rulers, all of whom committed, or served to call attention to, variations on a single crucial error. No matter how much power one had, one had to know when and how to exercise it. Failure to discern the right response to the exigencies

---

130. On this practice, see Gherardo Ortalli, *La pittura infamante. Secoli XIII-XVI* (Rome: Viella, 2015).

131. See below, p. 223.

of the moment would have fatal consequences. These might be abrupt, coming in the form of rebellion or betrayal, but they might also take the form of the gradual erosion of the very foundations of one's power. A good governor had to be able to maximize incomes without appearing predatory, do justice without veering into cruelty, offer mercy without being foolish, achieve balance between ceremonies of power and one's own personal comportment, and show judiciousness in whom they honored and shamed. The reins of power were slippery, and inattention to that fact invited catastrophe.

Taken on their own, the chapters of the Anonimo's chronicle that depict the life of Cola di Rienzo easily take on the tenor of a morality tale. In the Anonimo's telling, the tribune began as an example of the moral virtue and acumen integral to the virtues of good governance. Once in power, he became ever more inconsistent and self-serving. He evinced an ever greater belief in the security of his position, in the inherence of his own power and authority, which, the Anonimo stresses, blinded him to the results of even his most egregious missteps. He paid for his mistakes with his life. This is a simple, satisfying story of the importance of clear-eyed moral rectitude. If the virtue and justice of a man like Ianni Macellero could lead to God's gift of miraculous prosperity, Cola's failures led to injustices and the collapse of his state. The corrupt ruler sows only chaos and dissension, and his harvest is violence and death. The simplicity and clarity of this story is undeniably alluring. Indeed, the Anonimo's vivid style makes it all too easy to forget that one is reading a reconstruction of events, rather than looking through a window to the past. But reading the chronicle as a whole makes clear that this is a far simpler interpretation than the one the Anonimo was offering.

The Anonimo's description of Rienzo is often contradictory, as both heroic and fallen; and the reader is just as often hard-pressed to reconcile these extremes. While one solution is to take the Anonimo's account as a reliable psychological report, on the model of a modern clinical diagnosis, a more reliable approach is to see that the Anonimo is constructing a fairly consistent moral story about Cola along the model of his classical sources. Such was also the grand trajectory of his contemporary Boccaccio's *De casibus virorum illustrium*,[132] filled with

132. See Giovanni Boccaccio, *The Downfall of the Famous,* Louis Brewer Hall, trans. (New York: Italica Press, 2018).

dozens of examples of such virtuous ascendencies and then disastrous falls.

In chapter 27, for example,[133] Cola is presented as a reformed man while imprisoned, reading piously in his cell. He seems a respectable man while with the papal army, behaving appropriately. But once he is back in power, he devolves into a drunken tyrant. The Anonimo seems to suggest that Cola did not have a ruler's temperament, and that he did best when he was either denied unfettered access to power and privilege or when he was safely ensconced within a larger effort that someone else controlled. Even his first significant act, as part of a larger embassy to Avignon in Chapter 18, is marked by this pattern. Cola gives an admirable speech as part of the embassy, but once he is left alone in Avignon the Anonimo describes him as rapidly emboldened by Clement VI's favorable treatment of him, which served to fan the spark of ambition that had been smoldering in Cola's breast since his brother's death. Like so many of the moral portraits painted by the Anonimo in this work, this one is surely an invention, but an invention likely derived equally from classical sources and from the complicated memory of Cola that surely lived on in those who had known him.

Time and again, the Anonimo demonstrates a discerning eye for nuance, complexity, and the multi-faceted character of human nature. In the barons, those cartoon villains of the day, he saw the evils of tyranny, greed, and violence but also the virtues of courage, competence, and honor. In the *popolo*, the political class from which he himself hailed, the Anonimo saw discretion, acumen, and the capacity for the kind of good governance that could ensure justice, peace, and prosperity. But he saw also saw in the *popolo* the dangers of miscalculation and missteps born of naiveté, credulousness in the face of political flattery, and inevitable human susceptibility to the corrupting influence of power. So attentive a student of human nature would hardly follow up such nuanced observations by reducing the most important part of his work to a facile morality tale. Morality mattered to the Anonimo. He did not doubt that God rewarded the just and punished the unjust. The Anonimo's presentation of Cola's flaws as so glaringly apparent, in the Roman chapters of the chronicle, served in part to appeal to his audience, the

133. See below, p. 274.

very elites who so often appear as skeptical observers in his account. But in truth the Anonimo recognized that the interaction of moral virtues and the virtues of good governance was complicated. Each on its own was difficult; and the necessity of managing them both at once, as anyone who wielded power had to do, was more difficult still. The Anonimo's Cola di Rienzo had embraced high ideals and thereby risen to great power, but he had forgotten that he was only a man, and he lost sight of that power's practical limits.

The Anonimo's narrative offered a challenge for Rome's ruling elite. If they wanted to restore and sustain stability and prosperity in Rome, they needed to emulate Cola at his best while avoiding his missteps. In his chronicle, Anonimo provided them the tools to do so, not only by reflecting on Cola's career but by doing so within a larger context, one in which both moral virtue and the virtues of good governance recurred again and again as guiding themes. That the first half of the chronicle addressed the very themes that were most pressing in his study of Cola strongly suggests that they were intended to work as preparatory material. He presented all this to his audience in ways that were designed to draw them in and impress these lessons upon their minds in a lasting way. All the more tragic, then, that his work has so often been read piecemeal.

It is not clear that the Anonimo achieved his end. Within a few decades of the Anonimo's death, Rome's ruling elite made the decision to give up the sovereignty of their commune and serve instead as administrators under the power of the papacy.[134] As we have seen, one cannot say with any certainty that very many people read the chronicle in the intervening years. It would be easy, as a result, to dismiss the chronicle of the Anonimo Romano as the fragmentary remains of an incomplete and ineffective project. But to do so would be to turn a blind eye to the refreshing optimism of the Anonimo's commitment to popular communal ideology, and to turn one's back on his chronicle's literary innovation, rhetorical eloquence, and historical value. This last, above all, should not be forgotten. The history of failures can be as instructive as that of successes. The chronicle of the Anonimo Romano may not have succeeded in the ways its author perhaps hoped, but his work offers us a glimpse into the mind of Rome's governing class during a

---

134. Palmer, *Virtues of Economy*, 196–216.

period about which we otherwise know far too little, revealing the challenges with which it struggled and the possibilities that some, at least, could imagine. These are the sorts of rewards on offer to the reader willing to grapple with this splendid but challenging work in its entirety, as readers are now invited to do.

EDITORIAL NOTE

Overall, this translation is based on Giuseppe Porta's definitive edition. The manuscripts on which Porta based that edition include numerous lacunae. Some of these are places where specific dates or sums have been left blank, perhaps to be filled in later. In other cases, however, the material missing is more substantial. In what follows, these lacunae have largely been preserved and signaled with bracketed ellipses, [...]. The one major exception to this rule comes in chapter 27, when, in the midst of his siege of Palestrina, Cola di Rienzo imprisons Fra Morreale and his brothers. Porta's edition has a lacuna here. Ghisalberti's edition, however, fills the gap with material taken from Biblioteca Marciana di Venezia, Cod. Cartaceo 4802. Ghisalberti discusses this issue in the introduction to his own edition (pp. xxxiv–xxxvi). Because Anglophone readers will likely already have encountered this material in Wright, who based his translation on Ghisalberti, and because it supplies important details pertaining to Morreale's story and the dire financial situation that Cola was in at the time, I have opted to incorporate the passages Ghisalberti included, working in that case from his edition rather than Porta's. The passage has been italicized in order to signal this, and a brief explanatory note included.

The Anonimo — or the surviving manuscript of this text — uses many variants of proper and place names. We have attempted to regularize these whenever possible, providing important variants in footnotes or in parentheses in the Index.

The Anonimo's text also contains many passages, and individual words, in Latin. In what follows, all such instances have been left in Latin and italicized. Translations are provided in the footnotes. Including translations of these passages in the main text would only serve to erase the uncertain relationship they have to that text due to the chronicle's unfinished state.

※

# CHAPTER ONE: PROLOGUE
## The Reason Why This Work Was Undertaken

THE GLORIOUS SCHOLAR-SAINT, Messer Isidore, says in his *Etymologies* that the first Greek to discover writing was a man named Cadmus.[1] Before that man's day, no one knew the use of letters. As a result, when they needed to memorialize something, they couldn't write about it. Instead, they made memorials of things in sculptures of stone and etched images, which they would place in prominent locations where a great many people were to be found. Alternatively, they placed them in the very place where the memorialized events had taken place, such as the site of a great battle or victory [...], defeats or tragedies [...] and various animals in stone, as well as armed men, in reference to the thing memorialized. They erected these stones in the places where famous things had happened, as a sign of perpetual remembrance. They produced no books, because prior to the Greeks there was no writing. This was also the way of doing things among the Romans throughout Italy and France, and especially in Rome. Because they wished that their descendants should know [...] their deeds, they created triumphal arches and funerary inscriptions, with battles, armed men, horses, and other things as one finds today in Perugia and Rimini.

Once Cadmus made known the art of writing, people began to write down their deeds and various other things, particularly famous and magnificent things, in order to overcome the inadequacy of memory. In just such a way Titus Livy wrote a book that described the period from the founding of Rome to the age of Octavius.[2] Lucan wrote the deeds of the Caesars.[3] Sallust and other writers refused to let any of Rome's past deeds fade away.[4]

---

1. Isidore of Seville, *Etymologiarum sive originum libri XX*, I.3.

2. Livy, *Ab urbe condita libri*, written in the final decades BCE. Like the Anonimo's own chronicle, it survived only in part but was well known during his day.

3. Lucan, *Pharsalia*. This was an epic poem recounting the civil wars fought in the time of Caesar, written in the first century CE, during the reign of Nero.

4. Sallust was a late first-century BCE figure, a contemporary and supporter of Caesar. He wrote multiple histories, most famously his *Bellum Cataline*, which recounts the conspiracy of Cataline against the state, and its thwarting by Cicero.

In the same way, should I [...] allow to go unrecorded the things that I have seen in this world by the grace of God and that are worth remembering for their notable excellence and novelty? It would hardly be acceptable for the shadow of ignorance to prevail due solely to reluctance to write. In fact, I would like to produce a truly special narrative in this book. It is a great and beautiful undertaking, which I have taken on for many reasons. The first is so that people might find written records of events similar to those they have seen themselves, and so come to see the truth of the words of Solomon. Solomon said, "There is nothing new under the sun, whatever seems new is not."[5] Another reason for this work is to record many examples, beautiful and good, so that people might wisely shun what is dangerous and instead choose and adopt what is not. I hope therefore that reading this work will not be without some fruitful utility. The third reason is my own respect for the magnificence of these events, as I already said. There is no reason to trouble oneself with trivial matters. Leave them be! One should write about great matters.

My fourth reason is the same that moved Titus Livy. Titus Livy explains this in his first decade, where he discusses Alexander of Macedonia: how many foot soldiers and cavalry he had, how long his rule lasted, and how much of the world he conquered. Then he says that Alexander's greatness was nothing compared to that of Rome. By saying this he responds as if to a question that someone might have asked him, namely, "In recounting the history of the Romans how is it that you feel the need to discuss Alexander?"

In response Titus Livy says, "I do this to set my mind at ease." As if he were to say, "My mind was inspired to write these things. I wanted to treat them so that I might satisfy my mind." So I say, "By God, my inspired mind could by no means rest until I had put down in writing these beautiful things and novelties that I have seen in my life."

The fifth reason is another that Titus Livy writes in the beginning of his work, in the first decade.[6] He says, "When I am engaged in writing these things, I stand apart from and do not see the cruelties that our city has been witnessing for so long." So I say, "As I took pleasure in this work, I stand apart from and do not feel the war and

---

5. *Ecclesiastes* 1:9-10.
6. Livy, *Ab urbe condita libri*, *Praefatio*, 5.

# ✳ CHAPTER ONE: PROLOGUE

miseries which afflict my land, due to which profound tribulation not only those who witness them are sad and despondent but also those who only hear of them."

What I write is absolutely true. As God is my witness, and those who were with me are too, the things written here are all true. I saw and heard them. This is the case above all with things that took place in my own land and were noted by trustworthy people, whose accounts corroborated one another. I have therefore placed certain indications within the flow of the text that indicate when such people agreed about something. Let these signals reassure the reader so that they do not suspect what I've said. Furthermore, I have written this chronicle in the vernacular, so that even folk who only read simple things may partake in its utility, for example the simple merchants and other good people for whom loftier writing is not intended. I therefore undertake this vernacular work for the common good and for common enjoyment, insofar as I have already produced a version in a very [...] Latin.[7] Yet that piece was not so orderly or complete as this one is.

Moreover, I have broken this work into chapters[8] so that, should someone wish to find something, it might be readily found.

CHAPTER TWO.[9] The people drive Senator Giacomo Savelli from the Campidoglio. The knighting of Messer Stefano Colonna and Messer Napoleone Orsini.

---

7. There is a word missing here. Campanelli, "'Benché io l'aia fatta per lettera'," 4, argues that the word is probably *luculento*, derived from the rhetorical term elocution (*elucutio*), and meaning something like brilliance. He notes that the Anonimo uses the term repeatedly to describe Cola di Rienzo's eloquence as well. This would suggest that the earlier, Latin version, was written in a higher style, while the surviving vernacular text is rather more colloquial.

8. The Anonimo's use of chapter headings is indicative of the works thematic rather than chronological organization. See Musto, *Writing Southern Italy*, 100.

9. The Anonimo is not providing a modern table of contents here but rather a sketch of things to come in his chronicle. As a result, he begins with chapter two. The first chapter, already underway, was, after all, not yet to come but rather already before the reader's eyes.

CHAPTER THREE. The prince of Morea is defeated at the Porta Castel Sant'Angelo. The origins of the Guelfs and Ghibellines. The character of Dante and how he died.

CHAPTER FOUR. Pope John and the coming of the Bavarian to Rome, his departure, and the antipope that he created.

CHAPTER FIVE. The monster born in Rome. The papal legate is slain in Bologna.

CHAPTER SIX. Fra Venturino comes to Rome with the Doves. The bell tower of St. Peter's is burned.

CHAPTER SEVEN. Pope Benedict and the roof of St. Peter's in Rome, which was rebuilt.

CHAPTER EIGHT. The comet that appeared in parts of Lombardy. The defeat of the tyrant Messer Mastino by the Venetians.

CHAPTER NINE. A very cruel famine. The Battle of Parabiagio in Lombardy. Various new fashions.

CHAPTER TEN. The death of King Robert and the coming of the queen of Hungary to Rome.

CHAPTER ELEVEN. The battle for Spain, the destruction of Algeciras, and the siege of Gibraltar.

CHAPTER TWELVE. The duke of Athens is driven from Florence. Pope Benedict dies. Pope Clement is elected.

CHAPTER THIRTEEN. The crusade carried out at Smyrna in Turkey.

CHAPTER FOURTEEN. The battle for France, in which the king of Bohemia dies and the king of England defeats the king of France.

CHAPTER FIFTEEN. A great flood and the extent of the waters.

CHAPTER SIXTEEN. A ship run aground and robbed on the Roman coast.

CHAPTER SEVENTEEN. Leonardo of Orvieto is captured by Rome.

CHAPTER EIGHTEEN. The great deeds of Cola di Rienzo, August Tribune of Rome.

CHAPTER NINETEEN. The death of Andrew, king of Puglia, by hanging. How justice followed after this death.

※ CHAPTER ONE: PROLOGUE

CHAPTER TWENTY. The king of Hungary enters Italy. The death of the duke of Durazzo, who is beheaded.

CHAPTER TWENTY-ONE. The cruel mortality that afflicted the whole world. The steps of Sta. Maria in Aracoeli.

CHAPTER TWENTY-TWO. The earthquake in Italy.

CHAPTER TWENTY-THREE. The fifty-year Jubilee in Rome. The king of Hungary's return to Rome and Puglia.

CHAPTER TWENTY-FOUR. The Perugians lay siege to Bettona, raze that place to its foundations, and behead the traitor, Messer Crispolto.

CHAPTER TWENTY-FIVE. The bell tower of St. Peter's in Rome burns. The pope loses control of the Senate. Pope Clement dies.

CHAPTER TWENTY-SIX. A senator is stoned by the Romans. The magnificent deeds of Messer Egidio Conchese of Spain, cardinal legate, to retake the Patrimony, the March of Ancona, and Romagna.

CHAPTER TWENTY-SEVEN. Messer Cola di Rienzo returns to Rome and reassumes power amid much rejoicing. He is cruelly slain by the people of Rome.

CHAPTER TWENTY-EIGHT. Emperor Charles comes to Rome. His coronation and his departure for Germany.

※

# CHAPTER TWO

THE PEOPLE DRIVE SENATOR GIACOMO SAVELLI FROM THE
CAMPIDOGLIO. THE KNIGHTING OF MESSER STEFANO
COLONNA AND MESSER NAPOLEONE ORSINI

AND SO, with what novelty ought I to begin? I shall start in the time of Giacomo Savelli. Holding the office of Senator solely due to King Robert's support, he was driven from the Campidoglio by the syndics.[1] The syndics in question were Stefano Colonna, lord of Palestrina, and Poncello Orsini, the son of Messer Orso, lord of Castel Sant'Angelo.[2] These two men went to the Aracoeli and called together the people, the many armed knights and infantry of Rome, by ringing the bell.[3] All of Rome armed itself. I remember the sound well. I was standing in Sta. Maria in Publicolis[4] and I saw the train of armed knights pass by, summoned to the Campidoglio. So proudly they went! There were many of them, well mounted and armed. The last of these, if I recall rightly, wore a coat of red silk and a silken yellow headdress, with a horseman's mace in his hand. They passed directly down the street, past the fish-market, where the blacksmiths are found, alongside the house of Paolo Giovinale. The train was long. The bell was ringing. The people armed themselves. I stood there in Sta. Maria in Publicolis. Of all these things I am sure.

---

1. The king referred to here is Robert of Anjou, or Robert the Wise, of Naples. He named Savelli and Matteuzzo Orsini to the senatorial office in 1325, as his vicars. The term "syndics" refers to municipal officials. On Robert, see Samantha Kelly, *The New Solomon: Robert of Naples (1309–1343) and Fourteenth-Century Kingship* (Leiden: Brill, 2003).

2. Poncello is a nickname for Napoleone, making this the same man named in the chapter's title.

3. That is, the church of Sta. Maria in Aracoeli. On the use of bells — and the soundscapes of cohesion and rebellion — in Italian communes, see now Atkinson, *Noisy Renaissance*.

4. Sta. Maria in Publicolis, known in the twelfth century as Sta. Maria de Publico, is located in *rione* Regola, not far from Campo de' Fiori and near the Palazzo Santacroce.

❋ CHAPTER TWO

The senator, Giacomo Savelli, stood on the Campidoglio. He erected a stockade around his position. But his fortifications were useless. The syndics of Rome, his uncle Stefano and Poncello, sallied out. Gently, they took him by the hand and removed him from power, in such a way that no one was in any danger.

There were some who thought (and said), "Stefano, how could you shame your own nephew this way?"

Stefano's response was superb. He said, "I will pay him back with two denari worth of cherries."[5] But those denari were not forthcoming.

I WILL ALSO BEGIN from the moment that these two barons were made knights by the people of Rome, anointed in rosewater by the Twenty-Eight Good Men in Sta. Maria in Aracoeli, to their great honor.[6] One became Messer Stefano, the other Messer Napoleone. The celebration on the Campidoglio that day was great, as was the honor bestowed. In the Piazza of Sta. Maria tents and pavilions were pitched. There were trumpets, shawms,[7] and all manner of instruments played. Lances were broken, horses raced, and breastplates rattled. Many banners flew. Even more coats of arms were seen. The celebration was tremendous. It was a day for honors. In the church of Sta. Maria in Aracoeli stood two daises for the ones most honored of all. It seemed a truly regal event.

---

5. Roman coinage, in this period, included silver *lire provisini* (a money of account that was used in reckoning value but not actually minted), *soldi provisini*, and *denari provisini*. There were twelve denari to the soldo, and 20 soldi to the lira. Also common was the ubiquitous gold florin of Florence, worth approximately 47 soldi. Two *denari* was a trivial sum, so the implication of this wry statement was that Savelli's dignity wasn't worth all that much.

6. This appears to be an odd mistake. The Good Men were officeholders in Rome's popular communal government, each responsible for one of its districts (*rioni*). Thus, they were always in multiples of 13, at least one for each *rione* of Rome.

7. A type of woodwind instrument.

I remember these things as if from a dream. It was the year of our Lord, 13[…].⁸ Later, these two anointed knights went to King Robert of Naples, who dubbed them both with his sword, a thing most upsetting to the Roman people.

Of course, I was not part of these events because, though I was alive, I was still very young, not yet having reached adulthood. All the same, I wanted to start my account with something significant. Now, by the name of God, let us turn to the defeat of the prince of Morea, which happened as follows.⁹

---

8. There is a lacuna in the text here, which makes the year uncertain. Porta, 207 suggests 1325, with the next paragraph's voyage to Naples in early 1327.

9. "Morea" was the late medieval way of referring to the principality of Achaea, which was originally a vassal state of the Latin empire founded after the Fourth Crusade and based in Constantinople. During this era, it was usually given in fief by the Angevin kings of Naples to their various relatives and allies.

# CHAPTER THREE

THE PRINCE OF MOREA IS DEFEATED AT THE PORTA
CASTEL SANT'ANGELO. THE ORIGINS OF THE GUELFS AND
GHIBELLINES. THE CHARACTER OF DANTE AND HOW HE DIED

IT WAS IN THE YEAR OF OUR LORD 1327, in the month of September, during the vigil of the Archangel at harvest time, when the Romans had a great victory at the Porta Castel Sant'Angelo, which happened in the following way.[1] The imperial electors of Germany elected as emperor Lewis, duke of Bavaria, who was not obedient to Pope John, as I shall explain.[2] When it was understood that this newly elected man was coming to Rome, Pope John, who was alive at that time, and King Robert of Apulia[3] took measures to brace themselves for his arrival. At their command, Messer Giovanni della Rascione,[4] prince of Morea and brother of King Robert, as well as Messer Giovanni Gaietano, legate in Tuscany,[5] therefore marched with many men to Rome to aid in the defense. They rendezvoused in the city of Narni. It was a splendid and well-equipped host. There were seven hundred knights and innumerable infantry. All the barons of House Orsini were there: Messer Napoleone, the new knight of the people, Bertoldo de Francesco dello Monte, nephew of the legate and champion of the Guelf Party,[6] Messer Andrea de Campo di Fiori,[7] and many others. The army grew immeasurably large as it prepared to occupy Rome.

1. Notably, Castel Sant'Angelo is named for the Archangel Michael, whose feast day it was. See Gardiner, *Marvels*, 6, 84

2. The disagreement between Lewis and Pope Giovanni XXII seems to have been discussed in chapter four, which was either lost or never completed.

3. This is the same King Robert of Naples as in the previous chapter. "Apulia," "Puglia," and "Sicily" were medieval Italian terms for the kingdom of Naples.

4. This is Giovanni di Gravina, duke of Durazzo, then also titular lord of Morea in Greece. The title "della Rascione" is complementary and perhaps indicative of cunning or savvy.

5. Giovanni Gaetano Orsini, cardinal legate in Tuscany at the time.

6. The Guelfs were one of the two great factions in Italian politics, along with the Ghibellines. They ostensibly favored papal causes, while the Ghibellines were allied with the Holy Roman Emperors. In reality, things were far messier.

7. This is another Orsini. The family had several branches, which were

The Romans, seeming as though they meant to ready a good defense, prepared themselves and named as captain of the people a most virtuous baron of House Colonna — Sciarra was his name, one of the most experienced and skilled men in the arts of war then living. Before the legate drew near, Sciarra took control of all the fortresses of Rome. He held Castel Sant'Angelo firmly. Then he put the people in order, naming neighborhood commanders. He made twenty-five captains in total, all of them Romans. He organized all the constables. He kept them all on alert. He guarded the gates well. He heard reports often. He had many spies. Giacomo Savelli, Tebaldo Santo Stati, and many other barons were there alongside the people.[8] The closer the approaching legate came, the more alert the Romans became.

So it was that the night of the vigil of the Archangel arrived in Rome. The enemy entered the Leonine City, but not through the gate, which was well guarded. Instead, they came in through a hole in the wall.[9] They broke through the wall where it stood near the Incarcerata. Knocking the wall to the ground, they created a large opening near the well.[10] Through this opening they brought through their banners and their legions of troops. Once they had entered, they occupied the zone between the Castel Sant'Angelo and St. Peter's. The whole area was blanketed in armed men. Proudly they sounded their horns and trumpets, shawms and drums, making a great display. They wrote witty declarations about their entry into Rome, which they incised upon the bronze gate.

When the valorous captain, Sciarra, saw that the enemy had arrived, he did not hesitate for a moment. He armed himself and

---

sometimes distinguished by association with different holdings or with parts of Rome where their power was centered.

8. The Savelli we have already met. Porta points out that "Santo Stati" was a bastardization of the names of the counts of Sant'Eustachio, which had become common usage by this time.

9. The Leonine City, named for the ninth-century Pope Leo IV, includes the region of the Vatican. It was not part of Rome and had its own circuit of walls. Though the walls of both were in equally poor repair during this period.

10. This is a reference to a specific neighborhood, in the parish of Sta. Maria in Traspontina. See Gardiner, *Marvels*, 86, 108.

# CHAPTER THREE

commanded the warning bell be sounded. It was midnight when the first toll sounded. He sent a crier with a trumpet across the city, so that all the people would arm themselves and assemble at the Campidoglio, knowing that the enemy had entered the Puortica.[11] The sleeping populace quickly awoke. Everyone took up arms. The crier's name was Coscia. The bells rang terribly. The populace came to the Campidoglio. The barons and the people came together there. The good captain spoke, declaring that the enemy had come to enter Rome and kill babes still at the breast of Roman mothers. He highly inspired the people. Then he divided them into two parts. Of one part he was leader, while the other was led by Giacomo Savelli, who was sent to the Porta San Giovanni, called the Porta Maggiore. This he did because he knew the enemy was actually split in two, one part planning to enter by way of the Porta Castello and one by the Porta Maggiore. But it did not turn out that way for, as God willed, the feast of the Archangel had come.

The attackers entered on the day following the Holy Angel's feast. So the plan failed, for they did not arrive at the gates at the same time, on the same day. When Giacomo went to the gate, he found no one there. There he held fast, despite facing no organized opposition. On the other hand, there was the group following Sciarra and his banner. The cavalry was numerous. Seven armed *rioni* were represented.[12] The host contained innumerable people. They marched on the Ponte San Pietro. I remember that during the night an armed Roman knight, standing mounted on the bridge, heard the blowing of an enemy horn. Wanting to flee, he was thrown from his horse. He left the horse behind and continued on foot. A wise man does not lack caution!

When day broke, the Roman people came to the bridge. It was dawn. Sciarra gave the command that the bronze gates be opened. The crowd was large. The enemy was stunned to see the many banners. For they knew that every banner indicated twenty-five men. And so

11. "Puortica" is the way that the Anonimo refers to the Vatican Borgo, that region already described as occupied by invading imperial troops.

12. As it still is today, medieval Rome was divided into administrative regions called *rioni* (singular, *rione*), which were themselves subdivided into neighborhoods known as *contrade*. *Rioni* were the primary means by which locations were specified in Roman records and were commonly used to identify individuals as well.

the gate was opened. The men of *rione* Monti were at the front. Men were deployed at the porticoes, along the Piazza de Castello. There the soldiers and other folk were assembled. Then the horses charged. One tumbled over the other. One man delivered blows, and another took them. Trumpets sounded here and there. Great was the noise and great the clash. One attacked and the other defended. Sciarra and Messer Andrea of Campo dei Fiori came together, shouting curses at one another. First they shattered their lances on one another. Then each hammered the other with his sword. Neither had any fear of death. Eventually, though, they each fell back to their own people. There were blows exchanged, javelins hurled, and rocks thrown. It seemed a truly vicious battle. The people of Rome battled back and forth like waves on the sea. The enemy gradually gave way and the Romans advanced halfway across the piazza.

Then something unusual happened. A man by the name of Ianni Manno of *rione* Colonna bore the banner of the Roman people. When he arrived at the well that stood in that piazza in front of the Incarcerata, where the opening in the wall was, he took the banner and hurled it in the well. He did this intending to bring about the ultimate defeat of the Romans. The traitor really deserved to die. Yet, because the prince had already been driven back, the courage of the Roman did not falter. One moment there was fleeing and the next there was fighting. So it was clear who was the son of a good mother. Sciarra Colonna inspired his people highly and achieved something truly notable, causing him to change his colors so quickly. He caused him to show good judgment.[13]

A large number of the people were moving along the river, on the Santo Spirito side.[14] There, due to the crowd, five Roman foot

13. This passage, relating to Ianni Manno and Sciarra, is a difficult one. The Anonimo's language makes it unclear whether "the Roman" is Ianni or some generic figure representing the Roman forces more generally. The clear indication is that there was doubt about the outcome of this battle, but Sciarra's quick success boosted the confidence of his men, leading them to fight on when they seemed on the verge of retreat.

14. That is, on the same side of the Tiber River as the Hospital of Santo Spirito in Sassia, near St. Peter's. The hospital had its own docks, the Porta Arcella or Arzeli. See Pietro De Angelis, *L'ospedale di Santo Spirito in Saxia,* 2 vols. (Rome: Tipografia Dario Detti, 1960–62); and Andreas Rehberg, "I papi, l'ospedale e

## CHAPTER THREE

soldiers were drowned. And then there was another remarkable thing. There was a prominent Roman, Cola de Madonna Martomea degli Annibaldi was his name, a very ardent fellow, as youthful as fresh water.[15] He was struck with the audacious notion that he might capture the prince himself. He spurred his war horse and broke through the mighty enemy host to where the prince was being defended. He saw him there and he stretched out his hand to strike him. Well, if you can believe it, the effort was a failure. The prince swung an iron mace and struck his horse with it. Such was the might of the prince's steed that it launched itself and carried the prince beyond Nicola.[16] Nicola did not have enough room for his horse to move. Attempting to turn about it took a bad step and tumbled into the great moat in front of the hospital of Santo Spirito, which had been dug for the defense of the garden. Into the ditch he and the horse tumbled, staggered by the force of the prince's mount and trying to turn about, and there he died. How great was Rome's sadness at the loss of this famous baron. Indeed, it inflamed the people. The prince fell back. His troops relented. They began to flee. They went by way of the Porta Verdara.[17] That was the road by which he fled.

It was the hour of terce.[18] The retreat was great. Greater still was the slaughter. They were slaughtered like sheep. They gave no resistance. Many people were killed. The Romans took tremendous spoils. A few Orsini barons, who put up a fight, were captured. As many were put in prison as the captain wished. Among them was Bertoldo, leader of the Orsini, captain of the Church and of the

---

l'ordine di S. Spirito nell'età avignonese," *Archivio della Società Romana di Storia Patria* 124 (2001): 35–140.

15. Porta suggests that this is Madonna Bartolomea in the local dialect. That would identify this young man as Nicola Annibaldi, son of Pietro and Bartolomea and husband of Maria Orsini. For his precise situation in the Annibaldi family, see the family tree appended to the chapter on the Annibaldi in Carocci, *Baroni di Roma*, 311–16.

16. "Cola" is simply the short form of "Nicola," so this is the same opponent.

17. Porta notes that the gate near the Vatican Gardens was known by this name during this period. See also "Porta Viridaria" in Gardiner, *Marvels*, 6, 85.

18. 9:00 AM.

Guelf party. If Sciarra had not been there to carry him away on horseback, the Romans would have killed him.

Other people he did not defend, namely the Neapolitans, Provençals, French, and the Puglians. There were so many dead, stripped bodies that one cannot even guess at the number. From the piazza of Castel Sant'Angelo all the way to St. Peter's, around Sta. Maria in Traspontina and Piazza Santo Spirito, at all the gates, all the way to the piazza of the Armenians,[19] in every street they lay like scattered seeds, cut down, naked, and dead. Among them lay the count of San Severino and many other notables: it was a stark sight. Ultimately, the prince vanished with what people he could gather together. For days dead bodies were found among the vineyards, still armed, laying inside shelters and in the shade of trees, having been wounded in the battle. They had died while fleeing.

Sciarra returned to the Campidoglio in great triumph. He commissioned a beautiful pallium for Sant'Angelo in Pescheria and a lovely chalice too, in thanks and celebration of this Roman victory.[20]

IN THAT TIME were born the two cursed parties, the Guelfs and the Ghibellines, who had not existed before. The Blacks and the Whites appeared too. One evening, as the people were finishing their daily work, near the dinner hour, in the city of Florence two dogs fought. One was named Guelf and the other Ghibelline. They struggled mightily with one another. The young people were drawn to the ruckus the two dogs made. One group favored Guelf, the other Ghibelline.[21] When the dogs were...

---

19. Although it no longer exists, Porta, p. 210, notes that a Piazza of the Armenians was attested in this part of Rome from at least the late thirteenth century and is also attested in the fifteenth-century account of Antonio di Pietro dello Schiavo.

20. Sant'Angelo in Pescheria was an important church not far distant from the Campidoglio. It was, and remains, located near the Theater of Marcellus, on the site of the ancient Portica of Octavia, and took its name from the fish market that operated just outside. It was a special church of the Colonna. See Gardiner, *Marvels*, 103.

21. This origin story for the Guelf and Ghibelline parties is both utterly fanciful, misleading about when the parties originated (they were much older), and

※ CHAPTER THREE

[The remainder of the chapter is missing.²²]

---

conflates their emergence with that of the Blacks and the Whites, originally of Florence, which were two opposing Guelf factions and had also originated well before these events. It is entirely possible that the Anonimo took this tack as a sign of his general disgust for factional politics of this sort, condemning such conflicts by depicting their origins as ridiculous. The Italian names of the factions derive from the original German factions: Guelf (generally pro-papal) were those of the dukes of Welf (Bavaria) and Ghibelline (generally pro-imperial) of the faction of the Hohenstaufen of Waiblingen.

22. Among these missing sections is the Anonimo's discussion of Dante's life and character. This was also a celebrated passage in Giovanni Villani's *Cronica Nuova* (X.136); copied almost verbatim in Agnolo di Tura's *Cronaca Senese*, 387. See Musto, *Writing Southern Italy*, 89.

# CHAPTER FOUR
## POPE JOHN AND THE COMING OF THE BAVARIAN TO ROME, HIS DEPARTURE, AND THE ANTIPOPE THAT HE CREATED

[This chapter is missing.[1]]

1. Born Jacques Duèse du Cahors, Pope John XXII (r. 1316–34) was the candidate of both the future King Philip V of France and King Robert of Naples. He is best known for his suppression as heretics of the Spiritual wing of the Franciscan Order. These reformers found powerful supporters in anti-papal forces, including Marsiglio of Padua, William of Occam, and Emperor Lewis IV of Bavaria. Lewis entered Rome on January 1328, was crowned emperor by Sciarra Colonna, and declared Pope John deposed. In his place Lewis named as Antipope Nicholas V, the Franciscan Spiritual Pietro Rainallucci da Corbara. Pope John was also embroiled in the controversy over the nature of the Beatific Vision, and his position was later condemned. Emperor Lewis and Cardinal Napoleone Orsini called for a general council to depose John, but he died before their plans came to fruition.

# CHAPTER FIVE
## THE MONSTER BORN IN ROME.
## THE PAPAL LEGATE IS SLAIN IN BOLOGNA

[The beginning of this chapter is missing.]...

THERE IS A CITY twenty miles from Bologna, called Ferrara. Certain noble citizens, known as the da Fontana, were driven out of Ferrara [Map 2]. This happened because they had sold Ferrara to the Venetians. Now the marquises d'Este are the lords in their place. The da Fontana beseeched the papal legate to return them to their homes within three years.[1] The marquises of Ferrara sent the legate fourteen thousand florins annually, so that those who had sold their homeland to the Venetians might not return.[2]

After four years of this tribute, in the seventh year of his rule,[3] the legate did not feel himself to be lord if he did not have a lord's freedom to act. He called up an army and set it upon Ferrara. Ferrara was of considerable size, a mile long, and stood on the banks of a great and noble river known as the Po. Across from it was another branch of the Po. The city, as I've said, was ruled by the marquises d'Este, who are noble men, well-liked by the tyrants of Lombardy. The army of the legate was extremely imposing. In one fell swoop it seized the whole countryside of Ferrara. Then it erected a wooden bridge over the Po. Then it took the parts of Ferrara that lay outside the walls on the Venetian side of the city. It was easily done. The whole land was lost. By land and by water they were besieged.

The two sides began to provoke one another. The captain of the army was the count of Armagnac, who hurled insults at the barons of Romagna[4] and called them traitors who, as a result of their greatness, failed to be on their guard when they ought to have been. The people

---

1. The papal legate, Bertrand du Pouget, governed in the city of Bologna.

2. Porta notes that we do not know the da Fontana side of this story, knowing only that the Este obtained the right to rule Ferrara as papal vicars in 1329, in return for annual payments.

3. Porta notes that the legate, Bertrand, had been conceded *signoria*, i.e., rule, over the city in 1327.

4. This refers to the Este, who hailed from the Romagna, in which region these events took place.

of Bologna where there, who are always reluctant to step out of their house. There were many troops there as well, who had not been paid, having been denied the pay they requested. Also present were the lords of Romagna. The legate kept the army poorly supplied. He gave them no provisions. Whenever he was asked for something he would respond: "*Bene. Faciemus.*"[5] Note well the matters that those who wish to be lords but lack the means ought to consider!

Inside of Ferrara there were two thousand heavy troops. Marquis Rinaldo did not hesitate.[6] At the hour of Terce[7] he burst out of Ferrara and set upon the army. The army was in the midst of eating. Then began the slaughter of men, flight, bellowing, and crying out. The count of Armagnac was captured and ransomed for eighty thousand florins. The lords of Romagna allowed unchecked plundering. Many men were killed or captured. Many spoils were taken. A great catapult called the Ass was captured without opposition.[8]

The Bolognese people took shelter on the bridge. The bridge was held together with cords. It fell into the river. You can well guess how many people died. There were a few who clung to the ropes and dangled above the water. Behold, someone came with an axe and cut the line. All those people who had been hanging there drowned in the Po. You see what a son of the devil that man was! Twenty thousand people perished in the battle. The *carroccio* returned to Bologna nevertheless.[9] When the news reached Bologna the wails of mourning were great.

5. "Very well. We shall do it." The Anonimo renders the legate's speech in Latin, and in the second person plural, playing up the pomposity of this clerical lord.

6. Rinaldo d'Este was the brother of Niccolò and Obizzo III d'Este. The three ruled Ferrara together at first, hence the Anonimo's plural "marquises," but eventually Obizzo ruled on his own.

7. 9:00 AM.

8. For the context of this battle of Ferrara in April 1333, see John Larner, *The Lords of Romagna: Romagnol Society and the Origins if the Signorie* (Ithaca, NY: Cornell University Press, 1965), esp. 76–80. On the Papal States at the time, see Jean-Claude Maire Vigueur, "Comuni e signorie nelle province dello Stato della Chiesa," in *Signorie cittadine nell'Italia comunale,* J.-C. Maire Vigueur, ed. (Rome: Viella 2013), 105–72.

9. A *carroccio* was a stylized cart bearing a standard that Italian cities would bring

## CHAPTER FIVE

The legate did not waste a moment. First, he wrote a letter to Messer [Galeotto I] Malatesta, who held back with the other tyrants.[10] The sense of the letter was this: "Why have you rebelled against the Church of Rome?" Messer Malatesta replied with his own letter. It said nothing but, "*Bene. Faciemus.*"

After this the legate prepared to outfit another army, even more fearsome. He summoned from his own land five hundred Saracen light cavalry, dressed in yellow, long-legged, and wielding javelins.[11] He levied a heavy grain tax to raise money for his army. When the people of Bologna learned of this, they were angered, both due to the tax and because of their many dead, and they began to murmur seditiously. A doctor of law — Messer Brandelisio delli Gozzadini by name — stood in the piazza of the commune with a sword in his hand.[12] He roused the people and drove the marshal of the legate from the Palazzo della Biada,[13] killing a few and robbing them. Then he besieged the beautiful and noble fortress of the legate, of which I spoke earlier.[14] The siege lasted fifteen days. The water was cut off because the conduit that carried it there was broken. Within, there were provisions of bread, wine, salted meat, and many other things. The Bolognese hurled dung into the palazzo with catapults and fired crossbows at it.

Seeing that the whole world had risen up in rebellion against him, the legate was urged to save himself. The bishop of Florence came. The legate put himself in the hands of the Florentines. The Florentines carried him out of the fortress. They traveled along walls on the road

---

into battle. It has a quasi-sacral aspect, often being stored in the cathedral when not in use, and its capture was a great coup. That the Bolognese *carroccio* was not captured despite the legate's failure indicates that they were not utterly defeated.

10. The Malatesta were the lords of Rimini. The legate had expected their aid.

11. The term for these troops is *iannetti*. The Anonimo uses the same term when describing forces more readily identified as Muslim in other chapters, so there is no reason to assume he means anything else here.

12. This would be the modern Piazza Maggiore, the seat of communal government in Bologna.

13. This palazzo, parts of which dated to the twelfth century, stood in the same piazza and was used for municipal grain storage.

14. This refers to the lost initial part of this chapter.

that leads to the Florentine gate. All the people of Bologna shouted at him, made rude gestures, and hurled insults. The sinners gestured rudely and shouted injurious things at him. They lifted their robes and showed him the first *Decretal* and the sixth *Clementinae*.[15] They made a great tumult. How they would have shown their teeth if he had not been in the custody of the Florentines! The legate made his way along the Via delle Alpe with his little band and hardly any supplies. He traveled to Pisa and from there to Avignon.

The Bolognese robbed everyone from Languedoc. Many of them they killed.[16] Then they razed to the ground the noble fortress of which I've spoken. They left nothing but the church. They tore the walls down to their foundations. This occurred in the year of our Lord, 1334, in the month of [...]. The bell of the legate went to the order of the Hermits of St. Augustine. The noble icon from the altar, which was of alabaster and made in Pisa with a value of ten thousand florins, went to the Dominican preaching friars. The circular golden lamp, which burned in the choir of the legate, went to the Franciscans. They also took all the dried meat, as much as they could eat. During that time, Sir Giovanni de Andrea, a doctor of canon law and a man of great wisdom, of acknowledged courtesy, lived there. He was the one who wrote the book known as the *Novella*.[17]

15. This appears to be a lewd joke, indicating the flashing of genitals (the first *Decretal*) and bare behinds (the sixth *Clementinae*, of which there were only five parts). These were texts of canon law, on which the authority of men like the legate rested.

16. That is, they robbed and killed those from southern France, whom they associated with the Avignon papacy and the legate who served it.

17. Giovanni (d.1348) was a well-respected canon lawyer. He is the author of the *Glossa Ordinaria* or standard commentary on canon law. He is reputed to have had a daughter, named Novella (b.1312), who also taught canon law in her father's place. The collection title may be either a mistake on the Anonimo's part or — like the other canon law collections cited — an anti-clerical joke. The *Novellae* themselves are a sixth-century collection of the civil law code of Emperor Justinian.

# CHAPTER SIX

FRA VENTURINO COMES TO ROME WITH THE DOVES.
THE BELL TOWER OF ST. PETER'S IS BURNED

IN THE YEAR OF OUR LORD, 1334, in the month of March, in Lent, one of the preaching friars, named Fra Venturino da Bergamo of Lombardy of the order of Saint Dominic, moved the greater part of Lombardy to devotion and penance by means of his devout sermons, and led this mass of people to Rome to seek forgiveness.[1] Among them were folk from Bergamo, Brescia, Como, Milan, and Mantua. Some of them were noble and respectable men, while a tenth of them were from rural parts.[2] These people, who traveled with Fra Venturino, were innumerable.

Most marvelous of all was the way they were dressed. Their garb, which Fra Venturino had given them, consisted of a long white gown, down past the mid-leg. Over the gown they wore a sky-blue tabard down to the knee. On their legs they wore white stockings. Over the stockings they had leather boots up to the mid-leg. On their heads they wore a cap of white linen cloth with another of sky-blue wool over it, on the front of which there was a Tau.[3] The top part was white, the middle part pink. On their breasts they wore a white dove, which

---

1. Movements like this one happened repeatedly in Italy during the communal period and were closely tied to the values of justice and peace that undergirded popular communal politics. See James A. Palmer, "Peace Movements: Peace in the Communes," in *A Cultural History of Peace in the Medieval Age (800–1450)*, Walter Simons, ed. (London: Bloomsbury Academic, 2020), 101–18; and Katherine Jansen, *Peace and Penance in Late Medieval Italy* (Princeton, NJ: Princeton University Press, 2018), esp. 46–48, with complete bibliography. For comparison, Giovanni Villani also treats Fra Venturino in his *Cronaca Nuova* XII.23.

2. The Anonimo's language is unclear here, as Porta notes in his edition. He writes that this last group of people came from the *"vescovata,"* a term of uncertain meaning. I take him to be comparing the people from various towns, noble and respectable, to those who were otherwise, perhaps from rural communities on ecclesiastical lands. That is the translation used here. Alternatively, this may refer to clergy under episcopal authority, who would be neither mendicant nor lay, and would therefore need permission to travel.

3. The tau is a Greek letter, the cruciform shape of which — T — carried association with the cross. It is most associated with the Franciscans, but the Anonimo does not mention this.

had in its mouth an olive branch as a symbol of peace.[4] In their right hand they carried a staff, in their left, a paternoster.

With these people, Venturino descended through Lombardy preaching. Many followed him. He came to Florence. The Florentines received him and his followers graciously. Charitably they housed them in their own homes, gave them food and beds, washed the people's feet, and carried on in this charitable manner for three days without any thought of reward. Then many of the Florentines were moved to take up the same garb and follow Fra Venturino. He came next to Viterbo. From Viterbo, he came to Rome.

By now the fame of Fra Venturino had preceded him in Rome. He declared that he hoped to convert the Romans. When he arrived, he was received in San Sisto. There he preached. His great crowd of followers was orderly and well behaved. In the evening they sang lauds. They processed in an orderly manner. They had a silken banner, which they donated to the church of Sta. Maria sopra Minerva. To this day it hangs in the vault of the Minerva above the chapel of Messer Latino.[5] It is of green silk, long and ample. On the front is depicted the image of the holy Mary. There are little angels depicted here and there, playing harps, as well as Saint Dominic, the martyred Saint Peter, and other prophets. He left that sign. Then he preached in Sta. Maria sopra Minerva on the day of the Annunciation.

Afterwards, he preached on the Campidoglio, in the council chamber. All of Rome came to hear his sermon. He had a firm grip on the attention of the Romans. They stood silent. They listened attentively to see if he erred by using false Latin. So he preached, saying that they should remove the shoes from their feet because the land where they stood was holy. He declared that Rome was a land of great sanctity because of the bodies that lay in it.[6] But the Romans are an evil people. For then the Romans began to grin. Then he requested a boon and a gift from the Romans. He asked that the games of the Agone not be held.[7]

4. This dove (*palomma*) is the origin of the term by which the Anonimo calls this group, the *palommelle*, or doves.

5. Porta identifies this as the chapel of Latino Malabranca, who died in 1294.

6. That is, the remains of the martyrs, for which Rome was justly famous.

7. This refers to important annual games, including various competitions and

✳ CHAPTER SIX

Fra Venturino said, "My lords, you intend to hold this festival of yours at the cost of much money. For the love of God and the saints, do not do it, lest you commit idolatry in service to the Devil. Give this money to me. I will dispense it as God intends, to needy folk who do not have time to go see the *sudario*."[8]

At this the Romans began to ridicule him and say that he was mad. As they said this, they did not remain in their seats but rather got to their feet and began to depart, leaving him there alone.

After this he preached at San Giovanni.[9] The Romans had no desire to hear any more and they drove him out. In anger he despaired and cursed them, saying he had never seen a people so perverse. He made no other appearances. Instead, he left in secret and departed from Rome. He journeyed to Avignon. The pope then forbade him to preach.

IN THIS SAME PERIOD, a lightning bolt struck the bell tower of St. Peter's, and the whole upper part burned. The bells were undamaged. Also, around this time, Pope John, of whom I've spoken previously, died. As his death approached, he retracted his erroneous claim that the souls of the blessed do not see God face-to-face. And he declared that he had only said this for the sake of argument.[10]

---

ritual combat, that took place in what is now the Piazza Navona and in Testaccio. They were among the most important civic events of the year, celebrating both the commune and its domination of lesser communities in the vicinity.

8. The *sudario*, or the Veronica, is the cloth with which Veronica is said to have wiped Jesus' face, and on which a miraculous image of his face was thereby imprinted. It was an important relic that people came on pilgrimage to see. Venturino is pointing out that the poor could not avail themselves of the time or resources to do such a thing.

9. That is, at the Lateran.

10. Even prior to his papacy John XXII is known to have argued that the souls of the dead do not see God until after the resurrection, and he continued in the same vein until the last year of his life, despite considerable opposition to the idea. For discussion of the broader context of this debate in late medieval Italy, see Virginia Brilliant, "Envisaging the Particular Judgement in Late-Medieval Italy," *Speculum* 84.2 (2009): 314–46.

# CHAPTER SEVEN
## Pope Benedict and the roof of St. Peter's in Rome, which was rebuilt

IN THE YEAR OF OUR LORD 1334, Pope Benedict was elected.[1] He was an ultramontane and a white monk of the Cistercian order of Saint Bernard. At the time of his election, he was known as the White Cardinal. His election was more divine than human, for cardinals ranked him fourth among those who might be pope, and the person in fourth is in a very weak position. All the cardinals agreed that he was in fourth position, so that everyone considered his case hopeless. His election was truly divine. For ultimately all the votes were in favor of the White Cardinal, so that the one considered most hopeless was selected as pope, astonishing them all.

This man known as the White Cardinal was a very large fellow, huge and fat with a ruddy complexion. His likeness, as is customary, is found inside St. Peter's over the great gate leading into the nave. This pope was a most holy man, and he adhered to the principle that he would never give dispensation to marry to those bound together by kinship.[2] He was deeply opposed to such unions. He would never consent to them. He was also extremely thrifty, a real pennypincher when it came to the assets of the Church, and not only with respect to its wealth but also its benefices. He was very concerned to have a good sense of anyone on whom they were to be conferred, insisting that their character and their life be carefully scrutinized. Many such cases he examined himself. He had no patience for fools. If some unworthy priest came before him, one truly ignorant or of ill-repute, he would strip the fellow of his benefice and confer it upon someone of better character who was better suited to the task. He frequently traveled in search of good quality, trustworthy clerics. He treated any such one with great honor. And because he

---

1. This refers to Benedict XII (1334–42), the famous theologian and inquisitor Jacques Fournier. See Irene Bueno, ed., *Pope Benedict XII (1334-1342): The Guardian of Orthodoxy* (Amsterdam: Amsterdam University Press, 2018).

2. This is more rigorous than it sounds. According to standard practice, the ties of kinship included those created by marriage, not just biology, which meant a great many possible unions might run afoul of them and require a papal dispensation.

# CHAPTER SEVEN

found so few, he was tightfisted with such grants and not overeager to distribute them.

A monk of San Paolo of Rome[3] by the name of Manosella came before Pope Benedict because he had been elected abbot after the death of his predecessor in that office. This fellow took pleasure in wandering about Rome at night singing songs and playing a lute, for he was a talented musician and singer of love songs. He would walk the streets at night and the vineyards during the day. So the Romans say. How it must have made holy Benedict despair when his monk lept and danced.

When this newly elected fellow appeared before Pope Benedict, he said, "Holy Father, I am the one elected by San Paolo of Rome."

Now, the pope was well aware of the quality of the person who had come before him. He said, "Do you know how to sing?" To which the elected one replied, "I do know how."

Then the pope said, "I mean religious songs."

"I know the songs," the elected one declared.

Then the pope asked, "Do you know how to play?"

"I do," the elect declared.

The pope said, "I mean to say, do you know how to play the organ and the lute?"

"All too well," the elected one replied.

Abruptly the pope changed his tone and asked, "And is it suitable that the abbot of the venerable monastery of San Paolo should be a buffoon? Get out of here and look to your affairs!" So he returned home with his head on straight.[4]

This same Pope Benedict reconfirmed everything his predecessor had done in opposition to the Bavarian.[5] Then he had the entire

---

3. That is, the venerable church of San Paolo fuori le Mura.

4. Here the Anonimo uses an idiomatic phrase that doesn't translate easily into English: "Così tornao collo capo lavato," or "And so he went back with his head washed."

5. That is, Lewis of Bavaria, the German emperor excommunicated by John XXII.

roof of San Giovanni in Laterano restored, which was half missing. Then he had the roof of St. Peter's completely replaced with a noble and clean structure.

❈

IT WAS IN THE YEAR OF OUR LORD 13[41], in the month of [...] that these works were completed.[6] It cost eighty thousand gold florins.[7] The overseer of this whole endeavor was an extremely talented carpenter by the name of Master Ballo of *rione* Colonna, who was so skilled that he could anticipate down to the day, the hour, and even the very moment that the whole roof would be completed. Such was his acumen that he was able to remove the old beams and hoist the new ones right up so quickly it was like he was a bird. A man was mounted on each end of the beam. I wouldn't have wanted to be one of them!

When the old roof had been removed, they found an incomprehensibly large beam, ancient and of stupendous size. I saw it myself. It was ten feet in thickness. It was bound in place with ropes because it was so old. This beam had held due to its great size. Like the others, it was made of pine. They found carved into it the letters CON, which means "This is one of the beams that the good Constantine put into this roof." It was as ancient as the Hallelujah! The beam was taken down and within it were found gaps and cavities caused both by old age and by the gnawing of creatures who had made nests within. This was clear from the fact that a tremendous number of mice were found nesting within it, martins were found there too and, what is more, the nesting places of foxes. Even someone seeing it had a hard time believing it. This noble beam was cut up and used to make planks needed for completion of the renovation. Furthermore, many noblemen of Rome used it to make dining tables.[8]

6. Here the year and month have been omitted. I have supplied the year that Porta identifies for the completion of the work.

7. Porta points out that this is a wild exaggeration. Contemporary documents indicate that price to have been not more than 15,000 florins, which was still a very large sum.

8. This practice — though similar to modern recycling chic — was both a symbolic and practical aspect of Roman reverence for the ancient past that

## CHAPTER SEVEN

I wish to relate a marvel. In order to make the new roof, all the masters that could be found both inside and outside Rome were brought together. Among them was one of the good people of the world, whose name was Nicola de Agniletto de Vetralla. This fellow stood up on an architrave to work. The beam was located up on a high wall. Hatchet in hand, this master did the work needed there. He stood on his feet. Perhaps the beam was not balanced properly, or it was hanging. The weight was very great. The beam came loose, and when it did, it began to rise. As it rose it began to rock and spin. The master barely managed to avoid falling to the ground. He scrambled nimbly and managed to keep his feet. The master was terrified that both he and the beam would crash to the ground. Nor could he hide his fear, for suddenly half his beard turned white. He often shaved it after that. He would often say that its whiteness was due to the fear he had felt that he and the raised beam would fall.

The same thing happened to King Conradin. After he was defeated and captured at Astura, King Charles had him beheaded.[9] His hair was so lovely that, when he shook his head, it resembled gold thread twirled around a column of silver. During the night that he passed in prison, his golden hair turned white. When he was decapitated the next day, he seemed to have gone from blonde to silver-haired. And this change took place in one night!

Some might ask how fear can cause such whiteness. To this Avicenna responds, saying that when a man stands in a very high

saw the appropriation and incorporation of many *spolia* of ancient monuments into the fabric of both secular and religious buildings in order to add prestige and lineage to such holdings. For recent summations of research, see Richard Brilliant and Dale Kinney, ed., *Reuse Value: Spolia and Appropriation in Art and Architecture from Constantine to Sherrie Levine* (New York: Routledge, 2016); and Peter Cornelius Claussen, "Marmo e splendore: Architettura, arredi liturgici, *spoliae*," in Andaloro and Romano, *Arte e iconografia*, 193–225. For Cola's symbolic re-use of the timbers of the Senate Palace fortifications as dining tables, see chapter 18, pp. 219–20.

9. This refers to the defeat and execution in 1268 of Conradin, Hohenstaufen duke of Swabia, son of Conrad IV of Germany (d. 1254), heir to Emperor Frederick II (d. 1250), by Charles of Anjou, who went on to be King Charles I of Naples (1265–85). Astura, where Conradin was captured, is on the coast of Lazio.

place all his virtues are absorbed by the need to comfort the mind's animal virtues, that he not [...]¹⁰ For this reason the members of the body tremble, because they are stripped of their ruling virtue. In similar cases, the heat of the skin moves from the outlying areas and moves inward to preserve itself. In this way the skin loses its vigor to such an extent that it cannot maintain its temperature. A sign of this is when one feels a part begin to tingle. One encounters this often with those who work in the sea. One might also ask why this fellow's beard whitened more on one side than on the other. I would say that this change happened with great rapidity. The part that was closer to the danger was the one that received the impression from it;¹¹ the other part was safer and so did not whiten.

10. This paraphrase is probably from Avicenna's, *The Canon of Medicine*, which the Anonimo may have studied as part of his medical education. Porta notes it is impossible to identify precisely. This is probably due in part to the gap in the text here. "Virtue," as the Anonimo uses it here, is a medical term referring to the various functions or capacities of the body, all of which stem from the life, or vital virtue, provided it by the soul via the beating of the heart and the action of *spiritus*. See James J. Bono, "Medical Spirits and the Medieval Language of Life," *Traditio* 40 (1984): 91–130; and Nancy G. Siraisi, *Medieval and Early Renaissance Medicine: An Introduction to Knowledge and Practice* (Chicago: University of Chicago Press, 1990), 107–8. Medieval medicine understood many influences on the body and mind to be transmitted through spirits (*spiritus* or *pneuma*), an idea that was primarily derived from Galen. Famously, such impressions could be transmitted by the eye — Galen's theory of ocular intromission — but also in other ways.

11. Here, again, we see the idea that an event could impose itself, or make a kind impression upon the bodily *spiritus*, with physical results (e.g., whitening, in this case).

# CHAPTER EIGHT
## THE COMET THAT APPEARED IN PARTS OF LOMBARDY. THE DEFEAT OF THE TYRANT MESSER MASTINO BY THE VENETIANS

IN THE YEAR OF OUR LORD 1337, in the month of August, there appeared in parts of Lombardy a most splendid and beautiful comet that remained visible for three days. Then it disappeared into the air. This comet appeared to be a star, more brilliant than the others, with a distinct tail extending behind it, pointed like a sword, the tip of which hung over Verona. This tail extended from one side. It moved neither up nor down but extended straight out like a burning flame. It greatly inspired folk to admiration, so that everyone wanted to talk about this novelty.

Aristotle, in his *Meteorology*, says that this is not really a star. Instead, it is a [...] developing in the upper reaches of the air, and made up of hot, humid matter, which moves and burns for as long as it takes to consume all the material that makes it up. He also says that this hardly ever happens without it signifying some great change, especially regarding the rulers of the earth, the commotion of realms, and the death or downfall of the powerful.[1]

In good faith, it was so; for after the comet had disappeared the news reached Lombardy that Padua had fallen. The Venetians had taken it and cast out Messer Alberto della Scala of Verona, who was imprisoned in Venice. Also following this was the destruction and ruin of Messer Mastino della Scala, who was so powerful and tyrannical that he hoped to wear a king's crown. Then he lost everything and was reduced to a state that suited him. This novelty occurred in the following way. After the death of Messer Cane della Scala he was succeeded by his nephew, Mastino by name.[2] This Messer

---

1. Aristotle, *Meteorology*, I.6-7.

2. This refers to Cangrande della Scala. See A. Castagnetti and G.M. Varanini, ed., *Il Veneto nel medioevo: Dai comuni cittadini al predominio scaligero nella Marca* (Verona: Banca Popolare di Verona, 1991); Louis Green, "The Image of Tyranny in Early Fourteenth-Century Italian Historical Writing," *Renaissance Studies* 7.4 (1993): 335–51; and Alexander Lee, *Humanism and Empire: The Imperial Ideal in Fourteenth-Century Italy* (Oxford: Oxford University Press, 2018), esp. 31–88.

Mastino della Scala was one of the greatest tyrants of Lombardy who held the most cities, the most power, the most castles, the most communes, and the most grandeur. He held Verona, Vicenza, Treviso, Padua, Civitale, Crema, Brescia, Reggio, and Parma.[3] In Tuscany he had Lucca and Lunisciana. He was lord of fifteen great cities. He conquered Parma by force of arms. When his army took up a position outside a city, he would aim more than forty catapults at it. He wouldn't leave until he had become lord of the place. He was content to be lord due either to fear or to love. Then he entered Tuscany. He took Lucca and tricked the Florentines, whence they arranged for him the ruin described above. After this he threatened to take both Ferrara and Bologna.

He had a way of handling the noblemen who handed their cities over to him. Namely, he kept them with him and looked after them in grand fashion. There were many barons, many foot soldiers and cavalry, many buffoons, falcons, palfreys, steeds, and destriers for jousting. There was a constant commotion. One saw caps doffed, Germans bowing, and boundless feasts. There was the sound of trumpets, shawms, pipes, and drums. One saw tributes flowing in, pack mules being unloaded, jousts, tournaments, and a lovely bustle of singing, dancing, leaping, and every lovely and delightful thing. Folk wore French fabrics and Tartar [...], embroidered velvets, artfully worked cloth, decorated with images and gold.

When this lord rode out, all Verona shook. When he threatened, all of Lombardy trembled. Among his many magnificent deeds, it is said that he had eighty dishes at once when he dined in court. Each plate had its own tray, carried by two barons. Judges, doctors, men of letters, and skilled men of every sort found patronage in his realm. His fame resounded in the court of Rome. There was no one like him in Italy.

Messer Mastino basked in his own magnificence. So he gloried, thinking himself so mighty, not understanding human frailty. When he had reached this lofty condition, he had an enormous palace built in Verona. To lay its foundation he destroyed a church called San Salvato. No good would come from that. Then he began to slander

---

3. Porta points out that the Anonimo is wrong about both Civitale and Crema.

the tyrants of Lombardy. He had no interest in traveling to confer with them. Then he had a crown made [...] adorned all over with pearls, sapphires, rose spinels, rubies, and emeralds, and worth twenty thousand florins. He had this crown made because he intended to see himself crowned king of Lombardy. He had it fashioned of iron in fact, due to his great subtlety, to signify that he had won his realm by force of arms.[4] Once he had fashioned this crown, the hearts of the Lombard tyrants were deeply troubled, and they began to think intently about how to avoid becoming subjects to one of their peers.

Messer Mastino was a knight of the Bavarian, a cunning man and a just lord.[5] One could travel throughout his realm with gold in one's hand. He wrought great justice. He was a swarthy, hairy man, bearded with a big belly. He was a master of war. He had fifty palfreys under his thigh. He swapped them out every day. When he rode out, two thousand knights rode with him. Two thousand armed foot soldiers, handpicked swordsmen, went everywhere with him. While he remained attentive to virtue, he grew great. But as he began to grow proud, he became gluttonous and began to be corrupted by luxury. He became extremely hedonistic. He boasted that he had despoiled fifty maidens in a single Lenten season. These vices brought about his fall from his honorable state. He began to eat meat on Friday, on Sunday, and during Lent. He had no fear of excommunication.

The manner of his fall from grace was as follows. He had a brother named Messer Alberto della Scala. This Messer Alberto was sent to rule Padua, which he commanded like a king. He had with him counts, barons, soldiers, and many other people. His company was quite splendid. Messer Alberto's behavior was as follows. He would enter a cloister of nuns and dally there for three or four days. Then he would visit another. Each time he would despoil some beautiful nun. He used foul language crudely and constantly.

---

4. Although the Anonimo describes this crown as a kind of metaphor conceived by Mastino, the crown of Lombardy was traditionally of iron and had been since the early medieval period.

5. That is, he had been knighted by Emperor Lewis IV of Bavaria. There were other ties between the two. Lewis's daughter Elizabeth married Cangrande II della Scala, Mastino's son.

The leading men of Padua were Messer Marsilio da Carrara and Messer Ubertiello da Carrara, who were his kinsmen and had handed the city over to him. Messer Ubertiello had a beautiful wife. Every hour of every day Messer Alberto teased him, saying, "Watch out, Messer Ubertiello, I twice made you a cuckold tonight."

He would never leave off. He said it at every opportunity. Messer Ubertiello just smiled. He went about smiling and never stopped laughing. Messer Alberto had with him a pack of stupid vulgar men. The braggarts paid no heed to what they did or said. They had the same manners as their lord. And so, Messer Alberto continued to chatter at him in this uncouth way, not knowing when to stop. Instead, he said, "Oh Messer Ubertiello, tonight I made you a cuckold three times!"

He wouldn't cease this villainous slander on account of the man's nobility, nor for honor, kinship, kind regard, good character, or any other reason, so that eventually Messer Ubertiello burst. He couldn't bear it any longer. [...][6]

Marsilio was a cunning knight, shrewd and subtle. At once he rode to Verona and spoke with Messer Mastino. He told him that he intended him to be the greatest man that had ever been in that land, so that he might subdue even the pride and grandeur of the Venetians. And he told him how to do it, saying, "Messer Mastino, you have in your territory of Padua a village called Bovolenta. This Bovolenta includes the marshland along the coast. Long ago there were pools there for making salt. If you produce salt in your own lands, oh great lord, no one would be able to deny your wisdom. When the Venetians see you doing this, they will either have to pay you a great deal of money in tribute or their own salt will be worth less. The income that the Venetian Camera has from salt will then be yours, making you twice as great and putting the Venetian pigs at your mercy. Send an ambassador to them to make your excuses, explaining that you aren't doing this to harm the Venetians: by doing so you will clearly demonstrate your wisdom, since you

---

6. Here this is a lacuna in the text. The sense of what is happening here is clear enough, and Porta, p. 218, notes that it is corroborated in by Giovanni Villani. Having had enough of della Scala's taunting, Ubertiello (i.e., Ubertino da Carrara) set about conspiring with his lord's enemies.

## ❋ CHAPTER EIGHT

don't want to lose the support of the Paduans. You aren't coercing anyone. Rather, you simply wish to produce salt on your land so that you can collect taxes on it in order to cover the great expense of maintaining your soldiers and other grand matters."

This is the bone he lodged in the throat of Messer Mastino.[7] The tyrant was swayed by these treacherous words, believing he could rise higher even than God would allow. Greedily he commanded that in the village of Bovolenta, along the coast, a beautiful castle of wood should be built near the pools, so that his salt operation might be well guarded. And he caused the salt pools to be readied and put into operation. Then he began liberally to produce some of the loveliest and finest salt in the world. Oh, what a lucrative operation this was! Everything went according to plan.

And so, Messer Marsilio went to Venice as he was ordered, well informed of all these matters and appointed as an ambassador just as he had requested. He stood before the doge and the patricians and spoke the words he had suggested, but with the delivery and tone changed so that they sounded altogether different. He said, "My lords of Venice, Messer Mastino intends to produce salt in his land in order to have your wealth for himself, to take you in hand and rule you, and to outdo your own salt-production operations. If this happens there will be no more incomes from the salt trade. The Venetian Camera's most precious commodity is salt. You had best be mindful of your affairs." He said no more. By doing and saying this, he had kindled a fire between the Venetians and Messer Mastino.

In response the Venetians assembled a magnificent and splendidly adorned embassy. There were twelve Venetian patricians, the greatest merchants and richest men, savvy and subtle, all dressed in the same costume, velvet garb, part scarlet and part green, fur-trimmed and quite becoming. Their robes went to their feet, with an overcoat to the mid-leg [...] short at knee length, their hoods had a slight point at the top and a silken cap underneath, embellished with silver lace, with image-adorned belts about their waists. They were costumed in really exotic attire. With noble familiars and other attendants, they

---

7. The Anonimo's wonderful style is in evidence here. The della Scala were inclined to dog-related names like Cangrande (Big Dog) and Mastino (Mastiff). So now, of course, Mastino has a bone lodged in his throat.

crossed the sea, mounted their little palfreys once on land, and made their way to Verona. They sped along like doctors, each hot on the heels of the others.[8] Many came out to see them. Folk marveled at their exotic attire. It was like seeing the games of Testaccio in Rome.[9] When the ambassadors entered Verona the whole city came out to see them. Folk stared at them unblinkingly like wolves. This was because their attire was quite different from the men of the court. Their garb was of noble cloth, tight in the Catalan fashion, embellished with silken twill on top, fur-lined German capes, and cowls hung over their faces, fastened at their shoulders with clasps of gold. At their wastes were belts fastened with silver gilt bars. On their feet stockings.

Unhesitatingly, they headed for the court. They rode boldly through town. The twelve ambassadors appeared before Messer Mastino. The speech of Venetians is inherently prideful, and they spoke coldly that way to Messer Mastino, saying, "Messer Mastino, the commune of Venice requests that you not lose the friendship of Venice in exchange for salt, and that you not seek to do what your ancestors never did and what has never been done in our own times. Salt comes from the Venetians, not the Paduans. You should leave off making this salt, if you do not wish to anger the men of Venice, and if you would like to remain our friend." To this embassy, Messer Mastino responded, saying, "Come tomorrow to dine with me in my court and you will have my answer."

The next day a truly grand feast was prepared. In the great hall preparations for more than eight hundred people were made. On the high table every bowl and vessel was of silver. To this feast the Venetians came, and all twelve of them were positioned together at a table at the foot of the room, in full view of all the attendees. After washing their hands, they did not remove their huge garments, even as they sat down at the table. Folk made great sport of them. They stood there astonished as if the Venetians were Patarines or

8. Here the Anonimo deploys an interesting turn of phrase indicative of hasty urgency.

9. This refers to the pageantry of the municipal games that took place in Rome each year, which included participants from the city and the areas under its dominion. These are the very games Fra Venturino had failed to cancel.

## CHAPTER EIGHT

excommunicates.[10] Folk gawked at them like owls. Messer Mastino stood at the head of the room, higher up than the rest of the nobles, served at table like a king. All the nobility of his court saw him. Upon his arrival nothing was held back. The dishes began to come in. Knights with golden spurs served before him. Lutes, violas, pipes, and various other musical instruments played pleasant music. It was like being in paradise. After the food came richly dressed buffoons. How they sang, danced, and jested. Each one of them tried [...][11]

[...][12] They did not allow themselves to be driven from the walls. They showed heart. They feared neither siege engines nor threats. The noise was tremendous. Lances and arrows flew. Oh, how terrible it all was! Then Messer Pietro Roscio, with his beautiful company, slipped quietly and secretly through the gate called the Porta di Santa Croce. Of this gate, which led to the Cuorvo Bridge, Messer Marsilio of Carrara was the guard. At half terce,[13] the servant of Messer Marsilio opened the gate and lowered the bridge, letting Pietro Roscio in without a single sword blow. On the street leading to the piazza he spied the Venetian captain with a large troop of soldiers and knights.

It was then, at the hour of terce, that Messer Alberto woke from sleep.[14] Wearing only his nightgown, he mounted a beautiful steed, accompanied only by Messer Marsilio. In his hand, he carried a club. He rode arrogantly along. *Omnis armatorum eius multito pugnans resistebat ad portam.*[15] When Messer Alberto arrived at the head of the street, he saw that in the piazza a large force had arrived, a great

---

10. The Patarines were a heretical group, whose name was often used to mean simply "heretics."

11. Here there is a gap in the text but what is happening here is plain. Mastino has hired a pack of buffoons to mock the Venetians, positioning them so that everyone would see their humiliation.

12. Here the action has shifted from the court of Mastino back to the Padua of Alberto. We can see that Mastino's behavior had the effect Marsilio had hoped, infuriating the Venetians and provoking war. We return to the action at the moment that Marsilio's betrayal of Mastino becomes total.

13. 7:30 AM.

14. 9:00 AM.

15. "His whole host of troops was fighting to hold the gate."

host of men. He heard trumpets and horns. He saw the enormous Venetian battle standard of Saint Mark. At this he marveled and asked Messer Marsilio, "Who are all these people?"

To this, Messer Marsilio replied, "This is Messer Pietro Roscio, who would like a word with you."

Alberto said, "Am I to die?"

Marsilio replied, "No. Turn back. Go to my chambers."

And so it was done. Messer Alberto hurried away to the chambers of Messer Marsilio, and there he locked himself in with a key. The Venetians took the piazza and seized the mounts and weapons of all Messer Alberto's men. They seized him and his nobles and imprisoned them in Venice. There they remained until the war was over.

Then it was that the comet appeared of which I spoke before. The Venetians took control of the gates of Padua. *Sine mora*,[16] they rode out and made terrible war on della Scala. Messer Pietro Roscio marched through the land plundering and burning. He took Monsilice by force and was slain there. The Venetians didn't need to carry on this harsh war for long. Soon the city of Brescia was lost. Everyone there rebelled. There was no resistance.

Messer Mastino, desperate and fixated on his ill fortune, slew the bishop of Verona with his own hand, a man who was of his own kin, killing him on the steps of the episcopate. Albuino, the bastard of Messer Cangrande, murdered him.[17] Under the head of this bishop's bed a steel mirror was found with strange characters etched on it. On its handle a figure was depicted, with letters that read, "This is Fiorone."[18] Then a little book was found there, on which there was

16. "Without delay."

17. Cangrande was the uncle of Mastino and Alberto, whose successes had paved the way for Mastino's rule. The murdered bishop was Bartolomeo della Scala, Mastino's uncle. The Anonimo attributes the murder of the bishop to both Mastino and Albuino and seems justified in doing so given that both were later made to do an elaborate public penance for the act. See Giuseppe Cappelletti, *Le chiese d'Italia dalla lore origine sino ai nostri giorni* (Venice: Antonelli, 1854), 10:770–72.

18. This mirror appears to have been a device for communicating with a demon, Fiorone, and is clearly described in a manner evocative of the

※ CHAPTER EIGHT

one of the enemies of God was depicted holding a man as another demon stabbed him in the breast, in the very place where were that man was wounded. Messer Mastino did this because he suspected that the bishop planned to usurp him.

All told, the war lasted two years. In the end, Messer Mastino was exhausted and could fight no longer. He came to an agreement with the Venetians and made peace. The terms were as follows. First, that he give up all the wealth he had in Verona, which he had taken from the Venetians. Second, that he send these personal effects, which amounted to 24,000 florins or 2,000 a set, to the commune of Venice. Third, that the Venetians were to have Treviso, which Messer Mastino gave them for their trouble. They allowed him to keep Verona and Vicenza out of love of God and mercy. His other lands, like Padua and Civitale, returned to the control of their own people. Then the Venetians freed Messer Alberto, his brother, along with the other nobles they had imprisoned. Throughout the course of this war, the Florentines gave their aid, offering as much money as was needed.[19]

In this way Mastino della Scala went from a lofty status to a humble one; though he wasn't too terribly humbled, as he died an old man and lord of Verona and Vicenza. The warlike fellow had a monument to himself made in marble while he was still alive, where he was eventually entombed in the house of the Franciscans, where he lay alongside his wives. On that monument there were inscribed no words dedicated to God or the saints, but rather game animals, horses, dogs, hawks, and other worldly things.[20]

---

necromantic arts. See Richard Kieckhefer, *Forbidden Rites: A Necromancer's Manual of the Fifteenth Century* (University Park: Pennsylvania State University Press, 1998). For a similar incident of mirror sorcery in the career of Cola di Rienzo, see below, chapter 27, p. 298.

19. Here the Anonimo finally explains what he meant previously when he alluded to Florentine involvement in Mastino's downfall as vengeance for his trickery.

20. This is not true, though the monument does include mastiffs that were symbolic of Mastino, Cangrande, and the della Scala line. For recent discussion of this monument, with bibliography, see Irving Lavin, *The Art of Commemoration in the Renaissance,* Marilyn Aronberg Lavin, ed. (New York: Italica Press, 2020), 121–23, 138–39.

In their handling of this tyrant, the Venetians were like the Romans, who sent an embassy to Benevento. The Beneventans sprayed the backs of the ambassadors with urine. The Romans were enraged by this, and as a result the whole province of Samnium was destroyed and made subject to the commune of Rome, as Titus Livy says.[21]

---

21. The Anonimo is paraphrasing Livy, *Ab urbe condita libri*, VII.31, to which he has added the more colorful details and the explanation that Samnium is that part of southern Italy where Benevento is located.

# CHAPTER NINE

A VERY CRUEL FAMINE. THE BATTLE OF PARABIAGO IN
LOMBARDY. VARIOUS NEW FASHIONS

AFTER THE COMING of the comet of which I spoke above, there followed a particularly wet and rainy year.[1] Ailments and sickness abounded among the people. There was enough snow for three winters. So much fell that an unfathomable depth of it covered the cities. The roofs of many houses in Bologna collapsed under the great weight. The summer too was wet, so that one could hardly leave one's house to practice one's trade or do business. The fields lay unworked. All the grain and beans planted in them were lost, unable to overcome the smothering wet that drowned them. From this came infertility and a poor harvest, and then hunger so awful that it is hard to speak of or even to believe. Dearth was everywhere. In Rome, grain came to twenty-one *libri provisini* per *rublum*.[2] This was in the year of our Lord 1338.

Titus Livy writes that there was once a famine in the Roman countryside so terrible that a great many people fell prey to it, preferring to die rather than live in hunger. They covered their eyes with their cowls so as not to bear witness to their own deaths and threw themselves into the Tiber where they drowned. By dying they finally alleviated their hunger.[3] In all honesty, I did not see such things transpire in our own time. But there were innumerable women who cast aside their honor in exchange for bread. Many people sold their freedom for bread.[4] Great houses, fields, and

---

1. See chapter 8, p. 87.

2. A *rublum*, or *rubbio*, was a dry goods measure commonly used in Italy and corresponding roughly to 290 lbs. See Ronald Edward Zupko, *Italian Weights and Measures from the Middle Ages to the Nineteenth Century* (Philadelphia: American Philosophical Society, 1981), 231–35.

3. Livy, *Ab urbe condita libri*, IV.12.

4. The precise meaning of this statement is unclear. It most likely indicates not actual slavery but rather the taking on of new obligations or debts and thus the loss of independence. It must be said, however, that a certain measure of debt was utterly normal, so the emphasis was likely on new obligations in addition to old ones, rather than to some starker change of status. On the kinds of credit–debt relations common to urban societies in late medieval Italy, see

vineyards were sold — given really — for next to nothing, simply for bread. The lack of food resulted in tremendous poverty. Many ate cooked greens without bread. The very poor gnawed thistles cooked with salt and such plants as pigs eat. They harvested tall spears of grass and the roots of aquatic plants and ate them cooked with mint. They roamed through the fields begging for turnips to eat. There was one father who gave each one of his children a turnip daily, to eat as if it were bread. People ate meat without bread too, if they had it. Of wine, there was a good supply. It weighs on me to recount such sad things. Women cast down their jewels, belts, and adornments, seeing themselves assailed by so terrible a hunger. If one possessed grain, one could obtain every woman's treasure.

During this time, I was in Bologna[5] and I saw the folk of the countryside came into town hoping to avail themselves of bread from the official stores. Oh, how sadly they returned home when nothing was to be found! Folk ate withered pears, chopped and mixed with farina, as well as the heads, guts, and blood of animals. Many were found dead from hunger. At night, people roamed about crying out "Bread! Bread!" They did this at night so that during the day no one would recognize them, for they were folk of some standing and did not wish to bring shame to themselves. Back in Rome the entire city would have died were it not for the arrival of a grain ship, which came from Pisa.

There were two miracles related to grain during this period of dearth. In the city of Piacenza, in Lombardy, a nobleman of the

---

Richard K. Marshall, *The Local Merchants of Prato: Small Entrepreneurs in the Late Medieval Economy* (Baltimore, MD: The Johns Hopkins University Press, 1999). John F. Padgett and Paul D. McLean, "Economic Credit in Renaissance Florence," *Journal of Modern History* 83.1 (2011): 1–47, distinguish between transactional credit–debt relations, which were to be paid back, and ongoing credit–debt relations rooted in ties of friendship (*amicizia*), in which payment was not necessarily the main point. For actual slavery in Italy, which was not primarily debt slavery, see Sally McKee, "Domestic Slavery in Renaissance Italy," *Slavery and Abolition* 29.3 (2008): 305–26.

5. It is likely that the Anonimo was in Bologna pursuing his medical studies at this time, as discussed above, pp. 10–11.

## CHAPTER NINE

Visconti family from Castiello Nuovo[6] had in his possession twenty thousand baskets of grain. This was in the month of May, when fava beans are in season. One Monday, all of Piacenza made its way to his house, seeking grain. "I want six lire per basket," the nobleman declared. The people returned with six lire on Tuesday and he denied them, saying "I want seven lire for it." They came on Wednesday with seven. "I want eight lire," he said. Thursday, they came with eight. He asked them for nine. On Friday they came with nine Bolognese lire. The wicked fellow came out and declared, "Go home, you pests. I will not sell this grain of mine for less than ten lire."

With tremendous grief, the people returned home still hungry. But God the good and gracious would not have it so, and on Saturday a knight and citizen of Piacenza by the name of Manfredo de Lando arrived with a grain shipment. Suddenly the price was five lire. Then the favas began to fruit. After another day, the price of grain dropped to four lire. On the third day it was three. When the Visconti nobleman saw this, he was despondent. Wracked with anxiety, he went home and entered the storeroom where he kept his grain. He contemplated all the profit he could have made had he simply been slightly more generous with those in need. Then he said to himself, "Oh grain of mine, I am ruined." With his mind bent more on avarice than mercy he strung a strap from one of the ceiling beams and there, in the midst of his granary, he hung himself by the neck.

IN THE ROMAN COUNTRYSIDE, in a fortified place called Castiglione delli Alberteschi, there was another miracle that I heard about from trustworthy sources.[7] During this time of terrible dearth, the entire mass of Roman paupers — men, women, and children alike — flocked to that place. They covered the whole land. In Castiglione

---

6. Porta speculates that this refers either to Castelnuovo Scrivia, in Piedmont, or the Lombard location called Castelnuovo d'Adda, both of which were Visconti possessions.

7. The location of this miracle may have been an agricultural holding located outside the Leonine City's Porta Cavalleggieri. See Antonio Coppi, *Discorso sull'agricoltura del'agro romano*, 2nd edition (Rome: Monaldi, 1841), 25.

there was a man named Ianni Macellaro.[8] He was the first one to have offered charitable donations of livestock to Santo Spirito in Rome.[9] He was a rich landowner. He had no children and much wealth, including serving men and women, sheep, cattle, pastures, cultivated fields, and granaries bursting with grain. All of these things he had been given by God.

When fava season came, and the favas were green in the fields, all the landowners issued announcements that no one should trespass in their crop. Ianni, conversely, let it be known that everyone should come and make camp in his fields. Of the fava plants, from which they could eat as they wished, nothing but the stems were spared. So the starving people were drawn in. *Corvinam servant pauperes famelici.*[10] A host descended on his fields. All day long they lingered there eating.

8. While by no means certain, Ianni's last name, which translates to "the butcher" likely identifies him as a well-to-do member of what can be called the *popolo*, a class of relatively new elites whose wealth derived from their business enterprises, in his case trade in livestock and meat, rather than from feudal title or high ecclesiastical office. This group is commonly known as the *bovattieri*. See Isa Lori Sanfilippo, *Roma dei Romani*, 95–122; Clara Gennaro, "Mercanti e bovattieri nella Roma della seconda metà del trecento (Da una ricerca su registri notarili)," in *Bullettino dell'Istituto storico italiano per il Medio Evo* 78 (1967): 155–87.

9. The hospital of Santo Spirito, a pious institution well established in Rome by this time. See De Angelis, *L'ospedale*; Rehberg, "I papi, l'ospedale"; Diana Bullen Presciutti, "Dead Infants, Cruel Mothers, and Heroic Popes: The Visual Rhetoric of Foundling Care at the Hospital of Santo Spirito, Rome," *Renaissance Quarterly* 64.3 (2011): 752–99. The order of the hospital was founded by Gui de Montpellier in Provence, c.1200. It grew rich of both pious donations and on *"male ablate,"* that is, restoration of ill-gotten gains. It seems unlikely that Ianni inaugurated the tradition of giving to the hospital, so perhaps he was an early donor during this particular period of dearth. On donations to the hospital, see now Andreas Rehberg, "Gestire l'assistenza: L'ospedale di Santo Spirito e l'ospedale di SS. Salvatore a confronto," in Ait and Esposito, *Vivere la città*, 225–42, at 226–32.

10. "The hungry poor are the same as crows." This phrase, written in Latin rather than the vernacular, is likely a proverbial reference, rather than one to a specific text. See Maurizio Campanelli, "'Benché io ià fatta per lettera': Gli inserti latini nella *Cronica* dell'Anonimo Romano," *Filologia & Critica* (2012): 3–29, at 9–10.

# CHAPTER NINE

Each day, the patron, astride his horse, visited and greeted them there amid his crops. He exhorted them to eat their fill and to bring beans home as it suited them. Furthermore, he gave each man a small loaf. Then he returned home. In this way he gave consolation to the needy.

With time the famine came to an end and a period of felicitous fertility began. The Roman paupers departed. The favas of the place had all been taken. They were utterly devastated. The plants of this good man, on which no fruit remained, lay in the fields. Yet even as the stalks were struck down, God showed his great abundance, and they produced fruit. Suddenly fava beans abounded. There were so many, on those very stems from which they had all been taken, that it really seemed that the beans of the other landowners had left their fields and come to the one of trampled plants. So God showed clearly how well pleased he was with the mercy of a pious heart in times of need and the grace given to those who succored the needy, and from one, one hundred issued, just as the Gospel says.[11]

IN THE MONTH OF FEBRUARY, in the year of our Lord 1338[/9], on the first Sunday of Lent, there was a terrible conflict in Lombardy between Como and Milan, in the field of Parabiagio.[12] It happened like this. Venice had defeated Messer Mastino della Scala of Verona and had taken Treviso, driving away all the infantry and cavalry. The defeated and fleeing soldiers, left with no money, undertook a grand campaign. Their leader and commander was a famous German, with a great reputation and skill at war, Malerva was his name.[13] He had with

---

11. Matt. 19:29; Mark 10:29–30.

12. This battle saw two uncles of Azzo Visconti, the rebel Lodrisio on one side and Lucchino, captain of Azzo's armies, on the other. For a recent summary of the battle and its sources, see Guido Cariboni, "I Visconti e la nascita del culto di Sant'Ambrogio della Vittoria," *Annali dell'Istituto Storico italo-germanico di Trento* 26 (2000): 595–613. The best account of the battle is that of Galvano Fiamma, *Opusculum de rebus gestis ab Azone Luchino et Johanne Vicecomitibus ab anno MCCCXXVIII usque ad annum MCCCXLII*, C. Castiglioni, ed., in Rerum Italicarum Scriptores, t. 12, pt. 4 (Bologna: Zanichelli, 1938), 26–31. See too, Villani, *Nuova Cronica*, 3:205–8.

13. Raynald von Giver, called Malherba or Malerba in Lombard and Tuscan accounts. He was commander of the Company of San Giorgio, put in the

him many knights with golden spurs, among them Count Orlando and Count Guarnieri, who were later leaders of the company. He had three thousand cavalry and around four thousand infantry troops, thugs, and innumerable camp followers and hangers on.

One of these men, Messer Lodrisio Visconti, who had been driven from Milan, contemplated marching on that city with the company and other forces. He did so. He swore solemn oaths to Malerva and spirited away his band of brigands. Paduans and Veronese marched side by side across half of Lombardy. *Nullo contradicente*,[14] they passed between Milan and Brescia and then to Bergamo. Eventually they arrived at a place called La Colomma de Chiaravalle. It was a marvelously rich spot, belonging to the white brothers of Saint Bernard.[15] There they halted. He called allies and those well inclined toward them to aid in their endeavor. They pitched their pavilions in the open field. It was February of the year of our Lord 1338[/9]. The cities trembled with fear as this massive host marched across the countryside. They were on their guard both night and day. After the army halted at Colomma, it was declared that Messer Lodrisio desired to return home in force.

At that time, Messer Azzo Visconti was lord of Milan and of house Visconti.[16] Quickly Messer Azzo called for aid from all the cities of Lombardy that were subject to Milan. Then he called on his kinsmen. Thereafter he called upon his friends. Not content to send out letters and ambassadors, he also called on the people of Milan. He marched a great force of cavalry and infantry into the field. There were men from Brescia, Trent, Bergamo, Como, and Lodi. Great was the disorder. Most of them were commoners.

---

service of Lodrisio by Mastino della Scala. For the mercenary companies, see William Caferro, *John Hawkwood: An English Mercenary in Fourteenth-Century Italy* (Baltimore, MD: The Johns Hopkins University Press, 2006).

14. This phrase appears to indicate that the diverse body of troops did all this without any conflicts among themselves, i.e., in good order.

15. As the chronicler notes, this was a famous Cistercian monastery.

16. On the Visconti, see Francesco Cognasso, *I Visconti: Storia di una famiglia* (Bologna: Odoya, 2016).

## CHAPTER NINE

In the field the two hosts, those of Messer Lodrisio and Messer Azzo Visconti, confronted one another. Between them stood the field of a village called Parabiago. It was winter, and there was a great deal of snow due to how wet that year was, as mentioned before. There was so much snow, in fact, that it was impossible to fight an orderly battle. Men staggered through snow up to their knees. They were terribly mired down. Arms and raiment alike were covered in mud. Again and again, the two armies clashed. Then they fell back to their pavilions. The conflict raged for three days. The banner of both sides had a white field with a black serpent holding a naked man in its mouth.[17]

One night, the men in the army of Messer Azzo were so exhausted that more than seven hundred of them had fallen asleep. The next day there was no hesitation. One army hurled itself against the other. Trumpets sounded and captains maneuvered. Then they came together ferociously. The whole field of Parabiago was full of combatants. The battle lasted all day. There were blows with lance, sword, and mace. The fighting was vicious. It made a tremendous uproar. Messer Lucchino, uncle of Messer Azzo and leader of that side, was defeated in battle and captured, and Messer Lodrisio and Malerva, his captain, were victorious. Forty-four hundred men were killed, not counting those who drowned in the river or perished in the swirling snow: men of Como, Trent, and Bergamo; country folk and foot soldiers mostly, who because of the impediment of the snow could not flee. Thirty-six hundred horses were slaughtered, and many more were injured. Now you see how Messer Lucchino's endeavor turned out!

Messer Azzo remained well armed in Milan, the whole people with him. No one dared to go out. One of his relatives, Messer Giovanni Fieschi of Genoa, his cousin, along with the five hundred Burgundians of good quality that were in his company, was tasked with aiding his kinsman.[18] When news came of the defeat, he hurried out of Milan with the five hundred Burgundians and four hundred Germans and he rushed to the field of Parabiago. First, he rounded up all those who had fled the battle. He gathered those together

17. The two armies, both fighting for a Visconti, were both flying the traditional Visconti banner.

18. Porta notes that Giovanni Fieschi (Ianni dello Fiesco) was count of Lavagna and the brother of Lucchino's wife Isabella.

that he could. Second, he surveyed how things stood with the army, and he noted that the country folk were not well organized, and that they were scattered across the field, some here and some there, picking over the spoils of battle. Third, he sent word to Malerva, telling him not to engage and bribing him with ten wine flasks full of ducats, so it looked as if he were simply sending him some of the fine wine of Malvasia. The money was like a strong leash. Then trumpets sounded and he descended on them. There was hardly any resistance. The banners of Lodrisio and Malerva were cast down and Lodrisio was captured. Messer Ianni dello Fiesco of Genoa was slain in the fighting. Once Lodrisio was taken and his ranks broken, the rest of the field was won without further resistance. They returned to Milan in triumph but having suffered gravely as well; for, as has already been noted, forty-four hundred people had died, not counting those who were in peril for their lives due to their wounds. They carried back as many of these as possible on carts. They had carts piled with dead bodies, which they gathered from the field of battle and transported to their tombs.

Messer Lodrisio did not die, but he was locked away in perpetual imprisonment, in a castle called San Columbano.[19] There he was provided with every pleasure he could have wished for: music, singing, food, and women, save simply that he could never leave his prison. The soldiers of the company were totally stripped of what they had. Their arms and their mounts they lost. After this I saw a good two hundred fifty of them wandering on foot. This one had spurs strapped on. That one had a shield.[20] This one a helmet and that one a scrawny horse, according to their condition. The Burgundians were given double pay and great gifts. Malerva was released.

Only a few days later, Azzo Visconti died and was succeeded in his dominion by Messer Lucchino Visconti, who held most of Lombardy, including Parma, Piacenza, Lodi, Bergamo, Brescia, Milan, Crema, and Civitale. He ruled for [ten] years with such peace and justice that no one in all that land had reason to fear. A man

19. Porta notes that Lodrisio was released in 1351 by Archbishop Giovanni of Milan, a fact apparently unknown to the Anonimo.

20. It is unclear where precisely the Anonimo saw these survivors. He may have spent some time in or around Milan, or he may have seen them elsewhere in northern Italy, for example near Bologna.

could walk freely with gold in his hand. Messer Lucchino was a harsh man without mercy. He never forgave. He punished each according to their sins or failings. The man was so cruel that he once fed to his dogs a young German boy who had brought him cherries, because the lad had struck one that had barked at him. He refused to relent, neither due to the boy's youth or the pleading of his father — who was his constable and friend— nor for money.

Messer Lucchino, despite the fact that he had a personal guard like a king's that was made up of both foot soldiers and knights, kept with him a special and novel defense. It consisted of two huge and terrible hounds, enormous as lions and shaggy as sheep. Their eyes were red and terrible. These two dogs were always with him at court, one on his right and one on his left. In the midst of his palace he had a strong tower. Within it was a spacious chamber. When Messer Lucchino rested in that room, the dogs stood guard. They constantly circled the tower. No one could come near the door. There was always a guard at the gate. Another was at the gate that led through the wall to the court. Yet another stood in the piazza. When Messer Lucchino took his meals alone, he stood at the table, the dogs ever with him, and he fed first one and then the other big chunks of meat. When he was standing there the numerous members of his court crept about in silence for fear of the dogs. No one moved. No one spoke. For if the lord so much as looked at a man with disfavor, the dogs were instantly at his throat, wrestling him to the ground.

There is no reason to marvel too much at these guardians, for this was nothing new. Valerius Maximus writes of Massinissa, who was the one-time king of Numidia and was a trusted and faithful friend of Rome. This King Massinissa always had two great dogs guarding him, enormous mastiffs, and he never felt safe without them.[21] This was despite the fact that he was guarded by both foot soldiers and knights, controlled the whole rich country of Numidia, and had the good friendship of the Romans by whose will he ruled, safe, secure,

---

21. That Lucchino had a stern sense of justice is corroborated by Galvano Fiamma, *Opusculum*, 8.2, but no mention is made of the fearsome dogs that the Anonimo describes. It seems likely that the Anonimo has introduced this story, borrowing from ancient sources, in order to emphasize the ease with which a just man might inadvertently slip into cruelty, which was an important them for him. See above, pp. 47–51.

and feared. Sometimes he was asked why he did this. In response he said, "Man, who wishes naturally to be free, is incapable of keeping faith. A dog, who knows nothing of liberty, is faithful to his master."[22]

Anyway, Messer Lucchino was a very just man. Neither gold nor silver could hinder him from doing justice, so that his whole land was free. He had a bastard son, Messer Bruzo by name. He gave this Messer Bruzo command of Lodi. He sent him to rule that city. It happened that one nobleman there killed another. He was seized and was to be beheaded.

The relatives of this evildoer approached Messer Bruzo and said to him, "Messer Bruzo, you have a great need of money. Don't kill this prisoner of yours. Here are 15,000 florins ready for the taking."

Hearing this, Messer Bruzo was unsure what to do. He rode from Lodi to Milan. He knelt before his father and asked permission to take the money, for he was only a poor knight. He could earn 15,000 florins simply by sparing the evildoer's life. Hearing all this, Messer Lucchino, his father, gave a sign to his servant that his helm should be brought in. The helm was cunningly wrought and shining. On the top there was a lovely crest, covered in vermillion velvet. On it were written letters of gold.

When the helm was brought in, Lucchino said, "Bruzo, read these letters." So, he read them. They said: "Justice."

Then Lucchino said, "Should we give the impression of justice but not the real thing? Are 15,000 florins worth more than this helm, which is itself worth more than my whole lordship? Go, return to Lodi, and do justice there. If you do not, I will do justice to you."

Messer Lucchino wanted very much that pure-hearted men should come to his realm. He loved the ordinary people. He ruled [ten] years, and when he died in the midst of his reign and passed the baton there was none better or greater than he to take it up.

---

22. See Valerius Maximus, *Factorum ac dictorum memorabilium libri novem*, IX.13, ext. 2. Massinissa was the first king of Numidia and an ally of the Romans at the famous battle of Zama.

# CHAPTER NINE

IN THOSE DAYS people's customs began to change tremendously, both with regards to clothing and behavior. They began wearing hoods with long points [...] They began wearing clothing that was snug and had large collars in the Catalan fashion, bearing purses on their belts, and wearing caps on their heads on top of their hoods. They began sporting long flowing beards, as if in imitation of Saracens or Spaniards.[23] Before this time, one never saw such things. Instead, people shaved their beards and wore clothing that was less clinging and more virtuous. If someone did sport a beard, they would have been seen as suspect unless they were either a Spaniard or a penitent. But now everything has changed, so that folk parade about with little caps on their heads to give themselves an air of authority, and with flowing beards as if they were hermits, and with purses at their sides as if they were pilgrims. There you have it insofar as the new fashion is concerned! What is more, anyone who didn't wear a little cap, sport a great beard, or dangle a purse from their belt was given short shrift, hardly noted, or even treated as if they were nothing! Great captains had beards. Anyone who had one was feared.

I want to make this point a bit more fully.[24] There was, in a certain land, a king who highly honored philosophers and wise men who spoke eloquently. This king deliberately sought to build up a company of virtuous men. A great philosopher came to his court. The king was quite delighted to have the presence of this good

23. Significantly, Cola di Rienzo grew a beard later in his career as well. This passage suggests that the Anonimo would have seen his beard negatively, as a sign that he embraced fashions stemming from unwholesome foreign influences. Fashion and dress were consistently of interest, and sometimes of concern, to the Anonimo. On fashion in trecento Italy, and its relationship to the changing elite values of the late fourteenth century, see Susan Mosher Stuard, *Gilding the Market: Luxury and Fashion in Fourteenth-Century Italy* (Philadelphia: University of Pennsylvania Press, 2006).

24. The story that follows derives originally from Diogenes Laertius, who tells a much simpler anecdote along these lines about the philosopher Aristippus in his *Lives of Eminent Philosophers*, II.8, 75. A version of it was then told by the fabulist Babrius. See Babrius and Phaedrus, *Fables*, Ben Edwin Perry, trans. (Cambridge, MA: Harvard University Press, 1965), 554. Such fables were heavily mined for exempla during the medieval period, but the precise source of the fable for the Anonimo is uncertain.

man and all the more so when it became clear that this philosopher comported himself well and answered every question put to him. As a result, the king wished to honor the goodness, knowledge, and virtue that he found in this man. He invited him to a formal dinner that included various tasty and intricate dishes, with all his noble court in attendance. The room where the event was to be held was spacious and grand. The tables were arranged all about. The whole place was covered in tapestries of fine, pure silk. The walls were hung with draperies elaborately decorated with baboons made from golden silk thread. The ceiling above it all was hung with cloth decorated with golden stars. There were various oriental rugs scattered about. The king wanted this dinner to be very formal. At the head of the room there was a small table. At this table, only the king and the philosopher sat. The servants came in, bearing tasty things to eat. As he ate, the king wasted no time, urgently asking the philosopher's thoughts about various things he had been wondering about. The philosopher, like a prudent fellow, answered as appropriate. His replies had a great impact on the king, for they seemed true. "You speak well. It pleases me," the king repeatedly responded.

Meanwhile, the philosopher began to feel the urge to spit. He clutched in his mouth a huge mouthful. Eventually he could hold it in no longer. It had to come out. The philosopher searched the walls and the area thereabout, looking for somewhere to spit. But he found nowhere because, as I said, everything was covered in noble draperies. Then the philosopher raised his head and spied the face of the king. He saw that the king had a beard: bushy, large, and very black. It came to the middle of his chest and its sides came to his shoulders. He looked like some satrap.[25] The philosopher concluded that this beard was the ugliest thing in the room, the best possible receptacle for his spit. The wise philosopher steeled himself and then spit right into the middle of the king's beard.

---

25. Porta suggests the word used here *(varvassore)* be translated as "vassallo," meaning vassal or liegeman. But the *Vocabulario della Crusca* recommends it be understood as equivalent of the Latin *satrapa* or "satrap." This is in keeping with the Anonimo's association of big beards with Muslims, so I've rendered it that way here.

## CHAPTER NINE

When the king felt this, he was shocked and angry. "Why have you done this?" he demanded.

The philosopher responded, saying, "On all sides — below, beside, and above — I found myself surrounded by cloth woven with gold. There is nowhere foul enough to spit aside from your beard. It's the nastiest place there is, so I spit there. It is fitting that one spit only in the ugliest places."

To this, the king had no reply; he was dumbstruck. So the philosopher put his hand on the king's shoulder and said, "Say that I speak well. Say that it pleases you." So as for those who wear beards, let them stand alongside this philosopher and receive what the king received.

# CHAPTER TEN
## THE DEATH OF KING ROBERT AND THE COMING OF THE QUEEN OF HUNGARY TO ROME

IN THE YEAR OF OUR LORD 1342[/3], the illustrious and glorious man, Robert, king of Sicily and Jerusalem, ended his days.[1] He was entombed honorably in the city of Naples, in Sta. Chiara. He lay in the place where his predecessors slept. As a result of his death, the kingdom of Puglia was disconsolate, as I will explain. This king Robert was a most wise man, so wise that through his wisdom he won a crown despite the fact that he should not have become king.[2] He arranged that his brother by blood, Charles, to whom the crown should have gone, should become king of Hungary instead, and so it happened, after which he himself was crowned.[3] This man Robert preserved his realm in such peace that throughout Puglia, Lavoro,[4] Calabria, and Abruzzo the country folk neither bore nor knew the use of weapons. They carried only wooden clubs, to fend off dogs. Even this was only sometimes needed.

When this king heard reports that said, "You have lost five hundred troops in battle," he responded, "Five hundred carlini are lost."[5]

1. There was no longer an actual kingdom of Jerusalem. After the fall of Acre in 1291, no crusader polities remained in the Levant. The title, however, continued to be claimed by the Angevins after their defeat of the heirs of Frederick II Hohenstaufen, who had adopted the title after a treaty with the Muslim conquerors of the Holy Land. The Angevin rulers of Naples styled themselves kings and queens "of Jerusalem and Sicily," and their coats of arms bore both the French fleur-de-lis and the Jerusalem cross.

2. On Robert, see Kelly, *New Solomon*.

3. Here Porta observes that the Anonimo believes contemporary rumors that suggested Robert had poisoned his eldest brother, convinced the second to become a monk, and tricked the third to become king of Hungary. Modern historians do not find this credible. Several late medieval chroniclers, including Froissart, attributed necromantic and other magical powers to King Robert, and other accounts of the Angevins include magical rings and poisonings.

4. The Terra di Lavoro, the region of southern Lazio and northern Campania, corresponding to ancient Liburia.

5. Carlini were Neapolitan gold coinage, roughly the equivalent of Florentine florins and Venetian ducats. Robert's concern was for war's expense in terms

# CHAPTER TEN

This king was so industrious that during his lifetime the power of the empire was never able to make inroads into his realm. Two emperors exhausted themselves before the walls of Rome: namely, Henry the count of Luxembourg and Lewis the duke of Bavaria, as I said above.[6] This king was also count of Provence and a man of letters, particularly learned in the medical arts. He was both a great medical mind and a great philosopher. Some things about his handling of money made him seem avaricious. What is more, he converted bodily penalties into monetary fines.

This king had a son, who was duke of Calabria.[7] He was deeply concerned with justice, and used to say, "Our great-grandfather, King Charles [I], by his skill acquired and maintained this realm. My uncle did so by largesse and my father by means of his wisdom. I will do the same by means of justice." The duke worked diligently to uphold the highest justice. It happened that a baron of his realm murdered a knight. He was accused in the court of the king, in Naples. There he was imprisoned and sentenced to be beheaded. Then the king changed the sentence from a bodily one into a monetary fine, condemning him to pay 15,000 ounces.[8] The money was pledged. The man was taken out of the unpleasant place he was being kept and put instead in other lodgings, large and less restrictive. When the duke heard this, he angrily went to the prison from which the fellow was removed. There he clapped his own legs in irons. He stood there like a wretch that was waiting to die. He refused to leave. When his father heard about this, understanding his son's desire, he agreed that justice should be done contrary to his own wishes. The murderer lost his head. Once it was done, he went to his son, the duke, and said, "Duke, we have conceded to your

---

of treasure rather than blood. He had a reputation among contemporaries for his parsimoniousness.

6. That is, emperors Henry VII and Lewis IV. Some of this would have been in the missing fourth chapter.

7. Charles of Calabria (1298–1328), Robert's heir to the crown, who predeceased his father. Charles was renowned for his justice. On Robert's death, Charles's daughter inherited the crown as Giovanna I.

8. *Oncia*, a Neapolitan unit of account worth about 60 carlini at this time, with substantial variations over time.

wishes in good faith, but justice that is too harsh, where no mercy is to be found, is the worst kind of cruelty."

This king had a galley equipped for travel to Provence. It was made by skilled craftsmen who named it the Red Galley. The king, once crowned, wished to recover Sicily, which his father had lost due to his luxurious ways.[9] He put together a great host of troops. He had one hundred thousand men. He armed his navy for a voyage to recover Sicily. Prior to departure, he consulted his arts, the lot-casting of geomancy.[10] The result suggested that he would capture Sicily. Then he took to his ship, and the host cast off for Trapani. There at Trapani, in a raid, a woman traveling to meet her husband was captured. She was asked her name. She responded, "I am the sad Cecilia." Upon hearing this the king was powerfully disturbed. He felt his arts had deceived him.[11] The prediction had been fulfilled. There was no point in going forward. He hastened to depart but was unable to do so, nor could he prepare to go, for the sea was disturbed. A great tempestuous storm blew in. Fortune would not allow him to depart, nor would it allow him to provision his army. There, in the land of his enemies, he seemed likely to die of hunger.

Behold the cruel methods he deployed so that he and his army might escape! They had little bread. He divided it up equally. The people pondered what they would eat, for they needed more bread than they had. *Eadem actio prava fuit et studiosa*, as Aristotle says.[12] Across from them, out at sea, there was a small wooded

9. Charles II of Naples had lost Sicily to the Crown of Aragon after a long struggle initiated by the Sicilian Vespers of 1282. Its recovery was a constant policy initiative of King Robert.

10. Here again the Anonimo recounts Robert's reputation for the magical arts.

11. Cecilia was a common enough woman's name, but it was also the word for Sicily (Sicilia in modern Italian but Cecilia in the Anonimo's rendering), hence Robert's worry. It was foretold he would capture Cecilia, but which one? The Anonimo's account may be a tactful elision of Robert's military failure and political inability to rouse former Angevin adherents in Sicily.

12. "The deed was both wicked and wise." Campanelli points out that the Anonimo refers here to Boethius' translation of Aristotle's *Categories*, but that he reverses the meaning of the original, which says "neque eadem actio et una numero erit prava et studiosa." Whereas Aristotle says something cannot

## CHAPTER TEN

island, standing perhaps ten miles from where the host was. They took boats and loaded them with a force of six thousand people, giving them hatchets and hooks, tools to cut wood, and sending them to the island as if gathering wood was their task. As soon as these six thousand people arrived there, they were abandoned. The boats turned back. They were left without bread. There they starved to death. Imagine the cruelty! To survive the storm six thousand were condemned to starvation. No one visited them or comforted them. The mantle of Sant'Alberto would have suited their need, transforming itself into a raft for them, so that they might return home.[13] Having freed himself of this great host of men, the king now sought to depart. As soon as the ships set out, the storm assailed them, tossing them to and fro. All night long they were at the mercy of the sea.

Twelve ships, including the king's, were driven by the violent winds of Fortune to the port of Messina. At break of day came the dawn. The sailors made a tremendous noise. Don Federico, kinsman of King Robert, disturbed by the noise, which did not seem to be that of merchants, rose from his bed, and going to look out from his balcony, he saw there the royal insignia. He then understood that his kinsman King Robert, who had come to retake Sicily, was being buffeted by fortune. The queen followed the king and, understanding what had happened, said, "Oh, king, what do you intend to do to my brother?"[14] The king had mercy and did not take

---

have two opposing qualities at once, the Anonimo insists that in this case the king's act was simultaneously wicked and wise. Campanelli, "Benché io l'aia fatta per lettera," 6–7. It must be noted, however, that wickedness and wisdom are not obvious opposites in the same way as are the colors black and white or the qualities of goodness and badness, which comprise Aristotle's examples. Aristotle, *Categories*, I.5. Indeed, the Anonimo is consistently keen to emphasize that apparent virtue could easily slip into vice. See above, pp. 44–54.

13. Porta speculates that this refers to the blessed Alberto degli Abati di Trapani, who died in 1307, and was famous for bringing miraculous aid to Messina when it was reduced to starvation by the besieging forces of Charles of Calabria.

14. The king here is Federico of Sicily, not Robert. Federico's wife was Eleanor of Anjou, King Robert's sister. The Anonimo's sense of the ironies of Fortune has Robert's ships blown to the very land he had originally intended to invade.

advantage of the fact these twelve ships had been lost and could not escape his grasp. In that moment, at half terce, fortune was satisfied.

The king, with his galleys, withdrew a bit and then returned home to Naples. He went back to his palace. Never again did he take up arms, neither by sea nor by land. He had a private garden created alongside his palace and there he spent his time at archery. As he shot, he considered matters relating to his realm. While doing it he put his signature on this and that, gave audiences to and answered the concerns of the people, and did all the various things that he was obliged to do.[15]

AT THAT TIME, in the year of our Lord 1343, the holy queen of Hungary — mother of Lewis, king of Hungary and of his brother Andrew, king of Puglia — came to Rome to visit the bodies of the saints and the basilicas.[16] She lingered in Rome for three days, visiting all the sanctuaries and giving great gifts to all the churches. Fra Acuto, one of the little brothers of Assisi who had established the Hospital of the Cross in Sta. Maria Rotunda, was the first to request alms from her in order to fund repairs to the Ponte Mollo, which had fallen to the ground.[17] The queen donated so much money

---

15. We have been unable to locate what appears to be the fabulistic source of these remarks.

16. This is Elizabeth of Poland, queen of Hungary. Andrew, her son, would marry Giovanna I of Naples, the granddaughter of Robert of Anjou. Elizabeth's husband, who died in 1342, was King Robert's aforementioned brother, Charles. According to the explicit terms of King Robert's last will and testament, his granddaughter Giovanna would become the sole ruler of Naples. Andrew would become only prince consort. This tension in Andrew's status would lead to his eventual assassination. Many contemporary writers, including Villani and Petrarch, however, also continued to call him "king." For these developments, see Ronald G. Musto, *Medieval Naples: A Documentary History, 400–1400* (New York: Italica Press, 2013), 234–302; Elizabeth Casteen, *From She-Wolf to Martyr: The Reign and Disputed Reputation of Joanna I of Naples* (Ithaca, NY: Cornell University Press, 2015); and Musto, *Writing Southern Italy*, 207–11, 220–21, 229–52.

17. Acuto was a Franciscan friar who did indeed found a hospital in Rome, sometimes known simply as the Hospital of Acuto. Sta. Maria Rotunda is the

## ✻ CHAPTER TEN

that the bridge was rebuilt with a little help. New supports were built, and towers too, and arches would have been made, if there had been no impediment. But then the numbers of the poor of Rome began rapidly to increase, and so much was asked that her gifts were not enough. Such was the importunity of the beggars that the queen grew concerned, and it suited her to depart. *Nam pauperes habent mores corvinos. Rustici montani mores habent lupos.*[18] The women of Rome did her great honor. She greatly admired Roman garb.

She departed and traveled to Naples intending to visit her son, King Andrew, and visit him she did, and was received by Queen Giovanna and by the counts of the realm who did her honors of which I will speak when I touch on the death of King Andrew. This queen [Elizabeth] traveled in a carriage. Four palfreys drew it. She was accompanied by eight countesses. Everyone was focused on her. In another carriage there were other damsels with Hungarian veils and coronets of pure gold on their heads. Fifty knights with golden spurs, as well as other servants, attended her.

This woman had had four fingers severed from her right hand. A Hungarian baron by the name of Feliciano had severed them. The thing transpired like this. Feliciano had a daughter named Elisabetta, who used to dwell in the royal court as a companion of the queen. The kinsman of the king *carnaliter illam mediante regina cognovit.*[19] The time came when the father wished to withdraw her from the queen's service, saying that he wished to have her marry. Elisabetta said, "It is not suitable that one who has lost her honor in the shadow of the king should have a husband."

Hearing this, Feliciano was enraged. He said nothing more. Rather, he went with one of his young sons, a knight, to speak with the king. The king was in a military camp. Feliciano entered the camp and went right past everyone there. He passed through the stockade that surrounded the king's position and went to the royal pavilion. There, before the door of the pavilion, he found a friar who

---

name of the church located in the Pantheon of Rome. The bridge in question is the Ponte Mollo, the Milvian Bridge.

18. "For paupers have the manners of crows. Mountain rustics have the manners of wolves."

19. "had carnal knowledge of her while she was serving the queen."

was the king's confessor. He knelt on the ground and confessed, saying, "I must take up a matter with the best knights in the world and so there is risk of death for two people. I pray that you absolve me." The friar did not understand him. He darkened the door, made his sign of the cross, prayed for mercy, and absolved what he did not comprehend.

Meanwhile, the guards announced to the king that Feliciano had come. The king was at table, dining with the queen and with their son Lewis, currently the king, who was at that time still a young child. The king gave permission that Feliciano should enter. Feliciano, now permitted, said to his son, "Stay here. Don't come in. If you hear any ruckus mount up and get out of here. Your horse will carry you to safety."

Feliciano entered. When the king saw him, he raised his voice and said, "Oh ho, you madman, have you found for me the good Bohemian sword that you promised?"

Feliciano responded, saying, "No. I'll find it. But how would you like a wound, a cut, from this dagger of mine?"

He then raised his dagger two feet above the king's head. The king raised his eyes to the dagger's edge. Feliciano brought his hand down, letting fortune decide where it would land. The blow would have split the king's head in two. Trembling and afraid, the king dove under the table. The queen raised her hand. The blow severed her four fingers, which fell to the ground. The thing was unheard of. The uproar enormous. The damsels, who were serving at table, slew Feliciano with their serving knives. Then they fell upon his son and slew him. Father and son died in one moment thanks to the tongue of Elisabetta. And the queen lost half her hand.

# CHAPTER ELEVEN
THE BATTLE FOR SPAIN, THE DESTRUCTION OF ALGECIRAS, AND THE SIEGE OF GIBRALTAR

IT WAS IN THE YEAR OF OUR LORD 13[40] in the month of [October], when a great and terrible battle between Christians and Saracens occurred.[1] *Duce Deo*,[2] the Christians were the victors. The Saracens were defeated in Spain in a place called Cornacervina, in the territory near Seville, where 60,000 Moors died.[3] The event transpired as follows.

There was in Spain a noble and glorious king. In our day, there has been none better. He bore the name Alfonso, son of King Duranno of Castile.[4] This King Alfonso was most victorious. He held the frontier against the Saracens resolutely. He defeated a great duke of the Saracens, Picazzo by name, in a rout, capturing him.[5]

---

1. This refers to the Battle of Rio Salado between Abū al-Hasan 'Ali, ruler of Marinid Morocco and Yusuf I of Granada, on one side, and the Christian kings Alfonso XI of Castile and Alfonso IV of Portugal, on the other. For the battle and subsequent events in the context of late medieval crusading in Iberia, see Joseph F. O'Callaghan, *The Gibraltar Crusade: Castile and the Battle for the Strait* (Philadelphia: University of Pennsylvania Press, 2011), 162–217. See also Map 3 above. It should be noted that Cardinal Giles Albornoz, who will be discussed in the chronicle's final chapters, participated in this battle. See Enzo Petrucci, "La Chiesa nell'azione del Cardinale Egidio de Albornoz durante la campagna in Italia," *Rivista di Storia della Chiesa in Italia* 1 (2011): 57–99, at 72.

2. "With God in command."

3. Spanish sources identify the place as Peña del Çiervo (the Hill of the Deer). This hill was the location from which Alfonso's forces launched their attack, not the location of the besieging forces. See O'Callaghan, 180.

4. "Duranno" is Ferdinand IV.

5. This seems to refer to one of the sons of the Marinid ruler of Morocco. Likely, Abū Mālik 'Abd al-Wāhid, who was indeed slain by Alfonso, but in battle. Porta cites various sources making similar references to a man named Pytazius or Picaço. The intended marriage and baptism appears fanciful, perhaps reflecting rumors that reached the Anonimo's ears, or they may be borrowings from the standard tropes of chivalrous romance literature, so popular in trecento Italy. For the Roman context and reception, see Internullo, *Ai margini*, 369–82.

This Picazzo had one eye. Thinking nothing of Picazzo's nobility or power, King Alfonso decided to spare his life if he would willingly receive baptism and take his daughter to wife. These things were promised and carried out. When Picazzo came before the baptismal font, he reneged. Scorning baptism and Christianity, he spit most foully into the baptismal basin. Seeing this, the good King Alfonso was angered. He didn't hesitate. His hand flew to his sword and without mercy he separated Picazzo's head from his body. The body was thrown to the dogs.

The mother of the young Picazzo was a queen named Ricciaferra. Ricciaferra's husband was named Salim, king of Bellamarina, whose origins were in a city called Trebesten.[6] Hearing of the murder of her handsome son Picazzo at the hands of King Alfonso, Ricciaferra contemplated vendetta against the Christians and King Alfonso alike. And because she couldn't carry it out without a great military force, she decided to call a crusade against the Christians. She arranged it with her own pope, the caliph of Baghdad, the sultan of Babylon, who issued a general call to crusade and offered an indulgence throughout the Saracen world — among the Parthians, Medes, and Turks — summoning a great host to take back lands from the Christians, occupy and destroy the churches of Christ, and replace them with temples to Muhammad.[7] And so it was done.

---

6. King Salim was the Marinid ruler of Benamarin (Bella Marina), Abū al-Hasan. His wife, here called Ricciaferra, was named Fatima. Trebesten is modern day Tlemcen, in Algeria.

7. The word translated here as "crusade" is "*passaio*" or "*passaggio*" in modern Italian. This is a general term that was commonly used to refer to Christian crusades, for which there was no consistently used official term in the medieval period. Note, "Babylon" refers not to the historical Babylon but to Cairo, ruled in this era by Mamluk sultans and home to the Abbasid caliphs who had previously reigned from Baghdad. The contents of this letter reflect those of one described in contemporary sources. It is attributed to a Muslim author, but that attribution was likely Christian propaganda. The Anonimo seems to have had some knowledge of it. The actual involvement of the Mamluks seems unlikely, and the indulgence supposedly on offer was a Christian norm, rather than a Muslim one. See O'Callaghan, *Gibraltar Crusade*, 171.

## CHAPTER ELEVEN

Throughout the Saracen world, the *alfaquecqui*,[8] that is to say the priests, traveled about preaching, bearing letters from the caliph, their pope, which urged the crusade against the Christians. The people came together in a great force of infantry and cavalry. There were at least 400,000 warriors. All of them bore maces and slings: among them were Persians, Arabs, black Saracens, Parthians, and Andalusians. All these people were moved to be part of the host preparing to cross the sea. There were four crowned kings who guided the host. The first was the king of Garbo, along with the king of Morocco, the king of Bellamarina (another name for Trebesten), and the king of Granada.[9] These were the kings of the Saracen realms. It is true, of course, that the king of Granada did not voyage with the rest, because his realm was inside Spain. But when he heard of the approaching Saracen host, he rebelled and began to make war within Spain itself.

These four kings and their great host approached, crossing the sea and taking up positions on land. For six days they arrayed themselves in the land of the Christians with horses, asses, mules, camels, countless women, servants, weapons, grain supplies, and other accoutrements of war. They passed freely through the land, taking up positions outside a Spanish city called Taliffa,[10] which they claimed as their own. In the wide-open fields they erected their

8. If we take seriously the Anonimo's assertion that these are priests, this term may be a reference to fakirs, or Sufi ascetics, whom the Anonimo is treating as comparable to Christian clergy here. The role ascribed to them, preaching and bearing formal letters calling for crusade, again echoes Christian norms. This is complicated by the fact that from at least the thirteenth century on, in Castile, the alfaqueques (from the Arabic al-fakkāk) was an official charged with redeeming captives ostensibly taken in war, usually in exchanges of Christian captives for Muslim ones. See William D. Phillips, Jr., *Slavery in Medieval and Early Modern Iberia* (Philadelphia: University of Pennsylvania Press, 2014), 49–50.

9. Garbo refers to al-Gharb, a name commonly used for the Moorish ruler of the North African zone opposite Gibraltar. Morocco and Benamarin were in Marinid hands. The king of Granada was Yusuf I.

10. This is Tarifa, near the Rio Salado. This event is sometimes referred to as the Battle (or Siege) of Tarifa rather than the Battle of Rio Salado, as the Anonimo and others refer to it.

pavilions and pitched camp. They brought with them engines and trebuchets for the purpose of mounting a vigorous siege. The host was vast. They had no worries at all. Rather, they ate and drank. Their drums pounded. How great a noise they made! They had with them engines for raising ladders and throwing boulders. Their camp, where they resided, was called Cornacervina, a spacious field, well supplied with water, wood, and pasture. It was strong too, for a river called the Rio Salado defended it. This river separated Taliffa from Seville.

They really would not have approached nor would they have been able to move through the narrow route along the coast had they not, as soon as they arrived, come to an agreement with a great and powerful baron of the realm by the name of Don Ianni Manuelle.[11] This Don Ianni Manuelle was among the strongest pillars of Spain. The mountains were under his control. This Don Ianni had such a dispute with King Alfonso that he was unwilling to speak to him and raided him, for he despised the king for being unwilling to remain with his queen and instead keeping by his side a whore named Madonna Leonora, as I will explain later.[12] To this Don Ianni Manuello the Saracens paid a great sum in gold coins so that he would allow them to pass, and so it was. By the power granted him by King Alfonso, Don Ianni Manuello allowed the Saracens to pass, and they came to the field of Cornacervina, as I have said, and there the host undertook its merciless siege. They aimed their trebuchets and arrayed their engines for hoisting up ladders by means of wheels and ropes.

The host kept up the siege for three months. Taliffa was utterly lost if it did not find help. It could not endure. When the good King

11. This refers to Juan Manuel, who did indeed have rocky relations with Alfonso XI and had in the past gone so far as to ally himself with the Nasrid king Muhammad IV and make it easier for him to make war on Castile. But the Anonimo is wrong to believe this animosity played any role in the battle here described. Juan and Alfonso's relationship was patched up in time for Alfonso's earlier crusading effort in 1330. Juan Manuel was present at the Battle of Rio Salado and led the vanguard. See O'Callaghan, *Gibraltar Crusade*, 142–61, 177.

12. The Anonimo refers here to Eleanor de Guzmán, Alfonso's mistress and mother to Enrico II of Castile.

## CHAPTER ELEVEN

Alfonso heard of this host and its great strength, he was not afraid, and he set out for the frontier near Seville, the royal city. It is said that the holy Madonna Maria was born in that city.[13] King Alfonso did not sleep. He sent to the pope for aid. He sent word as well to the kings of the lands nearby, that is, to his uncle, Don Dionisio of Lisbon on the sea, the king of Portugal,[14] and to the king of Navarre and to the king of Aragon. He sent orders to all his barons that they should follow him. He sent commands to Don Ianni Mannuello that he should not move, and that he should instead remain to close off the line of retreat, barring the way when he heard the sound of battle. Earnestly did the king call for aid. He summoned all of Spain. The kings made no reply but rather came in haste with their cavalry and infantry. They demonstrated their good will and their strength.

The first help came from Pope Benedict [XII]: 700 well-equipped men-at-arms, Germans and Frenchmen, with mighty steeds and well-armed, they came marked with the cross, absolved of their penances and of sin.[15] The second to respond was the king of Navarre with the men of Pamplona, with 5,000 well-bedecked knights, wearing fine steel helms on their heads, shields on their arms, sharp swords at their sides, and bearing shining spears in their hands. He brought with him as well 20,000 foot soldiers. The third was the king of Aragon, with 5,000 knights, including men of Provence and France. With him came the men of Toulouse. He also brought 20,000 foot soldiers. Don Dionisio, his uncle, came too, with the men of Lisbon. The fourth to arrive was the king of Portugal, with 15,000 Spanish knights, mounted on horseback and carrying light spears. Fifth was Alfonso, king of Castile, with 30,000 good knights, well-equipped, with Spanish steeds from Castile, which are considered the noblest of all destriers, and with countless infantry.[16]

13. No certain identification is known.

14. This is another error in which the Anonimo, as with Juan Manuel, blurs the battle of Rio Salado with events of preceding decades. King Denis (Dionisio) of Portugal died in 1325; and it was his son, Alfonso IV, who participated in this battle.

15. The mark of the cross and the absolution of penances and sin indicates that the Anonimo understood these men to be crusaders.

16. The Anonimo is probably inflating the numbers here. See O'Callaghan, *Gibraltar Crusade*, 187.

As the siege of Taliffa went on, King Alfonso remained in Seville with his barons. Hunger and dearth were everywhere in Seville. The people who had come to help had nowhere to stay. They couldn't afford anything. The people began to murmur about the great delay. Scolded by his barons, King Alfonso therefore decided to go to battle and see what fortune had in store. He rested his hopes on God, who had never failed him. He took to the task with vigor. He arrayed his forces as follows. He had 30,000 well-accoutered knights, no more, and 100,000 foot. Between his forces and the Saracen host ran the river known as Salato. On one side of the river was Cornacervina. Here were the trebuchets and pavilions, the tents and banners, and a mass of people, as I mentioned, with many drums. To the right side of the host stood the mountains of Ilerda, the old land.[17] On the other side stretched an open plain. Behind it was a narrow pass, through which they had come by means of bribery, as I noted. Above that valley were the mountains controlled by Don Ianni Manuello. Before them was the river and their enemies. They monitored the river's fords with care.

King Alfonso proceeded in this way. First, he commanded 700 crusading knights sent by the papacy to cross over the river. Three hundred of them managed this and engaged the guardians of the crossing. Two hundred of them arranged themselves to absorb the force of the river's current and enable the foot soldiers to cross over. The remaining 200 remained there to guard the crossing, focusing entirely on that task. There was no small danger in making the passage, crossing the river. All of them were on specially chosen steeds. The troops bore no banner except one with a vermillion cross on a white field. Upon the cross was the crucified one.

After the seven hundred knights, King Alfonso followed, mounted on a dappled steed. It is said that it was the best and most beautiful in the world. With him came 10,000 knights who, once the river was forded, were the first to join the battle, along with the king. After King Alfonso came the king of Aragon with 5,000 knights and 20,000 foot. These headed for the mountains to create blockades, occupying the passes and byways, the routes up and down, so that

17. Porta points out that this is an error. Lérida, to which the Anonimo is taken to be referring here, was far from the site of this battle. It is unclear precisely what the Anonimo means when he calls this "the old land."

the Saracens might not draw strength from them, either as a refuge or an escape route. On the other flank the king of Navarre was sent with 10,000 knights and 5,000 foot, so that the Saracens could neither flee that way nor stretch out their force across the field. After these people came the king of Portugal with 40,000 foot and all the rest of the host, to reinforce them.[18] This was the overall formation. From the rear, Don Ianni Manuelle was to strike with his mountain men.[19] This was their cunning plan. This is what was lain out in a letter sent to Rome to Messer Stefano Colonna, written in a strange script, difficult to decipher.[20]

With the order of battle and password given, the 700 knights headed into the river. They broke through the waters and passed over. They were exposed. Three knights, mounted high on horseback, were the first to cross the water: an archbishop and two knights with golden spurs, nobles close to King Alfonso, men who knew the area and the nature of the ford. These were the first ahead of all the rest. As they crossed, they were captured by the perfidious Saracens and their heads were quickly separated from their bodies. There in that ford they became glorious martyrs of Christ. Then the cavalry arrived. First one and then another made the crossing. They had little protection. The whole Christian host was arrayed as one force on the other side of the river. None, aside from the archbishop and the two knights, received glorious martyrdom due to the danger of the crossing.

Even after the host had crossed over the river the Saracens, that perfidious people, remained unaware of the size of its multitude.

18. Here the Anonimo uses a delightful idiom that does not render well in English. The king of Portugal and his men are there to *"sostenere le spalle"* or "support the shoulders" of those who joined battle first. A modern idiomatic translation might be "they had their back."

19. Here again the Anonimo mistakes Juan Manuel's role. He was in the vanguard, among the first to ford the river.

20. This would indicate that, in addition to the eyewitnesses mentioned below, the Anonimo had a first-hand, written account of the battle — probably hastily composed in an Iberian handwriting unfamiliar to Italians — and that he may have had enough access to the Colonna to use their records of this and other events, including those in Rienzo's Rome.

They remained by the riverside, eating and celebrating, playing their tambourines and making a general ruckus. Eventually, they looked up. Then they seized their weapons, bows, maces, and slings, offering full and robust defense. It was the hour of terce.[21]

Trumpets and other instruments sounded. Each side could hear the noise of the other. The shrieking was so loud it seemed no human voice could have produced it. The terrible sound echoed off the mountainside. It could be heard ten miles away. One heard shouts and cries. They crashed together, body upon body. They were hand-to-hand. Some gave ground and some pushed forward. One heard cries of "Come on! Let's go!" Other cries were silenced by powerful blows upon armored heads. Lances were thrown, swords raised, and arrows loosed. Stones, splashing into the river, slapped down like snow. The Turks who were there were armed mostly with slings and stones. They were a danger to many.

I asked a Spanish pilgrim if he had any knowledge of this battle. He replied that he was there. He removed his cap from his head to reveal a large round scar in the midst of his forehead, saying it was from a stone. Another, of whom I inquired along the same lines, removed his cap and revealed three scars from sword blows and another from a stone at the fore. You can well imagine how the Saracens rose up and rallied to one another's aid. There was a flood of horses, cracked heads, and breasts punctured by arrows and spears. The dead were trampled by horses. There was tremendous wailing and crying out. The blood ran like streams of water. Those who were sons of a good mother showed their worth there.

Then one witnessed the Saracen cavalry's admirable martial prowess and skill at arms. They rode across the battlefield fighting, striking blows with blades and missiles. No one could pin them down, such was their speed and agility. They carried shields on their arms that were two feet long and one foot wide, covered in linen, such that they were protected from their head to their feet.[22]

21. 9:00 AM.

22. The measure translated here as "feet" is *"piedi,"* which has that literal meaning and corresponded to a measure of somewhere between one third to half a meter, depending on local variation. See Zupko, *Italian Weights and Measures,* 195–200.

# CHAPTER ELEVEN

They had short stirrups [...] waxed linen garb, and steel helmets on their heads. In their hands they bore javelins. These they hurled. Whosoever lifted one of them would not want to lift another. When they ran out of javelins, they could lean from their horses while riding, as far as the ground. With javelin and lance they landed blows in front, behind, below, and above, however they wished. Their dexterity was great. This is the game of the Saracen cavalry. These mounted warriors are the royal scouts.

The battle lasted until nones,[23] no longer, for the Saracen force heard the approach of Don Ianni Manuello, descending from the mountains to strike them from behind and cut off the passes. Once they heard this host and spotted its dust cloud and also saw its shining lances and banners, their heart and virtue quickly broke. They were entirely routed. They couldn't resist. They turned heel and fled. Their flight was a terrible thing. They fled without letting up. They had no hope if not in their legs. There was killing and butchery all around. A great wound was inflicted on the wretched Saracen force. Such was the noble battle for Spain, among many few so memorable. There were 60,000 Saracen corpses and 40,000 prisoners.

The king [of the Saracens] was not present for these things, nor did he hear of them, due to the confidence he had regarding the strength of his army. He fought until word reached him of the mighty host, and he began to have doubts. There stood guarding the entrance to the royal pavilion one man — Serafin by name — three feet taller than anyone else, slender and very muscular with long legs and a black face, wearing a great coat and a silk tunic. In his hand he bore a gilded iron mace. This Serafin, to whom the person of the king was entrusted, was reluctant to announce the poor turn of events. Instead, he told the queen of it. The queen, Ricciaferra by name, took action. She went before the king. From her eyes flowed rivers of tears. She said, "Up king, for the day has been won by Don Alfonso."

The king was playing chess. When he heard this, he was troubled. She said no more, and he heard no more. Two words were enough.

---

23. A monastic hour corresponding to 3:00 PM. The Anonimo thus suggests that the entire battle lasted about six hours.

Dressed in a [...] of gold that came to his feet, with a golden cap on his head covered in precious stones, and bearing a golden rod in his hand, he mounted his horse and took the road that led to his home. He was defended by 7,000 Turks with gilded iron rods in their hands, dressed in satin tunics and capes of fine Eastern silk, armed in imperial array. There went with him other knights with lances as well, with great shining points. Ahead of these came many tambourines and innumerable other musicians playing. Both host and sound seemed regal. Still further ahead came 10,000 Saracen cavalry riding with javelins aimed in all directions, like a porcupine would with a pack of dogs. No one confronted them, such was the thicket of javelins. And there were many other soldiers, both on foot and mounted, of imposing strength and with incomparable arms, who followed him. In this way, did Salim, king of Bellamarina, flee from battle. He broke through and overcame all obstacles due to the might of his cavalry. He left behind Ricciaferra, his wife and queen. He left everything in a desperate state. His flight lasted for six days. Six days the chase continued. The bodies of the dead lay in the fields like sheep.

After the king had departed, the queen caused white silken cloth to be laid out on the ground. On them she had all her money and royal jewels placed. She sat there too, with fifty of her king's lesser concubines. A Spanish knight — Arcilasso by name — armed and well mounted with lance in hand, rode across the field. In his furor, he charged into the Alfanic, which is to say into the pavilion of the king. He happened upon the queen. When this Spaniard saw her sitting there in grief (though her face still demonstrated her dignity), he lost control of himself and struck her with a lance. It passed through her from one side to the other. With that blow, she died. He turned back and did terrible deeds in the field of battle.

There was one marvel, namely that the steed of King Alfonso, the beauty of which has already been noted, could not be restrained or controlled from the moment it entered the field. Contrary to the will of those who held its reins, it bore the king to the pavilion of the king of Bellamarina and there began to rage. It carried on in this way as if possessed of human sensibilities. When King Alfonso entered the royal pavilion, he found the queen dead and lying among her subordinates, who stared at her corpse and wept.

## CHAPTER ELEVEN

There was among them a Christian girl named Maria, born in a settlement called Obeda.[24] This Maria was a slave, and a concubine of the king due to her beauty and manners. She spoke and asked the king to show mercy, saying that Arcilasso had killed the lady. When the king understood that the queen was dead by Arcilasso's hand, he was much aggrieved and said, "Arcilasso! Why couldn't you temper your rage? My victory would have been twofold." Then he mourned over the lady. She was big and fat. You wouldn't believe it. On her legs and arms, and at her throat, she had rings of pure gold, decorated with precious stones. At the king's command, the lady was picked up. Then she was preserved, put in a coffin filed with aloe, and placed in a high tower out of respect for her dignity. Then the body was ransomed back to her husband for an inconceivable amount of money. After this, King Alfonso seized the treasure of the king who had fled, which included *doppie* [...], so that thousands of mules exhausted themselves carrying arms and other things, as I described.[25] Maria from Obeda, guardian of the queen, was freed. She said that the *doppie* found were not even a quarter of the whole, three quarters of which were stolen.

Let us return to the flight of the Saracens. This flight lasted for six days. There was no limit to the butchery. On the sixth day they found a town alongside the sea that received them. It is called Ziziria. The Christianity of Ziziria lapsed. For the town gave itself over to plundering. There were 60,000 Saracen dead. All of their bones were piled in a field so that there was a great mountain of them. It remains there to this day. What is more, even today when laborers plow the fields, they discover heads, legs, arms, and a great many bones. Hardly any escaped. Moreover, there were many days to come in which travelers going about their business happened across bones lying at the base of trees in the shape of a sleeping man. This was due to wounded men who fled the battle and positioned themselves at the base of trees in order to lean on the trunks, for they were exhausted, and as they rested there both their spirit and their lives abandoned

---

24. Porta identifies this as Úbeda in southern Spain.

25. *"Doppie"* were likely gold coins of double the value of the typical gold coinage. The details of the treasury's contents fall within a lacuna in the manuscript, however, so our sole measure of its value is that it was enough to exhaust thousands of pack animals.

them. So the fleshless bones remained. In their jaws men found gold glimmering. This was due to the fact that the Moors placed coins and their golden *doppie* in their mouths.[26] The gold of these *doppie* sparkled. So whoever found one battered the skull with sticks and stones in order to dislodge the mandible and smash the bones of the head to the ground. So the happy travelers snatched up the money.

The plunder from this battle was great. Forty thousand Saracens were captured, men and women, who to this very day remain slaves of the Spaniards.[27] They hoe and plow, spin and weave, cook and do other tasks according to their capacity. They do every trade. Such an infinite number of them were available that they were sold like goats. Throughout Spain they were sold with crowns on their heads, even though they had been reduced to servitude. They performed every service for their lords, the Spaniards. *Hortos et vineas colunt dominorum precepto solo victu contenti.*[28] All manner of things were plundered: money, gear, arms, clothing, copper vessels, horses, mules, donkeys, camels, pavilions, trebuchets, ever so many provisions and supplies. Imagine how many people there were! King Alfonso claimed the royal pavilion with all its contents.[29] This

26. Why dying men would hide coins in their mouths is unclear. Nor would "fleshless jaws" be able to contain them. More likely gold was found scattered among the remains and the Anonimo is either supplying a fanciful explanation or reporting uncritically what others have told him.

27. On slavery in late medieval Spain, see Philips, *Slavery in Medieval and Early Modern Iberia;* and, for a slightly later period, Debra Blumenthal, *Enemies and Familiars: Slavery and Mastery in Fifteenth-Century Valencia* (Ithaca, NY: Cornell University Press, 2009).

28. "They cultivated the fields and vineyards by the command of their masters, content simply to be fed." Campanelli, "Benché io l'aia ià fatta per lettera," 17–18, notes that this particular Latin line, like some of the previous sentences, is specific in a way that creates a tension with the general servitude depicted in other lines. Did the Saracens perform all manner of tasks or were they, in fact, primarily used as agricultural laborers? The surviving account never really resolves this.

29. Here, after a lengthy digression, the Anonimo returns to the topic of the Alfanic and the royal treasury, which he began discussing above but describes in more detail here. The lacuna above, and the version now presented, give the stark impression of a work in progress, the precise structure of which the author had not yet worked out.

✻ CHAPTER ELEVEN

pavilion was known as the Alfanic. It had three hundred rooms. It was made of linen cloth covered by red leather and had silken gold-painted ropes. You have never seen a more marvelous or beautiful thing. From its highest peak to its outer edges, everything was decorated with moons inside moons of various colors. The craftsmanship cannot be put into words. Within the Alfanic was found Ricciaferra, the queen slain by Arcilasso, as was said, who was sold to her husband, sealed in a casket, for a great deal of gold. In addition, the royal treasury was found, a fourth of it since the other three quarters had been stolen. Twelve hundred mules carried the treasure, which was made up of *doppie*. I was told by someone who saw and spent them that the *doppie* were of gold in the form of little silver discs, of a quality hardly less than that used for the paten of an altar chalice.[30]

Also included in the treasure found there was the letter of indulgence, which their great pope — the caliph of Baghdad by name — had granted them, in which it was promised that whosoever should die as part of this great endeavor would be resurrected on the third day.[31] Then it promised seven virgin wives in holy paradise. Then it promised that they would be embraced by holy Muhammad and holy Elinason.[32] Then it promised that they would be able to feast on milk, cheese, savory confections, butter, and melons.[33] These were the promises of the sultan caliph of Baghdad in his letter. Then

---

30. The interchangeable use of gold and silver here is confusing at first glance but perhaps refers to a white gold that appeared similar to high quality silver. The paten is the small plate, or tray, that accompanied a communion chalice and was used to hold the host.

31. While the Anonimo's meaning here is unclear, O'Callaghan, *Gibraltar Crusade*, 171, understands the propaganda referred to here to promise resurrection of the dead in paradise within three days.

32. This pairing recurs later in the text. Porta notes that it corresponds to references to "santo Mahomat" and "santo Alinoechacan" or "Alinochaçan" in a Spanish chronicle. It occurs also in *chansons de geste*.

33. Porta suggests that *"lagane,"* rendered here as "savory confections," should be understood to mean lasagna. Because the dish in question may have taken various forms — none of which would resemble the most familiar modern version that includes tomatoes, as yet unknown to Europeans — I have instead rendered it in a more general way.

he commanded them to exterminate all Christians and occupy the entire world.

Also found in the Alfanic were a great many weapons, as well as royal garments of Tartar or oriental cloth and decorated with gold and precious stones. From this treasure the good King Alfonso sent one tenth of the golden *doppie* to Pope Benedict [XII] in Avignon, who was alive at that time. The total value was 160,000 florins. He also sent to him the royal banner that was at hand for the victory, the very one he had carried in battle. He also sent the beautiful horse that he had ridden into battle, which Pope Clement [VI], Benedict's successor, gave as a gift to Philip [VI] Valois, the king of France, due to the great affection he had for him. Along with these things he sent twenty Saracen prisoners with their arms, along with the clothing and mounts they had when they were captured. These captured Moors were sent to Avignon. Due to the change of environment and loss of freedom all died but one, who became a devout Christian and servant of the pope. He still lives to this day.[34] Alfonso also sent twenty banners captured during the rout of the Turks and Persians, which were displayed along with the great royal banner in the chapel of Pope Benedict within the papal palace of Avignon. These days they are no longer displayed there.

When the battle was over, the king of Granada feared that his realm would become a tributary of Castile.

I can truly say in good faith that I beheld some of these arms in the following way. Emperor Charles [IV] came to the city of Tivoli in 13[55], as I said.[35] There were a lot of people. I stood on a bridge, in the spot where one goes to buy wax candles, sweets, and

---

34. On the life and survival of Muslim captives in medieval France, see now William Chester Jordan, *The Apple of His Eye: Converts from Islam in the Reign of Louis IX* (Princeton, NJ: Princeton University Press, 2019).

35. This is one of the few auto-biographical details we have of the Anonimo's life. Charles IV entered Italy late in 1354, perhaps at Cola di Rienzo's and Petrarch's urging, and was crowned in Rome on January 5, 1355. He remained in Lazio for only a few days, earning Petrarch's criticism for his retreat (*Familiares* XIX.12). For Charles's journey, see Matteo Villani, *Cronica* IV.92, V.2, Porta 1:605–6, 608–10. For Charles IV, see Iva Rosario, *Art and Propaganda: Charles IV of Bohemia, 1346–1378* (Woodbridge: Boydell Press, 2000).

## CHAPTER ELEVEN

spices. A man held a sword under his arm. The pommel was gilded, embellished with lilies and other flowers. I asked, "Do you want to sell that sword?"; and he drew it from its sheath. The blade was like one of ours, with a shape somewhere between that of a dagger and a sword. It was not overly large or lengthy but, like ours, quite suitable, made in a Genoese fashion. The pommel was like a flat plum in size, the hilt shaped like a half-moon, and most of it — pommel, hilt, blade, and all —was gilded. The sheath was decorated with tendrils of cunningly worked iron and the hilt fastened with well adorned straps. It seemed to me that the blade was not so simple as one of ours.

The good fellow responded, saying "I don't want to sell it, not even for fifty florins." He reinforced the claim with a solemn oath.

The people standing nearby asked, "Why?"

He responded, saying, "This sword was earned during the rout in Spain, when the king of Bellamarina was defeated by the king of Castile. I found it there. So, although it is very fine, it is so dear to me that I will not sell it for any price."

With this victory achieved, the battlefield plundered, and the kings and other allies rewarded, King Alfonso did not rest. He gathered together the people of his realm and the crusaders and set out after the evil and perfidious foe. Fiercely he harried them. He sought to capture their territory. Around this time, Pope Benedict [XII], the white monk, died and Pope Clement [VI], the black monk was raised up.[36] There was a noble city by the sea, on the border of the Saracen lands, that was called Ginzera.[37] The region was named Ginzera. It was among the best, noblest, and richest cities in the Saracen world when it came to spices, silk, and Tunisian cloth. King Alfonso lay siege to this city by land and by sea. The siege was grueling. There were one hundred thirty galleys at sea and on

---

36. This is to say that a former Cistercian monk was replaced by a Benedictine.

37. This is Algeciras, which remains a major port to this day. The Anonimo is again in error here. Due to a shortage of supplies for his armies, Alfonso did not take Algeciras following the Battle of Rio Salado. Indeed, Cardinal Albornoz, who will appear later in this text, laments that fact in one of his letters. See O'Callaghan, *Gibraltar Crusade*, 183. The siege of Algeciras began almost two years after the battle of Rio Salado and lasted until 1344.

land innumerable cavalry and foot. The siege lasted eighteen months and was assisted by hunger. King Alfonso and his host entered the city. He captured whoever he liked, killed those for whom that was preferable, and drove out the whole wicked lot. He seized all their supplies, which were of an inestimable quantity. He filled the city with Christians. Churches were built, as well as houses of religious orders, and two bishoprics were founded. To this day, that city serves the glorious and blessed Christ.

Now take note of this novelty. Once the king had captured Ginzera, he had no need of such a great host. He freed the troops from his command. They had been expensive. Among the others so freed were thirty Genoese galley crews, who had served him well. These galleys returned to Genoa. When they entered the port, trumpets, castanets, and shawms were played, as is customary. The sounds and festivities exceeded even imperial grandeur. Then they entered the port and docked. Very slowly the whole host disembarked, well dressed and bedecked with rich accessories. They had greatly enriched themselves. Among other novel things they brought into the port and carried through it were six Moors, all shabbily dressed. Their bodies were covered with yellow cloaks. They had irons on their legs. These revealed that they were prisoners. All of Genoa ran down to the port to see the newly arrived galleys. The entire populace was there. They surrounded these Moors. Everyone wanted to see these people of an alien faith. The six Moors stood there amid the throng, wretchedly afraid. They muttered a great deal to one another and then lifted their heads, raising their faces to marvel at the beautiful buildings and towering palaces that stand near the port of Genoa. The crowd could not understand them. There was present a servant of the Genoese, who was a Saracen. He was Christian, raised in Genoa. He knew the Latin language.

The crowd called out, "What are they saying?"

He responded, "They say this: It is hardly surprising that we Saracens were defeated and conquered, since we placed ourselves in opposition to all Christendom and to Genoa." When they arrived in Genoa, they looked about marveling at the palaces of the Genoese port. They believed Genoa to be the most beautiful and well-fortified place in Christendom, with nothing like it elsewhere. From this we can gather that their dwelling places are not so fine as ours.

## CHAPTER ELEVEN

The bishop of Perugia, who had been in the company of the crusaders, also returned from Gizera and brought eight Turks with him. They were mounted, white and beautiful like us, attired like us and with steeds like ours. On their heads they wore hats that came down to their ears, shaped like a papal miter. It is true that they had in the center a straight bill, long and soft like the neck of a gru, covered in white linen cloth.[38] On their backs they wore a white linen doublet, like one of ours. It is true, however, that the sleeves came to the fingertips. Over the doublet they wore a mantel of linen cloth similar to the cope of a priest. The point of the right side extended from the left shoulder, and that of the left from the right.

After this, King Alfonso did not rest. He gathered together an army from his lands and lay siege to a beautiful and noble castle, the last fortress of the Saracens. This castle bears the name Iubaltare.[39] The regions is called Alcacuc. In this castle, Muhammad wrote his laws and gave them to the Saracens, and produced the book called Alcorano.[40] The king positioned his army in opposition to this castle and swore on the majesty of his realm and the height of his crown that he would never lift the siege until the castle fell. He planted his standard in the ground. It was a narrow space. He positioned his army and guards believing he could take the place by starving it out. It was a most beautiful and mighty castle. It was called Iubaltare. It stood on the pinnacle of a tall stone outcropping. At the top of the outcropping, eagles made their nests. From that peak the heights dropped down to a plain. There, on the flat land, there was a mighty wall with many little towers. Picazzo, of whom I spoke before, had it hewn out of the rock. Behind the wall there was an abundant fountain of water. Along the flat land there was a mosque. There trees of every sort could be found. A more pleasant fortress has never been seen. The Christians lost it due to neglect.[41] King

38. A gru is a kind of crane, hence the use of its characteristic neck as a comparison.

39. Gibraltar. Despite the fact that the Anonimo claims Alfonso "did not rest," his siege of Gibraltar began five years after the fall of Algeciras.

40. Needless to say, the Anonimo's sense of the writing of the Qur'an is strikingly incorrect.

41. Gibraltar, first conquered by the Muslims in 711, changed hands a few times over the centuries. It was last taken by the king of Castile in 1309 and had been passed into Muslim hands again in 1333.

Alfonso intended to retake it by means of his siege, but it did not turn out that way, for he was overcome by that great and terrible mortality of which I spoke and which inflicted upon him a disease of the lungs.[42] So it was that, with his siege lifted, he died during the time of great mortality in the royal city of Seville.

This King Alfonso was the noblest, most glorious, most just, and most pious king that there ever was in Spain. The Spaniards have mourned him ever since. He was possessed of every virtue. He had not a single defect. He had only one fault, which was that he did not love his queen and did not wish to stay by her side, despite the fact that they had a son. Instead, he kept a mistress — Donna Leonora by name — whom he loved over all other things, who was his comfort, and by whom he had sons and daughters. Without her he could not go on. Many times the pope admonished and excommunicated him. He wanted the king to send this whore off packing. The king responded sweetly by means of a letter, carried by an emissary, which said, "Holy Father, if it please you that I should die and live no more, I will let it be so; at any rate, I would not be able to go on living if I had to do it without her." After this, the pope harassed him no more. He did not want him to die prematurely.

I was living in the city of Bologna, at the university, where I was in my fourth year studying medicine, when I heard this tale related in the chambers of the rector of medicine, from one of his caretakers.[43]

42. Alfonso died of plague in 1350. This description may indicate that he died of a strain on pneumonic plague.

43. Being in the fourth year meant that the Anonimo had nearly completed his studies at this time. Four years of study were the norm, with the fourth being devoted to study of specific works by Avicenna, Galen, and Hippocrates. See Vern L. Bullough, "Medieval Bologna and the Development of Medical Education," *Bulletin of the History of Medicine* 32.3 (1958): 201–15 at 214.

# CHAPTER TWELVE
### The Duke of Athens is driven from Florence.
### Pope Benedict dies. Pope Clement is elected

In the year of our Lord, 1342, a thunderbolt struck the bell tower of St. Peter's in Rome, burning the entirety of its roof. This happened during the hour of vespers,[1] when the canons sing the office in their choir. It was in the year of our Lord 1342 that Pope Benedict, the white monk, died and Pope Clement VI was elected.[2] This Pope Clement was a black monk and a person of such talent that he had no equal. He was a great theologian and an eloquent preacher. When he took his seat to preach or debate, all of Paris rushed to see him. Goodness, what a skilled preacher he was! He was a Frenchman and very generous, so that when he was at university the incomes from his prebendaries could never meet his expenses. He had achieved every rank of dignity. First, he was a black monk of Saint Benedict, a conventual, and sub-prior, then a deacon, then a prior, then an abbot, then a bishop, then archbishop of Rouen, then cardinal under the *titulus* of Saints Nereus and Achilleus; and then, finally, he was made pope.[3] What more is there to say? If he was aware of some rank higher than his current one, he desired to achieve it.

Once he had been raised to the papacy, the roof of St. Peter's was destroyed by fire, as I mentioned before. A most honorable delegation of Romans came before the pope, made up of twelve people: six laymen and six clergymen.[4] Their leader was Stefano

---

1. 6:00 PM.

2. See Diana Wood, *Clement VI: The Pontificate and Ideas of an Avignon Pope* (Cambridge: Cambridge University Press, 1989).

3. This list indicates Clement's steady ascent through the ranks of both monastic life and that of the secular clergy. Every cardinal was associated with a particular Roman church. In this case, the fourth-century church of SS. Nereo e Achilleo.

4. Porta notes an error here, observing that this group numbered at least eighteen. It included various Roman barons and ecclesiastics, including the young notary Cola di Rienzo, who delivered the oral presentation of the delegations's requests to the pope.

Colonna, commander of Santo Spirito.⁵ These twelve ambassadors entreated the pope, in the name of God and the Roman people, that he should come and visit the seat of his bishopric in Rome. Furthermore, they asked him to grant them a general indulgence and jubilee, so that that it might happen every fifty years rather than every hundred, for life was short and few lived to be one hundred years of age.⁶ After a few days, the pope responded to the ambassadors.⁷ To begin with, he admitted that their petition was just, listing twelve reasons why he was compelled to visit his bishopric, the city of Rome. Then he conceded a fifty-year jubilee in Rome, granted a general remission of sins, penalties, and guilt for those penitent and confessed, and declared what the conditions of the jubilee were to be.

IN THE TIME of this pope, in the year of our Lord 1342/3, on St. Anna's day, Sir Walter, count of Brienne, duke of Athens, and perpetual lord of Florence, was driven from that city and the lunatics there did many shameful things, much that was regrettable, to be condemned, and damaging. Men were slain and their flesh butchered. The turn of events transpired as follows. The Florentines purchased Lucca from Messer Mastino della Scala and entered into possession of it. The Pisans, troubled by this transaction, set upon Lucca with an enormous and memorable siege. The cavalry numbered [...]. Around the besieging force there were numerous trenches, stockades, and wooden towers. They also cleared and fortified the road by which one travels between Pisa and Lucca, for a distance of twelve miles. This they did so that one could freely travel to the army with aid and supplies, without impediment. The siege lasted [...] months.⁸ In

---

5. This title relates to the Hospital of Santo Spirito, in Rome, of which another Colonna was then preceptor. See above, chapter 3, p. 71 n. 14; chapter 9, p. 100 n. 9.

6. Boniface VIII had created the first jubilee in 1300, with the intention that it be held once each century. The Romans, for a variety of reasons, hoped that it might become more frequent. On the jubilee, see Arsenio Frugoni, *Il giubileo di Bonifacio VIII* (Rome: Laterza, 1999).

7. For his response, the sermon *Desidero videre vos*, see Wood, *Clement VI*, 43–73.

8. This lengthy siege is described in detail in Giovanni Villani, *Cronaca*, XII.131–134, 139–140.

order to keep the siege going, the Pisans created the *gabella* known as the Seca.⁹

In short, they defeated the Florentines, drove them from the field, and would not permit Messer Malatesta, who was the captain of the Florentines, to reach them with supplies of food. They also did another notable thing; for Messer [Galeotto I] Malatesta, who was bringing supplies and men, arrived one evening at a river called the Serchio, which flows near Lucca. In the night the Pisans dug a trench, incredibly deep and wide, between the Serchio and the city of Lucca, its depth was [...] and its width [...]. They did all this labor in a single night. When in the morning Messer Malatesta, *paratis omnibus copiis tam ad pugnam quam etiam ad grasciam, transivit aquam diluculo, non potens transire ex impedimento valli, miratus stupefactusque retrocessit meavitque, per ripam fluminis ascendens, deditque circuitum miliaribus decem ferme, ibique improvise pisanum exercitum invasit. Tum vero, facta resistentia factoque ingenti Florentinorum impetus, fessi Florentini terga dederunt. Multi cadunt, multi capiuntur. Vix Malatesta cum aliquibus evasit. Omnis eorum copia militibus preda fuit.*¹⁰ In the end, the Pisans took Lucca by starving them out.¹¹ They still hold it to this day.

The Florentines, finding themselves in a state of confusion, called for a captain of war, the lord Messer Walter, count of Brienne, duke of Athens, for he was a wise and powerful man of the French royal

---

9. A *gabella* was a kind of tax, sometimes on a particular trade good, like salt. Porta suggests that the *"Seca"* should be read as *"Sega,"* which was a head tax that was fairly common in Tuscany.

10. "crossed the water at an early hour, well supplied in every respect, with troops and victuals alike. Finding himself unable to cross due to the obstacle of the trench, he turned back and departed, amazed and astonished. Climbing the bank of the river, he stationed a guard of nearly ten thousand, then he launched a surprise attack on the Pisans. But then, with the mighty Florentine attack met resistance, and the men of Florence were driven back exhausted. Many fell, and many were captured. Malatesta himself barely escaped with a few others. All the rest were prey for soldiers."

11. Porta notes that the Anonimo's chronology is flawed. The Pisans took Lucca, but the captain of the Florentine forces was Maffeo da Ponte Carradi of Brescia. Malatesta became captain at a later date.

house.[12] When Messer Walter received their letters he was delighted. He took to his horse with his men, at least five hundred knights, with a great baggage train and many supplies. He rode straight and true. He entered the city of Florence and was granted perpetual rule of the city, in a peaceful manner with the consent of the council and without any tumult.[13] Then the duke commenced his reign. He ruled firmly. The first thing he did was release from prison Messer Pietro 'Zaccone' Tarlati, lord of Arezzo, liberating him from a captivity to which he had been perpetually condemned.[14] Then he received large rich embassies that came from all over Tuscany. He took control of Arezzo. He held Pistoia, San Miniato, Volterra, and Prato. He seemed to have taken all of Tuscany, with hopes of making himself its duke. Things stood this way with the Pisans that, so long as he was troubling people elsewhere, they weren't bothered by it. He ruled quite harshly and filled the Florentines with high hopes. Once he had assumed command, he demonstrated his glory liberally in various places.

Among other things, he sent a French bishop to King Philip, his kinsman, in Paris.[15] The bishop described how the duke had taken control of Florence. To this King Philip replied, "This pleases me a great deal." Then he asked, "Has Duke Walter done anything of note?"

The bishop responded, "He has upgraded the gates, getting rid of the old ones and putting new ones in their place, and over the

---

12. He had also married Beatrice of Taranto, King Robert of Naples' niece. He was closely tied to the Angevin Guelf affinity in Italy and was named vicar of Charles of Calabria, Robert's son and the Florentines' appointed *signor*.

13. There is a gap in the text here, but I take this to be the intended meaning.

14. This was Pier Saccone Tarlati di Pietramala (1261–1356), who ruled Arezzo from 1327 to 1336. Tarlati was a Ghibelline, whose brother had also ruled Arezzo as its bishop, and who had actually sold the city to the Florentines once his own situation became untenable. He then found himself imprisoned after attempting to take it back in a coup. See Robert Black, *Benedetto Accolti and the Florentine Renaissance* (Cambridge: Cambridge University Press, 1985), 1–3.

15. This is King Philip VI of France, to whom the Anonimo will return in future chapters.

gates he has constructed lovely tall towers." To this the king said, "Tell Walter, the duke of Brienne, that Philip Valois exhorts him to contemplate how to make himself lord of the hearts of men, and not merely of towers."

As another of his ambassadors he enlisted a knight, whom he sent to King Robert of Naples, of whom I have spoken before. At this point Robert was still alive. The knight announced to the king the noble lordship attained by his kinsman, Duke Walter. The king responded, "We'd like Walter to rule for a long time." Then he asked, "Where does he reside? Is he living in Sta. Croce?"[16] The knight responded, saying "No. He dwells in the Palazzo degli Anziani." The king shook his head and said, "He has not done well. Go and tell him to return the priors of Florence to their palace and their proper nobility. Tell him to do honor to the people."[17]

This duke was lord of Florence for ten months before he was shamefully driven from the city.[18] The reasons why he was driven out were these. First, he was extraordinarily cruel. He killed people without a thought. He had with him an official, called his conservator, Messer Guglielmo of Assisi. He was a knight and a judge.[19] This Messer Guglielmo was a red serpent. As he dined he had people mercilessly tortured right in front of him, having them dismembered and tortured to death. He had a son, a young knight only twelve years of age and a most angelic creature, but simple.

16. Sta. Croce was the main Franciscan church in Florence. The Anonimo does not explain why Robert asked this, but its neighborhood was among the more popular districts of the city at the time.

17. The priors were the members of Florence's highest ruling council and their palace, which Walter had appropriated for himself, is now known as the Palazzo Vecchio.

18. For the best recent treatment of the events described here, see Najemy, *History of Florence*, 135–37. For a recent analysis of this incident as related in the Anonimo and other contemporary writers, see Musto, *Writing Southern Italy*, 202–7.

19. When city communes brought in a foreign executive, generally called a *podestà*, which was far from uncommon, it was normal for the man selected to bring along others to serve as his officials. That would have been part of the purpose for the knights who accompanied Walter to Florence.

When the man was engaged in torture this son of his would cheer him on, saying "Hey, give him another shake for the love of me! Hoist him up!"[20] He did this to a great many people, consigning them to death. His father was worse than Dionysius, the tyrant of Sicily.[21] Then the cruel conservator took to cutting off heads, hanging people, and killing without mercy. What is more, he hung the good people of Florence, dressed in various fancy garb, in front of their own houses. Nardo de Cenne, a potter and one of the most eminent of the Florentine *popolo*, a man who had loaned to the commune 100,000 florins each time he was asked, he hung for his wealth.[22] There were many others. Then this *signore* turned to true avarice. He gobbled up every penny the people had and consumed all that each man possessed. He snatched every coin from the hands of the merchants.

The duke had in his service a man most terrible and cruel, a Florentine by birth but one who long before had been cast into perpetual exile for his falsity and treachery. This fellow was one of his companions in arms and in his travels. The duke had restored his status, both in his own grace and in that of the Florentines. His name

---

20. The "angelic" son's words indicate the use of the *strappado*, a common torture method whereby the victim's arms were bound behind their back and they were then suspended from a cord tied to the wrists, resulting in the painful dislocation of the shoulders. Sometimes, as here apparently, the victim was repeatedly dropped.

21. Dionysius, an ancient Greek tyrant, ruled Sicily and parts of southern Italy from Syracuse from the late fifth through the mid fourth century BCE. The Anonimo was not on the scene, but his reference to Dionysius reveals a possible source for his own account of details of this incident. See Musto, *Writing Southern Italy*, 204.

22. Nardo's identity as one of the *popolo* indicates that he was hardly a simple potter, rather, this was the trade that determined his guild membership and hence his membership in the Florentine governing class. The *popolo* were often just as wealthy as the old political elites who were their rivals. The government of Florence was under considerable financial duress in the fourteenth century, above all due to war costs. In order to keep the commune afloat, the Florentines collected "forced loans" (*prestanze*) based on an individual's overall wealth. Najemy, *History of Florence*, 35–62, 120–23.

## CHAPTER TWELVE

was Messer Arrigo Fei.[23] This Messer Arrigo Fei was in charge of the *gabella* and was possessed of a truly cunning talent for finding money. Where he was able to find a florin, other men couldn't have found a single grain of millet. All day long he came up with new *gabelle*. You never saw such a diabolical soul. The fellow was subtler when it came to *gabelle* than Aristotle was with regards to philosophy. By his innovations, every bit of income, every private patrimony, came into the possession of the commune. Due to all this, the merchants felt they had been abandoned.

Furthermore, the duke dawdled when it came to pursuing the interests of the Florentines. About Pisa, he did absolutely nothing of note. He completely ignored Lucca and did nothing to restore the honor of Florence in that regard. The hostages that Messer Mastino had taken for the purchase of Lucca he did not recover. In fact, he never even mentioned them. His soldiers provoked conflicts all over Florence, rather than making peace. He demanded every penny the region had. Three hundred thousand florins were taken, spirited away by sea to Monaco, that great castle between Genoa and Marseille. Then he undertook to construct himself a noble castle. He had strong walls built within the city. He wished to enclose the Palace of the Priors within them.

Given all this, the citizens of Florence began to really wonder whether they should continue to suffer his rule. In secret they began to look for ways to cast him down. It could not be easily done, due to the large personal guard he had with him.

The first to bring word of this conspiracy was an armorer, who came before the duke as he was dining and said, "You are going to be killed."

The duke asked, "By whom?"

"By the *popolo*."

"When?"

"On the day of St. James."

"How?"

23. The Anonimo reads "Errigo Fegi."

"As you ride through the land, a currier will come to you with letters. As you read them, a man will bend his Turkish bow and shoot you with an arrow. From one side will come a man with a pike. From the other will come a man with a dagger. Then they will cry out, '*Popolo! Popolo!*'."

The duke replied, "How do you know this?"

The armorer answered, "From my wife." The wife knew it from the woman of a priest.[24] The priest's woman then came, and the priest as well, and stood alongside the armorer. They didn't have any proof. The armorer was dragged through Florence being tormented with hot pincers. Then, behind him, came the priest, mounted on an ass, his tonsure shaved, a crown of olive leaves on his head, and soft leather gloves on his hands. They were accompanied by the sound of trumpets and horns. The armorer was hung by the neck. The whole people trembled at the sight of this farce.

On the next feast day, [the duke] armed his personal guard, and along with two of his nephews he galloped through Florence. He had the Florentine nobility brought before him and disarmed. Then work on his castle increased.

One Saturday, at vespers,[25] in the year of our Lord 1342/3, a fight broke out near the Palace of the Priors. Quickly voices began to call out, "To arms! To arms! *Popolo! Popolo!*" The entire Florentine *popolo* was armed. The *popolo* clashed hand-to-hand with the soldiers. The soldiers were overcome. They abandoned their horses in the piazza of the Palace of the Priors and forced their way inside using crossbows. Fourteen hundred people sealed themselves inside that beautiful palace. The streets thereabout were emptied of the stalls of butchers. That night, the first to emerge from the palace was a simoniac judge — Messer Simone of Norcia was his name — alone and heavily

---

24. The passage reflects the rapidity of urban gossip and rumor, so often recorded in trecento sources. It was not uncommon for priests to have female consorts, who sometimes appear to have been their servants. The ambiguity is preserved here insofar as it is not entirely clear which of the two this woman was. See Roisin Cossar, *Clerical Households in Late Medieval Italy* (Cambridge: Harvard University Press, 2018).

25. 6:00 PM.

armed.²⁶ Once the guards noticed him, his defenses amounted to nothing and he was killed. He had two hundred florins on him. He was chopped into four pieces. To each of the four *Anziani* of the *popolo*, a piece was delivered. Four popular *Anziani* were established, who were charged with overseeing all things.²⁷

When day came, the *popolo* attacked the palace. They set fire to the door. Nothing could prevent them, neither water nor other means. The entire door burned and was consumed. For some days, the duke remained sealed inside the palace with his men. By the end the stink of excrement and piss was awful. It was better to go out and die than to die from the stench. They couldn't escape. The soldiers began to mutter seditiously against the duke. Due to all this, they made a deal. The *popolo* stood outside the palace, armed, and shouting out vulgarities. Then they demanded that the conservator be handed over to them, the cruel Messer Guglielmo of Assisi. Seeing this, the duke, who had no other way out, ordered Messer Guglielmo to go out.

Note well what this cruel father did out of his desire to escape. He ordered his son to go out before him so that by his son's death he might diminish the anger that the *popolo* was directing at him.²⁸

---

26. A simoniac was someone guilty of the crime of simony, the purchasing of office. The term emerged centuries prior in an ecclesiastical context. The Anonimo is clearly indicating the questionable character of this judge, who he suggests wouldn't be a judge at all if not for his wealth.

27. The Anziani were leaders of the *popolo*, an office that went back to the Primo Popolo of the thirteenth century. The Anonimo is indicating here that this old office was revitalized in this moment, though he presents them as already existing first, and then mentions their establishment. Musto, *Writing Southern Italy*, 204–7, questions the reliability of details of dismemberment and, later on, of ritual cannibalism in several of these accounts, including those of the Anonimo, Villani, Agnolo di Tura, and Boccaccio. He notes that they are all based on hearsay. None claimed to have witnessed them, and only Villani and Boccaccio were in the city at the time. All were explicit about other events that they *had* witnessed.

28. Here the Anonimo refers to Guglielmo's son who, the Anonimo reports, had been present for his torture sessions.

The young son, *patris precepto*,[29] went out, approaching the door like a pig going to slaughter, knowing he would die and knowing too the heartlessness of his father. He turned his head and said, "Father, where are you sending me?" His father replied, "Go in safety."

When the boy reached the door, he was received by the enraged *popolo* at the point of a sword. A priest was the first to lop off his arm with a sword, saying "Here's for my part! I wish no longer to perform the mass!" See how much the priest hated the young fellow! What a cut! What a blow!

He was pierced a thousand times. Then the boy saw his father dressed in fine garments and bearing in his hand a silver chalice that held the Host.[30] He came out reluctantly, but those behind him gave him a shove as those before him pulled him out. They cut him into bits like little leaves. His flesh, and that of his son, were carried through Florence, sold by the piece, and roasted, and there were people who ate it. Take note how much these men suffered when they received what was due them.

No harm was done to the duke's person, for Count Simone of Casentino along with the commune of Siena made a deal to take him out of his palace by night, saving him along with fifty people. This happened on the day of St. Anne.[31] Then he escorted him to his own land and made him renounce his power over Florence. The duke rode off to Bologna, arriving in poverty, totally stripped of his possessions. From Bologna he went back to his own land.

29. "By his father's command."

30. As he does at other times, the Anonimo here switches his point of view to the first-hand impressions of characters who soon died, and therefore could not have reported what they saw. His account also contains several other unconfirmed details, not reported by other sources. Here, he may be suggesting that Guglielmo was disguised, perhaps as a priest, which would parallel Cola di Rienzo's own failed attempt to escape the Roman mob by disguising himself. Alternatively, the Anonimo may be describing the use of liturgical objects as a kind of flag of truce, suggesting that Guglielmo hoped carrying them would protect him from immediate violence.

31. This feast day fell on July 16, while the siege of the palace lasted until August, when Guglielmo of Assisi and his son were killed. It was not until August 6 that the duke was forced to abandon Florence.

He suffered great shame and damage. More than four hundred of his soldiers were dead and plundered. Messer Ianni de Braio[32] and Messer Caucassaso, two great barons and kinsmen of his, died by the sword. Messer Ceretieri Visdomini, his councilor, fled and then turned up a short while later. Messer Arrigo Fei, his cunning tax collector, was captured in the habit of a white friar, humiliated, and stripped naked. He was larger and fatter than even a terrible pig. He was killed and hung by his feet. Little boys made tremendous sport of him, throwing rocks and mud at him, and battering him with sticks.[33] Florence was returned to the *popolo*, to a peaceful communal state. The duke went to France, to his own land. In the end, he died in the battle fought between the king of France and the king of England; in which battle John [II], the king of France was captured, as I will describe. It was the year of our Lord 13[…]. The duke of Athens was slain in that battle.[34] Such was the end of the duke of Athens, lord of Florence.

32. Jean of Broy, or Gian de Brai, appears to have been a celebrated knight, and is recognized as such in the verse of Antonio Pucci. See Cesare Paoli, "Nuovi documenti intorno a Gualtieri VI di Brienne Duca d'Atene e signore di Firenze," *Archivio Storico Italiano* 16.70 (1872): 22–62, at 55.

33. This passage foreshadows the desecration of Cola di Rienzo's body. See below, chapter 27, p. 297.

34. At the Battle of Poitiers on September 19, 1356.

# CHAPTER THIRTEEN
## The Crusade Carried Out at Smyrna in Turkey

A CRUSADE was carried out against Turkey, directed at a place in Outremer[1] that is called Smyrna, an endeavor that shook all Christendom. It happened like this.[2] We know that the inhabitable world is divided into three parts: Asia, Africa, and Europe. The sea separates these three parts of the earth, in a manner resembling a half cross [Map 4]. In Asia there is a province, small but also beautiful and wealthier than the others, which is known as Turkey [Map 5]. Said Turkey is first among the other provinces of Asia and borders us. It has seven cities. The first is called Smyrna. This city stood near the sea on an outcropping of earth, was razed to the ground, and was relocated to a mountain five miles from the old city.[3] The second city was called Aito Luoco and was the place where the tomb of the blessed Saint John the Evangelist is, the place where Saint John

---

1. The Anonimo here uses *oitra mare*, the Italian version of the French *Outremer*, which for late medieval Europeans meant the Crusader States of the Levant, including the Holy Land. For a general introduction see Malcolm Barber, *The Crusader States* (New Haven: Yale University Press, 2012). For Outremer itself, see Laura K. Morreale and Nicholas Paul, ed., *The French of Outremer: Communities and Communications in the Crusading Mediterranean* (New York: Fordham University Press, 2018).

2. Here the Anonimo likely exaggerates the impact of the Smyrna Crusade on Christendom. For the crusade efforts of this era, see Norman Housely, *The Later Crusades, 1274–1580: From Lyons to Alcazar* (Oxford: Oxford University Press, 1992). See too Kenneth M. Setton, *The Papacy and the Levant (1204–1571)* (Philadelphia: American Philosophical Society, 1976); James Muldoon, "The Avignon Papacy and the Frontiers of Christendom: The Evidence of Vatican Register 62," *Archivum Historiae Pontificiae* 17 (1979): 125–95. Petrarch, a contemporary of the Anonimo, certainly felt that many of these campaigns were driven by the rivalry between the Venetians and the Genoese, rather than being truly aimed at the Turks. See Nancy Bisaha, "Petrarch's Vision of the Muslim and Byzantine East," *Speculum* 76.2 (2001): 284–314.

3. Old and New Smyrna are both ancient sites, corresponding to the modern city of Izmir. Pliny indicates that "New" Smyrna was created by Alexander the Great, while Strabo says it was established by Antigonus. See Pliny, *Natural History*, V.29; Strabo, *Geography*, XIV.1.

wrote the Apocalypse.[4] In this sense to call it Aito Luoco is to refer to lofty speech, as in the lofty manner in which John spoke his prophecies. The third city is named Pergamum, the birthplace of the famous doctor, Galen. The fourth is called Ephesus. The fifth is named Philadelphia. The sixth is known as Phrygia. The seventh is Pamphylia.[5] These seven cities were Christian and were endowed with well-ordered episcopates by the blessed Saint John the Evangelist. But in our own day, due to our sins, six are now held by the infidels. The seventh, Filadelfia, remains Christian. It is separated from the others a bit by a bay. It serves the glorious Christ.[6]

In the region of Romania, there was an emperor of Constantinople named Parialoco. His son was named Catacucino.[7] This Parialoco had great faith in a Christian named Messer Martino Zaccaria of

4. The Anonimo's source for the name Aito Luoco, which simply means "high place" is unclear. Neither of his subsequent identifying markers is correct. See Setton, *Papacy and the Levant*, 192. John the Evangelist was thought to have written the book of Revelations on the island of Patmos and to have been be buried in Ephesus. In all likelihood, the Anonimo is giving a formal name to what was simply the acropolis of Smyrna, which remained in Turkish hands. Such questionable etymologies were common to medieval writers, many of whom cited Isidore of Seville, one of the Anonimo's sources as well.

5. The Anonimo's confusion here is notable. The seven cities, as he lists them, are Smyrna, the so-called Aito Luoco (probably not a city at all), Pergamum, Ephesus, Philadelphia (modern Alesahir), Phrygia (the ancient name of an inland region in central Anatolia not a coastal city), and Pamphylia (actually a region to the southeast, rather than a city). The "seven cities," however, refers to the opening passages of the book of Revelations, in which the author addresses the Christian communities of each.

6. Philadelphia remained Christian in the Anonimo's day despite being surrounded by Turkish emirates. It fell under Turkish control in 1390. See Nevra Necipõlu, *Byzantium Between the Ottomans and the Latins: Politics and Society in the Late Empire* (Cambridge: Cambridge University Press, 2009), 129n.

7. By *Romania*, the Anonimo means Byzantium. The imperial line referred to here is that of the Paleologoi. The last was John VI Kantakouzenous. The latter succeeded John V Palaeologos, whose regent he had been. The Anonimo omits the fact that John was actually allied with Umur Bey, the ruler of Smyrna and primary villain of this chapter. See Housely, *The Later Crusades*, 65.

Genoa, a noble and valiant master of war. He made him his admiral of the sea. He defended that whole part of the sea on behalf of Parialoco. He did great honor to his lord. He had as many ships and men as he wanted. Then, as payment, Parialoco gave Messer Martino a most noble and lovely island, extremely fertile, that was called Chios.[8] This island is the source of nearly all the mastic there is. There grow the trees that weep tears, from which mastic is made. Great was Messer Martino's barony. There he resided with his family and a large, powerful force.

It happened that the Turks captured from the Genoese a region near the sea, known as Fogliara Vecchia. Then they captured Metellina, which borders Athens and Greece, where the Academy was.[9] Then they lay siege to the city of Pera by both land and sea. They were everywhere. There was no escaping them. Messer Martino, considering the shame of his citizens, and the damage inflicted on them, could take no more. He armed his galleys with crossbowmen and loaded them with a splendid army of skilled young warriors. He took to the sea, reinforced Pera, broke the siege of the Turkish army, and did significant damage to them. Then he forbade all Turkish merchants from doing business in his territory on the isle of Chios.

Three great barons ruled on the tip of the Turkish province. They were brothers by blood. The first was named Morbasciano, the second Cherubino, and the third Orcano.[10] These men ruled the cities of Smyrna, Aito Luoco, and a large territory. Morbasciano caused tolls and taxes to be collected from any merchants who

---

8. The Genoese conquered this island in 1346. By the time of the Smyrna Crusade, Zaccaria had lost Chios to the Turks, and the papacy was keen that he not get it back in hopes that restoring it to the Byzantines would encourage the reunification of the Christian church. See Setton, *Papacy and the Levant*, 191.

9. The Anonimo again reveals some knowledge of the Aristotelian tradition.

10. The first is Umur Ghazi, emir of Aydin and also known as Umur Bey or Umur Pasha. The third is Sultan Orhan Gazi, son of Osman I, who was married to Theodora, daughter of John VI Cantakouzenous. These men were not brothers. The second "brother" listed here as Cherubino is difficult to identify but is perhaps Orhan's brother, Çoban Bey.

passed near his lands by sea. He collected these tolls on the spit of land where today the Venetians have built the city of Smyrna, on the plain alongside the sea where the ancient city was. These tolls and taxes were disliked by all, and particularly by the Venetians merchants. Whenever they wished to raise the toll, they raised it to whatever they liked. Every Venetian considered the tolls extortionate. We hardly need recall what they did to Morbasciano. It happened in that [...] Venetians.[11]

The army stood outside Negroponte.[12] They devastated the lands there about, the olives, vines, and orchards. They blocked the roads. Because of its large population, Negroponte starved. The patriarch of Jerusalem was in Negroponte — Don Manuello Camorsino was his name — a Venetian, Franciscan friar, and magnificent man of great wisdom and honest ways.[13] He was deeply ashamed to be under siege along with so many good people. He saw no way to escape. After a little while, really not long at all, he saw ships appear at sea. There were twelve galleys under the Venetian banner of San Marco. Messer Pietro Zeno, the bold and victorious captain, was their commander. When the Turks saw the Venetian armada, which was hastening toward them, they raised camp and fled back to their cities. First, they fortified the point of Smyrna, so that the Venetians would not be able to access the port there.

With the besieging army gone, Don Manuello, the patriarch, left Negroponte with knights and infantry, with rations of hard baked bread and favas, dried meat, and wine. He took to the sea in pursuit of the Turks. He knew the point of Smyrna was guarded. It was impossible to go that way. He therefore took his whole force and moved about twelve miles off, to an island in the sea known as

---

11. It is unclear what should be present in this gap in the text, but the intent, based on the previous sentence, is clear. The Anonimo is transitioning to an account of the conflict.

12. This is the name by which Italians knew the ancient city of Chalcis, in Euboea, and which was sometimes also used to refer to the entire region.

13. The Anonimo is mistaken here. It was the patriarch of Constantinople, Henry of Asti, whom Clement VI named as his legate and who led the victorious early stages of the first Smyrna crusade, not the patriarch of Jerusalem. See Setton, *Papacy and the Levant*, 186.

the isle of Cervia. There he positioned himself. For three days he lingered warily. Then, on the third day, the galleys of the Venetians and Genoese joined him. They ordered themselves in a beautiful naval formation and set out to capture Smyrna. They could not enter the port. It was a strong point. Ballista bolts and arrows rained down. There was no way to enter.

As a result, some of the galleys broke off and proceeded along with the coast on their left, loaded with wood and the makings of a wooden castle [...] the patriarch had his counsel.[14] He didn't delay a single moment. He didn't want to be left with no option but to retreat by sea. Around the place he had a wall of stone constructed. Everyone gathered lime, earth, and stones from the ancient, ruined buildings, in order to raise high the wall. The patriarch, along with a noble French knight named Fiore de Belgioia, laid the foundations by hand. They created only one entry point in the wall, facing toward Turkey. It defended the coast. On that side there was no wall. They carved out enough territory to constitute a little town. There they stationed their men. Small dwellings were erected, a piazza, a marketplace, and a moneychanger's table. In this way they obtained supplies and engaged in buying and selling. They also enclosed within the walls a bubbling spring, a source of fresh water. Then, for improved fortification, a very large trench was dug around the wall so that, if there was need, the sea could be let in to fill it. Whenever a ship came carrying grain it was unable to approach, for Turkish corsairs also sailed those seas. They inflicted a great deal of damage. Once it was known that this foothold had been established at Smyrna, grain was brought in from the settlements thereabouts.[15] Men from Modone, Corone, Patras, Malvasia, Fogliara, and Philadelphia came with supplies.

When Morbasciano learned that the point of Smyrna had fallen to the Venetians, he sent ambassadors throughout Turkey. All Turkey hastened to reclaim it. The Turks gathered in fortresses in the

---

14. Again, it is unclear what might have been intended for this gap in the text. The sense is that faced with the insurmountable problem of entering the port of Smyrna, the patriarch took counsel from those with him, leading to the construction of their own strong point some distance down the coast.

15. Porta suggests that by this time Smyrna had been taken, and that this event was intended for one of the prior gaps in the text of this chapter.

# ❋ CHAPTER THIRTEEN

mountains near Aito Luoco. They came no closer except in raiding parties. Raiding was a daily affair. The Christians rode out, pillaging and plundering. The Turks did the same. There were ambushes, sudden furious attacks, and equally rapid retreats. They did great damage. Cunningly men ascended the mountains single-file, one after the other. They rode small steeds, quick with small heads, their back hooves shod and their front bare. That is how they rode. They resembled Alexandrian deer. Most of these Turks, as is their custom, wore tunics of white linen that ended at mid-leg and had large, long sleeves. They were just like the garb of the clergy. On their heads they had white caps with long points like the neck of a stork. They had big beards and long hair. On their arms they bore a kind of round buckler, worked all over like a great plate and decorated with gypsum. These are their shields. At their sides they wore well-made Turkish swords. They have no points and the cutting edge curves at the thigh. Furthermore, most of them also carry a lance with a shining steel point, remarkably large and some of them gilded. At their sides they bear bows and quivers of arrows. Oh, what evils they carry out with their archery! Among their arrows are some wrapped with a gold thread, which are the most excellent. Furthermore, there are some among these many armed Turks who wear a doublet of waxed fabric, large and intricately worked, covered with sendal and fine Arab cloth.

So began the war, hard and harsh, by land and sea. Messer Pietro Zeno of Venice took to the sea and seemed to surround the whole land of the Turks. He burned the lands close by the sea. Wherever his forces appeared, there was no hope. Then by a stroke of luck he found new fishing grounds. Five Turkish ships sailed the seas, menacing the men and women of Greece, who were captured along with their possessions, sheep, clothing, and other goods. These Greeks were from villages near the coast. They were captured by the Turks and plundered. Their villages were burned. When Messer Pietro saw these ships in the distance, he knew just what he would do. He hoisted the sails of his galley to the winds. He swooped down on them as the sparrow hawk does on the quail. Knowing what cargo they bore, he said, "Are we to tolerate such insults?" He had twelve galleys. They rammed their prows into the bellies of the Turkish ships and sank them into the sea. The ships were not large. Three were sunk in deep water with all they contained. Not one living soul escaped. Then two ships were surrounded and captured. In one was the *ameli* of the sea, who came forward to acknowledge him as master and lord.[16] His name was Mostafa. These two were not sunk, for they put up no resistance. It seemed they might be more useful alive. When all the Turks had been taken off their ships each was tied to the other with a rope around their neck. Each one crossed their hands over their breast and bowed down, as if showing reverence, and they said, *"Ano stavròs, stavròs,"*[17] almost as if to say, "Please spare us, for we desire the cross and wish to be Christians."

After this, the valorous warrior, Messer Pietro Zeno, returned with this prize to Smyrna. While Mostafa languished in prison, a letter arrived for him from his wife. In the letter was a lock of hair that was most blonde.[18] Messer Pietro then carried out raids by land, doing great damage. He went about menacing every Turkish locale and habitation. He had them trembling in fear. When Messer Pietro Zeno rode out, Messer Martino Zaccaria fought at sea. Indeed, whenever one was on land, the other was at sea, buffeting and menacing the land of the Turks. The fortresses above Aito Luoco were unable to withstand them. The Turks prepared themselves to put up a resistance. Messer Pietro Zeno of Venice and Messer Martino Zaccaria of Genoa were valorous captains, up to any task, long and tall like two spears, slender and swarthy, well-armed and well-prepared. The weakness of the Christians was that they lacked cavalry. There were too few mounted warriors among them. Present was the capable German captain, Malerva of whom I spoke before, who after the battle of Parabiagio, on the plains of Milan, had elected to come and serve at his own expense for one year, along with twenty-five men. There too was Messer Nolfo, nephew of the king of Cyprus, with fifty cavalry, all knights with golden spurs and known for great deeds. The patriarch, the Franciscan Messer Manuello Camorsino of Venice, was there. So too was a most noble French baron, Fiore de Belgioia by name. This Fiore of Belgioia was

16. The term *ameli* denotes a Turkish official. The precise nature of the office is unclear.

17. Porta identifies this as a neo-Greek phrase meaning, "long live the cross, long live the cross."

18. One wonders how the Anonimo knew this detail. Does he imply that Mostafa's wife was a Christian?

## CHAPTER THIRTEEN

one of those who erected the walls along with the patriarch, as I've said. There were 15,000 infantry, though they were not sufficiently armed, as I've mentioned. For this whole endeavor was not planned adequately and took place over a large area.

It was the month of January in the year of our Lord 1345, on the day of the festival of St. Anthony.[19] The patriarch heard that the Turks had multiplied, and he believed an attack on his position was imminent. Of this he was convinced. He heard the counsel of the Christian leadership, that is of Messer Pietro Zeno, Messer Martino Zaccaria, Fiore de Belgioia of France, Messer Nolfo of Cyprus, and Malerva the German captain. It was decided that they would show no fear but rather put up a stalwart resistance. There was an ancient church there called Santo Ianni. It was said that the blessed Saint John had built it. This church was the episcopal seat of the region around the city, when Christians dwelt there prior to the city being destroyed. After the destruction, it was left abandoned. The church was two crossbow lengths distant from the new wall. It was not located inside the wall. The patriarch entered this church along with forty of the above-mentioned barons. They gave great thanks to God for enabling them to reclaim a Christian church that had been lost. They admired its walls, its pulpit, and its height, and they praised God and Saint John whose church had been recovered. Then the mass was celebrated there with great solemnity. With tears, devotion, and happiness, they prayed to God that similar accomplishments might be achieved throughout the Turkish lands.

Men describe this event in two ways.[20] Some say that while the patriarch was singing the mass along with the aforementioned forty barons, a great multitude of Turks came down from the hills, hidden among the trees, and entered the church of Santo Ianni where, in

19. That is, St. Anthony of Egypt, the desert father. His feast day is January 17.
20. Here the Anonimo's account is at least partially corroborated by John VI Cantacuzenus in his *History*. It seems likely that d'Asti insisted on this mass despite the misgivings of the other leaders, who saw exposing themselves like this as a needless risk. Setton, *Papacy and the Levant*, 192–93, notes, however, that the Anonimo's account is a clear blend of fact and fiction and that — as with several cases in the Anonimo's narrative — finding the line between the two is challenging. See Seibt, 37–107; Musto, *Writing Southern Italy*, 19–20, 213–20, et passim.

the midst of the mass, they killed and decapitated all present. No help came, for the infantry was too far off. Another person told me that it happened another way, though similarly. They said that they personally witnessed these things, swearing an oath that they were telling the truth. According to this person, on Saint Anthony's day in January, in the church of Santo Ianni outside Smyrna, the mass was sung with great solemnity. After the mass, the patriarch gave a very good sermon, comforting the Christians and exhorting them to persecute the infidels, recover the lands of the Christians, and liberate the seven churches from the hands of those dogs. Then he said, "Know that such was the force by which God compelled me to come to this place that my right leg bears a scar." Then he made the sign of the cross and gave his blessing to everyone present. There were at least 15,000 Christians there from among the infantry. After this he armed himself with a fully panoply of arms: cuirass, faulds,[21] and gauntlets, a helm upon his head, and greaves of steel, all well-wrought. Over this armor he draped a rich episcopal mantel, that article of clothing that is known as a cope, which was made of silk and fine gold thread and adorned with pearls and precious stones, as suited a prelate of his high rank. In his hand he bore a naked shining sword. Mounted on a powerful destrier he well resembled a baron. He dug in his spurs and went boldly to his martyrdom. There followed after him Messer Pietro Zeno of Venice and Messer Martino Zaccaria of Genoa, armed and adorned just as you would expect.

The decision of these men to charge into battle was totally unplanned. Their forces were disorganized. They had heard the approach of the Turks, but they did not believe that the ambushers were so near or their traps so well lain. So they sallied out, not taking the direct path but rather moving to the left in order to open up more space. The majority of the force that hastened out after them went instead to the right, believing that they were following after leaders who were not actually ahead of them. The further they went the more lost they became. The region was uninhabited and perilous due to the many obstacles created by ruined walls and the foundations of houses and towers. It was a pathless place, one

---

21. In contrast the cuirass, which covered the chest, the faulds covered the abdomen and upper leg.

## ✽ CHAPTER THIRTEEN

where men could easily lose themselves. Once the first three — the patriarch, Messer Pietro Zeno, and Messer Martino Zaccaria — were some way off, they realized that they were alone without any support within a labyrinth of ruined buildings. There they quickly fell into the Turkish trap. Without a sound they were surrounded. It availed them nothing to draw their swords or put up a defense. They were pulled down from their mounts to the ground. Their heads were expeditiously separated from their bodies. The three barons received holy martyrdom and were made knights of Christ. Those Turkish dogs carried off their heads. They carried off their gear and beautiful adornments. They even made off with their horses. Only their naked bodies were left on the ground. *Ad presulem tamen plangibilior casus fuit. Nam eques insuper – Dardo nomen erat – in virum sacrum sceleratas primum manus iniecit clavaque ferrea ictus ictibus cumulans moribundum semianimemque pontificem leva tenuit arreptoque gladio caput obtruncat, nudatumque cadaver ad terram prolapsum dimisit venerabilem que calvariam ornato involvens pallio ad suos abiit.*[22]

By this time the army was fully in the field. Once they came out, the death of the patriarch and the two champions was discovered, for the bodies were found by the rearmost of the host. Great was the grief and great the lamentation, greater the shame of falling back. Each one wished himself dead. Out into the empty field went the elaborately adorned French knight, Fiore de Belgioia, decorated in gilt silver that had been crafted with noble mastery. Joyfully he went to take the crown.[23] Messer Nolfo, nephew of the king of Cyprus, went out too, clad in a royal manner. Malerva the German went out, that good captain of sixty knights. After these men came the rest of

---

22. "Upon the patriarch an even more lamentable fate was visited. For a knight — Dardo was his name — lay his wicked hands upon the holy man, with his right raining down blow after blow upon the dying man with an iron club while holding the half-dead man fast with his left. Then, after seizing his sword, he struck off his head, cast the denuded body down on the ground, and carried the venerable head back to his companions wrapped in the ornate cloak." Campanelli, "Gli inserti latini," 19–20, hypothesizes that this text was originally a marginal note, meant to be translated into the vernacular and then integrated properly with the other text, perhaps because the Anonimo was contemplating giving a fuller account of the patriarch's final moments.

23. That is, the crown of martyrdom.

the army. They arrived in the desolate fields. Horses charged, arrows flew, javelins were hurled, and swords clashed. Many fell on all sides. Nowhere was respite to be found. Fiore de Belgioia had no desire to flee. He spurred on his destrier. With sword in hand, defending himself, he fell dead among the foe. Messer Nolfo, nephew of the king of Cyprus, was pierced by two arrows and died. Malerva the Germon was captured alive. He was flayed alive by the dogs. Many Christians died, many were captured, many were crowned with holy martyrdom. Some were burned not far from Smyrna, some flayed, some decapitated. In the end, the Christians could bear no more. They turned tail and returned to Smyrna, let the sea water into their defensive ditch, and saved themselves from the fury of those dogs who came hacking and killing Christians, or capturing them. And so the killing concluded. The gates of Smyrna were closed, and the sea water made to surround it. *Tamen*,[24] countless Turks were slain, captured, or flayed.

Listen to this beautiful occurrence! A man who saw it all himself told me that many Turks were captured, among them one who was hugely fat. They flayed this fat man alive so that his skin hung down around his waist like skirts and they left him like that.[25] Left there, he went wretchedly on his way. Once he was safe (imagine this if you can) the flayed Turk turned and with both hands gave the *ficora* to the Christians, so round that it might as well have been August.[26]

Then the Christians sealed themselves inside Smyrna. They had no leader. The news spread to the city of Venice, to the Roman curia, throughout Christendom, and to the ears of the pope and the cardinals. The curia deeply mourned the death of the patriarch

24. "Nevertheless."

25. The text compares the man's skin to a *"braca,"* an article of clothing that hung from the waist and covered the legs.

26. The *"fica"* was a rude gesture of ancient origin, common in the Mediterranean, the name of which referred to a fig. The joke here is that the obese Turk made for a particularly plump fig. The Anonimo does not comment on the plausibility of this reported incident. The reference to August indicates the Italian season for the ripest figs.

and the rout of the Christians.²⁷ A great council was held in Venice by the patricians and the doge. It was determined that they would turn all their might to the task of avenging the humiliation of their citizen and to win the war and seize Smyrna with a firm hand. This they could not do without papal approval. A Venetian embassy came before the pope in Avignon and humbly requested a crusade against the Turks. Pope Clement [VI] received the ambassadors graciously and granted them his approval. The call to crusade went out across Christendom: remission of penance and of sin for those who participated, for those who died in the effort would travel directly to the feet of God, turning neither left nor right.

The crusade was not preached from the pulpits, nor was it handled with the care that it should have been, but the news alone was enough to move people.²⁸ There was a great commotion. Many prepared themselves, hoping to die for God: men, women, friars, and priests alike. So much property was sold and so many supplies acquired. Whoever could afford it began to prepare, while those who could not sought some means of doing so. They went about begging in God's name so that they might pay their way to the front. There was in Christendom no city, no castle, no community from which many did not come. Two hundred came from one city, three hundred from another. From this city came five hundred and from that a thousand. Imagine what a multitude it was! They dressed themselves in white tunics with the sign of the cross in red. Many stood in the piazzas in this garb. Every street was full of people dressed this way. Each made the pilgrimage to Ancona. From there, they took to the sea and headed for Smyrna. And another thing

27. These events took place during the period of the Avignon papacy, so that the curia was in Avignon rather than in Rome. It appears that, for the Anonimo, it remained the Roman curia all the same. As it did for Clement VI, who strongly stressed its remaining "Roman." See Wood, *Clement VI*, 43–95.

28. Despite the Anonimo's claims, Clement did have this crusade preached as part of an effort to raise funds for it. See Housely, *The Later Crusades*, 59. Indeed, the effort here described was part of a papal project that had begun years before. Venturino da Bergamo, whom we met in chapter 6, pp. 79–81, preached this crusade in 1343. See Setton, *Papacy and the Levant*, 190; Wood, *Clement VI*, 177–201 et passim.

happened too, namely that enemies made peace with one another before donning that uniform.

Once Pope Clement saw everything that was happening and understood that he couldn't control it, it seemed better to him to provide the multitude with a leader, for without leadership such a large assembly might easily go wrong. He ordered Messer Guido, dauphin of Vienne, to take up this burden.[29] The dauphin obeyed the holy father. Taking up the banner of the cross he traveled with his cavalry into Provence. He entered Italy. He then arrived at Ancona and went from there to Negroponte. During the course of this pilgrimage his lady wife died.[30] Eventually the entire host arrived at Smyrna. All day long Venetians ships brought them in. Such money those ships made! What a fleecing![31] They wouldn't do a thing for mere chump change. Folk came from Modena, from Corone, from Foggia, from Patras, and from Malvasia.[32] The beautiful and honorable people of Philadelphia were there, well mounted and well-armed. Among this throng of people many scuffles broke out due to the need to blow off steam, not without ill effect.

The Venetians decided it was best to negotiate a truce before the arrival of the dauphin. An embassy from the Venetians went to Aito Luoco for the purpose of the truce. They demanded total control of Smyrna. When the embassy arrived, Morbasciano was eating, reclined on the ground and leaning on his left arm. He was

29. This Guido is Humbert II of Vienne, the last to bear the title "dauphin" before it began instead to refer to the heir apparent of the French throne. Humbert was not actually supported by the curia at first, having instead taken it upon himself to join the effort in Smyrna. By May of 1345, Humbert successfully convinced Clement to name him "captain of the holy Apostolic See and leader of the whole army of Christians against the Turks." He is notorious for his ineptitude. See, Housely, *The Later Crusades*, 60.

30. Setton, *Papacy and the Levant*, 210, notes that Humbert's wife, Marie des Baux, died at Rhodes in 1347, after his efforts in Smyrna were already over.

31. The Anonimo uses the same verb used to describe the flaying of the fat Turk, *scorticare*. "Fleecing" captures this sense.

32. Some of these are Italian towns (Modena, Foggia); while others are in Greece (Malvasia, Patras). The majority of the recruiting for Humbert's effort, which drew thousands, came from the cities of northern Italy.

so immensely fat that his stomach resembled a wine cask. He was clad in linen that was most nobly embellished with silk. Before him were brought bowls decorated with sparkling gems, full of candies, almond milk, and eggs with spices and rice. He held in his hand a golden spoon with which he voraciously devoured it all.

Hearing that an embassy had come, he did not get up from his meal, instead saying, among other things, "We are well aware that the dauphin is coming. As long as we have our two prosperous friends among the Christians, we need have no fear."

The ambassadors asked, "Who are these friends of yours?"

Morbasciano replied, in Latin with no interpreter, saying "They are the Guelfs and the Ghibellines."[33]

In time, the dauphin of Vienne arrived in Smyrna. He had thirty knights and no more. As soon as he arrived, without delay, he entered the gates and took the people by the reins. He would permit none to leave. Pillaging raids were undertaken. Many Turks were captured. Many of the people came from Rome, Germany, France, and Picardy. No city remained unaccounted for. Eighteen [...] this siege and battle lasted. Fifteen thousand Christians gathered together in one place. After this, things began to go badly. The heat was tremendous, and the dusty earth was such that men trudged through loose dusty earth up to their mid-leg. The people began to take seriously ill and die like sheep. There was also a terrible famine there. The master of the Hospital of Rhodes forbade Venetian ships to come and also provided supplies and arms to the Turks.[34] As a

---

33. As noted above, pp. 67, 72, 73 n. 21, the Guelfs and Ghibellines were factions that supported the papacy and the empire, respectively, but should be understood here to indicate factional divisions more generally. According to the Anonimo, Morbasciano felt that so long as Christendom remained at war with itself, he had nothing to worry about. These factions were likely not nearly so important a factor as was the rivalry between the Venetians and the Genoese.

34. This is a reference to the Knights Hospitaller, also known as the Knights of St. John. The implication is that this military order was allied with the Turks, rather than the Christian forces under the dauphin. This seems difficult to reconcile with what we know. The Hospitallers were a part of Clement's collaborative enterprise, and Humbert himself took refuge on Rhodes when he became ill in

result, the people were deeply troubled. A great many took to the sea and went back home. The majority left. Few remained. When people left, they withdrew all the money they had there from the Venetians. They were pursued everywhere.[35] The dauphin erected a new wall of good strong stone, larger than the first, with towers, gates, and moats. The Venetians were chosen as the defenders of that place, and to this day they hold that territory. With this new, secure wall completed, the dauphin saw no further reason to remain. He left Smyrna and returned to his own country. There was nothing of particular note done after this.[36] So ended the crusade to Smyrna.

---

1346. See Housely, *Later Crusades*, 61. On the other hand, Setton, *Papacy and the Levant*, 207–8, reports the Anonimo's assertions, despite his skepticism about the account, but observes that it is unclear how the Hospitallers could have exerted such control since the Venetians controlled the settlement.

35. The sense one gets here is that the Venetians were holding people's money in deposit and that something like a fourteenth-century "run on the bank" was happening here.

36. The Anonimo omits the fact that prior to his departure Humbert likely negotiated a truce with Morbasciano. See Setton, *Papacy and the Levant*, 209.

# CHAPTER FOURTEEN
THE BATTLE FOR FRANCE, IN WHICH THE KING OF BOHEMIA
DIES AND THE KING OF ENGLAND DEFEATS THE KING OF FRANCE

IT WAS THE YEAR OF OUR LORD 13[46] that a horrible defeat occurred in France, eight leagues from Paris, at the mountain of Crécy. Philip [VI] Valois, the king of France, was defeated and king Edward [III] of England was the victor.[1] It happened this way.

The reason for the war between the king of France and the king of England was this and nothing else than this. There was a French king who was most wise, good, and just, whose name was Philip the Good.[2] This Philip truly bore the mark of the cross on his right shoulder. He played with the lion as easily as one would play with a puppy.[3] When he reached old age, Philip found himself with no heir. He had only a daughter, whom he gave as wife to King Edward of England. This queen's name was Isabella. When King Philip died, having no son, he did not wish to leave his realm with no governor. There was in France a noble count, by the name of Philip, the count of Valois.[4] This was a relative of his, though not of direct lineage. He was the savviest, wisest, and most sophisticated man in France. He

1. The original leaves a gap where the date would be, but the battle of Crécy took place on August 26, 1346. For recent studies, see the essays in Andrew Ayton and Philip Preston, *The Battle of Crécy, 1346* (Woodbridge: Boydell, 2005). For consideration of the Anonimo's account in particular, see Campanelli, "The Anonimo Romano at his Desk. See above, p. xiv, Map 6.

2. That is, Philip IV the Fair.

3. Philip's piety is praised here, as the Anonimo expressed it, he bore the mark of the cross on his shoulder (i.e., from carrying it like Christ). The inveterate enemy of Boniface VIII and destroyer of the Knights Templar, Philip's piety was at best complicated. As for the lion, the arms of the Plantagenet kings of England and their kin depicted one or more rampant lions, and it is likely to this that the Anonimo refers. On Philip IV, the classic account is Joseph Strayer, *The Reign of Philip the Fair* (Princeton, NJ: Princeton University Press, 1980); but this work has been supplanted with new research. See, for example, the work of Elizabeth A.R. Brown on the Capetian monarchy.

4. There is a sort of continuity here with the previous chapter. In 1349, Phillip VI Valois purchased the Dauphiné from Humbert II, the "dauphin" of the previous chapter, who sold it due to his own desperate need for cash.

was a bold man, and he had fought as a mercenary in Lombardy. The king left this count of Valois as his executor and the governor of his whole realm. He entrusted everything to him. Then he died and passed from this life. Philip Valois remained. He began to rule the kingdom well and wisely. And since he had no rivals, and the king had no male heir, he arranged with the barons of the realm, and with the pope, to be crowned. He was anointed and consecrated in Rouen, and his son John was made duke of Normandy.

When King Edward of England learned that Philip had taken the crown of France, he swore on the majesty of his kingdom that he would give the French no quarter until he had taken back the realm that should have passed to him from his mother.[5] He was little concerned with embassies, with flattery, or with the pope and his curia. So he rallied his great power, his mighty army, and left England, crossing the sea with his royal navy and landing in the land of France. His force numbered 18,000 knights and no more, 30,000 archers including servants, infantry, cooks, and all the others together. It is the English custom that every member of the household has a bow. When they leave off their normal duties, they use their bow and serve as archers. There King Edward stood. His son, the younger Edward, prince of Wales, was with him. The queen, counts, knights, and many barons were there too. They had at least 3,000 wagons full of everything an army needs. Once the English had crossed the sea and taken up positions on land, the first noteworthy thing King Edward did was to send his entire navy back to England.

His people were unsure what to make of this and asked, "Why have you done this?"

The king responded, saying, "I would not have you hoping to return home. Be stalwart." Then he lay siege to a powerful region that was the center of the lands thereabout — Salluppo by name — taking it by force and holding it as his own.[6] Then he marched along the coast of Normandy, alongside the sea. He marched more than two hundred miles, torching and burning villages and castles as

5. This is Edward III (r. 1327–77), son of Edward II and Isabella.

6. Porta suggests that "Salluppo" may correspond to Saint-Lô, which Edward captured soon after landing. He notes that Villani refers to this same place as "Sallu," which lends credibility to the reading.

# CHAPTER FOURTEEN

he went, pillaging and killing. He met no resistance. Eventually the damage he was inflicting became clear to King Philip. He had seized and robbed a great many people. Fortresses and towers that stood in his path he cast down. Then he wrote to King Philip, declaring that he awaited him, longing to meet him on the field of battle, and asking how long it would be. King Philip requested fifteen days and no more, so that he might send for his son John.

Duke John of Normandy was positioned in Gascony with his army, laying siege to a castle called Aiguillon.[7] There, alongside a river, stood his mighty host. As soon as they heard his father's command, they left standing in the field tents, pavilions, and every kind of gear. They delayed not a moment. He and his great army immediately set out. They took with them only weapons and horses. They marched hard for fifteen days. But their efforts were for naught, for when they arrived thirty days had passed; the battle was underway. He was unable to offer his father succor. He missed the battle.

Let us turn now to the details. King Philip, after promising to appear on the field, knew well that his barons had made deals with the English and given them access to the heart of France. He found it unbearably painful to see his enemies traveling freely throughout France, with no defenses. So he gathered together many good men. He had at least 100,000 cavalry. He had at least 12,000 infantry. He had the king of Bohemia, John, with thousands of Germans. King John enjoyed going to war for pay. He had the king of Majorca, named John, who had been driven out of his own realm.[8] He stayed and fought for pay too. He had Louis, count of Flanders, as well, who had been driven from his own land. He also had Messer Otto Doria and Messer Carlo Grimaldi, with 5,000 Genoese crossbowmen. He had many other counts, barons, and troops as well.

The king of England arrived at night in a large valley eight leagues from Paris. The valley lay near a castle called Mount Crécy. At the other end was a village of 4,000 people, called Abbeville. Between these two points, on the flat plain at the foot of Crécy, he arrayed his forces and positioned his host. Once the army had arrived and

---

7. The Anonimo names this Arpiglione.

8. This is James III of Majorca, who had recently lost his kingdom to Aragon but enjoyed a good relationship with King Philip.

positioned itself, it was night, the hour when the small bell rings.⁹ His outriders, who rode ahead of him, and his spies who approached Paris and Saint Denis, heard the bells of Saint Denis of France and those of the Sainte-Chapelle¹⁰ when they rang the small bell. They also heard, following these, the matins of the religious and of the chapels.¹¹ When the news reached Paris that the English had made camp, all the royals took up arms. There were so many that their arms were valued at two hundred florins.¹²

It was the break of dawn. It pleased King Philip to make the king of Bohemia captain of all his forces and send him out to see to his defenses. And so it was done. He sent from Paris John of Majorca, Louis the count of Flanders, and all his other barons. The English watched all this from the long road that led to Paris, which offered a good view. Watching, the English understood the course of the French forces making their way onto the field. They could see this from the glinting of their shining helmets and the shimmering of their banners as they reflected the rays of the morning sun. With this clear view, Edward new without a doubt that battle was unavoidable. And when one considers the size of the French host, it is no surprise that he was somewhat concerned. He hesitated, raising his voice and saying, "Oh God, help me."¹³ Very rapidly, within little more than an hour, he had his army surrounded by a good iron chain, fixed to iron

---

9. This is a reference to the ringing of the monastic hours. Smaller, quieter bells were used during the night.

10. Campanelli, "The Anonimo Romano at his Desk," 76, identifies the Anonimo's Santa Maria delle Sciampelle as the Sainte-Chapelle, which he notes had a lower chapel dedicated to the Virgin.

11. King Edward's eyes and ears were in place in and around Paris by daybreak.

12. This is a small sum for it to be the value of all the arms of the royals here described. The Anonimo may be repeating bad information or may have misread the sources he relied on for this passage.

13. On several occasions the Anonimo Romano relates a private thought or exclamation of his chief characters. These might be considered literary tropes, a form of rhetorical *amplificatio*, often used in chivalrous romances. See, for example, the hero's sighing calls to Jesus in *Huon of Bordeaux,* Catherine M. Jones and William W. Kibler, ed. (New York: Italica Press, 2021), ll. 1900–1916, 6797–6825; and Cola di Rienzo's similar calls in chapter 18, p. 237.

## CHAPTER FOURTEEN

poles that were planted in the ground at regular intervals. This chain was staked out in the form of a circle, like a horseshoe in that it was closed on all sides except one, which was left open like a gate for coming and going. Then he had a deep trench dug in spots where his position was weak. Every Englishman had a job. Then he surrounded the chains with the wagons he had brought. He placed one wagon next to another, with the shafts pointed upward. The wagons were so substantial that it really seemed like a well-walled city.[14] Then he arrayed his people accordingly.

On the left side, at the foot of Crécy, was a small rise. It was a lightly forested spot. There was grain there too, which was unharvested. It was the third day of the month of September. Due to the cold climate of that country, grain matures in September. There among the trees and the grain he placed in concealment ten thousand English archers. Near each wagon he placed a barrel of arrows. At each barrel he stationed two crossbowmen. Then he positioned 500 well-prepared knights outside his main force. Their captain was Edward the prince of Wales, his son. This was the first battalion. Behind these five hundred he placed two wings, each of 500 good knights, one on the right side and one on the left. Behind these 500 he placed 1,000. This was the third battalion. Behind this 1,000 and inside the chains he held in reserve himself and all his remaining cavalry. With this done, he comforted his people and commended himself to God, saying, "My lord God, defend and lend aid to the just." This was how he positioned his forces. This was his excellent ordering of things.

---

14. Here the Anonimo seems to be drawing on the account of Giovanni Villani, who also describes the creation of a wall of wagons. Villani's account, which must have been written within months of the battle, has been deemed quite accurate and seems to have influenced subsequent accounts in France. See Andrew Ayton, "Crécy and the Chroniclers," in Ayton and Preston, *Battle of Crécy*, 1346, 287–350. The same influence is clear with the Anonimo. Campanelli, "The Anonimo Romano at his Desk," 47–48, however, points out that the Anonimo seems likely to have drawn on several sources, not merely Villani from whom he sometimes differs. He speculates that some of his information may have come from eyewitnesses, though none are mentioned by the Anonimo.

It was Saturday, the third day of September. The king of Bohemia arrived at the field from Paris and took up a position not too far from the English. The king of Bohemia had weak vision. He did not see well. First, he asked about the positioning of King Edward. When he understood how he was positioned he quickly said, "We're lost. The English cannot be defeated except with great damage to us."

Then he asked what the weather was like. The crowd responded that the sky above the English was clear as a sapphire, while the sky over the French looked like rain. He replied, "This battle suits them rather than us."

He sent an emissary to King Philip in Paris. The emissary said, "King Philip, should it please your highness, let's not have this battle, for it cannot proceed without great loss and has no purpose. It would be better if we held firm in our positions. The king of England will decide to leave. When he goes, we'll be right behind him. We will have him marked."

King Philip was very angry and said, among other things, "When the best captain in the world is afraid, I feel like drowning in the Seine!"

The emissaries did not soften these words for the king of Bohemia. The king of Bohemia replied, "Today it will be clear that I am not afraid. It will also be plain that this battle is an act of madness rather than courage." Then he commanded the readied battalions to attack.

Before this attack (such as it was) he had grouped his forces into nine battalions. But the first three were the most renowned, the primary groups. The first battalion was that of Messer Otto Doria and Messer Carlo Grimaldi, the captains of 5,000 Genoese crossbowmen. The second was that of the king of Majorca along with the count of Flanders, with 3,000 cavalry. Then there were several battalions of various sorts. Then there was that of the king of Bohemia with 1,000 Germans, 4,000 Frenchmen, and his son Charles near at hand.

The first battalion to arrive on the field in the morning hours was that of the 5,000 Genoese crossbowmen. Their orders were to ascend the slope of Crécy so that they would be looking down on the English. But it didn't happen that way because the English had occupied the hills and placed obstacles amid the grain. The

※ CHAPTER FOURTEEN

Genoese therefore positioned themselves on a different hill further away. Then disaster struck, for they could not load their crossbows and were unable to shoot. There had been a sprinkling of rain. The land, soaked through, was soft underfoot. When they tried to load their crossbows they put one foot up on the stirrup.[15] That foot sank into the mud. They couldn't brace their foot against the ground. Whispering started up among the French, who fretted that the Genoese had turned traitor because they had not been paid. They said, "These fellows won't shoot, and if they do, they'll shoot blunt bolts. Let the Genoese die then!" So spoke the French who were moved to anger at their own troops. Cruelly they drew their swords and lances. The Genoese were slaughtered to the last man. Messer Otto moaned about the loss of his troops to the king, who responded saying, "We have no need of the foot. We have ample forces." That was the first argument. Five thousand Genoese were slain in a moment.[16]

Then the front lines smashed into each other, the battalion of John, king of Majorca, attacking Edward the duke of Wales.[17] So great was the shouting in this battle, so overwhelming the noise and the crash of arrows, that it was if two mountains were crashing together. Each struck and received blows in turn. Instruments were

15. Crossbows were loaded by pointing them down, putting one's foot in a stirrup at the front end, and using that as leverage. When the Genoese did this, the pressure simply made their planted foot sink into the mud, making it extremely hard, if not impossible, to load their weapons.

16. We do not know the source for the Anonimo's incorrect account of the Genoese role. The Genoese did engage but, unable to reload because of the mud, withdrew from battle. They were not slaughtered by the French. See Michael Prestwich, "The Battle of Crécy," in Ayton and Preston, *Battle of Crécy, 1346*, 139–57; and Russell Mitchell, "The Longbow–Crossbow Shootout at Crécy (1346): Has the 'Rate of Fire Commonplace' Been Overrated?," in L.J. Andrew Villalon and Donald J. Kagay, ed., *The Hundred Years War 2. Different Vistas* (Leiden: Brill, 2008), 233–57.

17. Here, my translation reflects the arguments of Castellani about the proper text of this passage, in which he offers a correction of Porta's edition. See A. Castellani, "Note di lettura: La 'Cronica' dell'Anonimo Romano," *Studi Linguistici Italiani* 13 (1987): 66–84. This suggestion has also been adopted by Campanelli. See his "The Anonimo Romano at his Desk," 76.

sounded, a great number of horns and pipes. During this battle a notable thing happened. The prince of Wales had spurred his steed toward the enemy. Being alone, he failed utterly. A count, known as Count Valentino, saw and recognized him. He recognized a chance at real profit. As if trying to catch a great fish he cast his hook. Quietly, he guided his steed toward Edward, prince of Wales, and embraced him. He seized him by the chain links of his armor and said, "You are my prisoner." Then he stopped and dragged him from the battle by force, holding him entirely at his mercy.

As Count Valentino was carrying off the king of England's son, the count of Alençon, who was brother by blood to King Philip, seeing Edward defeated and bound up like a sheep, angrily said these words, "Count Valentino! What makes you so bold as to drag my cousin off to prison?" He didn't wait for a reply. Springing into action he raised the gilt iron mace he held in his hand and struck Count Valentino on the head. The blows continued, one after another, and Count Valentino's strength abandoned him. He lost his grip on both his reins and Edward's armor and fell to the ground from his horse, dead. So young Edward *nimirum* glad, spurred on and returned to his side, which had already begun to falter.[18]

Louis, count of Flanders, saw all this transpire. As I have said, he had been driven from his own land and had been in Paris fighting for pay for some time. He was an old man, a good and honest person. He loved King Philip, and his honor, very much. He understood what betrayal had happened in the midst of the French barons. He could not restrain himself from speaking the truth. Nobly he raised his voice and said, "Count of Alençon! This is hardly the loyalty or goodness that you owe the crown! The war was won and now, because of you, it is lost!"

When the count of Alençon heard this, he did not wish to hear more. He leapt from his steed and with the very same mace he struck the count of Flanders, that old man, killing him. What a savage thing that we come to this, that a man should die for telling the truth and condemning evil. No one in the count of Flander's party was brave enough to speak up. Only one of his despairing dependents, a household servant and foot soldier of lowly birth,

18. *Nimirum* is a Latin adverb meaning "evidently" or "doubtless."

# ❋ CHAPTER FOURTEEN

seeing such cruelty, drew his dagger and thrust it into the belly of the count of Alençon so that it passed clean through him. And so the count of Alençon, traitor to his brother, died there on the field.

The servant who had slain the count of Alençon then went before King Philip and said that he had murdered his brother to avenge his lord and because of the betrayal that he had committed. He backed this up with good evidence. Hearing this, King Philip pardoned him and opted to take no vengeance himself.

While these things were happening, the English archers began to come down from the hillside amid the grain and ceaselessly fired arrows at the cavalry. They were raising their bows and saying, "Loose! Loose! Loose!" They were a danger to the whole force. On the left side, the horses were struck, severely weakening the army. Those injured began to flee. Horses fell dead. The English advanced. The battle was lost.

In the meantime, there were a great many skirmishes and maneuvers. Which was most famous? The English cavalry uses a certain technique. When they see that one of their number is dead, they put a live man in his place, a healthy one in place of one injured, and a rested man in place of an exhausted one. Then they changed positions so that the five hundred on the right wing came to the front. In their place came half of the thousand men of the third battalion. Then those in the front go back to the thousand. They change the left wing in the same manner. The rearguard, the large royal host, always stays in the same position. It does not move unless due to absolute necessity.

King John of Majorca did not die in this battle, but he was wounded in the face. He died most cruelly in his own land. Wishing to return to his realm, he did battle with his cousin, the king of Majorca, but was defeated and beheaded.

Once the battalions were put to flight, the king of Bohemia asked his aids how things were going on the field. They told him that no living person remained there but he and his people alone. All the French had been cut to pieces. The English stood strong, firm and unyielding with their standard raised. So the king of Bohemia commanded that the two powerful barons who were at his side prepare to attack. They said, "What do you want to do? The whole

French host is slain. The English stand strong. We're not some extra sauce!¹⁹ It's madness to go up against so many!"

The king responded, "Then you are not the sons of my two friends, who were the bravest in all Germany!"

The two barons replied, "There is no need for courage here, for we are nothing compared to our enemies!"

Then the king said, "I want us to go. Let us go and die with honor."

To this they replied, "What does your death, or ours, benefit you?"

The king replied, "By good faith I say what I say because I am trying to speak truthfully." At this the two barons were convinced.

Like lambs they lowered their voices and said, "Your majesty. Do what pleases you." And so the king had certain barons brought before him, those who were the greatest in Luxemburg and in the realm of Bohemia, and he commanded them to be as obedient to his son Charles as they were to him and to honor him as king and lord.²⁰ He commanded them as well to ensure that Charles survived the battle. Then he commanded the nobles who stood before him to charge with him into the English and drive into them so that, if they did their jobs, there would be no turning back. Then he chained himself between the two aforementioned barons, and they linked the chains of their armor so that they might share one death and one honor.

The first rank comprised one thousand Germans from Luxemburg, quality men, Bohemians and gentlemen from Prague. Behind them

19. The text literally reads, "we are not sauce" (*saiza*, or *salsa* in modern Italian). I take this to be a figure of speech. The whole terrible dish (the battle) has been cooked and the barons feel that the king of Bohemia is tossing them in as an afterthought.

20. John of Bohemia or Luxemburg was the son of Emperor Henry VII and first of the Luxemburg line of kings of Bohemia, the father of Emperor Charles IV. John had sent Charles to Paris from his early years to be brought up at the French court. The Anonimo's account matches what we know of John's character and career; but since all the interlocutors in the above dialogue died in this battle, we might assume that the Anonimo made up the conversation.

## CHAPTER FOURTEEN

followed four thousand French, Burgundian, and Picards. His son Charles he held back. Then the trumpets and horns sounded in each battalion. They lowered their lances and spurred their steeds. They struck without mercy. There were two vicious tactics that benefitted the English. First, they refreshed their five hundred forward cavalry with the one thousand stationed in the rear. Second, that their two wings of five hundred could fan out and fill the field on the left and the right, flanking the front lines. Once the Germans had engaged the English front line, the wings were activated and attacked them from each side. The king of Bohemia was attacked from the front and from both sides. The king's horse stumbled. The king fell and was trampled to death by the steeds of the two barons at his side. First to fall was Messer Haundello Tornello, a noble French knight who bore the king's banner. He was among the first of the king's men to be unhorsed and killed. The thousand Germans did not retreat. They put up a spirited resistance despite having no king and no banner. Many Englishmen died. Ultimately, the ranks of the king of Bohemia were worn down, like spices are ground down by a great pestle.

Charles, son of King John, stood some distance off. When he understood that his father was slain and defeated, he could not contain his tears. In his grief he said, "Let us die with him!" He positioned his banners for a charge. The act was pointless and futile, for the English position was stronger than ever. Anger, grief, and passion drove him on. Then his barons surrounded him, seizing his horse's reins and turning its head back toward Paris, and dragged him unwillingly back to Paris, where he halted. He allowed himself to be led away without too much force, doing what really mattered by showing that he would have preferred to act.

Now no one remained in the field in service to the king of France. The English held the field uncontested. They did not give themselves over to plundering. In fact, they did a most noteworthy thing. Even three days after the battle they neither disarmed nor dismounted. Nor did the royal standard depart from the field. They did not let down their guard in the slightest. Then, once they saw that there was no one to resist them, that their position was secure and there was no threat of ambush, they set one part of their force to plundering in an orderly way, taking supplies and stripping the bodies of the fallen.

So transpired the noble battle that took place near the town of Crécy in France. Sixty thousand men were dead on the field. Many prisoners were taken. The king of Bohemia, commander of the whole army, was dead, as were the count of Alençon, of Valois, Louis of Flanders, and many other barons. The English collected fifteen hundred sets of golden spurs, and a further thirteen hundred banners were taken in the rout. The thousand Germans were carried to Paris in wagons. Most of the king of Bohemia's body was taken as well, for most of it was intact. These stripped corpses were taken from the battlefield to Paris for burial. The bodies of the rest were not taken and lay in the field for four days, a spectacle for all to see.

AFTER THIS, the English struck camp, loaded all their gear back onto wagons and, arranging themselves in good order, remained there no longer. They turned away and departed. They marched to Calais, that great fortress by the sea, in order to lay siege to it.[21] The men of Calais were perfidious, loyal servants of the king of France. They are fishermen, living alongside the sea, wicked people and pirates. When people traveled by sea from England to France, they would rob them. King Edward therefore went there and laid siege to the castle of Calais for three months, by both land and sea.[22] At sea he had his ships block the way so that nothing could get in or out. On land he carried out the siege. He had a fearsome ditch from his position up to the castle. Then he surrounded his forces with another great ditch, covering them with planks so that nothing could harm his forces. That is how the siege proceeded. Then he hurled huge stones and iron balls at the gates. They were smashed and shaken. The stones were thrown by trebuchets. He never ceased, night or day. He set the land ablaze. Siege engines, catapults, and other horrible things threatened the castle and its inhabitants.

The people of Calais put up a spirited defense. They too had trebuchets and other means of tormenting their enemies on land.

21. The Anonimo's treatment of the capture of Calais is extremely abbreviated. On Calais, especially after the English capture of the city, see Susan Rose, *Calais: An English Town in France, 1347–1558* (Woodbridge, Suffolk: Boydell Press, 2008). For the siege itself, see pp. 7–22.

22. Porta observes that the Anonimo's chronology is off here. The siege of Calais lasted nearly a year.

## CHAPTER FOURTEEN

They fired both on land and sea, like a porcupine. One ball flew out of Calais and struck a good large ship. It smashed it and sank it to the bottom of the sea. Both the castle and the army were low on supplies. One side refused to give up. The other would not relent in their siege. The hunger was great. The men of Calais had begun to cast lots to decide who would eat the other. In the besieging army starving men began to eat their horses. Coerced by hunger, the men of Calais, with the permission of King Edward, sent a letter to their own king asking for aid. The king of France came with 200,000 men.[23] His son John, the duke of Normandy, had arrived. When the host of the king drew near to Calais, it found the army of King Edward well defended by its ditches and planks. They were unable to advance nor could their many arrows find their targets. So King Philip called for King Edward to come out and face him on the field of battle.

Edward responded, "I move according to my own will, not according to yours."

To this King Philip replied, "Great is your shame! Here I am in the field. You lack the courage to come out and face me!"

Edward replied, "There is no shame in this, for I do not hold fast for no reason. My stance has a purpose. This way I will capture Calais. On the first possible day after the task of Calais is completed, I will meet you in battle."

King Philip replied, "I will give you Calais. Don't hesitate on that account. From this moment it will be yours."

Edward answered, "I do not need you to give it to me, for I do not need given to me what I can earn myself with sword in hand."

And so King Philip, unable to advance, gave his permission to the people of Calais to do whatever they must to secure their own well-being. He then turned away and returned to Paris. Hunger consumed the folk of Calais. They asked the king of England for mercy.

---

23. The actual number seems to have been between 15,000 and 20,000. For background, see John A. Wagner, "Calais, Siege of (1346–1347)," *Encyclopedia of the Hundred Years War* (Woodbridge, Suffolk: Greenwood, 2006), 73–74.

The king said, "How can I have mercy on those who have cost me all my silver?"

The gates were opened. The king wished to have all the people of Calais killed, but at the request of the queen, and of some theologians, he forgave them. He drove out the inhabitants of Calais, letting each man leave in a gown and with nothing else. Calais, with its gold, silver, cloth, and livestock came into the possession of the English. Its castle was stocked with Englishmen. It serves the English crown well, right down to this day.

# CHAPTER FIFTEEN
A GREAT FLOOD AND THE EXTENT OF THE WATERS

WE'VE MADE a great journey so far, we have wandered through many moments, and we have sought out many strange places. We have been to Lombardy and Spain, to Turkey and France. Now is a good time to go back home. Let us return to Italy. Let us return to the magnificent and unheard-of events that for their novelty have drawn the attention of all Italy.

We will speak first of a great flood that took place in Rome. Never had the waters of the Tiber so abounded. Never had the Tiber overflowed its banks so badly or caused so much damage. It was in the year of our Lord 13[…], during the pontificate of Pope Clement VI.[1] In the city of Rome the river known as the Tiber swelled; and as a result of its increase there was a deluge of water so deadly and so marvelous that few, perhaps none, could recall a similar thing having happened. For the entire summer God opened the cataract of the heavens and sent frequent heavy rains, though not large ones. Then, in the autumn, as the grapes were being harvested, beginning on All Saints Day,[2] it seemed as if the fountains of the abyss had been opened so that they might vomit water. So the Tiber began to swell, and it would not recede for anything. During the period between All Saints and Christmas, especially after the eighth day, the rising of the waters continued so that it overwhelmed the usual bounds of its riverbanks. And so the whole plain that surrounds the city of Rome was inundated, and then the bulk of the region both within it and without. It was a marvel, a thing the likes of which no Roman had ever heard. The entire low-lying part of Rome was submerged. Only the seven hills were visible, not overcome by the waters.[3]

The following were the limits and extent of flood in Rome, briefly stated. First, the piazza of Sta. Maria Rotunda was so flooded that one

---

1. Clement VI's papacy lasted from 1342 to 1352. Porta suggests that the precise date of this flood, left obscure by the surviving text, was likely 1345 or 1346.

2. November 2.

3. On the history of Roman flooding, see Rabun Taylor, Katherine W. Rinne, and Spiro Kostof, *Rome: An Urban History from Antiquity to the Present* (New York: Cambridge University Press, 2016), 241–50, with bibliography.

could not enter it either on foot or on horseback. The neighborhood of Sant'Angelo in Pescheria was flooded up to the neighborhood of the Jews, which extends to the piazza of the Jews from a point near the arch near the piazza of the Savelli.[4] In *rione* Colonna the waters came all the way to Folserace, which is near Sant'Andrea de Colonna, where the great column stands.[5] The Porta del Popolo was submerged similarly, so that it was utterly impassable. *Item*, the field of Austa was totally flooded.[6] *Item*, at San Trifone[7] the water came up to the altar and totally filled the church. It also flowed into the monastery and church of the nuns of San Silvestro in Capite.[8] Anyone who wished to visit the women there had to take a raft. *Item*, it came into the monastery of San Giacomo in Settignano by way of Via Trastevere in the following way: it filled the whole place, and the church was flooded up to the altar, covering the

4. These two references refer to the Piazza Giudea and the Portico of Octavia, just outside the church of Sant'Angelo in Pescheria and near the Theater of Marcellus. This was a zone dominated by the baronial Savelli family.

5. This is less easily understood. The church referred to is no longer extant and the meaning of "Folserace" is lost to us. The Anonimo here most likely refers to the area on the present Via del Corso between Sant'Andrea della Valle and the Piazza Colonna further north, the heart of the Colonna district of medieval Rome where the column of Marcus Aurelius still stands. The Via del Corso (the medieval Via Lata) carried on north to Piazza del Popolo. The Anonimo is listing sites from the Tiber bend northward through the central *abitato*, to the northern walls, and then back to the Campo Marzio, and the outer *rioni* of the city.

6. The "campo dell'Austa" is a reference to the location of the Mausoleum of Augustus and the Campo Marzio, the most frequent area of Roman flooding. The use of "Item" preceding each item on this list is an instance of the Anonimo slipping from a literary mode into a more documentary one. This was the customary way of denoting a new item in a list in a wide array of documentary forms, from last wills and testaments to legal statutes. The Anonimo may have had access to official documentation and — like many medieval historians — incorporated this information into the body of his narrative.

7. Also near the Campo Marzio, at Via della Scrofa. See Cesare D'Onofrio, *Visitiamo Roma mille anni fa: La città dei Mirabilia* (Rome: Romana Società Editrice, 1988), 135–36.

8. Further up the Via del Corso (Lata), past Piazza Colonna and Montecitorio.

whole choir and the altar itself.⁹ To those standing on the hill of San Brancaccio¹⁰ it seemed that they had at their feet a terrible lake, in the midst of which the monastery seemed to stand. The zone around San Paolo Maggiore was also flooded, the vineyards and the planted and sown fields.¹¹ Also flooded were the vineyards near the Porta San Paolo, in the area called Ostiense, as well as all the vineyards near the Porta San Pietro. Simply put: every low-lying area alongside the river.

Such being the case, the whole area of Santo Spirito, the piazza of the Castel Sant'Angelo, and the houses of Puortica were swamped with a huge amount of water. It came in at the gate of the bridge, which was metal, and rose all the way to the second gate, which was wooden. Flooded too was the area from the gate of the Leonine City alongside the Castel Sant'Angelo, which initially blocked the waters coming from Santo Spirito. From there, because the whole place was like a lake, one couldn't pass without a raft. If one approached the bridge by the direct route, from the houses of the Vaiani,¹² one found oneself submerged up to the saddle cloths of one's horse.

This overwhelming water consumed and drowned all the planted and sprouted crops it encountered. It buried the vineyards in sediment. It pulled trees up by their roots. It cast down walls and houses. It drowned livestock. It damaged the territory of Rome to a cost of more than 100,000 florins. It broke the chains and engines of the millers and swept away five good stones, which were washed out to sea¹³ and so lost.

9. This is the modern-day church of San Giacomo alla Lunghara.

10. Given its location toward San Paolo Maggiore, this probably refers to the San Brancaccio district on the Oppian Hill.

11. That is, the zone around San Paolo fuori le Mura, outside the city walls.

12. The Vaiani (also spelled Vayani, Vagiani, or Vigiani) were members of Rome's urban nobility, residing in *rione* Ponte. Paolo Vaiani, a legal expert, was an ally of Cola di Rienzo and served him as an ambassador to Florence and other places. He remained important after Cola's fall, serving at various times as *podestà* of Florence, Todi, and Arezzo. See Sandro Notari, "Vaiani, Paolo," in *Dizionario Biografico degli Italiani*, online at https://www.treccani.it/enciclopedia/paolo-vaiani (Dizionario-Biografico).

13. Roman millers used floating mills, situated on the Tiber, many between the Vatican and the Arenula. The Anonimo refers to their millstones here. For an image of these mills, from c. 1495, see Krautheimer, *Rome: Profile*, 273, fig. 209.

Others were recovered with great difficulty. Along with the water came trees, ships, stones, planks, animals, and houses that had been violently swept up by the raging waters. Some of these things were salvaged, but others washed out to sea, including doors, tables, and casks both full of wine and empty. So it was that some found casks of wine and others found chests full of money. One person saw a house made of wooden boards, in which a baby boy was heard, wailing in his crib. These things, and innumerable others, the running waters stole away. They even swept away cattle along with their ploughs and ploughshares.

It rained for a long time. For a long while the Tiber remained engorged. Once it began to swell, it remained so for five days. On the fifth day it grew. On the sixth day it went no further. On the seventh day it began to recede, and the river returned to its usual channel.

Pisciainsanti, a Roman butcher, had a herd of gelded rams in a house alongside the river.[14] When he saw the river rising, he moved them to a house far enough away that it seemed impossible to him that the river could reach them. At night the river swelled and flooded so much that it submerged even that house. Pisciainsanti, when morning came, found the house full of water and the rams floating there drowned.

IN THE CITY OF FLORENCE, in the year of our Lord 13[...], in the month of November, on the fourth day, the city of Florence was flooded nearly as much by a great deluge.[15] The bridges were knocked down and the ovens ruined. It was impossible to bake bread there for a long time. The wells were filled with water. The river swelled, and the waters rose. The flood waters did not extend beyond the vicinity of the river.

14. It must be noted that this butcher's name translates to "pisses on the saints." There is perhaps a moral to this story.

15. This is the flood of November 4, 1333 recorded by Giovanni Villani in his *Nuova Cronica*, III.12.

# CHAPTER SIXTEEN
A SHIP RUN AGROUND AND ROBBED ON THE ROMAN COAST

IT WAS IN THE YEAR OF OUR LORD 13[..], in the month of [...], on the [...] day, that a merchant ship ran aground on the Roman coast, between Porto and Ostia, on the Tiber. The thing happened this way. Merchants of the Regno had come from the west and had loaded in Marseille and Avignon a shipment of French cloth.[1] The ship belonged to Queen Giovanna.[2] The captain, officers, and sailors were all from Ischia.[3] The merchandise belonged to Neapolitans and Ischians.

The galley set out and raised its sail to the wind. It passed Marseille and Monaco, and it crossed the sea of Genoa. Then it passed Pisa. Then it came to Piombino. Then it reached Civitavecchia. Once the coast of Civitavecchia was behind them, they were expecting to reach home. But then a pestilential wind arose. The sea raged without mercy. The winds were so wild that the captain lost his wits. It was the dead of night. The darkness was horrible. You've never seen such a hellish torment. There was nothing to be done but to turn back toward the port of Civitavecchia. It was terribly hard for the sailors and the passengers to turn back and lose so much time. Yet, if they returned to Civitavecchia, they could save their ship. It was decided to take a middle course and look for shelter on the Roman coast, escaping danger and recovering in the Tiber of Rome. So it was done.

The sailors used all their craft and skill. They took their time entering the Tiber. What peril there is in that entry! Finally, the ship entered the river, and they believed themselves safe because the rage of the sea could not touch them once they passed the river's mouth. But it wasn't so. Once the ship was in the midst of the Tiber channel, in the spot between Ostia and Porto, it stuck fast and would not move. There was an unfortunate spot where the water was shallow. They blundered into those cursed shallows. They didn't keep to the deeper channel.

1. The Regno was the kingdom of Naples.
2. Giovanna I. See above p. 111 n. 7, 114, n. 16. The Angevin monarchs of Naples were also lords of Provence, and until Giovanna I's sale of the city to Pope Clement VI in 1348, also lords of Avignon.
3. An island just off the coast of Naples.

The experienced sailors of Genoa and Sicily avoid the place. So some of the sailors disembarked to see why the ship was stuck and they found that it was touching the bottom. There was nothing they could do with mere pails carried by hand. The river was raging too. The ship had run aground in the sand. Waves battered the ship, rocking it from side to side. It seemed like it might capsize. The grief of the sailors and their captain was great. The passengers wept. Everyone thought they were going to die.

Day came and brought helpful clarity. The noise was heard at the castle of Porto and at Ostia. Rafts came from Porto and carried the passengers to shore for money. They saved the master, the sailors, and the passengers along with their personal possessions. The merchandise remained on the ship. There was, in the castle of Porto, a noble Roman named Martino da Porto.[4] Martino had his servants strip the ship and carry off all the merchandise, both cloth and spices. The cloth he sold without giving a share to those who had lost it. He would have rather been excommunicated than give anyone their due.[5] He held to the old proverb: "Those who err at sea are imperiled on land." For this reason, and due to other excesses, he was hung by the neck, as I will describe later.

In the ship was the money and other payment from Provence, which was on its way to Queen Giovanna from her own lands. In it there was cloth worth 20,000 florins. Also on board were passengers from Provence, both men and women, who were on their way to Naples. There were sacks of pepper, cinnamon, and canella. There was also a brother of Saint John by the name of Fra Morreale, a Provençal from Narbonne, a knight of golden spurs, who was still very young.[6]

---

4. This was Martino di Francesco Stefaneschi, member of a baronial family and relative of the Orsini.

5. The Anonimo is being somewhat misleading here. Rome's communal leadership would certainly have considered this a crime, but some barons would have seen the plundering of shipwrecks in their territory as their right under the dubious *ius naufragii*. See Palmer, *Virtues of Economy*, 57–60.

6. It is impossible to know if the Anonimo is correct here, but this would be the infamous Montréal d'Albarno — Fra Morreale — future captain of famous mercenary band known as the Great Company. His career began as a Hospitaller of St. John in Jerusalem. See below, chapter 27, pp. 275–77, 285–89.

## ❋ CHAPTER SIXTEEN

He found himself on the Roman beach by chance and lost everything he had, right down to his purse of florins. He escaped with only his person. He entered Roman territory at a tender age and was a martial fellow that became a most virtuous captain, a man of great deeds and great valor, leader of the Great Company. In the end, he lost his head in Rome, as I will describe.

❋

# CHAPTER SEVENTEEN
## Leonardo of Orvieto[1] is captured by Rome
[The entirety of this chapter is missing.]

※

1. There is no information to identify this person.

# CHAPTER EIGHTEEN
## THE GREAT DEEDS OF COLA DI RIENZO, AUGUST TRIBUNE OF ROME

COLA DI RIENZO was of base origins.[1] His father was an innkeeper named Rienzo.[2] His mother was named Matalena and made her living washing cloths and carrying water. He was born in *rione* Regola. His home was near the river, among the millers, on the street that runs from Regola straight to San Tommaso,[3] near the temple of the Jews. From a young age he was nourished with the milk of eloquence, and was a good grammarian, a bettor rhetorician, and a skilled writer. Goodness, how quickly he could read! He was very familiar with Titus Livy, Seneca, Cicero, and Valerius Maximus. He took great pleasure in recounting the magnificent deeds of Julius Caesar. All day he would study the marble reliefs one finds around Rome. There was none other than he that could read the ancient carvings. He translated all the ancient writing into the vernacular. He correctly interpreted these marble forms. Oh, how often he would say, "Where are these good Romans? Where is their lofty justice? If only I might find myself in such times as theirs!" He was a handsome man and on his face there was always an odd smile. He was a notary.[4]

It happened that one of his brothers was killed and no one sought vengeance for his death. Cola could not help him. He thought long about how to avenge the blood of his brother. He pondered at length about how to reform misguided Rome. He arranged to have himself sent to Avignon as an ambassador to Pope Clement [VI] at

1. For the most recent review of research on Rienzo, see Musto, "Cola di Rienzo," *Oxford Bibliographies Online*. For an analysis of the Anonimo's treatment of Rienzo, see above, Introduction, pp. 55–58.

2. Cola di Rienzo is the local and less formal rendering of Nicola di Lorenzo.

3. That is, the church of San Tommaso ai Cenci near the medieval Jewish Ghetto.

4. Medieval Italian notaries were highly educated legal experts, with deep knowledge of Latin style, who frequently held important roles in civil governments, often acting as officials, historians, orators, and ambassadors. See, for example, Marino Zabbia, *I notai e la cronachistica cittadina italiana nel trecento* (Rome: ISIME, 1999). For Rome, see Internullo, *Ai margini*, 199–213.

the behest of the Thirteen Good Men of Rome.[5] His speech was so refined and beautiful that Pope Clement quickly began to favor him. Pope Clement deeply admired Cola's lovely way of speaking. He wanted to see him every day. So Cola spoke more freely and said that the barons of Rome were highwaymen, that they permitted murder, robbery, adultery, and every evil. They were content for their city to remain in this sorry state. He succeeded in raising the pope's ire against the powerful.

But then, by the doing of Messer Giovanni Colonna, a cardinal, he came into such disfavor and such poverty that he was almost like someone straggling into a hospital.[6] With his overcoat on he stood in the sun like a snake. But the one who cast him down eventually raised him up again: Messer Giovanni Colonna brought him once more before the pope.[7] He returned to favor and was made a notary of the Roman Camera, gaining many advantages and benefits thereby. He returned to Rome most happily, muttering to himself about his intentions.

Once he had returned from the papal court, he began to exercise his office dutifully. He well recognized and understood the robberies perpetrated by the dogs of the Campidoglio, the cruelty and injustice of the powerful. He saw that it threatened the commune itself and that there seemed to be no good citizen willing to help matters. For this reason he rose to his feet in the council chamber of Rome, where all the councilors stood, and said, "You are not

---

5. Rome was somewhat notorious for changes of regime. The government of the Thirteen Good Men was a popular one, along the lines of *popolano* governments in other Italian communes in the late thirteenth and fourteenth centuries. It was overthrown while Cola remained in Avignon. See Musto, *Apocalypse in Rome*, 58–82; Collins, *Greater than Emperor*, 132–38.

6. The Colonna were one of the greatest baronial clans in Rome, controlling significant territory both inside and outside the city, and with ties to both the Neapolitan court and, like most barons, the college of cardinals, of which Giovanni was a member. On the Colonna, see Rehberg, *Kirche und Macht*.

7. The Anonimo is wrong on the details here. It is commonly understood that Cola was returned to favor by the efforts not of Cardinal Giovanni but of Petrarch, who leveraged his own ties to the Colonna in order to help bring this about. See Musto, *Apocalypse in Rome*, 75–77.

good citizens, you who consume the blood of the poor and have no interest in helping them." Then he admonished the officials and the rectors who should have been maintaining their Roman city in a good state.⁸ Once his elaborate discourse was complete, one of the Colonna by the name of Andreozzo de Normanno, who was the chamberlain, rose to his feet and gave him a loud slap. Then one who was a senatorial scribe, a man named Tommaso de Fortifiocca, rose and made a rude gesture. So Cola's speech concluded.

ON A SECOND OCCASION Cola admonished the rectors and the people to behave rightly by means of an image which he caused to be painted on the palace of the Campidoglio, facing the market. On the outer wall of the council chamber he painted the following image.⁹ A great sea was depicted, much disturbed by frightful waves. In the midst of this sea was a small boat, barely afloat and lacking both rudder and sail. In this ship, which was in such peril, was a widow dressed in black, clad in a mourning belt, her gown ripped from her breast and her hair torn as if she had been weeping. She was kneeling, her hands crossed piously at her breast, as one praying to be delivered from danger. Above her was written, "This is Rome." All around this ship, just below it, were four ships that had foundered,

8. The Anonimo uses the phrase *"buono stato,"* a common enough political slogan in trecento Italy, used by Pope Clement VI himself, which became a hallmark of Rienzo's new government. See Musto, *Apocalypse in Rome,* 143–59, esp. 147–49.

9. This and the following images and their sources in the visual culture of trecento Italy have been analyzed at great length over several decades. For analysis and bibliography see Amy Schwartz, "Images and Illusions of Power in Trecento Art: Cola di Rienzo and the Ancient Roman Republic" (PhD diss., State University of New York at Binghamton, 1994); Musto, *Apocalypse in Rome,* 104–29; Musto, *Writing Southern Italy,* 163–78; and Serena Romano, "L'immagine di Roma, Cola di Rienzo e la fine del Medioevo," in Andaloro and Romano, ed. *Arte e iconografia a Roma,* 227–56. The first image is a secularization of Giotto's *Navicella* mosaic, prominently displayed over the atrium entrance portal of the Old St. Peter's across the river. The image of Rome as Widow was a common theme running through Bernard of Clairvaux, Dante (*Purgatorio* VI.112–14), and Petrarch. Neapolitan court artists had visualized it in the *Panegyric to Robert of Anjou from the Citizens of Prato* in the 1330s.

their sails fallen, their hulls shattered, and their rudders lost. On each ship was a drowned, dead woman. The first was named Babylon, the second Carthage, the third Troy, and the fourth Jerusalem. Above them was written, "Due to injustice these cities were imperiled and diminished." A message issued from these dead women which said:

Once you towered on high over every government.

Here and now we await your collapse.

On the left side there were two islands. On one little island a humiliated woman sat and her label said, "This is Italy." The woman spoke, saying:

You took away the authority of every land

and kept me alone as your sister.

On the other island there were four women with their hands over their eyes or clutching their throats in gestures of great sadness,[10] and they spoke as follows:

Once you were accompanied by every virtue.

Now you drift on the sea, abandoned.

These were the four cardinal virtues, namely temperance, justice, prudence, and fortitude. On the upper right side there was a small island. On this little island was a kneeling woman. Her hand was raised to heaven as if she were praying. She was dressed in white. Her name was Christian Faith. Her own verse was as follows:

Oh, father most high, my master and lord,

if Rome falls, where shall I reside?

On the upper right side there were four ranks of various winged animals, holding horns to their mouths and blowing as if they were

---

10. Here we can imagine the stereotypical posture of a woman in the ritual mourning of the *pianto*. For this behavior, see Carol Lansing, *Passion and Order: Restraint of Grief in the Medieval Italian Communes* (Ithaca, NY: Cornell University Press, 2008). Giotto deployed it for his image of *Ira* in the Scrovegni Chapel, Padua. On trecento language of gesture generally, see Jean-Claude Schmitt, *La raison des gestes dans l'occident médiéval* (Paris: Editions Gallimard, 1990); and Moshe Barash, *Giotto and the Language of Gesture* (Cambridge: Cambridge University Press, 1987).

the winds that caused the sea to be so tempestuous and afflicted the struggling ship. The first rank included lions, wolves, and bears.[11] Their label read, "These are the powerful barons and wicked rectors." The second rank was made up of dogs, pigs, and stags. It was labeled, "These are the evil councilors, followers of the nobles." The third rank comprised sheep, dragons, and foxes. They were labeled, "These are the false officials, judges, and notaries." The fourth rank contained rabbits, cats, goats, and monkeys. Their label read, "These are the mob, the thieves, murderers, adulterers, and plunderers." In the upper part was the sky. In the midst of it was the Divine Majesty as if coming to pass judgement. Two swords ushered from his mouth, pointing this way and that. On one side stood Saint Peter and on the other Saint Paul, both at prayer.[12] When the people saw the image of all these figures every one of them was amazed.

WHEN COLA DI RENZO WROTE, he did not use a goose quill. Rather, he used one of fine silver. He said that such was the nobility of his office that the pen should be silver.

NOT LONG AFTER THIS he admonished the people by means of a beautiful sermon in the vernacular, which he delivered in San Giovanni in Laterano. Behind the choir, on the wall, he had mounted a great and magnificent metal tablet covered in ancient script, which no one but he knew how to read or interpret.[13] Around this he caused to be painted figures depicting the Roman senate handing power over to Emperor Vespasian. There, in the midst of the church, he had

11. The Anonimo here refers to the armorial *sigla* of the great Roman families.
12. The imagery here refers to the Apocalypse. Saints Peter and Paul are the patrons of Rome.
13. This was a copy of the *lex de imperio Vespasiani*, which Cola had discovered in the Lateran, where it was being used as an altar top, not long before. It survives and is currently in the Capitoline Museums. On the history of the tablet(s), see Carrie E. Beneš, "Cola di Rienzo and the *Lex Regia*," *Viator* 30 (1999): 231–51; and J.-Y Boriaud, "Cola di Rienzo et la mise en scène de la *lex Vespasiani*," in *La* lex de imperio Vespasiani *e la Roma dei Flavi: Atti del Convegno (Roma, 20–22 novembre 2008)*, Luigi Capogrossi Colognesi and Elena Tassi Scandone, ed. (Rome: L'Erma di Bretschneider, 2009), 115–24.

a stage made of planks, and he had built a very high wooden stairs for ascending to it. He had ornate tapestries and draperies placed all about. Many of Rome's powerful assembled, among them Stefano Colonna and his son Giovanni Colonna, who were among the savviest and most magnificent men in Rome. Many wise men were also present: judges, experts of canon law, and many other men of authority.

Cola di Rienzo ascended to his pulpit before all these good people. He was dressed in a sleeveless German robe and about his throat he wore a cape and hood of fine white cloth. On his head he had a white cap. On top of this cap there were gold circlets, of which the one that was in the front was divided in half. From the hat's top protruded a naked silver sword, the point of which thrust into that circlet and divided it in two. He climbed up boldly. When silence fell, he began his eloquent sermon, his beautiful speech, and said that Rome lay cast down on the ground and could not see where she lay for her eyes had been plucked from her head. Those eyes were the pope and the emperor, who were lost to Rome due to the iniquity of her citizens. Then he said, "Behold how magnificent was the Senate, which granted authority to the Empire."

Then he had a parchment read, on which were written the sections on the authority that the people of Rome had conceded to Emperor Vespasian. In the first place, that Vespasian was empowered to make laws as he saw fit and alliances with whatever people or groups he wished, and that he could reduce or increase the garden of Rome,[14] that is to say of Italy. He could grant or retract territory. He could raise men to the status of dukes or kings and depose or demote them as

14. This odd assertion is due to a late medieval error of translation. Vespasian's powers were to increase Rome's *pomerium*, which Seibt describes as "the sacred, military, and political boundaries of classical Rome." He observes that medieval readers commonly misunderstood this as referring to the orchards just outside the city's walls and hence we see it rendered here in a term that denotes that. See, Seibt, *Anonimo romano*, 151. Seibt and Porta note that Dante makes this same error when he refers to the garden of the emperor in *Purgatory* VI.105. On these interpretations of the *pomerium*, see Marta Sordi, "Cola di Rienzo e le clausole mancanti della 'lex de imperio Vespasiani'," in *Studi in onore di Edoardo Volterra* 2. Università degli Studi (Roma), Facoltà di Giurisprudenza, ed. (Milan: A. Giuffrè, 1971), 303–11; and Anna Modigliani, "*Lo ogliardino de Roma*: Il progetto italiano di Cola di Rienzo," *Roma nel Rinascimento* (2014): 241–52.

# ✳ CHAPTER EIGHTEEN

well. Also, he could unmake and remake cities, block up the rivers and redirect them elsewhere, and impose or cancel taxes at will. All these things the people of Rome conceded to Emperor Vespasian in that agreement, which had also been conceded to Tiberius Caesar.

Once these sections of the parchment had been read, he said, "My Lords, such was the majesty of the Roman people, that they conferred authority to the emperor. Now we have lost that authority." Then he stepped forward and said, "Romans, you have no peace. Your lands are not cultivated. Knowing full well that the Jubilee is coming, you have not set aside food or provisions, so that the people who come to the Jubilee will find the cupboard bare and carry off the stones of Rome due to their mad hunger. Even the stones will not be enough for such a multitude." Then he concluded, saying, "I beseech you to make peace among yourselves."

After this speech he said, "Lords, I know that many people mock me for the things I say and do. And why? Due to envy. But I thank God that three things consume themselves. The first is luxury, the second fire, and the third envy." His sermon complete, he descended and was praised enthusiastically by everyone.

IN THOSE DAYS he attended meals with the lords of Rome, with Giovanni Colonna. The barons would make fun of his speeches. They would make him stand up and force him to speak. He said, "I will be a great lord, or an emperor. I will prosecute all these barons. That one I will hang, and that one I will behead." He passed judgment on them all. At this the barons would burst out laughing.

AFTER THESE EVENTS, he predicted his own ascendancy, the state of the city, and his generous government in the following way. He had painted on the wall of Sant'Angelo in Pescheria, a place known to all the world,¹⁵ an image of the following sort. In the left corner burned

---

15. Sant'Angelo in Pescheria is a church in *rione* Sant'Angelo, near the theater of Marcellus and standing on the site of the Portica of Octavia. It was an important church and the site of Rome's great fish market, from whence it took its name. It was also a favorite church of the Colonna. See Isa Lori Sanfillipo, "Un 'luoco famoso' nel medioevo, una chiesa oggi poco nota: Notizie

a brilliant fire, the smoke and flame of which went up to the heavens. In this fire stood many people and kings, of whom some seemed half alive and others dead. Also in the flames stood an aged woman, and due to the great heat the two thirds of this old woman were blackened while one third remained unharmed. On the right side, in the other corner, there was a church with a tall bell tower, out of which came an angel, armed and dressed in white. His cape was of scarlet vermillion. In his hand he had a naked sword. With his left hand he took the hand of the old woman, in order to free her from danger. At the peak of the bell tower stood Saint Peter and Saint Paul, as if they were coming down from heaven, and they said, "Angel, Angel, help our housekeeper." Then there were many falcons depicted, falling from heaven into the midst of the roaring flames as if they were dead. In the highest heaven there was a white dove, which held in its beak a myrtle crown, which it gave to a little sparrow as it passed, and then cast the falcons from heaven. This little sparrow carried the crown and placed it on the head of the old woman. Below these figures was written, "Behold the time of great justice, which you await in silence."[16] The people who streamed into Sant'Angelo gazed at these figures. Many said that they were vain and laughed. Others said, "It will take more than pictures to set Rome straight." Some said, "This is a great thing, of great significance."[17]

He also predicted his rise in this way. He wrote a message and fixed it to the door of San Giorgio della Chiavica.[18] The message read as follows: "In a short while the Romans will return to their ancient *buono stato*."[19]

---

extravaganti su S. Angelo in Pescheria (VI–XX secolo)," *Archivio della Società Romana di Storia Patria* 117 (1994): 231–68; and Romano, "L'immagine," 253 n.64.

16. Porta calls our attention to the Book of Ecclesiasticus (or Sirach) 20:7, which says: "A wise man stays silent until the time is right."

17. For interpretations of this painting, see Musto, *Apocalypse in Rome*, 126–29; Musto, *Writing Southern Italy*, 171–78.

18. That is, San Giorgio in Velabro, in *rione* Ripa.

19. Cola's phrase, *buono stato*, might be translated as "good state," but its precise meaning was somewhat ambiguous, implying both a general status and perhaps also a political sense. Since this phrase is consistently used to characterize Cola's program of political reform, I have followed Musto in leaving it in the original. See also p. 187 n. 8 above.

※ CHAPTER EIGHTEEN

The message was put up on the first day of Lent, on the gate of San Giorgio della Chiavica.[20]

※

AFTER THIS he gathered together many Roman *popolani*, good and wise men. There were among them as well knights and those of good lineage, many wise and wealthy merchants.[21] He heard their counsel and discussed with them the state of the city. Finally, he assembled these good, competent people on the Aventine Hill, in a secret place. There he explained his plans for bringing about this *buono stato*. He rose to his feet among them and, weeping, recited the wretchedness, servitude, and danger into which the city of Rome had fallen. He also described the peaceful, lordly state the Romans had once had. He described the loyal subordination of the surrounding lands, which was now lost. He wept as he said these things, and he caused the people there to weep brokenheartedly. Then he concluded, saying that they had to work for peace and justice, beginning by hiring soldiers.[22]

Then he said, "Have no concern about money, for the Camera of Rome has inestimable sources of income. First, the hearth tax amounts

---

20. This church was one of the stations to which people came during Lenten pilgrimages. Cola had placed his message there knowing that it would be seen by many.

21. I have rendered *"Romani populari"* as Roman *popolani* because the phrase refers not merely to "people" but to the *popolo*, a term used to describe the non-noble political class, usually associated with guildsmen and the like, throughout communal Italy. The descriptors "good" and "wise" (*discreti*) are also telling. Both are terms used to describe the communal elite, with the latter most commonly used to refer to notaries and the like in Roman sources. Amanda Collins has argued that these terms refer to specific subsections of the Roman political class. See, Collins, *Greater than Emperor*, pp. 173–74, 182, 189–97. The classic article on social groups remains Massimo Miglio, "Gruppi sociali e azione politica nella Roma di Cola di Rienzo," *Studi Romani* 23.4 (1975): 443–61.

22. The text reads, *"commenzanno con sollanieri."* Wright renders this as "and comforted them" but Porta suggests that "sollanieri" should be understood to mean mercenary troops. Given that his next words are about how to finance things, I believe the latter to be more accurate, though it is unclear whether or not Cola or the commune were using mercenaries at this point.

to four [...] per fire, from the Ponte di Ceperano up to the Ponte della Paglia.[23] It amounts to 100,000 florins. *Item*, from the salt tax comes 100,000 florins. From the ports and fortresses of Rome come 100,000 florins. And from the livestock tax and from criminal fines come 100,000 florins."[24] Then he said, "We can begin, for now, with 4,000 florins, which the pope has provided, as his vicar knows." Thereupon, he said, "My Lords, do not believe that this is without the license and support of the pope, for many tyrants are violently laying their hands on the property of the church." With these words he sparked the spirits of those gathered together. He said many other things too, causing them to weep. Then he laid out his plans for achieving the *buono stato*, and to this end he bound them all with written oaths.

THIS DONE, the city of Rome was in great danger. It had no leaders. Each day they fought one another. Each robbed the other. When the opportunity presented itself, virgins were raped. No compensation was offered. Little girls were assaulted and dishonored. Wives were snatched from their husbands' beds. Laborers, when they went out to work, were robbed. Where? At the very gates of Rome. The pilgrims, who came for the good of their souls to the holy churches, were not protected but rather killed and robbed. The priests too partook in such evils. All was lechery. All was wickedness. There was no justice, no limit. No recourse remained. Everyone was dying. He who wielded a

---

23. The precise sum is left unclear in the original text, as Porta indicates. Wright suggests a tax of four *soldi*, which is a reasonable guess. The zone described here is large and is the medieval legal definition of the District of Rome. Ceprano lies southeast of Rome, between Frosinone and Cassino. The Paglia is a river that joins up with the Tiber far to the north, not far from Orvieto. See Carola M. Small, "The District of Rome in the Early Fourteenth Century, 1300 to 1347," *Canadian Journal of History/Annales Canadiennes d'Histoire* 16 (1981): 193–213.

24. Porta points out that either Cola or the Anonimo was exaggerating all these sums, which seem at least three times too high. He points out that Cola estimates the salt tax at thirty thousand in one of his surviving letters, which seems to indicate that the exaggeration was the Anonimo's. This latter estimate is also more likely, given the kinds of people Cola was speaking too, merchants and other savvy operators who probably had a good sense of their city's finances.

# ※ CHAPTER EIGHTEEN

sword decided what was right. There was no security except that each looked to his own defense among his relatives and friends.[25]

※

THE NOBLES AND THE BARONS were not present in Rome. Messer Stefano Colonna had gone with the militia to Corneto for grain. It was the end of the month of April. Then Cola di Rienzo decreed, with the sounding of horns, that every man should come unarmed to the *buono stato* at the sounding of the bell. The next day, over the course of the night, he heard thirty masses of the Holy Spirit in the church of Sant'Angelo in Pescheria. Then, at the hour of terce,[26] he came out of said church, fully armed but with his head bare. He came out openly and well. Many young boys followed after him shouting. Before him he had three banners carried by three good men from among his fellow oath-takers. The first banner was huge and red, with letters of gold, on which a figure representing Rome sat between two lions, holding in her hands the world and a palm leaf. This was the banner of Liberty. Cola Vallati, a man skilled in eloquence, carried it.[27] The second was white, on which stood Saint Paul with a sword in his hand and wearing the crown of Justice. This was carried by Stefanello, called Magnacuccia, a notary.[28] On

---

25. The Anonimo is certainly describing the corrupt condition of Rome, but his description also contains many stock tropes, ones that appear for example in Bartolo da Sassoferrato's *Treatise on City Government*; visually in Ambrogio Lorenzetti's frescos of *Good and Bad Government* in Siena; and in Cola di Rienzos own letters (e.g., Letter 7, May 24, 1347 to Viterbo).

26. 9:00 AM.

27. The Vallati were a prominent family in *rione* Sant'Angelo and had strong ties to the church, in which they had a private chapel and among the canons of which some of their family were included. The Anonimo calls Cola Vallati a *"buono dicitore,"* which indicates his skill in the *ars dictaminis*, or art of formal public writing. See Ronald G. Witt, "Medieval 'Ars Dictaminis' and the Beginnings of Humanism: A New Construction of the Problem," *Renaissance Quarterly* 35.1 (1982): 1–35.

28. Stefanello's status as a notary marks him as educated and of a type with Cola Vallati, but the fact that he was known by a nickname rather than bearing any kind of family name, suggests a slightly lower, if still respectable, social status. The fact that his nickname means "great bitch" doesn't detract from

the third Saint Peter was depicted, holding the keys of Concord and Peace.[29] He also carried another banner, which depicted the knight Saint George. Because this banner was old it was carried in a casing hanging on a raised spear.

Then Cola di Rienzo took heart, though he was not without fear, and proceeded alongside the papal vicar, ascending to the palace of the Campidoglio, in the year of our Lord, 1347. He had guarding him a force of one hundred armed men. With a great multitude gathered together, he ascended to the council chamber, where he spoke and delivered a beautiful speech about the wretchedness and servitude of the Roman people. Then he said that for the love of the pope and the salvation of the Roman people he was placing himself in danger. Then he had a charter read, in which the ordinances of the *buono stato* were set out. Conte, the son of Cecco Mancino, read them briefly.[30] Its sections were as follows:

First, that if any one committed murder, he would be executed, with no exceptions.

Second, that court cases should not be prolonged but rather brought to a close within fifteen days.

Third, that no house in Rome should be torn down for any reason, but rather handed over to the communal government.

Fourth, that in each *rione* of Rome one hundred infantry and twenty-five knights should be provided to serve in the communal army, and each was to be equipped with a shield worth five silver carlini and provided with a suitable stipend.

Fifth, that the Roman Camera, that of the communal government, should provide aid to orphans and widows.

Sixth, that in the Roman marshes and tidal pools, and on the Roman coastline, a ship shall be continuously stationed to protect merchants.

---

this, as Italian political elites had, for centuries, taken on shocking nicknames as a kind of bravado. See Wickham, *Sleepwalking into a New World*, 51.

29. All of these banners emphasized the traditional communal values of the Italian *popolo*, focused on liberty, justice, and peace. The conceptual pairing of peace and concord was also standard. See Jansen, *Peace and Penance*, 61–86.

30. Porta observes that Cecco was both a fellow notary and Cola's father-in-law.

Seventh, that all incomes from the hearth tax, the salt tax, the tolls from ports and gates, and from criminal fines shall be spent, if necessary, to maintain the *buono stato*.

Eighth, that the defense of Roman citadels, bridges, gates, and fortresses shall not be entrusted to any baron, except by the Rector of the People.

Ninth, that no noble shall be permitted to have any fortifications.

Tenth, that the barons must keep the roadways secure and should not receive robbers or other evil-doers, and that they should provide food supplies under a penalty of one thousand silver marks.[31]

Eleventh, that the wealth of the commune should be used to aid the monasteries.

Twelfth, that in every *rione* of Rome there should be a granary from which grain can be gotten when necessary.

Thirteenth, that should any Roman be killed in service to the commune, there should be payment of one hundred lire worth of provisions for a foot soldier and one hundred florins for a knight.

Fourteenth, that the cities and lands within the Roman district should be under the authority of the Roman people.

Fifteenth, that should someone bring charges, and then fail to prove those charges, they should sustain the penalty that would have been imposed on the accused, either in their person or their wealth.

Many other things were written there, which were very pleasing to the people, so that everyone raised their voices in happiness to demand that Cola should govern, together with the vicar of the pope. Furthermore, they conferred on him the power to punish, execute, or pardon, to grant offices, to make laws and forge alliances, and to determine boundaries. They also granted him absolute

---

31. This somewhat opaque ruling was part of an ongoing effort to ensure that grain and other foodstuffs produced in the Roman countryside would come to Rome, rather than being hoarded to drive up prices or sold outside Roman territory. The Roman commune generally struggled to control its own grain producing region. See Luciano Palermo, *Mercati del grano a Roma tra Medioevo e Rinascimento* (Rome: Il Centro di Ricerca, 1990), 55–60, 137–42.

authority anywhere that the jurisdiction of the Roman people applied.³²

ONCE NEWS OF THE EVENTS that had transpired in Rome reached the ears of Messer Stefano Colonna, who was at that time accompanying the militia in Corneto in order to obtain grain, he immediately set out with a small company and rode to Rome without delay. Arriving in the piazza of San Marcello, he declared that these things did not please him.³³ The next day, in the morning, Cola di Rienzo sent an edict to Messer Stefano commanding him to depart from Rome. Messer Stefano seized the message and tore it into a thousand pieces, saying, "If this lunatic makes me any angrier, I will have him thrown from a window in the Campidoglio!" When Cola di Rienzo learned of this, he immediately had the alarm bell rung.³⁴ The entirety of the enraged Roman people was summoned. Seeing that he was in great danger, Messer Stefano leapt onto his horse. Alone except for a single foot soldier, he fled from Rome. At great risk to himself, he paused briefly in San Lorenzo fuori le Mura to eat a little bread. Then the old man headed to Palestrina.³⁵ There, in the company of his son and his nephew, he bemoaned his situation.

THEN COLA DI RIENZO issued commands that all the barons of Rome should leave the city and go to their own castles, which was rapidly achieved. The next day control of all the bridges in the territory surrounding Rome was handed over to him. Following that, Cola di Rienzo named his officials. Then he had this man captured followed

---

32. The text specifies that Cola was granted *"mero e libero imperio,"* which is the language of sovereignty. *Merum imperium* was the kind of absolute authority, even over life and death, that was wielded by emperors or autonomous city governments. See Francesco Maiolo, *Medieval Sovereignty: Marsilius of Padua and Bartolus of Saxoferrato* (Delft: Eburon Publishers, 2008), 98, 153–56.

33. This piazza lay to the north of the Campidoglio, near the center of Colonna power in the city.

34. On the use of bells and other sonic cues, again, see Atkinson, *Noisy Renaissance.*

35. The fortress of Palestrina was the primary stronghold of the Colonna.

by that one. This one he hung. That one he had beheaded without mercy. He judged all the wicked men most harshly. Then he spoke to the people, and in that public address he caused to be confirmed and formalized all the things that had been done, and he asked the people to declare that he and the vicar of the pope were now to be called the Tribunes of the People and Liberators.

At this, the barons began to urge a conspiracy against the tribune and the *buono stato*; but they could not agree, and nothing came of it.[36] When Cola di Rienzo understood that the barons were failing to conspire against him due to the discord among them, he summoned them to appear before them and sent them an edict. The first to appear due to this command was Stefano Colonna, son of Messer Stefano. He entered the palace with a few men. He saw that justice was served to all there. Many of the *popolo* were there on the Campidoglio. He was afraid and much astonished by the enormous crowd. The tribune appeared armed before him and compelled him to swear on the body of Christ and on the Gospel that he would not act against the tribune or the Romans, that he would see to the provision of foodstuffs, that he would keep the roads secure, that he would not receive thieves or people of bad character, and that he would look after orphans and minors, would not defraud the commune of what belonged to it, and would appear, armed or unarmed as requested, whenever the tribune summoned him. Once Stefano had been given permission to go, Raynaldo Orsini came, then Giovanni Colonna, then Giordano [Orsini], then Messer Stefano [Colonna]. Let us be plain: all the barons fearfully swore obedience to the *buono stato*, and they pledged themselves, their castles, and their vassals to aid the city. Francesco Savelli was Cola's own lord, but he came and swore his obedience all the same.[37] Cola

---

36. The text states that the conspiracy failed to come together because the barons *"non fuoro in concordia."* This term, "concord," may indicate not only a failure to agree but a failure to set aside the violent enmities that marked baronial relations with one another.

37. It is possible that this refers to formal feudal ties of some kind between Cola and the Savelli, but it is more likely that the relationship being evoked here is that any resident of a Roman neighborhood would likely have had to the baronial family that dominated the area, as the Savelli did Cola's *rione*.

carried out his project cruelly, without mercy, even having a monk of Sant'Anastasio, who was an infamous fellow, beheaded.[38]

❋

THE OUTER CLOTHES of the tribune were of a blazing scarlet. His face and aspect were fearsome. He gave formal judgements in response to so many people that it was amazing that he was able to keep them all straight. After a few days the judges of the city came and swore their faith and offered themselves to the service of the *buono stato*. Then the notaries came and did the same. Then the merchants came. Simply put, to put their minds at ease, each one came unarmed and swore to the *buono stato* of the commune. And so these things began to take hold, and armed conflicts decreased.

After this, Cola established the House of Justice and Peace, placing there the banner of Saint Paul, on which the naked sword and the palm of victory were depicted. He installed in it the most just of the *popolo*, those who were tasked with keeping the peace, the good men, the peacemakers. Here is how they did things there. Two enemies would come and give assurances that they wanted to make peace. Then they would agree that each might do to the other what had been done to them, according to the nature of the injury. Then they exchanged a kiss on the mouth, and the one offended offered unequivocal peace. For example, a man might have blinded another in one eye. He would come and be led to the steps of the Campidoglio. There he knelt. Then the one who had been deprived of his eye came. The evildoer would weep and pray to God that he might pardon him. Then he would raise up his face so that, should he so wish, his enemy my pluck out his eye. But the offended man would not blind him, being moved by pity, but would instead forgive him his injuries.[39]

38. This person has not been identified.

39. It is possible, but unlikely, that Cola invented this process from whole cloth. Rome's residents availed themselves of a similar process for decades following Cola's downfall. It is most likely that Cola was formalizing a process already familiar to the residents of Rome, weaving an existing social practice into the fabric of his *buono stato*. See James A. Palmer, "Piety and Social Distinction in Late Medieval Roman Peacemaking," *Speculum* 89.4 (2014): 974–1004; idem, *The Virtues of Economy*, 167–95; and Jansen, *Peace and Penance*.

## ✳ CHAPTER EIGHTEEN

Civil cases were decided expeditiously. In those days terrible fear afflicted the hearts of thieves, murderers, evildoers, adulterers, and every person of bad repute. Anyone who was publicly accused slipped subtly out of the city, fleeing in secret. To bad people it seemed that they might be snatched out of their homes and threatened with execution. Wicked folk therefore sought refuge so far away that they left the region of Rome entirely. They had no hope of aid from anyone. They left their homes, their fields, their vineyards, their wives, and their children. The forests began to rejoice, for there were no bandits to be found within them. Oxen began to plow the fields. Pilgrims began to make the circuit of the sanctuaries. Merchants began to see to their business affairs and travels.

DURING THIS PERIOD a monster was born in Rome. In the neighborhood of Camigliano an infant was born dead from a woman of low status. It had two heads, four hands, and four feet, as if there were two babes joined at the breast. But one was larger than the other, and it seemed as if the smaller of the two had overtaken the larger, at which people marveled not a little.[40]

DURING THE SAME TIME, fear and terror assailed tyrants. Good people, as if liberated from servitude, rejoiced. The tribune held a general council and wrote most eloquent letters to all the cities and communities of Tuscany, Lombardy, the Campagna, Romagna, and Maremma; and to the doge of Venice; to Messer Lucchino, the tyrant of Milan; the marquises of Ferrara; the holy father Pope Clement; Lewis, the duke of Bavaria (who had been elected emperor, as I said earlier); and to the rulers of Naples. In these letters he adorned his name with a magnificent title in the following way: "Nicola the stern and merciful; tribune of liberty, peace, and justice; and illustrious liberator of the holy Roman republic." In these letters he declared that the *buono stato*, peaceful and just, had begun. He declared that

---

40. The Anonimo might be reporting an actual occurrence, or he might be using the story as a metaphor for the close bonds between the barons (the larger), and the *popolo* (the smaller), and the new primacy of the "smaller." Contemporaries like Bartolo da Sassoferrato had specifically labelled Rome's political situation as "monstrous."

the roads to Rome, previously so perilous, were now safe. Then he requested that they all send representatives with the authority to negotiate at a Roman synod on matters pertaining to the *buono stato*.[41] Then he comforted them and told them to rejoice and give thanks and praise to God for his great beneficence. The curriers who carried his letters carried in their hands a silver-painted wooden rod. They carried no arms. The number of curriers swelled, so that there was a great many of them, for they were received graciously and with great honor by every man. They received fine gifts.

One Florentine currier in particular was sent to the pope in Avignon, and to the cardinal, Messer Giovanni Colonna. He bore a wooden staff gilt with fine silver and decorated with the arms of the Roman people, those of the pope, and those of the tribune, which was worth thirty florins. Upon his return, the currier said, "I bore this rod openly through forests and on the road. Thousands of people knelt before it and kissed it with tears of joy because the roads had been made safe, liberated from highwaymen."

The tribune also had many scribes and masters of the art of letter writing, who never ceased writing letters both day and night.[42] Many were among the most famous in all the Roman lands. Then a great many buffoons and courtly knights began to be drawn to him, as well as musicians and singers. Vernacular songs and written verses about his deeds were produced.[43]

IN THOSE DAYS there was a powerful young noble by the name of Martino del Porto, nephew of the cardinal of Ceccano and of the cardinal Messer Iacovo Gaietano. In days past he had been senator,

---

41. These letters have been preserved and edited in both Burdach and Piur, *Die Briefwechsel;* and in a partial edition in *Epistolario di Cola di Rienzo*, Annibale Gabrielli, ed. Istituto storico italiano per il medio evo, Fonti per la storia d'Italia 6 (Rome: Forzani e Compagnia, 1890).

42. I've rendered the Anonimo's *"dittatori"* as "masters of letter writing" because the reference is to those skilled in *ars dictaminis*, the art of formal letter writing. Rienzo's chancellory, staffed by notaries, was typical of Italian communal governments.

43. Aside from the chivalric legend of Giannino di Guccio, purported son of Louis X of France and Cola's ally, none of this literature appears to have survived.

and his ancestors had many times enjoyed the dignity of that office. I made mention of this Martino earlier, regarding the galley that ran aground.[44] He was lord of the castle of Porto. He lived a life of tyranny. He besmirched his nobility with tyrannous deeds and theft. He took as his wife a most noble woman, Madonna Mascia delli Alberteschi, who was widowed and extremely beautiful. He lingered with this new wife of his for about a month, because he was no good at self-discipline. He was also terrible at temperance when it came excessive eating. He fell into dire and incurable ill health. Doctors refer to it as dropsy.[45] His belly was full of water. He looked like a wine cask. His legs were swollen, his neck soft, and his face drawn. He suffered a terrible thirst. He was shaped like a lute. He stayed quietly shut inside his house and had himself attended by doctors. Ostensibly as a security measure, Cola had this man of such nobility seized in his home, taken from the arms of his wife in his palace beside the river in the Ripa Armea, and taken to the Campidoglio.[46]

Once the robber baron had been conducted to the Campidoglio it was the hour of nones.[47] Cola did not delay. The alarm bell was sounded. The people were gathered. Martino was stripped of his frilly cape. With his hands bound behind his back, he was made to kneel on the stairs alongside the lion, in the usual place.[48] There he heard his death sentence. He was compelled to hastily make a full confession to a priest. He was condemned to the gallows because he had pillaged the galley that ran aground.[49] This magnificent man was

44. That is, in chapter 16, p. 180.
45. On the Anonimo's medical knowledge, see above, Introduction, pp. 10–11.
46. Porta notes that the "Ripa Armea" corresponds to the Ripa Romea, across the river in Trastevere.
47. Approximately 3:00 PM.
48. This is a reference to an ancient statue of a lion attacking a horse, which used to stand alongside the stairs and is now preserved in the Capitoline Museums. It was the traditional Roman site for executions.
49. That is, he suffered the humiliating execution of a common criminal, not of a nobleman, who would most often be executed by beheading. Traitors would be drawn and quartered, heretics burned. For a survey, with bibliography, see Andrea Zorzi, "Justice," in *The Italian Renaissance State,* Andrea

escorted to the gallows and hung on the terrace of the Campidoglio. His wife was able to see him from her distant balcony. For one night and two days he hung from the gallows, neither his nobility nor his Orsini relatives could help him.

In this way did Cola rule Rome and condemn many to similar punishment. This thing struck fear in the hearts of the powerful, who knew their own iniquitous deeds. Some wept piteously. Others trembled. So justice began to come into full force. Word of the thing terrified the magnificent so much that they could hardly trust themselves. And so the streets were open. Travelers went to and fro freely both night and day. No one dared carry arms. No one did injury to anyone else. A lord did not dare lay hands on his servant. The tribune was vigilant in all things. Out of happiness over such wonderful deeds some wept with joy and prayed that God would fortify Cola's heart and mind in his undertaking. The tribune's intention was, firstly, to exterminate the tyrants and confound them to such an extent that they could never more make trouble. The teamsters who transported shipments left their merchandise parked on the public streets and returned to find them safe and sound.

A fellow by the name of Tortora, one of the tribune's couriers, was branded on the throat for having taken money without permission when he was sent to the rulers of Naples. Word of a man of such virtue spread throughout the world. All Christendom was moved as if waking from slumber. There was a Bolognese fellow who was one of the slaves of the sultan of Babylonia.[50] As soon as he was able to free himself, he hastened to Rome. This man said that word had come to the great Racham[51] that a man of great justice had arisen in Rome, a man of the people, to which he responded, saying uncertainly, "Muhammad and holy Elinason help Jerusalem, by which he meant the land of the Saracens.

---

Gamberini and Isabella Lazzarini, ed. (Cambridge: Cambridge University Press, 2012), 490–514, 597–99.

50. That is, the sultan of Egypt, "Babylon" being the medieval name for Cairo.

51. The precise meaning here is not certain. The word appears to be the Anonimo's attempt to render an honorific title.

※ CHAPTER EIGHTEEN

IN THE DAYS after Martino was hung came the feast of Saint John in June.[52] All of Rome went to San Giovanni [in Laterano] in the morning. Cola wished to go to the feast like everyone else. His going was as follows. He rode with a large group of knights. He was mounted on a white destrier. He was clad in white silk, lined with sendal and embellished with gold thread. His aspect was strikingly beautiful and terrible. Behind his horse came one hundred sworn infantry men from *rione* Regola. Over his head flew his banner.

On another day he rode to St. Peter's in the afternoon. Men and women came to see him. His beautiful cavalcade was arranged like this. First came a militia of armed men on horseback, beautifully adorned, who would eventually take the field against the Prefect.[53] After these came the ranks of officials, judges, notaries, chamberlains, chancellors, the senatorial scribes, and all the other officials, peacemakers, and syndics.[54] Then came four marshals with their usual steeds. After this came Ianni de Allo, who carried a silver gilded cup in his hand with an offering like that made by the senator.[55] After this came the cavalry. After them came the trumpeters, who blew silver horns as they went. Playing silver cymbals, they made lovely honorable music. Then came the criers. All these people passed by in silence. After them came a single man — it was Buccio di Iubileo — who bore in his hand a naked sword as a symbol of justice. After him came a man who for the entire procession was

52. June 24.

53. While the office of the prefect of Rome was ancient, it was by this time a title associated with a single family, the di Vico. For more on Giovanni and Cola's conflict, see below. The militia referred to here is not specifically named but may correspond to the Felix Societas Pavesatorum et Balistrariorum, though these would not usually be mounted. See Jean Claude Maire-Vigueur, "La Felice Societas dei Balestrieri e dei Pavesati a Roma: Una società popolare e i suoi ufficiali," in *Scritti per Isa: Raccolta di studi offerti a Isa Lori Sanfilippo*, Antonella Mazzon and Isa Lori Sanfilippo, ed. (Rome: Istituto storico italiano per Medio Evo, 2008), 577–606.

54. These are mostly standard officials and legal professionals, with the exception of Cola's peacemakers and the special scribes of the senate.

55. Customarily, the senator would be the head executive official of Rome. We see here that Cola is appropriating some of the ceremonial behaviors of the office for himself.

203

tossing out money in the imperial manner. His name was Liello Migliaro. He had two people, one on each side, who bore the money sack. After them came the tribune himself. He was mounted on a great destrier, dressed in silk, specifically in velvet that was half green and half yellow. In his right hand he held a rod of shining polished steel. On its tip was an apple gilded in silver and above that stood a golden cross. On one side were etched letters that read: "*Deus*" and on the other "*Spiritus Sanctus*." Immediately after the tribune came Cecco de Alesso, who carried a standard in a royal manner. The standard had a field of white, in the midst of which there was a golden sun surrounded by silver stars. Atop the standard was a white dove of silver, that carried in its beak an olive crown. On his right and on his left he was accompanied by fifty vassals from Vitorchiano, the Faithful, with pikes in hand.[56] They looked like bears with their garb and their arms. After them came a large company of unarmed people: the rich, the powerful, councilors, companions, and many honorable people. With such triumph and such glory did Cola cross the Ponte San Pietro as everyone waved. The gates and the barricades had been cast down and the streets were open and clear. Once he arrived at the stairs of St. Peter's, the canons of St. Peter's came with all the clergy to meet him, formally attired in white surplice, bearing a cross and incense. They came to the stairs singing *Veni Creator Spiritus* and received him there with great happiness. Kneeling before the altar, he made his offering. The aforementioned clergy recommended the goods of St. Peter's to his care.[57]

The next day Cola gave an audience for widows, orphans, and the poor. He had two senatorial scribes seized and publicly denounced as forgers, punishing them with huge fines of 1,000 lire each. One

---

56. As both Porta and Wright have noted, for over a century the men of Vitorchiano had a special relationship with Rome and were known as the Faithful *(fideli)*. So here too Cola was emphasizing continuities with the traditional Roman regime, despite his various novelties.

57. On the canons of St. Peter's, their wealth, and their economic impact on the city of Rome, see Alexis Gauvain, "Romani e forestieri nelle case di San Pietro in Vaticano nel secondo Quattrocento," in Ait and Esposito, *Vivere la città*, 55–69.

was named Tommaso Fortifocca and the other Poncelletto della Cammora.⁵⁸ These two men were very powerful and popular.

❋

AT FIRST Cola led a very temperate life. Then his vices began to multiply: feasts, banquets, and overindulgence in diverse foods, wines, and confections. Then he had the palace of the Campidoglio surrounded with a palisade within the columns and enclosed in wood. He commanded that all the palisades of the barons' fortifications in Rome should be torn down, and it was done. He also commanded that those beams, planks, and wood should be transported to the Campidoglio at the barons' expense, and it was done. In the house of Messer Stefano Colonna he seized thieves, whom he hung. Then he condemned each person who had held the office of senator to a fine of one hundred florins, for he needed this to refurbish the palace of the Campidoglio. He took one hundred florins from each baron, but the palace was not refurbished, though work was begun. He had Pietro di Agapito arrested, who had been senator that same year, and he had him taken on foot to court by his marshals, as if he were a thief.⁵⁹ Then the embassies of various lands and nobles began to arrive. All of Tuscany had already sent embassies.

Cola organized the militia of Rome's knights in the following way. For each *rione* of Rome he established thirty foot and thirty knights, and he gave them a wage. Each knight was to have a destrier and a palfrey, gear for his horses, and fancy new arms. They looked just like barons. He also saw to it that the infantry were similarly adorned, and he gave them banners. He marked the banners according to the sign of each *rione*. He paid them a wage too. He commanded them to present themselves at the sounding of the bell and made them swear their fidelity. There were 1,300 infantry and 360 knights, young men specially chosen, well-armed masters of warfare.

Once the tribune was armed with his newly made militia, he began to make preparations to go to war with more powerful people. He sent his edict around and summoned all the powerful

58. Specifically, the Anonimo says Cola "mitered" (*mitrare*) these men, i.e., had them crowned with caps labeled with the nature of their crime. Again, this is was a standard practice in late medieval Italy.

59. Pietro di Agapito was a Colonna, the nephew of Stefano.

men within Roman territory. Essentially, he organized some of his servants and sent them to collect the hearth tax. They gathered in the ancient census of the people of Rome, and each day money came into Rome by this means, so that it was ever increasing, and it was a burden to count the payments of so many people. Soon enough the vassals of the barons agreed to pay one carlino for each hearth. The cities, lands, and communes that stood in lower Tuscany, the Campagna, and the Marittima all agreed to it. Astonishingly, the vassals of Antiochia paid. Once the edict had been sent to all the barons and cities thereabout, they sweetly obeyed, as I have said. To Rome, their mother and wife, they gave humble reverence.

Only Ianni da Vico, the prefect, tyrant of Viterbo, did not want to obey. He was summoned a thousand times and did not appear. Cola therefore passed a sentence against the prefect, and he was stripped of his dignity in a public assembly. Namely, Cola said that he was the murderer of his own brother, that he was engaged in factionalism, and that he would not hand over what was due to others, specifically the fortress of Respampano, and he was called by his name, Ianni de Vico.[60] Then Cola directed his army against the man. He made the young Cola Orsini, the lord of Castel Sant'Angelo, captain and named as his advisor Giordano Orsini.[61] Many allies were present in the army as well.

They set up camp near the city of Vetralla and besieged it for sixty days. They rode through the fields, burning and pillaging, right up to Viterbo. How they terrified the Viterbesi! Vetralla was surrendered willingly by its inhabitants. There was a strong fortress there. The fortress was not surrendered. Desiring to take it by force, the Romans built trebuchets and mangonels. They bombarded it with many stones. Then they made a wooden ram and brought it to the gate of the fortress. Night came. The people inside the fortress mixed sulphur, pitch, and oil; wood, turpentine, and other things,

60. That is, he was not called by his titles, of which he had been deprived. The fortress of Respampano, which was near Viterbo, had previously been a possession of the Roman commune.

61. These two were members of the baronial Orsini family. For that family, see Franca Allegrezza, *Organizzazione del potere e dinamiche familiari: Gli Orsini dal Duecento agli inizi del Quattrocento* (Rome: Istituto storico per il Medioevo, 1998).

## CHAPTER EIGHTEEN

and hurled this mixture down over the device. The ram was burned in the night. The next day only ashes were found.

The army included people from Corneto, with their lord Manfred. It included the might of the Perugians, of Todi, of Narni, and of many Roman barons. It was a most admirable army, powerful and noble. Once the Romans had laid waste to every field and had burned the farmland and flax right up to Viterbo, it was midsummer in July, when the heat becomes unbearable. At that point, the tribune decided to join the host personally and make a show of strength with knights and foot soldiers and destroy Viterbo's vineyards. When the prefect heard of this, he began immediately to consider obedience.

At that time, there were certain barons in the district that were being held on the Campidoglio, namely Stefano Colonna and Messer Giordano de Marino. The prefect first sent ambassadors there. Then he came personally to Rome. It was the hour of nones, at mid-day. He arrived on the Campidoglio and submitted to the power of the tribune. In his company were sixty men. Then the gates of the Campidoglio were sealed and with the ringing of the bell all the men and women of Rome were summoned. The tribune gave a speech, in which he said that Ianni de Vico wished to be obedient to the people of Rome. Then he reinvested him with the prefecture and said that he had turned over the property of the people. So it was done, for before the prefect left Rome, and before the army departed from Vetralla, the fortress of Respampano was handed over to the agents and syndics of Rome. Only then was the prefect released.

Now turn your ears to news of dreams. The night before the day of this accord, the tribune slumbered in his noble and triumphal bed. This was his first dream. As he slept, he began to cry out loudly in his sleep, saying, "Leave me be! Leave me be!"

Upon hearing this, the chamber servants rushed in and said, "Lord, what has happened? Do you need something?"

Then the tribune awoke and spoke, saying, "It seemed that as I slept a white friar came to me and said, 'Take your fortress of Respampano. Behold, I give it to you.' And as he said this to me in the dream, he took me by the hand. Then I cried out."

This dream more or less predicted how things went. Fra Acuto was a good and holy person.[62] One of the Hospitallers of Assisi, he had established the Hospital of the Cross of Sta. Maria Rotunda that I mentioned earlier in connection to the renovation of the Ponte Milvio. He mediated the peace between the Romans and the prefect. He came the next day to the tribune with the news of the peace and said, "Take the fortress of Respampano. I give it to you." The tribune spoke to the people in a public address. The whole market was packed.[63] At the head of the street Fra Acuto appeared dressed in white, mounted on a donkey covered in white, crowned with an olive wreath, and with an olive branch in his hand. Many flocked to see him. The tribune saw him from far off and said to his chamber servants, "Look. Last night's dream." In the Roman army at Vetralla there were 1,000 mounted warriors and 6,000 infantry. The host returned crowned with olive branches.

Now I want to consider something else. One might ask whether the dream could have been true. To this I would respond and say that it is true that many dreams are empty things, many are diabolical delusions, but nevertheless many dreams do turn out to be true, as if inspired by God, especially in temperate people who are not dissipated by overindulgence or troubled by unusual food. Furthermore, in that time of night called dawn, when night gives way to day, the mind is purified and the spirits tempered. The blessed St. Gregory tells us this in his *Dialogue*.[64] Holy Gregory says that in

---

62. Fra Acuto was a member of the Hospitallers of Assisi. See, Musto, *Apocalypse in Rome*, 200; Collins, *Greater than Emperor*, 229–30. He was well respected, and his foundation continued to bear his name and be the object of Roman piety decades later. See Archivio Storico Capitolino, Sez. 1, 785/1 f. 118v-120r and 785/11 f. 20v-23r for testamentary bequests dating to 1382 and 1396, respectively.

63. This is probably the public space on the Campidoglio outside the Senate House and next to Sta. Maria in Aracoeli, which was the main Roman market, where assemblies occurred. On the Campidoglio market, see Claudia Bolgia, *Reclaiming the Roman Capitol: Santa Maria in Aracoeli from the Altar of Augustus to the Franciscans, c.500–1450* (New York: Routledge, 2017), 98–100, 355–56, and passim.

64. Gregory the Great, *Dialogues*, IV.48 admits the same ambiguity to which

his monastery there was a monk of good and holy life who was named Merulus.[65] This Merulus had among his virtues this one, that he never stopped reciting psalms, except when he was eating or sleeping. One day he fell ill. As he slept, the sick brother Merulus dreamed that a beautiful crown of various flowers descended from heaven and alighted upon his head. He told the other monks of this dream. Then he died. Because he understood his dream to be a positive sign, he died happy. Fourteen years later, another monk dug a grave for a dead man in the spot where Merulus had been entombed. Once it had been dug up a fragrance arose, the sweetest odor, as if there were in that place roses, violets, lilies, and other flowers. So Merulus' dream that a crown of flowers came down from heaven was really true, and those flowers still gave off their sweet aroma from the grave after fourteen years.

Brother Martin also mentions this in his chronicle.[66] He says that Emperor Marcian, who was in Constantinople, dreamed one night that the bow of Attila was broken in two parts. Marcian took this to mean that Attila was dead, and this was true. This Attila was a great king and tyrant. He had many archers. He conquered all of Pannonia and Bulgaria. He depopulated many cities, including Aquileia and others. He killed his brother Bleda and was defeated by the Franks, Burgundians, Saxons, and Italians. In the course of his defeat, the king of Burgundy died and 180,000 men were slain, so that blood ran like a river. The defeated King Attila therefore returned to his own land and unified the many people of Hungary, as well as the Dacians, and then reentered Italy. Among the first territories he

---

the Anonimo refers, suggesting six kinds of dreams: those caused by too much food or too little, by illusion, by a combination of illusion and one's own thoughts, by revelation, and by a combination of revelation and one's own thoughts. See A. Smeets, "The Dazzle of Dawn: Visions, Dreams, and Thoughts on Dreams by Gregory the Great," in *Dreams as Divine Communication in Christianity: From Hermas to Aquinas,* B.J. Koet, ed. (Leuven: Peeters, 2012), 157–78. My thanks to Eileen Gardiner for this reference.

65. Gregory the Great, *Dialogues,* IV.47.

66. This is a reference to the thirteenth-century *Chronicon pontificum et imperatorum* of Martin of Poland. See Martinus Oppaviensis, *Chronicon pontificium et imperatorum,* L. Weiland, ed. *Monumenta Germaniae Historica,* SS 22 (Berlin: MGH, 1872), 397–475, at 454.

entered was that of Aquileia, which he destroyed. The most holy pope, Leo, lived during this time. He entreated Attila to leave Italy, and so it happened.[67] Attila departed Italy and returned to his own land, dying in Pannonia. On the night of his death, Attila's bow appeared in the dream of Marcian, the emperor in Constantinople, in Greece, from which Marcian concluded that Attila was dead, as indeed he was.

Valerius Maximus also mentions this phenomenon when he tells of the dream of Cassius Parmensis, who had slain Julius Caesar and then fled from Rome.[68] Octavian and Antony pursued him like a mortal enemy. This Cassius once passed a night in a small fortress. As he lay in bed he saw in his dream a terrifying man whose face was obscured, who threatened him. His threats were in the Greek language. He woke from this dream twice. The third time he called for light and ordered his servants to stand guard over him. The next day he had the same dream again. The legions of Octavian and the army of Antony were upon him. Cassius was captured and beheaded.

The philosopher Aristotle speaks of these things, particularly in his book that is called *On Dreams and Vigils*, in the chapter on dream divination.[69] Aristotle and those who accept his theory say dreams can be true by nature. He demonstrates this skillfully in the following way. First, the philosopher lays out the difference between wakefulness and dreaming. To the waking mind, large

---

67. This refers to Pope Leo I, whose papacy ran from 440 to 461. He was believed to have negotiated Attila's departure from Italy.

68. Valerius Maximus, *Factorum ac dictorum memorabilium libri novem*, I.7.7.

69. This refers to Aristotle, *De Divinatione per Somnum*, 462b–464b. The Anonimo more or less correctly characterizes what Aristotle says about phlegm and the tendency of dreamers to magnify sensations (463a, 11–20), and Aristotle does suggest that dreams may be caused by movements of air akin to the rippling of water, as the Anonimo suggests. Furthermore, he says that said ripples of air are more powerful at night and that sleeping souls are more receptive to them (464a, 6–20). Many details given here, however, and even specific things like the example of the fisherman, are not found in Aristotle at all; but the Anonimo's familiarity with Aristotle's theories of psychology and bodily influence also point to his medical training. See Musto, *Writing Southern Italy*, 56–57 for a summary of current research.

movements appear small in the imagination but when dreaming, such movements and other small things appear large. So is happens that in one person a little sweet phlegm is distilled in the mouth and seems to them to taste of sugar, honey, and cinnamon. In another person choler collects, and it seems to them that they see arrows flying through the air, fire, flames, and raging storms. A wind blows over someone, or even just a light breeze, and it seems to them that mighty gusts are blowing. The reason for this is that during sleep all the spirits are collectively drawn into fantasy and imagination, whence they are more attuned to comprehension, as well as because being unified they operate more powerfully. During wakefulness the spirits are dispersed, the objects of their attention are many and various, and when a virtue is unified it is more powerful than when it is dispersed. We've already said that at night the spirits are more attentive and focused, so that even small things can move them.

Aristotle makes a second point. He says, "What we run on is air, without which one cannot live. Air is within us. Human speech flows from person to person because the air is directed from person to person. Air shifts and moves according to the movements of people as does the density of forms reflected in a mirror." He gives another example: "Someone throws a stone into a lake. The stone moves the water. The water, moved in one part, moves the proximate parts in a circular form, and the strength of the throw determines how many circles it makes. The fisherman stands with his hook, fishing. He does not see the man throw the stone, but he sees the circles that the stone makes. He knows that someone is interfering with his ability to catch fish. He stirs himself and goes to ask the fellow not to throw any more rocks." In this way, Aristotle says, the human operation of speech stirs the air. The air moves from place to place and reaches the human senses and those of other animals, just as it happens that rotten meat and dead bodies exude corrupt vapors into the air and are sensed by wolves and vultures, whence it is written that a vulture will travel five hundred miles to a dead body. This happens for no other reason than the changes in the air that move from body to body. Now Aristotle would have it that not only do the movements of objects shift the air but so too do people's thoughts, so that, if one person should wish to kill another, the spirits within him become inflamed. These focused spirits change the air according to the quality of this inflamed choler.

The changed air extends to the person who is the object of this ire. Within the person who is the object of this ire the spirits are more attuned as he is sleeping and he senses the anger directed at him, in one form or another. This is the natural reason for prophetic dreams adduced by the Philosopher. It is not improbable therefore that the aforementioned emperor should see in his dreams the broken bow of Attila, for with the death of Attila the changes in the air of the hemisphere traveled from place to place unencumbered so that they reached the spirit of the slumbering emperor.

Now I would like to return to the matter at hand. Once the prefect gave in and handed over the fortress of Respampano, the strong and opulent castle of Cere, located in the Marittima, was quickly handed over to the tribune, then Monticielli near Tivoli, Vitorchiano near Viterbo, the fortress of Civitavecchia along the coast, Piglio in the Campagna, and Porto alongside the Tiber. The tribune therefore held in his hands all the bastions, byways, and bridges of Rome. Taking heart, he named Giovanni Colonna captain of those in the Campagna, should the people there rebel, and especially against the count of Fondi, Giovanni Caetani; to which Giovanni and the people of the Campagna acquiesced.[70] As a sign of his true obedience, the prefect sent his son Francesco, along with honorable company, as a hostage. Then Cola di Buccio di Braccia, a powerful man who dwelt in the mountains above Rieti, roused himself and fled from the lands of Rome.

Then Cola established on the Campidoglio a most beautiful chapel, enclosed in tin-plated steel.[71] Within it he had a solemn mass

---

70. The Colonna and the Caetani were old enemies and rivals for power and influence in the south, with a mutual dislike for one another that had its origins in the thirteenth century. Here Cola is showing his savvy by exploiting the enmity between them and turning members of the Colonna family to his cause.

71. Use of tin in this way resulted in a shiny silver appearance but was cheaper than actual silver gilding. My thanks to Claudia Bolgia for an explanation of the process. On the Campidoglio and its chapels, see Bolgia, *Reclaiming the Roma Capitol*, with various references to Rienzo.

performed, with many chanters and illuminations. Then he had all the barons of Rome stand before him as he himself sat, all standing on their feet with their arms folded and their heads uncovered. Oh, how afraid they all were!

❋

COLA HAD a most youthful and beautiful wife, who, when she went to St. Peter's, traveled in the company of armed youths. She was followed by various noblewomen. Young girls with soft feathers stirred the air before her face, fanning her attentively so that her face might not be troubled by flies. He had an uncle: Ianni Varvieri was his name. Varvieri was made a great lord and was called Ianni Roscio. He went on horseback accompanied in force by Roman citizens. All Cola's relatives went about in the same way. Cola had a widowed sister that he hoped to marry off to a castle-dwelling baron.

❋

COLA NAMED OFFICIALS and renewed their various duties. And so rumor and fear of so good a regime traveled through every land. People from distant cities and lands came to Rome to make legal complaints, and you would not believe how many made appeals and how many were punished. In the city of Perugia a Jew, a wealthy usurer, was secretly murdered along with his wife. At that time, an investigation into the matter was carried out in Rome. Many who had been afflicted by tyrants in the cities of Tuscany came to Rome to beg that their houses be returned to them.[72] For all such people Cola promised to do his best.

During this time many foreigners came, and the inns were packed due to the great crowd of visitors. Abandoned houses were refurbished. A great abundance of people flowed through the market. The lords of Montagna, those of Malieti, and Todino de Antonio, who almost never came to Rome, were all there. In this

72. Exile was a common result of political tumult in the Italian cities. Exiles commonly sought support that might allow them to return to their homes, and contemporaries seem to have thought that Cola's new regime had promise in this area. See Randolph Starn, *Contrary Commonwealth: The Theme of Exile in Medieval and Renaissance Italy* (Berkeley: University of California Press, 1982).

time of great prosperity, wishing to be the sole ruler, Cola dismissed the papal vicar, his colleague, who was a northern European, a great canon lawyer, and bishop of Viterbo, even though he was receiving many great prelates, letters, and embassies from Avignon.[73] Cola then sent an ambassador to the pope to notify him of this development. The ambassador, when he returned, reported that the pope and all the cardinals were deeply disturbed by this.

❋

NOW LET ME TELL YOU something about the splendid embassies that came to Cola. All of Rome was happy and smiling, for it seemed they had returned to the good old days. The venerable and triumphal embassies of the Florentines and the Sienese, as well as those from Arezzo, Todi, Terni, Spoleto, Rieti, Amelia, Tivoli, Velletri, Pistoia, Foligno, and Assisi all came. The embassies were made up of these and other men of obvious quality, honorable and well-established people: judges, knights, merchants, speakers witty and eloquent, and learned men. Every city and commune gave tribute to the *buono stato*. The cities of the Campagna, the Duchy, and the lands of the Patrimony all submitted themselves to Rome.[74] Not wishing to be under the dominion of the church, the people of Gaeta sent 10,000 florins along with their embassy and submitted themselves. The Venetians wrote letters sealed with hanging iron seals in which they offered themselves and all they had to the *buono stato*.[75] Messer Lucchino, the great tyrant of Milan, sent a letter in which he congratulated the tribune on his achievement with the *buono stato* and advised him to govern it well and keep an eye on the barons.

Most of the tyrants of Lombardy ignored him. Among these were Messer Taddeo delli Pepoli of Bologna, the Marquis Obizo[76] of

73. The vicar, Raymond, was bishop not of Viterbo but of Orvieto.

74. Much of Italy is represented here. The Patrimony refers to that of St. Peter (i.e., what are better known as the lands of the Papal States). The Duchy most likely refers to that of Spoleto. All of these are lands to which Rome, or the papacy, had some claim as within the late ancient District of Rome.

75. This refers to formal diplomatic correspondence in which the document was sealed as a measure to ensure authenticity and the seal itself hung from it. Needless to say, the total submission of the Venetians is likely overstated here.

76. Obizo III d'Este, marquis 1317–52.

## ❊ CHAPTER EIGHTEEN

Ferrara, Messer Mastino della Scala of Verona, Messer Filippino de Gonzaga of Mantua, the Carrara lords of Padua, Messer Francesco Ordelaffi of Forlì in Romagna, Messer [Galeotto I] Malatesta of Rimini, and many other tyrants, all of whom gave a crude, insulting response and then, after reconsidering, decided to send formal embassies. Lewis, the duke of Bavaria, by then already emperor, secretly sent ambassadors from Germany and asked in the name of God for Cola's help in reconciling with the church so that he might not die excommunicated. The duke of Durazzo wrote from the kingdom of Puglia to offer himself. In his salutation he wrote, "To our most dear friend." Messer Louis, prince of Taranto wrote too, along with many other royals. From Lewis, king of Hungary, came a great, honorable embassy. The two foremost of those ambassadors entreated the tribune and the Roman people to intervene in the vendetta they were obliged to carry out due to the cruel death of Andrew, king of Puglia, who the barons had hung as I will explain later.[77] These two were most noteworthy men, dressed in richly lined green cloth with German capes. When the tribune heard their request, he wanted to offer a response and ascended to the rostrum to address the people. It was Saturday. Various legal cases had just been completed. He had placed on his head the crown of the tribune, of which I made mention earlier. In his right hand he held a silver sphere with a cross.[78] Then he spoke, saying, "I shall judge the

---

77. Rienzo therefore found himself in the middle of a developing crisis in the affairs of the kingdom of Naples. Queen Giovanna I had been challenged in her rule and legitimacy from the start by the other Angevin cadet lines in the Regno: by her cousin Charles, duke of Durazzo; and by Louis, prince of Taranto, her cousin on the rival Angevin branch. With the murder of her husband, the prince consort Andrew and brother of Lewis of Hungary, both revenge and the set-aside claims to the Neapolitan throne by the Angevins of Hungary also came to the fore. For background and analysis of these confused politics, see Casteen, *From She-Wolf to Martyr,* 29–89; Musto, *Medieval Naples,* lxix–lxxi, 256–302; Musto, *Writing Southern Italy,* 229–52.

78. Seibt points out that this sphere, which Cola called the "orb of justice" *(orbis iusticie)* is none other than the very typical imperial globe emperors were commonly depicted as holding in their hand. See his *Anonimo Romano,* 178. Cola's reference to it is his correspondence. See BP 49, rr. 31–33; BP 57, rr. 583–94.

whole world justly and all people equally."⁷⁹ Then he said, "These are the Hungarian ambassadors, who seek justice for the death of the innocent King Andrew."

From Queen Giovanna, wife of the unhappy King Andrew, Cola received gracious letters, along with jewels and five hundred florins for his wife.⁸⁰ From the holy apostolic father he received letters wishing him well. From many prelates he received special letters exhorting him to suckle at the breast of the holy Church as if from a sweet and merciful mother. Then Philip Valois, the king of France, sent one of his archers with a letter. The letter was written in the vernacular and in simple language like that used in merchants' letters. By the time the letter arrived in Rome the tribune had fallen from power and his government was thrown down, so it went instead to the lords of Castel Sant'Angelo and eventually came into the hands of Agnilo Malabranca, the chancellor of Rome.⁸¹

I WOULD LIKE TO SAY something brief about the magnificent responses that Cola gave. The embassy of the prince of Taranto came to Rome. There were three ambassadors, an archbishop of the order of Saint Francis who was a master of theology, a knight with golden spurs, and a judge with all their splendid staff, baggage, and other goods. When the three ambassadors were before the tribune, the archbishop uttered these words, "*Misit viros renovare amicitiam.*"⁸² Then he spoke, saying how happy his lord was with what Cola had done. He comforted him. He offered himself as an ally. Then he asked that the Romans should be unified with him in opposition to

79. Here, as elsewhere, Cola speaks the words of Scripture, adapting Psalm 9:8 to describe himself, rather than God.

80. The Anonimo hints here at the formal status of Cola's wife, who he refers to as the *"tribunessa."*

81. Here is another indication that the Anonimo also relied on official, archival documents to round out his narrative, a practice widely used among trecento Italian civic historians.

82. The archbishop declares the embassy's purpose by quoting 1 Maccabees 12: "He sends men to renew friendship." Such scriptural references were common in trecento diplomatic oratory and underscore the close connection between religious sermons and secular political oratory at that time.

## CHAPTER EIGHTEEN

the king of Hungary, who had come to burn and reclaim the realm of Puglia. Having said these things, the archbishop concluded.

Upon hearing these words, the tribune responded without any prepared statement in the following way. First, he said this: "*Sit procul a vobis arma et gladius. Terra marique sit pax.*"[83] Then he said, "We have certain members of the *popolo* from whom to take council before we will give you an answer."

When the friar, that master of theology, heard these words he was so dumbfounded by the prompt response that he did not know what to say. The reason for this astonishment was this: that the tribune's response was an answer to his own opening words, with both coming from the same text, not too far apart, in the book of Maccabees. The passage is like this. A foreign people entered the kingdom of Judea by force of arms. The rulers of Judea put up a strong resistance. It was a great war. The fields went unplanted. Terrible famine swept the land. There was nothing to forage. The Jews were forced to look to the Romans, with whom they had an alliance, for aid. They therefore sent ambassadors to Rome to renew this relationship, hoping for aid and succor. They came as well to ask for grain due to the famine that afflicted them. As part of this effort they sent ships and money. The Romans responded with a letter, writing that they hoped there would be no war in their territory of Judea and calling for God to grant peace on land and sea. At the grain depot the Romans loaded the ships with grain and put the money in sacks. The grain they sent off and the money they kept. It was this that astonished the friar, so that in his heart he thought: "This tribune is a very wise man. So great is his learning that he responded to me with a biblical text from the same source as my greeting. He clearly has great wisdom, a capacious memory, and considerably savvy."

Now I want to tell you about the justice that Cola did. I have to admit that those who sell meat and fish in Rome are some of the worst people in the world. They swindle everyone. Now they said simply, "This meat

---

83. Clearly recognizing the archbishop's scriptural reference, Cola responds with one of his own, a paraphrase of 1 Maccabees 8: "May arms and sword be far from you and both land and sea be at peace."

comes from a sheep. This comes from a goat. This is old. This fish is good. This one is bad." The men of each guild simply told the truth.

Among the other ambassadors was a black monk who came to Rome from Città di Castello. He resided in Campo de' Fiori. There, after vespers, he got up from dinner and could not find his cape, which he had left outside. It had been stolen. The monk had some words with the innkeeper. The innkeeper said, "You didn't leave your cape with me."

Not wishing to spend time finding the cape, the monk came before the tribune and said, "Sir, I sat down to dinner. I left my cape outside the inn. I thought your rule would safeguard it for me. Then I was robbed. Now I cannot get it back. I am a sworn monk. I travel light like a sparrowhawk, dressed in a robe."

To this the tribune replied, saying, "Your cape is safe." He sent for cloth. That very moment he had a rich cape cut and made of the same cloth and color.

Then the monk went back to the inn quite content and said, "I have not lost a thing. Here is my cape." The notary of the tribune wrote down the location of the place. Had his later downfall not transpired, he would have fined the inn more than 1,000 florins.

In the region of the castle of Capranica a carter was robbed of his mule and of a quantity of oil. In good faith Count Bertuollo [Anquillara], who was lord of the castle, sent thirty florins to compensate for the oil and the mule and paid four hundred as a fine for having failed to keep his lands safe.

Once a currier was carrying letters for the tribune. As he was sleeping in an inn one night, another currier killed him and took his money. The evildoer was captured, he was buried alive, and above him in the grave the body of the one he had killed was interred.

More splendid still is how the question of King Andrew's death was addressed in Rome. The lawyers on the side of the king of Hungary and the lawyers on the side of Queen Giovanna appeared before the desk of the tribune's judge and put forward their questions. The lawyers of the king demanded justice. Those of the queen said that she was blameless in the death of her husband. The first group muttered to themselves about insults and insistently demanded

## CHAPTER EIGHTEEN

vengeance. The arguments of both sides were recorded in a book. This was, in no small way, an important and honorable affair.[84]

❋

NOW I WISH to tell you of the most honorable way that Cola was made a knight. Once the tribune saw that everything he had undertaken was going well, and that he ruled in peace without any resistance, he began to yearn for the honor of knighthood. He was therefore made a bathed knight on the night of holy Mary in mid-August.[85] The grandeur of this feast was of the following sort. First, during the night he prepared the entire papal palace and the area around San Giovanni in Laterano, and for several days before this he had dining tables made from the boards and planks taken from the fortifications of the barons.[86] These tables were placed throughout the hall of the old palace of Constantine, that of the pope, and the new palace, so that the sight astonished everyone who saw it. The walls of the room were knocked out and wooden stairs were built adjoining the opening so that food cooked outside could be brought in. In each room he had a supply of wine set up in one corner.

It was the vigil of Saint Peter in Chains. It was the hour of nones.[87] All of Rome, men and women alike, came to San Giovanni. Everyone gathered outside the gates to see the feast and in the public streets to watch the procession. Then came a great host of knights from many lands, barons, *popolani*, foreigners with bells ringing on their horses, clad in silk and bearing banners. They

---

84. Giovanna had ultimately to travel to Avignon to appear before a papal commission of inquiry, which eventually found her not guilty. See Casteen, *From She Wolf to Martyr,* 48–49; Musto, *Medieval Naples,* 278–83.

85. The reference to bathing here refers to ceremonial washing that sometimes preceded being raised to knighthood. The day in question is the Feast of the Assumption, falling on August 15. Wright and Porta point out that two events are being conflated here by the Anonimo. The event described here actually took place on August 1, 1347. On August 15 of that year, the day mentioned here, Cola was crowned, an event that the Anonimo doesn't discuss. On the coronation, see Musto, *Apocalypse in Rome,* 184–86.

86. On the appropriation of such materials, and their conversion to tables and other useful objects, see above chapter 7, p. 84 n. 8.

87. 3:00 PM.

had a great feast. They ran about and played. Then came an endless number of buffoons. One blew a trumpet and another a pipe. One played cymbals and another some other instrument. After this tremendous performance came Cola's wife, walking with her mother. Many honorable women accompanied her, hoping to become her intimate companion. After the lady came two young servants, who held in their hands the golden bridle of a most noble steed. One witnessed innumerable silver trumpets sounding. After this came a great number of cunning riders, among whom the Perugians and the Cornetani were the most skilled. Twice they tossed out silken clothes. Then came the tribune with the papal vicar at his side. Behind the tribune came one man carrying a naked sword in his hand. Overhead flew his banner that was born by another man. In his hand, the tribune carried a steel rod. Many noteworthy people accompanied him. He was wearing a white silken robe, *miri candoris*, embellished with gold thread.[88]

In the evening, between night and day, he ascended to the chapel of Pope Boniface [VIII] and addressed the people, saying, "You know that tonight I am to be made a knight. Return tomorrow so that you might hear things that will please both God in heaven and men on earth." At this the whole crowd was delighted. There was no fear and no clash of arms. Two people had words. In anger they drew their swords. Before a blow could be struck, they returned them to their sheaths. Each one then went on his way.

The inhabitants of nearby cities came to this feast and, what is more, old men, young girls, widows, and married women came too.[89] After everyone had left, the clergy celebrated a solemn mass.

88. Here the Latin phrase indicates that the robe was not only white but remarkably white.

89. The Anonimo may have found this remarkable because women of all ages were often excluded from participating in the public sphere, except for religious events. On the legal status of women, see Thomas Kuehn, *Law, Family & Women: Toward a Legal Anthropology of Renaissance Italy* (Chicago: University of Chicago Press, 1991); and his *Family and Gender in Renaissance Italy, 1300–1600* (Cambridge: Cambridge University Press, 2017). In some circumstances, however, women were treated as citizens and enjoyed the rights thereof. See Julius Kirshner, "Hidden in Plain Sight: Citizen Women in Late Medieval Italy," (unpublished paper, 2017), https://www.academia.edu/30770102/

# CHAPTER EIGHTEEN

After that was complete, Cola entered the bath and washed himself in the baptismal font of Emperor Constantine, which is made of most precious black jasper. This is an astonishing thing to admit. It provoked intense murmuring among the people. A Roman citizen, the knight Messer Vico Scuotto, girded him with a sword. Then he slept in a noble bed, laying in that place called the Baptistry of San Giovanni, within the circle of columns. There he passed the entire night. Now listen to this marvel. The bed and its bedding were new. When the Tribune climbed into bed one part of the bed fell suddenly to the ground *et sic in nocte silenti mansit*.[90]

When morning came the tribune arose dressed in fur-trimmed scarlet, with the sword from Messer Vico Scuotto at his belt, and with golden spurs like a knight. All of Rome, the entirety of its chivalry, came to San Giovanni — including the barons, foreigners, and citizens — to lay eyes on Messer Nicola de Rienzi, knight.[91] He held a great feast and made merry. Messer Nicola stood with his companions, adorned as a knight, above the piazza in the chapel of Pope Boniface. There a most solemn mass was sung. Nothing was lacking in terms of chanters or ornamentation.

Even as such a solemnity was being celebrated the tribune went before the people and said in a loud voice, "We summon Messer Pope Clement to come to his seat in Rome." Then he summoned the college of cardinals.[92] He also summoned the Bavarian. Then

---

Hidden_in_Plain_Sight_Citizen_Women_in_Late_Medieval_Italy, which emphasizes this complexity.

90. "…and it remained this way throughout the silent night."

91. Cola's name was, in common Roman fashion, the short form of Nicola. "Rienzo" was similarly short for Lorenzo, making him Nicola son of Lorenzo. As they grew nearer to noble status, Roman lines tended to develop family names. When they crossed over to that status those names often evolved so that the last name, "Gibelli," for example, might become "de Ibellis." On Gibelli, whose name began to shift to the more noble form by at least 1374, see Palmer, *The Virtues of Economy*, passim. By tweaking Cola's name this way, therefore, the Anonimo is saying something about Cola's aspiration to a change in status.

92. Porta argues that this detail demonstrates that the Anonimo was actually present for these events, suggesting that subsequent evidence shows evidence

he summoned the imperial electors in Germany and said, "I would have these men come to Rome. I would see for myself how these elections are carried out," for he had discovered writings indicating that in past times the right to carry out such elections had belonged to the Romans. With these summonses issued, letters and curriers were swiftly prepared and sent on their way.

After this Cola drew his sword from its scabbard and struck the altar so that it was divided into the three parts of the world, saying, "This is mine, this is mine, this is mine."[93] The papal vicar was present for all of this. He stood struck dumb, as if carved out of wood. He did not listen but rather, stupefied by this development, protested. By means of his notary he issued a public declaration, saying that these things had been done without consulting him, without his knowledge, and without papal license, and he had the notary produce a public instrument recording this.[94] As the notary was loudly giving voice to these protestations, Messer Nicola commanded that trumpets, horns, drums, and shawms should be played, so that their louder sound might drown out the notary's voice. The louder sound canceled out the quieter one. What a vicious joke! Once this was done, the mass and its solemnity were complete.

Understand something noteworthy. Throughout that day, from the morning dawn until nones,[95] red wine poured from the nostril of the bronze horse of Constantine, flowing through special lead pipes into

---

of a deliberate effort to erase any record of these summonses despite the fact that they do seem to have happened.

93. A standard way of making a map of the world was the "T and O" or "Beatine" form, which divided the world into three parts. See Map. 4. After having summoned both the pope and the emperor, each of whom was traditionally understood to hold a kind of universal authority, Cola, perhaps as a representative of Rome, is claiming such authority for the city.

94. This means that the notary drew up a formal document recording the statement. This was a common tactic and a step the vicar would have taken because he understood Cola to have put himself and the regime in legal jeopardy and wished to distance himself from the act.

95. 3:00 PM.

※ CHAPTER EIGHTEEN

a brimming basin. All the young men, citizens and foreigners alike, stood around it drinking happily when they had a thirst.[96]

Once word got out that Cola had bathed in the baptismal font of Constantine and then summoned the pope, the people began to be suspicious and doubtful. There were some who saw it as audacious but others who said that he was delusional and insane.

After the mass they went, many lords and ladies alike, to a solemn feast with a great variety of food and wine. Messer Nicola sat with only the papal vicar at a marble table — it was the papal table — in the room of San Giovanni, the old one. The whole room was full of tables. The tribune's wife ate with her ladies in the room of the new papal palace.[97] At this meal there was less water than wine. Whoever wished to attend was there. There was no order at all.[98] Abbots, clerics, knights, merchants and many other people were there. There were all manner of confections. There was a surfeit of sturgeon, the delicate fish,[99] as well as pheasant and young goat. Whoever wanted to take some of the less choice cuts was free to do so. The ambassadors who had come from various places were present at this gathering. As Cola had them sit down to dinner, there was, among the many buffoons present, one fellow dressed in the hide of a bull. He had horns on his head. He looked like a bull. He scampered and leapt about. When the meal was complete, Messer

---

96. Thought throughout the medieval period to be a statue of Constantine, this is actually the famous equestrian statue of Marcus Aurelius of c.175 CE, one of the few such statues surviving from Roman antiquity. It stood outside San Giovanni in Laterano from the eighth century and was only brought to the Campidoglio in 1538 for Michelangelo's redesign of the piazza. After a neo-fascist bomb attack on the Senate Palace on April 21, 1979, the original statue was placed in the Capitoline Museums, and a copy now stands on the Campidoglio. For background, see Krautheimer, *Rome*, 192–97; and Philipp Fehl, "The Placement of the Equestrian Statue of Marcus Aurelius in the Middle Ages," *Journal of the Warburg and Courtauld Institutes* 37 (1974): 362–67.

97. As was common in the trecento.

98. There is a clear sense here that an unusual amount of social mixing was taking place at the meal of Cola's wife. Traditional distinctions between noble and common, ecclesiastical and lay, were set aside for the event.

99. Usually reserved for royalty.

Nicola de Rienzi rode to the Campidoglio, dressed in fur-trimmed scarlet, with a large group of riders.

I SHALL NOT OMIT the things that he had done for himself during his ascendancy. He had a chest made with an opening in the top, which declined in value and eventually became worthless. He also had a little hat made, covered in pearls, which was very lovely and had a dove made of pearl on top. These various shortcomings weighed him down and led to his downfall in the following way.[100]

ONE DAY he invited Messer Stefano Colonna the Elder to dine with him, a man whose quality I discussed before. When the time came to dine, he had him brought to the Campidoglio by force and held him there. Then he had Pietro di Agapito, the lord of Genazzano, brought as well, he who had formerly governed Marseille and had at one time been senator of Rome. Also brought by force was Lubertiello, the son of Count Vertollo, who had also once been senator. These two senators were dragged to the Campidoglio as if they were petty criminals. He also held the prosperous young man Giovanni Colonna, who only a few days before he had made captain of the Campagna. He retained too Giordano Orsini of Monte and Raynaldo Orsini of Marino. He held Cola Orsini, the lord of Castel Sant'Angelo. He took Count Vertollo, Messer Orso of Vicovaro of the Orsini, and many others from among Rome's great barons. He did not have Luca Savelli, Stefano [the Younger] Colonna, or Messer Giordano of Marino. The tribune held all these barons under guard in his own small prison, he took them all by trickery, leading some to understand that he wanted to discuss something with them and others that he was inviting them to dine.

Evening came with the Roman people strongly cursing the maliciousness of the nobles and praising the goodness of the tribune. Then Messer Stefano the Elder raised a question: which is better in a rector of the people, prodigality or avarice? There was a great deal of

100. The odd transition between discussion of a box and a hat and then a reference to "these various shortcomings" has led Seibt, *Anonimo romano*, 182–83, to suggest that the Anonimo intended to fill out this part of the chapter with discussion of certain key events that he never got around to including.

## CHAPTER EIGHTEEN

argument about this point. Afterwards, Messer Stefano, taking hold of the tribune's fancy shirt, said, "It would better suit you, Tribune, to wear the honorable garb of a holy man than these pompous things."[101] Having said this, he released his hold on the shirt.

Hearing this, Cola di Rienzo was disturbed. It was evening. He had all the nobles seized and put under guard. Messer Stefano the Elder was shut up in the room where justice was served. He passed the whole night without a bed. He paced to and fro, coming to the door and entreating the guards to let him out. The guards refused to listen. This cruelty was inflicted on him all night without pity.

Day came. The tribune had decided to behead every single one of them in the great hall in order to liberate the Roman people.[102] He ordered that the room be decked out in silken cloth of red and white, and it was done. In this way, he hinted at blood. Then he had the bell rung and summoned the people together. Then he sent a confessor, a Franciscan friar, to each of the barons, that they might do penance and take the body of Christ.

When the barons learned of these developments and heard the ringing of the bell, they became so terrified that they were speechless, not knowing what to do. Most of them humbled themselves and took penance and communion. Messer Raynaldo Orsini and one other were not able to take communion because they had eaten fresh figs that morning.[103] Messer Stefano Colonna refused to

101. The term attributed to Stefano here is *vizuoco*. Wright renders this simply "a poor man," but that does not fully capture the sense. A lay holy woman, for example, was commonly called a *bizocca,* and the word used here is the masculine version of that term in the dialect of Rome. Stefano was shrewd enough to recognize the importance of the holy in Cola's personal charisma.

102. The Anonimo omits evidence that the barons were planning to assassinate the tribune, a conspiracy recorded by the *Chronicon Estense.* Rienzo was encouraged in this move to eliminate his enemies by none other than Francesco Petrarch, who provided both contemporary and classical precedents for the action. Petrarch later criticized Cola for his clemency. See *Familiares* XIII.6; and Cosenza, *Revolution,* 88–89. As the Anonimo reveals below, many among Cola's supporters also wanted them removed permanently.

103. This refers to the obligation to fast from the midnight prior to taking communion, which usually happened when mass was celebrated in the morning.

confess or take communion. He said that he was not ready and had not put his affairs in order. Meanwhile, certain Roman citizens, realizing what manner of judgment Cola was preparing to carry out, delayed it with sweet, soothing words. In the end, the tribune changed his mind and lifted the proposed sentence. This was at the hour of terce. All the despairing condemned barons were led into the hall. Trumpets were sounded as if they were about to be punished before the people.

His mind changed, the tribune climbed into the pulpit and gave a beautiful sermon. He based it on the line from the Lord's prayer: "*Dimitte nobis debita*."[104] Then he released the barons and said that they wanted to serve the people and make peace with them. One after another they bowed their heads before the people. Some of them Cola made patricians, some he made prefects in charge of grain, some dukes of Tuscany, and others dukes of the Campagna.[105] To each one of them he gave a lovely fur-lined robe, well adorned, and a banner marked with golden ears of grain. Then he caused them to dine with him and rode through Rome with them following behind. Then he let them go safely on their way. This deed greatly displeased the discreet men. People said, "This fellow has lit a fire and flame that he will not be able to put out." I would remind them of this proverb: "He who starts to fart and then squeezes his ass shut wears out his bum."

NOW I WILL TELL YOU how the castle of Marino was besieged. Once the barons had been freed, they had no taste for company. They departed Rome for their fortresses. Furiously, they muttered through clenched teeth. There was no agreement to begin hostilities with the Romans. Among others, the Colonna and the lords of Marino — Messer Raynaldo and Messer Giordano — fortified their strongholds.[106] Secretly they swore an oath. They made clear

---

104. That is: "Forgive us our sins."

105. Here Cola was formalizing roles that the barons already had, making them lords of the lands around Rome and putting them in charge of grain production and transport. On the Roman grain trade and baronial ties to it, see Palermo, *Mercati del grano;* and Palmer, *Virtues of Economy*, 60–65.

106. Marino, not far to the southeast of Rome, had been an Orsini holding for nearly a century by this time. See Carocci, *Baroni di Roma*, 43, 398–99.

that they planned to rebel. They fortified Marino and patched the holes in its defenses. They erected a strong double stockade of wood. Such was the tribune's lunacy that he never thought to forbid this. From the beginning he was utterly unprepared. He waited until the castle was strongly provisioned. The tribune became increasingly unfair. Many people began to mutter behind his back. Once the castle of Marino had been reinforced, provisioned with arrows, spears and men, provisions and defenses, wood and wine, he finally recognized the rebellion. An edict was issued demanding that the madmen present themselves in Rome. In the vineyards near Marino the messenger suffered no fewer than three blows to the head.

Then the rebels sallied from Marino and daily ravaged the countryside around Rome. They carried off cattle, sheep, pigs, and grain. All of this they carried back to Marino. In Rome there was tearing of cheeks. Everyone cried out with alarm. Anger and fear surged. Once again the tribune summoned the rebels and commanded them to come to Rome or face his wrath. Then he commanded that an image of Messer Raynaldo and Messer Giordano be painted outside the palace of the Campidoglio, depicting them as knights hanging upside down with their heads below and their feet above.[107] In response, Messer Giordano escalated his evils. He rode right up to the Porta San Giovanni and seized men, women, and herds of livestock. He took all that back to Marino. Messer Raynaldo, his brother, crossed over the Tiber and entered the city of Nepi, riding around, burning and plundering. He scorched the earth. He burned the fortress, houses, and men. He showed no reluctance to burn an old noble widow in a tower.

The rage of the Romans only grew with such cruelty. Many began to think ill of Messer Raynaldo and Messer Giordano. This was no mere monkey business. The perverse minds of the Romans turned against the Colonna.[108] It was harvest time. The grapes were

107. This is the use, common throughout trecento Italy, of painting *pitture infamanti* of traitors to the state. The inversion of their image indicating their upsetting the proper order of things. For recent research on *pitture infamanti*, see Ortalli, *La pittura infamante*; and Carolin Behrman, *Images of Shame: Infamy, Defamation and the Ethics of Oeconomia* (Boston: De Gruyter, 2016).

108. Although the specific malefactors here were two Orsini men, the Anonimo clearly understands the Colonna to be the ringleaders of baronial

mature. The people were pressing them. Then the tribune called the whole Roman people to arms, sent the Roman army and set it upon the castle of Marino, situating his forces in a place called Maccantregola. This is a forested valley, one mile distant from the castle. It was a splendid host, huge and powerful, comprising both foot soldiers and cavalry. There were 20,000 infantry and 800 knights. The weather was grim and rainy the entire time, which affected the army. It prevented them from doing any plundering. Ultimately, within about eight days, they plundered everything around Castle Marino. They utterly depopulated its lands. They cut down vines and trees; they burned mills; they uprooted the noble, previously untouched forest. They destroyed everything. For years that castle was a shadow of its former self. They took from its riches whatever plunder they could. All of Rome was there.

IN THOSE DAYS there was living in Rome a cardinal, a legate of the pope.[109] This legate assailed Cola with letters asking him to return to Rome so that he could discuss certain matters with him. The destruction completed, the tribune packed up his camp one morning and proceeded against the castle, not far distant from Marino. He took it easily, and *instanti*[110] the walls of the place were thrown down. He hoped to quickly assail the citadel and the round tower to which the garrison had retreated. To take the tower he had two wooden castles built, which rolled on wheels. He had ladders and other wooden structures made. You have never seen such splendid machinery. He prepared weapons of various sorts. Cola received many embassies in that place. A stream flowed from near the place. In that stream he washed two dogs and said that they were Raynaldo and Giordano, dog-knights. Then he destroyed the mill.

After this, Cola packed up his army and returned to Rome, because the letters of the legate concerned him. In the morning he expeditiously tore down the beautiful palaces at the foot of the

---

resistance to Cola. Cola was aware of this himself, suspecting the Colonna of targeting him for assassination. See Musto, *Apocalypse in Rome*, 211–12.

109. This was a new legate, Bertrand de Déaulx.

110. That is "immediately."

## CHAPTER EIGHTEEN

Ponte San Pietro, in front of San Celso.[111] Then he went with his riders to San Pietro. He entered the sacristy dressed, over his armor, in the dalmatic. This was the garb that emperors wear when they are crowned.[112] The whole thing was covered in little pearls. This was a lavish vestment. With this piece of apparel draped over his arm in the manner of Caesar, he entered the papal palace with horns sounding and appeared before the legate with his scepter in his hand and his crown on his head. His appearance was terrible and astonishing. When he had come before the legate, the tribune spoke, saying, "You sent for us. What does it please you to command?"

The legate responded, "We have certain information from our lord pope."

When the tribune heard this, he raised his voice and said quite loudly, "What information is that?"

When the legate heard the outraged tone of this response, he kept his peace and stayed silent. The tribune turned his back and returned to making war on Marino, and Marino against the Romans.

NOW I WILL DESCRIBE to you how the Colonna were defeated in Rome. It was a hard fight. The citizens of Rome seemed much afflicted by fatigue, discomfort, and damages. The tribune did not pay his troops as he was meant to. Whispers were heard across the city. The knights of Rome wrote letters to Stefano Colonna, saying that he should come with his people and they would open the gates. The Colonna gathered at Palestrina, numbering 700 knights and 4,000 foot.[113] They intended to return to Rome in force. Many barons were with them in this plot. Great preparations were made in Palestrina. In order to return to Rome they sent sweet sounding messages saying that they wished to return to their houses.

---

111. This is the church of SS. Celso e Giuliano. Wright observes that Cola is here breaking his own laws by tearing down the houses of the Orsini.

112. The Anonimo uses the word *dalmatica* for this item. A dalmatic was a long sleeved, formal tunic popular by the late Roman period and adopted by the clergy.

113. Palestrina was the main seat of Colonna power, slightly more distant than Marino and standing northeast of it.

The tribune was intensely frightened by this assembled host and became like a sick man, like a madman.[114] He would neither eat nor drink. One morning, about three days before the battle, he spoke to the people and comforted them, saying among other things, "Know that tonight Saint Martin appeared to me, he who was the son of a tribune, and he said to me: 'Do not be afraid, for you will slay the enemies of God.'"[115]

The next morning, when it was barely light, he sounded the alarm bell. The people assembled in arms. He spoke in a calm manner, saying, "Lords, I want to let you know that tonight holy Pope Boniface appeared to me and said to me that now, on this very day, we would take vengeance on his enemies, the Colonna, who so falsely slandered the church of God."[116] Then he said, "I have a son — his name is Lorenzo — who will come with me into battle against these perjurers and betrayers of the people." Next he said, "We know from our informants that these people are coming and have taken a position four miles from the city in a place called

---

114. The Anonimo's account is inconsistent. He portrays Cola as panicking one moment, and calmly in the control of the situation in the next. Here and throughout this battle account the Anonimo may have borrowed aspects his psychological portrait from available classical sources. Or, again, he may be attempting to reconcile differing first-hand accounts and rumors.

115. Saint Martin was an early fourth-century figure whose father did indeed hold the office of "tribune" within the Roman military, according to his hagiographer, Sulpicius Severus. See *Soldiers of Christ: Saints and Saints Lives from Late Antiquity and the Early Middle Ages*, Thomas F.X. Noble and Thomas Head, ed. (University Park: The Pennsylvania State University Press, 1995), 6.

116. Boniface VIII had been from the baronial Caetani family, between which and the Colonna there had been a long ugly feud in the opening years of the fourteenth century. The opening salvo was fired by none other than Stefano himself, then a youth, when he attacked and robbed a Caetani shipment of gold and silver in 1297. See Maire Vigueur, *L'altra Roma*, 200–204. Boniface's eventual arrest in Anagni, a Caetani center, by a combination of French and Colonna forces is generally understood to have led to his death. Cola himself was raised and received an early education not in Rome but in Anagni, and he may have developed a devotion to Boniface there.

## CHAPTER EIGHTEEN

Monimento. This is a true sign that not only will they be defeated but even slain and buried in Monimento."[117]

When he finished speaking, he had trumpets, cymbals and drums sounded, and he organized his forces, appointed captains for the battle, and called them Knights of the Holy Spirit. This done, quietly and without fanfare, he went with his legion, organized into cavalry and foot soldiers, to the Porta San Lorenzo, which is also called the Porta Tiburtina. With the people from among the barons were Giordano Orsini, Cola Orsini of Castel Sant'Angelo, chancellor [Agnilo] Malabranca of Pescina, Matteo the chancellor's son, Lubertiello the son of Count Vertollo, and many others.[118]

I do not want to leave out the way the tribune handled the prefect before the battle. The tribune sent for the prefect. Wishing to obey, the prefect came with one hundred knights to fight in service to the Romans. He brought with him around fifteen minor Tuscan nobles. He brought his son Francesco as well. This was the first time the young man had carried arms. He sent ahead of himself five hundred measures of grain to serve as a supply, as befitted a prefect. He had been coerced into allying with the Romans. Once he arrived, he was invited to dinner. As he sat down, he and his companions were stripped of their arms. Then he and his son were imprisoned. Their gear and horses were taken and given to the Romans. Then the tribune called an assembly and said, "Do not be astonished by the news that I have imprisoned the prefect, for he had come to betray the people of Rome and stab them in the back."

Now I will turn to the battle. The Colonna and their whole great force set out from Monimento at midnight, relocating to the monastery of San Lorenzo fuori le Mura. Unfortunately, the weather was rainy and bitingly cold. The barons assembled: Stefano Colonna, his son Giovanni, Pietro di Agapito who was the overseer

---

117. The Monument was the medieval name of the enormous pyramidal tomb on the Via Appia, near Sta. Maria Nuova, at the fifth milestone. Cola refers to the fact that the pyramid was badly decayed around its base and was kept standing only by a narrow column of foundation materials, making it a symbol of decayed baronial power.

118. The Anonimo acknowledges that many barons sided with the *buono stato*, even to the point of fighting against their own kinsmen.

of Marseille, [Oddone Colonna] the lord of Genazzano, Messer Giordano of Marino, Cola di Bucio de Braccia, Sciarretta Colonna, and many others. They came to discuss what they should do, for Stefano was afflicted by vomiting and was shaking like a leaf. Also, Pietro di Agapito, being somewhat exhausted, slept and seemed to see his wife a widow, weeping and crying. Afraid due to this dream, he wanted to leave the host. He did not want to be there for its defeat. They also heard the alarm bell ringing and knew that the people were aroused to a powerful anger.

Stefano Colonna, the captain general of the whole host, had gone before them all and, first thing, ridden up to the Porta San Lorenzo on his palfrey, accompanied by a single aid. He then began in a loud voice to call to the guard by name, asking him to open the gate. He argued in this way, saying "I am a citizen of Rome. I want to return to my house. I come for the *buono stato*." He was carrying the banner of the church and the people.

Upon hearing these words, the gate guard (Paolo Bussa was the good crossbowman's name) replied, saying "The guard you are calling is not here. The guards have been changed. I and my companions have come to take their place. You shall by no means find entry here. The gate is barred. Do you not understand how great is the anger of the people at you who have disturbed the *buono stato*? Do you not hear the bell? I ask you, by God, to depart. Do not insist on being so evil. As a sign that you will not be able to enter here, look, I am throwing down the key." He cast the key out and it fell in a puddle of water that had appeared there due to the bad weather.[119]

When the barons gathered in council and had considered all these things, it was obvious to them that they could not get in. They decided to leave honorably, divided into three groups, and prepared to march up to the gate of Rome sounding trumpets and other instruments before turning to the right and returning to their homes in honor. So it was done. Soon two of the battalions had already

---

119. This incident seems to indicate that the conspirators had expected one or more of their party inside the city to open the gates to them. Although the Anonimo does not draw this conclusion explicitly, he had indicated above that they did have allies inside the walls.

## CHAPTER EIGHTEEN

gone, the first and the second, made up of foot soldiers and knights. Petruccio Frangipane led them. They sounded their trumpets at the gate, turned to their right, and without any having shed a drop of blood, they turned away. Then the third group came forward. The bulk of the chivalry was in this group comprising many nobles, the proudest, most skilled horsemen, and the strong core of the host. There was a standing order not to do any harm under penalty of losing a foot. The first to approach were eight noble barons, among them the unfortunate Gianni[120] Colonna. This noble first rank rode ahead of the main group a good distance. Day was breaking.

The Romans behind the gate, because they didn't have the key, opened it by force in order to leap into the fray. Their axes made a tremendous noise. There was a great shouting and confusion. The right-side gate was opened, the left remained shut. Gianni Colonna, approaching the gate, noticed the ruckus within and believed, because there had been no order to open the gate, that his allies were the ones making the noise as they opened the gate by force. Believing this, Gianni Colonna quickly lifted his shield, set his lance, and spurred on his destrier. Adorned in a baronial manner, charging hard and not holding back, he entered the city gate.

Oh, what a scare he gave the people! The whole Roman cavalry turned to flee before him. In the same way the people hastily retreated the distance of about half the range of a crossbow's shot. But Gianni Colonna was not followed by his friends, instead remaining entirely alone like one called to judgement. The Romans therefore took heart, understanding that he was alone. And his misfortune got still worse. His destrier carried him to a pit located to the left just inside the gate. He was bucked off his horse into this pit and, realizing his misfortune, requested mercy of the people, swearing to God that they would not rob him of his armor. What more is there to say? He was stripped, wounded three times, and died. Fonneruglia de Treio was the first to strike him. The young baron was an energetic lad whose beard had not yet sprouted. He was renowned throughout the land for his virtue and glory. He lay naked, sprawled, wounded, and dead, on a little rise alongside the wall, just inside the gate. His hair was caked with mud. He was barely recognizable.

120. Giovanni the Younger.

Lo and behold! Immediately the horrible weather shifted, and the skies began to clear. Stefano Colonna came to the gate with a well-ordered host and asked anxiously after his son Gianni.[121] The response to him was, "We don't know what he did or where he went." Stefano suspected that he had entered the gate. So he spurred ahead, entered the gate alone, and saw his son lying on the ground amid the many men who were killing him between the pit and a watery bog. Then, fearing for his own safety, Stefano turned and went back out the gate. Losing all reason, he went wild. His love for his son urged him on. Saying not a word, he spun around and reentered the gate to see if there was some way to rescue his boy. Without drawing near he realized that he was dead. Then he thought of saving himself. He turned back grieving. As he was exiting the gate a huge stone fell from one of the towers overhead and struck him in the shoulder and his horse in the back. After that came a flurry of hurled lances flying here and there. His horse was wounded in the breast with a lance and lost its footing so that he could not remain mounted and fell to the ground. The people saw that he was defenseless, and so they killed him right in front of the gate, in the spot where there are images on the walls, right in the middle of the road. He lay there naked for passersby to see. He was missing one of his feet. He was covered in wounds. Between his nose and his eyes he had an enormous gaping wound so that it seemed like one was looking into the mouth of a wolf. His son Gianni had only two wounds: one in his groin and one in his breast.

Then the enraged people burst out of the city without order or restraint, looking for someone else to kill. The young men came across Pietro di Agapito Colonna, who had previously been governor of Marseille, a priest. He had never carried arms before that day. He was knocked from his horse. Due to the muddy ground, he could not escape easily. He fled to a nearby vineyard. He was a bald old man. He begged them in God's name to spare him. He prayers were worthless. First they took his money. Then they disarmed him. Then they took his life. There he was in the vineyard: naked, dead, bald, and fat. He didn't look like a warrior. Nearby in the same vineyard lay another baron from the lords of Bellovedere. Twelve men died

---

121. This is not Stefano the Elder, the head of the clan, but rather his eponymous son. Giovanni was, thus, his grandson.

in a short span. There they lay sprawled out. The rest of the host, both foot soldiers and knights, cast down their arms here and there in terror. They fled without looking back. Not one of them struck a single blow. Messer Giordano left in haste and didn't stop until he reached Marino. The host was defeated. The enemies were cast out and thrown dead to the ground, in plain view of everyone who passed by, among those that lay there the whole day were illustrious senators.

It is true that the standard of the tribune fell on the ground too. The terrified tribune stood with his eyes raised to heaven. In a high voice he actually said, "Oh God, have you betrayed me?"[122] But once victory was won by the people, the tribune had his silver horns sounded and took to the field in great glory and triumph, putting on his head his crown of silver olive branches. He returned triumphantly with the whole people to Sta. Maria in Aracoeli and there gave his steel scepter and his olive crown to the Virgin Mary. He placed his scepter and crown before the venerable image in the house of the Friars Minor.[123] After that he never again carried the scepter, wore the crown, or flew the banner overhead. After this he spoke to the people in the assembly hall and said that he wanted to sheath his sword. He took his sword and polished it on his clothing,

---

122. The Anonimo does not indicate how he heard or learned of many of these interior psychological details on both sides of the battle. The resemblance to Jesus's cry of despair on the cross (Matt. 27:46) here might indicate that the Anonimo was relying on standard medieval historiographical techniques to rhetorically amplify the drama of the situation. The expression comes from the Psalms (22:1), learned by heart by every trecento Roman literate in Latin. For this education, see Internullo, *Ai margini*, 19–113.

123. The Anonimo is reliable here. Rienzo deposited his regalia below the icon of the Virgin. In 1372 these regalia were incorporated into the Felici chapel monument as a memorial to Rienzo's *buono stato*. They were still there in 1444, when Giuliano di Coluccio Marcuzi wished in his will to be buried "in the place...where are the *arma* that are said to have belonged to the late Nicola, tribune of the City." See Claudia Bolgia, "The Felici Icon Tabernacle (1372) at S. Maria in Aracoeli, Reconstructed: Lay Patronage, Sculpture, and Marian Devotion in Trecento Rome," *Journal of the Warburg and Courtauld Institutes* 68 (2005): 27–72; idem, *Reclaiming the Roman Capitol*, 366–79.

saying, "I have cut an ear from such a head as neither the pope nor the emperor could touch."[124]

The three bodies were carried to Sta. Maria of the friars, covered with golden shrouds, and lain in the chapel of the Colonna.[125] The countesses came with a crowd of women, tearing their hair and wailing over the dead, that is over the bodies of Stefano, Giovanni, and Pietro di Agapito.[126] The tribune had them driven out, not wishing that the men should be honored or given funerary rights, and he said, "If those three cursed corpses cause me any problems I will have them cast into the common grave for hanged men, for they were oath breakers and don't deserve a proper burial!" So the three bodies were secretly carried to the church of San Silvestro in Capite during the night, and without any wailing they were secretly entombed by the nuns.[127]

HERE I WOULD LIKE to change topics for a time. The great author Titus Livy writes that a captain came from Africa that was the best

---

124. Here Cola evokes the gospels, specifically Matthew 26:51, Mark 14:47, Luke 22:50–51, and John 18:10–11, all of which relate the tale of Peter's attempt to prevent the arrest of Jesus in the Garden of Gethsemane. Peter famously lopped an ear off of Malchus, a servant of high priest Caiaphas, before being commanded by Jesus to stop and return his sword to its sheath.

125. That is, Sta. Maria sopra Minerva, a Dominican church.

126. This female mourning process was ancient and expected, especially for noble deaths. Cola's interruption of it would likely have been extremely offensive. See Thompson, *Cities of God*, p. 401, but see too the critique of Lansing, *Passion and Order*, 13–16 and passim.

127. San Silvestro in Capite (the Anonimo's San Silvestre dello Capo), just off the Corso, was a church with important Colonna roots. A community of women that grew up around Margherita Colonna (c. 1255–80), herself a holy woman that the family had failed to have canonized, had taken up residence there following her death in the late thirteenth century. It remained at this time a house of Poor Clares living under the same rule. See Lezlie S. Knox and Sean L. Field, ed., *Visions of Sainthood in Medieval Rome: The Lives of Margherita Colonna by Giovanni Colonna and Stefania* (Notre Dame: University of Notre Dame Press, 2017), 10–11, 17, 44, 59.

that ever there was in all the world.¹²⁸ His name was Hannibal of Carthage. This Hannibal broke the peace with Rome and destroyed the city of Saguntum in Spain to the displeasure and shame of the senate in Rome. Then he crossed the Alps into the Piedmont and entered Lombardy. There he defeated Sempronius, the Roman consul, at a river called the Tecino, alongside Pavia. Then he entered Tuscany and there, at the lake of Perugia,¹²⁹ he defeated the Roman army and cut the head off of the consul Flaminius. Then he tried to take Spoleto and could not. Then he turned toward Campania¹³⁰ and Montecassino and there he was met at the frontier by the great army of Fabius the Wise, who held him at bay for three years.

After three years there was a change in leadership. Fabius was removed. There were two captains: representing the nobility was captain Emilius Paulus and representing the people was captain Terentius Varro.¹³¹ Such was the cunning and energy of Hannibal that he brought these two captains to their feet and led them and all their strength of cavalry and foot soldiers all the way into Puglia, to a river called Volturno.¹³² There he defeated the Roman people, defeating both armies. There died one of the commanders, Emilius Paulus. Eighty senators died there. Servilius died there, who the year before had been consul. Tribunes and many good people died there. Forty-four thousand foot soldiers died there. Eight thousand eight hundred knights died there. Ten thousand were

---

128. The Anonimo refers here to Livy, *Ab urbe condita libri*, books XXI and XXII.

129. The battle of Lake Trasimene in June 217 BCE, one of the most famous in Roman and military history.

130. We here distinguish between the English usage of *"Campagna,"* meaning the Roman Campagna or hinterland; and *"Campania,"* meaning the bordering province of the kingdom of Naples.

131. The more standard translation here would be to refer to the *populari* represented by Gaius Terentius Varro as "plebians." Given his own use of the term, I suspect he had in mind the *popolo*, or "people" in the sense common to the Italian politics of his day.

132. That is, into Campania. "Puglia" was one of the terms used for the trecento kingdom of Naples, derived from the original Norman conquest of Apulia, which formed the base of the later kingdom.

taken prisoner. Uncountable plunder was taken there: horses and arms, gold and silver. The harnesses and coverings of the Roman horses were all of gold. Rome was horribly widowed. After the defeat had happened, the hour was late and the sun setting. The victorious Hannibal was quite happy. The leaders of his army made a circle around him and had a great feast and celebration of the triumph he had that day. Then they asked that he permit them and their chivalry to rest that night and the next day, for they were worn out an exhausted.

Among these leaders was a most valiant man by the name of Maharbal. He was the leader and organizer of the cavalry. Maharbal stepped forward and said these words, "Hannibal, my opinion is that you should not allow any rest either for yourself or your cavalry. Do you know what this victory has earned you? If you pursue your fortune without delay you will be eating and making merry as victor on the Campidoglio. Then you can grant a rest. Move your cavalry and your whole band and do not allow it to tarry. Let's go to Rome. We will find Rome in disorder and with its gates open. You will easily become lord. It is better that the Romans say, 'Hannibal has come' than 'Hannibal is coming.'" To these words Hannibal replied, "Maharbal, I praise you for your good intentions, but night gives its own advice. I want to think and take counsel." To this Maharbal responded, "Hannibal, Hannibal, you know how to achieve victory but not how to use it." So, Titus Livy says, "That delay was beneficial for the Roman people, for it freed them from servitude and returned ruling power to them from the Africans, into whose hands it had fallen."

NOW BACK to what we were discussing before. If Cola di Rienzo had followed up on his victory, he would have marched on Marino, taken the castle of Marino and utterly destroyed Messer Giordano, who would never again have raised his head, and the people of Rome would have retained their liberty free of tribulation.[133]

133. The Anonimo here uses classical precedent to criticize Rienzo for not following up on his victory. He was not alone. Petrarch (*Variae* 48; *Familiares* XIII.6) had also hoped for the barons' destruction. See also Cosenza, *Revolution*, 17–18, 130–48.

## CHAPTER EIGHTEEN

Now I will tell you how the tribune fell from power. The day after the victory, all the knights of Rome were called, those who were called "the holy militia," and he said to them, "I want to give you a double peace. Come with me."

No one knew what he was going to do. The trumpets sounding, he went to the place where the battle had happened. He brought with him his son Lorenzo. In the place where Stefano had died there remained a puddle of water. Upon arrival, he made his son dismount, and he anointed his head with water from the puddle, which was mixed with Stefano's blood, saying, "You will be the knight of victory."

As the others marveled among themselves, dumbfounded, he commanded that the knight constables should dub his son, touching the flat of their blades to his thighs. When this was done, he turned to the Campidoglio and said, "Go on your way. What we have done was done together. We are all lords of Rome. For us and you it is expected to fight for the fatherland." This statement deeply troubled the minds of the knights. From then onward, none of them wanted to carry arms.

Afterwards the tribune began to be the object of ill will. The people gossiped about him and said that he did not lack for arrogance. He began to become most terribly iniquitous, abandoning honorable dress. He wore fine things like an Asian tyrant. Already he began to show that he wanted to rule tyrannically by force. Already he began to extract money from the abbeys. Already he lay hold of whoever had money and took it from them. Upon those to whom he did this, he imposed silence. He ceased giving public addresses as frequently out of fear of the people's anger. He became red and fleshy, eating better than before and sleeping better too. He released the prefect, who was not in good health, and kept his son in his place. So the people began to abandon him and the barons too, and not so many people came to court to get his judgments as had done before. Then he imposed a tax on salt because he wanted money to pay his soldiers. At the same time, Messer Giordano of Marino never ceased pestering him daily, abducting and robbing the people. Due to all this the people murmured to one another.

It was autumn, after the harvest. Grain was scarce, costing seven *lire provesini* to the *rublum*. The tribune took money from anyone who had it. Messer Giordano continued his predations. The people became discontented. The cardinal legate, of whom I spoke above, cursed the tribune and declared him a heretic. He plotted with the lords, that is with Luca Savelli and Sciarretta Colonna, and favored them very much. Then the roads were closed. The great landowners stopped shipping grain to Rome. Every day brought a new clamor.[134]

❋

IT WAS DURING this period that a count that had been exiled from the kingdom of Naples came to Rome. His name was Janni Pipino, paladin of Altamura and count of Minervino. This paladin tarried in Rome because the rulers of Naples would not tolerate his bragging and boasting. *Cum familia sua degebat Rome.*[135] During this period, Messer Count Paladin erected a barricade in *rione* Colonna. He was the head of the rebellion within Rome.[136] The barricade was built under the arch of San Salvatore in Pesoli.[137] For a night and a day the

---

134. See above, p. 34.

135. "He dwelt in Rome with his armsmen." With this translation, I follow the suggestion of Campanelli that *"familia"* most likely refers here to a group of armed men associated with Pipino. See Campanelli, "Benché io l'aia ià fatta per lettera," 18. Giovanni Pipino has been declared a notorious brigand by King Robert of Anjou of Naples and was finally apprehended by Queen Giovanna I. He was released after Giovanna's consort, Prince Andrew of Hungary, intervened in his favor. Petrarch had been dispatched from Avignon by the Colonna, leaving Cola behind in the city, to attempt to secure Pipino's release on behalf of the Colonna, whose client he also was. Petrarch had failed in his mission. See Musto, *Writing Southern Italy*, 237–45.

136. Instead of accepting the Anonimo's claim that Pipino was the instigator of this unrest, Porta, 249, emphasizes the important role of Luca Savelli, whose family dominated Cola's own *rione*. Savelli, perhaps deliberately imitating Cola, posted a manifesto on the doors of Sant'Angelo in Pescheria on 14 December. Unrest in Rome was, then, already a problem, and Pipino's arrival simply seems to have exacerbated things.

137. San Salvatore was a church that stood where one now finds San Stanislao dei Polacchi. It thus stood in *rione* Sant'Angelo, very close to both the Campidoglio and the church of Sant'Angelo in Pescheria, where Cola had officially begun his movement to take over the city.

## CHAPTER EIGHTEEN

alarm bell of Sant'Angelo in Pescheria rang. A Jew rang it.[138] No one came to knock down this barricade.

The tribune quickly sent to the barricade a banner in defense. A constable named Scarpetta died, wounded by a lance while fighting. When the tribune heard that Scarpetta was dead and that the people had not assembled despite the ringing from Sant'Angelo in Pescheria, he began to sigh heavily and shake all over. He wept and did not know what to do. Shaken and struck to his core, he lacked the virtue of even a little boy. He could hardly speak. He thought that there might be ambushes lying in wait within the city, which wasn't actually the case because no one was openly in rebellion. There was no one threatening the people; it was he alone who was frightened. He thought he was going to be killed.

Why say more? In this way it became clear that he was no man of great virtue that would willingly die in service to the people, as he had promised. Weeping and sighing he gave an address to the people that were there with him, saying that he had ruled well and that the people were unhappy with him due to envy. "Now in the seventh month, I step down from my rule." Weeping as he said these words, he mounted his horse and sounded his silver trumpet, bearing imperial insignia and accompanied by armed men *triumphaliter descendit*[139] and went to Castel Sant'Angelo. There he sealed himself away, shutting himself in. His wife left the Lalli Palace dressed in the habit of the Friars Minor.

When the tribune descended from his grandeur those who were with him wept as well. The wretched people wept too.[140] His room

---

138. The church stands in what is now the Roman Ghetto and was in medieval times one of the main centers of Rome's ancient Jewish community. That a Jew was ringing the church bells, however, speaks clearly to the fact that no one else would do it.

139. "He descended triumphantly."

140. The Anonimo's account here relies on psychological, rather than political causation and is the basis for many later interpretations of Rienzo and his *buono stato* into the 21st century. The fact that the Roman people themselves mourned his departure complicates the Anonimo's image of an unpopular, unstable rule. So too does the archival record. See above pp. 41–42, 55–57; Musto, "Cola di Rienzo."

241

was found to be full of many baubles. You would not believe the number of written missives found there.

The barons knew of his fall but out of fear they waited three before returning to Rome. Rather than returning they hesitated fearfully.[141] The senators who were named after the tribune were weak governors and painted the tribune with his head down and his feet up in the way he had done the knights on the walls of the palace of the Campidoglio.[142] They also painted Cecco Mancino, his notary and chancellor. They painted his nephew Conte, who held the fortress of Civitavecchia. The cardinal legate entered Rome and began proceedings against Cola, condemning most of his deeds and saying that he was a heretic.

Then Cola di Rienzo secretly traveled to Bohemia, to the emperor Charles and resided in Prague, the royal city. Then he went to the pope in Avignon and there he managed to have the legal proceedings against him reversed, was named senator of Rome by the pope, came back to Rome, and did great and memorable things, as I will describe. Then he was killed by the people and harshly judged, as I will discuss in the chapter on his return to Italy.

THE PALADIN, who broke both Rome and the *buono stato*, *digno Dei iudicio*[143] ended up badly and died in disgrace. Eight years after these events he was hung by the neck in Apulia, in his own land of which he was a paladin, which is known as Altamura. On his head was placed a paper miter like a crown. On it was written, "Messer

141. This may well be, but the *Chronicon Estense* (RIS 15.3:158), which seems to have relied on diplomatic dispatches for these events in Rome, reports that Stefano Colonna kept the barons' party out and declared that "no one ought to presume or dare to break the peace previously made between so many by the lord tribune Cola di Rienzo, since the said Nicolo had brought peace among many; and great evil and scandal would follow otherwise." Again, the Anonimo did not have access to much of the diplomatic correspondence around Cola's *buono stato* and its fall.

142. Porta points out that these senators were none other than Bertoldo Orsini and Luca Savelli, barons both. Cola was portrayed in a *pittura infamante*, the visualization of traitors. See above, p. 54 n. 128.

143. "by the well-deserved judgment of God."

## ❈ CHAPTER EIGHTEEN

Giovanni Pipino, Knight, Paladin of Altamura, Count of Minervino, Lord of Bari, Liberator of the People of Rome."

Before he was hung, he made all kinds of arguments, saying "I am not of a lineage to be hung. I have not counterfeited money. Nor should I have to wear a miter. If it should be the case that I must die for my evil deeds, cut off my head."[144]

The response of the crown was this: "For your terrible deeds King Robert imprisoned you for life. King Andrew freed you and ended up cruelly slain. You could not have escaped royal punishment. Only Rome received you and so saved you. You destroyed their *buono stato*. You returned to the good grace of the crown. You made yourself leader of a great company. You gathered archers and robbers in your own lands. You preyed on the whole realm, plundered, and robbed. You made yourself king of Apulia.[145] Therefore it is right that you should end your life in a foul and disgraceful manner, as you deserve."

Such were the early deeds of Cola di Rienzo who had himself called the August Tribune.

---

144. That is, he requested the punishment of a nobleman, not of a common thief. The titles on his humiliating mitre were mocking, akin to the Romans' entitling Jesus "King of the Jews" above his cross. Pipino was a member of a highly respected southern family with a well-known record of patronage and pious endowments. See, for example, Caroline Bruzelius, *The Stones of Naples: Church Building in Angevin Italy, 1266–1343* (New Haven: Yale University Press, 2004), 163–72.

145. On events in Apulia during the civil war that followed the invasion of Naples by Lewis of Hungary, see Musto, *Writing Southern Italy*, 18–19, 211–13, with reference to the *Chronicon de rebus in Apulia gestis* by Domenico da Gravina.

## CHAPTER NINETEEN
THE DEATH OF ANDREW, KING OF PUGLIA, BY HANGING.
HOW JUSTICE FOLLOWED AFTER HIS DEATH

[This chapter is lost.[1]]

❋

## CHAPTER TWENTY
THE KING OF HUNGARY ENTERS ITALY.
THE DEATH OF THE DUKE OF DURAZZO, WHO IS BEHEADED

[This chapter is lost.[2]]

❋

## CHAPTER TWENTY-ONE
THE CRUEL MORTALITY THAT AFFLICTED THE WHOLE WORLD.
THE STEPS OF STA. MARIA IN ARACOELI

[This chapter is lost.[3]]

❋

1. For details of the events, see Casteen, *From She-Wolf to Martyr,* 29–66; Musto, *Medieval Naples,* 274–78.

2. For details of the events, see Casteen, *From She-Wolf to Martyr,* 67–76; Musto, *Medieval Naples,* 278–86.

3. This was the plague referred to as the Black Death, which first appeared in Italy in January 1348. The plan for monumental staircase of Sta. Maria, comprising 124 steps in front of the church, has long been associated with the end of the plague in Rome. The original project, however, was attributed to Rienzo in 1347 in preparation for the 1350 Jubilee. According to an inscription to the left of the church's central portal, it was designed in 1348 by Lorenzo Simone Andreotti, supposedly from the spoliated staircase of the Temple of the Sun on the Quirinal. The project costs of 5,000 florins were financed by a votive offerings for deliverance from the Black Death arranged by a Giovanni Colonna.

# CHAPTER TWENTY-TWO
THE EARTHQUAKE IN ITALY
[This chapter is lost.¹]

※

1. This was the series of quakes of September 1349, which struck central and southern Italy. In Rome it damaged the Torre dei Conti, San Paolo fuori le Mura, and the Lateran, among other buildings. Petrarch described it in a letter of June 11, 1351 (*Familiares* II.7).

# CHAPTER TWENTY-THREE
THE FIFTY-YEAR JUBILEE IN ROME.
THE KING OF HUNGARY'S RETURN TO ROME AND PUGLIA

IT WAS THE YEAR OF OUR LORD 1350 when Pope Clement granted to the Romans a plenary indulgence of both penance and sin for one year.[1] So all Christendom came to Rome without any restriction whatsoever. The cardinal de Boulogne-sur-Mer,[2] legate to Lombardy, was responsible for this indulgence and appointed Messer Annibaldo de Ceccano as cardinal legate for the pope in Rome, to guide the people and minister to the pilgrims. This cardinal legate wrote to his household and then left Avignon and came to Lombardy.

Messer Giovanni Visconti, archbishop of Milan and tyrant of Lombardy, appeared before him to pay his respects. Five destriers clad in scarlet and led by hand went before the archbishop. When the legate saw this, he was dumbfounded. He said, "Archbishop, what pomp, what vainglory is this?" The archbishop responded, "Legate, this is not pomp but simply due to the fact that I want the holy father to know that he has under him a little cleric who can get things done." The archbishop could only have gotten such destriers from among the great horses of the constables he had throughout the city.

Then the legate, Messer Annibaldo, came to Rome, dwelt in the papal palace, and began to provide for the governance of Rome and for the pilgrims. This Messer Annibaldo had four problematic qualities. First, that he was from Campania. Second, that he was squint-eyed.

---

1. The Anonimo's wording here is unclear. The Jubilee indulgence pertained to any who made the visit during the Jubilee year. That this was granted "to the Romans" refers to the fact that the Romans had been lobbying for another Jubilee earlier than 1400. Their interest was in the economic benefit of the increased pilgrim traffic. This had been one of the motivations for the embassy that first brought Cola di Rienzo to Avignon.

2. This was Gui de Boulogne, the subdean of the Sacred College of Cardinals. See Cosenza, *Revolution*, 121 n.11

## CHAPTER TWENTY-THREE

Third, that he was very pompous and full of vainglory. Of the fourth, I prefer to remain silent.[3]

This cardinal arrived in Rome and came into conflict with the Romans in the following way. He had a camel that he kept among the mules in his baggage train. One day the people came hoping to see it in the stable outside the palace. The foolish people made a great ruckus all around the palace. Some gazed at the camel. Some touched its fur, its head, or its testicles. They rode it. Then they wanted to lead it about. There was a tremendous amount of shouting and noise.

One of the legate's servants was there. He chastised the people because this disorderly behavior seemed wrong to him. To this chastisement he added threats. He made everyone go outside the enclosure. The people were not inclined to listen to him. They picked up stones in their hands, broke down the enclosure, and they headed straight for the servant. They threw stones at the place. They shouted like one would at a Patarine.[4] The people were drawn to this noise and came carrying sticks and rods. From the Piazza di San Pietro came the people of Puortica,[5] armed with every

---

3. Annibaldo da Ceccano was born c.1282 into an aristocratic family in Ceccano, in the northern Campania of the Regno of Naples, close to the border with Lazio. He was named archbishop of Naples in 1326, cardinal-priest of San Lorenzo in Lucina in 1327, and cardinal-bishop of Tusculum in 1333. He served as a papal legate to negotiate a truce between England and France in 1342 and was a trusted member of the papal curia in Avignon. He was known for his opulent entertainments, hosting the new Clement VI's reception in Avignon in 1343. The Anonimo's mention of his squint eye may have been a playful allusion to Annibaldo' treatise on the Beatific Vision, a controversial topic in trecento Italy that involved even Pope John XXII and King Robert the Wise of Naples. Pope John's interpretation — and that of Annibaldo who agreed with him — was declared faulty. See Internullo, *Ai margini*, 343–47. Contemporary Romans may have known the rumors about the Anonimo's fourth characteristic, but moderns must fill in the Anonimo's blanks. For details, see Musto, *Apocalypse in Rome*, 262–67; Marc Dykmans, "Le Cardinal Annibal de Ceccano (c.1282–1350): Étude biographique et testament de 17 Juin 1348," *Bulletin de l'Institut Historique Belge de Rome* 48 (1973): 145–315.

4. The Patarines were a heterodox religious sect in eleventh-century Milan. By this time, the term had become a generic one that meant simply "heretic."

5. The neighborhood near San Pietro.

kind of weapon, *clinora* of steel, shields, faulds, bucklers, and crossbows.⁶ At the palace they engaged in a massive battle. The gate was sealed. The noise was terrible. Stones flew, so did javelins and lances, hurled like a driving storm. It seemed like they wanted to take the fortress by force.

When the legate heard all this, he was astonished and terrified. He stood on his balcony above, looking down over everything. He had no idea why any of this was happening. He put his hands over his face and said, "What is the meaning of this? What did I do? Why are they attacking me like this? Look how you Romans give the holy father reason to come to Rome! In this land the pope would not be ruler, not even a just archpriest would be! I cannot believe I wasted my time coming here! The Romans are the most perverse and arrogant people in the whole world!" He held out his hand and gestured for them to stop the uproar. In the end, Brother Giovanni de Lucca, commander of the Holy Spirit, curbed and quieted the irrational citizens.⁷ Everyone went back to their houses. The cardinal was extremely afraid and would have preferred to stay in Avignon.

This legate did brilliant things. He placed in San Pietro the two beautiful draperies that are on the side of the choir, and he donated one to San Giovanni and another to Santa Maria Maggiore.⁸ He intended to reform the treasury of St. Peter. He gave absolution and penances to

---

6. Though it must be a weapon of some kind, the precise meaning of *clinora* remains obscure. The rest of the weapons and armor described here match what one would expect of the non-noble Roman militia, the Felix Societas Pavesatorum et Balistrariorum (Fortunate Society of Crossbowmen and Shieldbearers) which wielded considerable power in Rome during this period, sometimes rivaling that of the formal government. See Jean Claude Maire-Vigueur, "La Felice Societas dei Balestrieri e dei Pavesati a Roma: Una società popolare e i suoi ufficiali," *Scritti per Isa: Raccolta di studi offerti a Isa Lori Sanfilippo,* Antonella Mazzon and Isa Lori Sanfilippo, ed. (Rome: Istituto storico italiano per il Medio Evo, 2008), 577–606.

7. Giovanni was the head of the nearby Hospital of Santo Spirito in Saxia. For the hospital see above, chapter 3, p. 71, chapter 9, p. 100.

8. Wright's translation assumes that there were two draperies, dedicated to John and Mary respectively as a kind of offering. Given that the Anonimo does not refer to the Virgin but rather to "Santa Maria Maiure" suggests that these were donations of four draperies to three churches.

## ✼ CHAPTER TWENTY-THREE

provinces and cities, princes, and others. He punished penitentiaries, arresting and imprisoning them.⁹ He made knights, giving them honors and offices. He increased and reduced the number of days for penances, reducing the remission of fifteen days to a single day for the many people who were in Rome because, had he not done so, Rome could not have managed their numbers.¹⁰ He said the mass in a papal manner with all the ceremonies proper to the pope. To the sounding of silver horns he arrived in church and returned to his palace.

This legate wanted to do the fifteen-day penance and accrue the benefit to his soul like the others. But look what happened. One day, after saying mass, he rode off to make the pilgrimage circuit. He went to St. Peter's and then to St. Paul's. As he was going down the street that runs from the Armenians to Santo Spirito, in that spot between San Lorenzo *in Piscibus* and Sant'Angelo delle Scale, two bolts suddenly flew from the tiny window of a small house of the Incarcerata, alongside San Lorenzo. They had been shot to kill the legate.¹¹ One missed him and flew through air in vain, but the other struck his hat and stuck there. The cardinal was dumbstruck by such fare. The members of his household there rushed to his aid. They formed a ring around him. The noise was great: "Get him! Get him!" They ran here and there to find the one who had tried to kill the cardinal. The house had a rear exit, a back door. The shooters had left through that door, leaving their crossbows behind. They

---

9. A penitentiary was an ecclesiastical official with the power to impose penances and tend to other aspects pertaining to the care of souls. As with his attitude toward the treasury, we see here the cardinal's inclination toward reform.

10. Pilgrims were meant to visit the major basilicas (St. Peter's, San Giovanni in Laterano, and San Paolo fuori le Mura) daily for fifteen days. The Anonimo's mention of the large numbers of pilgrims points to the ultimate success of the Romans' 1343 mission to Avignon.

11. San Lorenzo in Piscibus stands near St. Peter's on the modern street of Borgo Santo Spirito, which leads to the Hospital of Santo Spirito in Saxia. Across from San Lorenzo is the church of SS. Michele e Magno, which Porta identifies with Sant'Angelo delle Scale. Armellini refers to this as San Michele or Sant'Angelo de Micinellis. See his *Le chiese di Roma dal secolo IV al XIX* (Rome: Pasquino, 1982), 363–65. The reference to the Incarcerata is obscure but may refer to a lesser chapel housed in a small building, which would explain the priest who was then questioned.

blended in with the crowd of penitents, all of whom were strangers. No one was found in the house. Two crossbows were found. The house was razed to the ground. *Iustus pro peccatore*[12] the priest was taken and tortured but did not reveal who the crossbowmen were.

Then the legate returned home. A pompous man who yearned for fame learned that he was not thought of highly. He was seething with anger. He was enraged. He could find no peace. Wringing his hands, he said, "Where have I ended up? In deserted Rome! It would be better for me to be a minor priest in Avignon than a great prelate in Rome. They attacked me at home in my palace, and now they have shot at me! I don't even know who to take revenge on!"

He couldn't control his wrath. He launched a major investigation to find the evildoers but was never able to identify them. He firmly believed that the tribune, Cola di Rienzo, was behind it. He wouldn't place the blame on anyone else. Then, hoping the pope would have mercy on him, he wrote letters to the court of the holy father, in which he recited his misfortunes, how he was attacked, and how potential assassins had tried to kill him. Along with the letter he sent one of the crossbow bolts. Then, to satisfy himself, he leveled a terrible sentence and curse upon those who had sinned against him. He cursed and excommunicated Cola di Rienzo, and whoever conspired with him, calling him a Patarine and a madman, annulling all his acts, and heaping on him every curse he could come up with. He stripped the guilty parties of every office, benefice, and dignity, even their right to water and fire.[13] He left nothing undone to confound his enemies. Being an expert in canon law, he knew how great the misdeed was, and how great a penalty to impose. From that time onward, the legate always wore a steel skullcap under his hat and a breastplate under his cape.[14]

---

12. "The just man in place of the sinner..."

13. These were follow-ups to the excommunication already leveled against Rienzo by Cardinal-Legate Bertrand de Déaulx. But here Annibaldo extends the excommunication to the officials of Rienzo's *buono stato* who were still in Rome, many still in office. Several would remain in office into the next decade. Denying people "water and fire" meant to condemn them to exile.

14. This may be a good indication that Rienzo still had many adherents in Rome.

✳ CHAPTER TWENTY-THREE

There was in Rome during those days the cardinal of San Crisogono, a Frenchman as well as a great prelate and baron.¹⁵ He came before Messer Annibaldo. To console him he said these words, "Whoever wants to set Rome straight would be best served by destroying it utterly and then rebuilding it anew." Once he heard this, the legate got back to work and continued with his legation.

✳

I WOULD LIKE to say something about how the legate died. It was in the month of July, and it was extremely hot. It suited Messer Annibaldo, by papal command, to absent himself from Rome and go to Naples to report on the desolation of the kingdom of Puglia, which was in ruin, as I will describe.¹⁶ Abruptly the legate left Rome. Once in Campania, he visited Ceccano, his homeland. He passed Montecassino and came to San Germano. There he rested. The next day he left San Germano, taking a short trip. He came to a castle not far off. In that castle he rested. As was customary, tributes came to him there from all over. Among other things, he was sent many flasks of good wine.

One man said that these flasks were poisoned, for the flasks had been poisoned by the Great Company, which was present in that land.¹⁷ This is not likely. Only a madman poisons his own wine.

15. Most likely Cardinal Gui de Boulogne, one of the four cardinals whom Clement VI would appoint in late 1351 to a commission to reform the government of Rome, and to whom Petrarch sent two advisory letters. See Cosenza, *Revolution*, 105–25, and p. 246 n. 2 above.

16. At no point in the surviving chapters does the Anonimo actually follow up on this promise. Frequent allusion to the political turmoil within the kingdom of Naples, however, suggests that he intended to and may well have done in one of the missing chapters. Following the murder of Prince Consort Andrew in 1345, the kingdom was torn by invasion and war. Queen Giovanna I of Naples, aided by her second husband, Louis of Taranto, defended the Regno against Andrew's brother, King Lewis of Hungary, who claimed the throne via descent from Charles II of Naples. For details, see Casteen, *From She-Wolf to Martyr*, 69–76; and Musto, *Medieval Naples*, lxix–lxxi, 274–86.

17. The Great Company was founded by Werner von Urslingen after his participation in the battle of Parabiago (above, chapter 9). Its initial members were largely veterans of the war between Pisa and Florence, (chapter 12, pp. 138–39. There were several different companies by the same name, including Fra

Of these various wines the legate, hot from his ride, drank full well, for he was thirsty. He was one of the greatest drinkers ever to grace the Church of God. He was at table in his room, having dinner. This man of Campania wanted his entire household with him as he dined. He ate in a happy, cheerful manner. At the advice of his doctors, Master Guido da Prato and Master Matteo da Viterbo, after dining he was accustomed to refresh himself by consuming fresh ewe's milk. He wanted to do this, as he was accustomed to do. One of his servants went to a barn yard and there milked an ewe. Once he had filled a large silver bowl of milk, he returned to the dining room. The legate had waited a long time as this milk was retrieved and whipped up. The cardinal, once the milk arrived, dug into it with his spoon and began to eat. He filled his stomach with it. A corrupting food. A long time after the meal, after the milk, came cucumbers soaked in vinegar, which he ate to refresh himself on the urging of these doctors. When night game, he went to rest. He could not find any rest, nor could he sleep. The food sat in his stomach, raw and undigested. The next day he began to feel tired, despite having ridden only a short distance. The first place he found was the village of San Giorgio. There he rested, for he could not ride any further. He rested that evening without eating. That night he passed from this life.[18]

Great was the sadness of his companions. They were abandoned, like sheep abandoned by their shepherd, in two ways. First, all their supplies were carried off by the barons of that land. Second, because the cardinal's nephew, one of two, died. Soon the entire household was sick. First this one, then that one died. The entire household died and not one was spared. One died in Campania, another at Rome,

---

Morreale's. See Michael Mallett, *Mercenaries and their Masters: Warfare in Renaissance Italy* (Totowa, NJ: Rowman and Littlefield, 1974), 29–35; and William Caferro, *Mercenary Companies and the Decline of Siena* (Baltimore, MD: The Johns Hopkins University Press, 1998), 4–9.

18. Another example of the Anonimo's medical expertise. Vittorio Formentin has analyzed the Anonimo's account here against contemporary medical theory of the physiological impact of certain foods, tracking the pacing of the Anonimo's prose with the progress of the cardinal's illness. See his "Approssimazioni al testo e alla lingua della *Cronica* d'Anonimo romano," in his *Leggere gli apparati: Testi e testimoni dei classici italiani* (Milan: Unicopli, 2012), 27–71, at 38–42. See also Introduction above, pp. 10–11.

## CHAPTER TWENTY-THREE

and another at Viterbo. Messer Giovanni, the other nephew, died in Santo Spirito in Rome. *Non remansit canis mingens ad parietem.*[19]

That was the novelty, the papal legate died while traveling in the village of San Giorgio, and after him his nephews and all his household, in the year of our Lord 1350, during the Jubilee. The body of the legate was opened. He was fat within like a nursing calf. His stomach was filled with a solid lump of wax. His body was anointed with aloe and dressed in the habit of the Friars Minor. He was carried in a chest by a mule like a load of baggage, *qua venerat via Romam rediit.*[20] He arrived in St. Peter's without any company, without wailing. Without aid of clergy his tomb in his chapel was prepared. He was tossed in. He was not placed, but thrown, face down, and so he remained. Consider, then, what human life, worldly glory, and honor amount to. A pompous man, a high-ranking prelate who desired money, honors, luxurious dwellings, and honorable company, lying alone in the habit of poverty, closed in his tomb. For all his wealth, not a servant even made the effort to lay out his sprawled body *secundum debitam figuram.*[21]

---

19. "Not a dog remained pissing on the wall." This is a biblical allusion to total destruction. See 1 Kings 16:11. This is discussed by Campanelli in "Gli inserti Latini," 7.

20. "He returned to Rome by the same road that he left it." Campanelli notes that this is not a reference to any other text. Instead, he speculates that these two Latin passages, and the one to come below, work to mark the three steps of the story he is telling. See "Gli inserti Latini," 7–8. The text might, however, be a paraphrase of the apocryphal *Acts of Peter* (XXXV), widely known through chapter 89 of *The Golden Legend* by Jacobus de Voragine. The Anonimo might be making a mocking comparison to St. Peter, returning to Rome to face his own death, by martyrdom, after his encounter with Jesus at the site now called *Domine, Quo Vadis?*

21. "in the proper way." Musto, *Apocalypse in Rome,* 266–67, speculates that these deaths might have been due to another onset of the plague and compares the Anonimo's account of such indifferent behavior to Boccaccio's in the Preface to the *Decameron*.

253

# CHAPTER TWENTY-FOUR
## The Perugians lay siege to Bettona, raze that place to its foundations, and behead the traitor, Messer Crispolto

[This chapter is lost.[1]]

✹

1. These events took place in 1352. The town was rebuilt by Cardinal Gilles Albornoz, who built a rocca there to maintain control of the region for the papacy. A San Crispolto, reputedly a first-century Christian martyr, was the town's patron saint, killed there among other Christians, who were beheaded. The Perugians removed the saint's relics in 1352, when they sacked the city. Cardinal Albornoz ordered their return in 1367. The Anonimo may have confused his account here, or he may have been referring to the saint as the symbolic personification of the town's rebellion against Perugia.

# CHAPTER TWENTY-FIVE
### The bell tower of St. Peter's in Rome burns.
### The pope loses control of the Senate.
### Pope Clement dies

[This chapter is lost.[1]]

1. It is difficult to know which tower is meant here. The first complete drawings of the Old St. Peter's were done in the early 16th century, in preparation for its demolition and replacement by the current basilica. But even in these drawings the western tower over the atrium remained intact. The papal loss of the Senate may refer to the Roman revolt of December 26, 1351 that brought Giovanni Cerroni to the city's rectorship on behalf of the *popolo*. Clement VI confirmed Cerroni in this office in May 1352 and died on December 6, 1352.

# CHAPTER TWENTY-SIX
A SENATOR IS STONED BY THE ROMANS.
THE MAGNIFICENT DEEDS OF MESSER EGIDIO CONCHESE OF
SPAIN, CARDINAL LEGATE, TO RETAKE THE PATRIMONY, THE
MARCH OF ANCONA, AND ROMAGNA

WITH POPE CLEMENT DEAD, Pope Innocent was elected, he who was called the cardinal of Claremont, a secular priest of the habit of Saint Peter.[1] When Pope Innocent was elected, God revealed his great vengeance on those who had corrupted the senate. It was the year of our Lord, 1353, a Saturday in February, during Lent. A shout arose suddenly in the Roman marketplace: "The people! The people!" From all over, the Romans rushed to that voice like demons, driven by a horrible anger. They hurled stones at the palace and seized whatever they could, especially the senator's horses.[2] When Count Bertoldo Orsini heard the noise, he decided to escape and fortify himself in his house. He armed himself completely: a shining helm on his head and spurs on his feet as suited a baron. He came down the stairs to mount his horse. The shouting and anger shifted its focus to the unfortunate senator. So many rocks and stones rained down on him that it was like leaves falling in autumn. Some struck him and others threatened to do so. The senator, stunned by so many blows, was unable to adequately shield himself with his armor. He was able to make it on foot to the palace where the image of Holy Mary is.[3] There, under pressure from the rain of stones, he lost his strength. Without mercy or restraint the people ended his days in that place, stoning him like a dog, raining stones down on his head as if he were Saint Stephen.[4] The count

1. Innocent VI, pope from 1352 to 1362.

2. Rome's largest market sat at the base of the Campidoglio. The palace referred to here is the Senate Palace on that hill.

3. There were several prominent images of the Virgin on the Capitoline Hill. See Bolgia, *Reclaiming the Roman Capitol,* passim. The Anonimo does not specify which this might be or its location.

4. Considered the first Christian martyr, stoned to death at a gate in Jerusalem. His death is recounted in Acts 7–8. In medieval art he was often portrayed with stones about his head and shoulders. Once again, it is difficult to know whether the Anonimo's comparisons are ironic, instructing by opposites, or sympathetic with the senator.

passed from this life excommunicated.⁵ No one said a thing. Once he was dead, they left him there and everyone went home. *Senator collega turpiter per funem demissus, deformis pileo per posticam palatii obvoluta facie transivit ad domum.*⁶

The reason for such severity was that these two senators lived like tyrants. They were already notorious for selling Roman grain abroad by sea. Grain was in terribly short supply. The commoners cannot bear great hunger and starvation. A starving people knows no fear. They do not wait for someone to say "do this." Such is the truth of famine that has brought down many powerful men. Another possible reason is God's disapproval that the goods of the Church were violated. Valerius Maximus speaks of this. He gives the example of Dionysius, the tyrant of Sicily, who cut the golden hair and beards from his gods and said that the gods should not resemble bearded goats. For this insult to his gods he was punished, so that he lived out his life in fear, and after his death his son became so wretched that he survived by teaching little boys the alphabet. Maybe that was all he was good for.⁷ Lo and behold! As soon as it became known that the

---

5. The Anonimo does not say why Orsini was excommunicated. He might have been one of the Orsini included among Rienzo's adherents excommunicated by Cardinal Annibaldo. See above, chapter 23, p. 251.

6. "His wicked fellow senator escaped by means of a rope, fleeing out the back of the palace shamefully with his face covered, and made his way to his house." This other senator was Stefanello Colonna. Campanelli, "Gli inserti Latini," 21–22, suggests from this passage and others in this late chapter that the manuscript copy we have is evidence that the Anonimo's translation between a Latin original and the surviving vernacular version was not yet complete.

7. The Anonimo derives this story from Valerius Maximus, *Factorum ac dictorum memorabilium libri novem*, I.1, ext. 3, but he mixes things up a bit. The original condemns Dionysius for stealing gold from the shrines of the gods, mostly golden garments and vessels but also the golden beard of Asclepius. In his *Tusculan Disputations* (V. 20.58), Cicero describes Dionysius' fear of assassination, saying that he would only allow his daughter to cut his hair and beard. This fear is also discussed by Diodorus (XX.63.3) and Plutarch (Dion IX.3). For discussion of this see, Lionel Jehuda Sanders, *Dionysius I of Syracuse and Greek Tyranny* (New York: Routledge, 1987), 27. The story told here seems to mix the two matters. Wright notes a supposed error, pointing out that Valerius Maximus describes Dionysius' son, Dionysius II, as a teacher of

senator had been stoned to death, the famine abruptly ceased in the lands thereabout and there was a ready supply of grain.

THE FIRST THING that Pope Innocent decided to do was to see to it that tyrants return to the church its holdings, which they had usurped and seized.[8] To achieve this, he sent into Italy his legate, Messer Egidio Conchese of Spain, a cardinal.[9] The deeds of this Don Gilio demonstrated clearly what a capable warrior he was. Earlier in life he had been a knight with golden spurs. Then he became the archdeacon of Conche.[10] Such was his skill that he was made the bannerman of the king of Castile. He was personally present at the route of Taliffa in Spain, which I described above.[11] Don Gilio descended into the Patrimony and arrived at Montefiascone.[12] He

---

literature, not the alphabet (6.9, ext. 6), suggesting that the Anonimo has mistranslated *litteras* in an overly literal way as *letters*. The Loeb translation of D.R. Shackleton Bailey, however, renders the passage similarly to the Anonimo, saying Dionysius II taught children their ABCs. For someone of the Anonimo's day, this would possibly have suggested a very low education on the part of Dionysius himself, as entry-level teachers were sometimes barely literate themselves. See Ronald G. Witt, "What did Giovannino Read and Write? Literacy in Early Renaissance Florence," *I Tatti Studies: Essays in the Renaissance* 6 (1995): 83–114, at 95. On literacy levels in trecento Rome, however, see now Internullo, *Ai margini*. That the Anonimo understood things this way is even more likely given his suggestion that this was all the man was good for. The use of this comparison to tyrannical barons was not unique to the Anonimo. His near contemporary in Rome, Giovanni Cavallini de Cerroni, had also deployed it. See Internullo, *Ai margini*, 270–71.

8. Our translation for *bieni della Chiesa* is broader than "goods" to get across the idea of the Patrimony of St. Peter.

9. That is, Gilkes Albornoz (Gil Álvarez Carillo de Albornoz), the former archbishop of Toledo. In 1350 he became cardinal of San Clemente. See Musto, *Apocalypse in Rome*, 312–14.

10. Albornoz had been archdeacon of Calatrava.

11. See chapter 11, pp. 119–25. Albornoz was present at the battle of Rio Salado and at the capture of Algeciras.

12. The Patrimony of St. Peter made up the core of the future Papal States and was long part of the late ancient District of Rome. See Peter Partner,

# CHAPTER TWENTY-SIX

could find nowhere but Montefiascone to go. Acquapendente, Bolsena, and all the other lands were occupied by Ianni da Vico, the prefect of Viterbo. He also held Terni, Amelia, Narni, Orvieto, Viterbo, Marta, and Canino. He was great. He was working to take Perugia. The legate was astonished at finding so few allies. Nevertheless, he wanted to parlay with the prefect. He sent for him, and they met. The prefect was characterized by an evil nature, so that whenever someone asked him for something he would quickly agree and say, "It will be done. It pleases us well." But he would not follow through on the promise. The more he promised you, the worse he treated you. This being his custom, he handled the legate the same way. He could not help himself. When they were together, the legate said, "Prefect, what do you desire?" The prefect said, "I want whatever pleases you." The legate then said, "I would have it that the Church rule what belongs to it and that you control what belongs to you." The prefect replied, "I would willingly have it so. I am content." And then he signed his personal sigil to a paper on which the agreement was written. He then headed back to Viterbo. He fulfilled none of his promises. He said, "I do not want to do this." To this he added, "The legate has a company of fifty priests and chaplains. My boys are enough to stand against his priests." This comparison inevitably made its way to the ears of the legate. To it the legate responded, saying, "Fine. He'll see that my priests will be more valiant than the prefect and his boys."

Once the legate understood the obdurate character of the prefect and saw his perverse obstinance, he did not call a crusade against him (things did not seem so grave as that). But he did call the aid of a league that included Tuscany, Perugia, Florence, and Siena. He created a great army, which he led himself. In this army was Cola di Rienzo, knight, who had arrived after being absolved by the pope in Avignon, as was said. The prefect cared little about this band of soldiers. Then the people of Rome

---

*The Lands of St Peter: The Papal State in the Middle Ages and Early Renaissance* (London: Methuen, 1972); Sandro Carocci, "The Papal State," in Andrea Gamberini and Isabella Lazzarini, ed., *The Italian Renaissance State* (Cambridge: Cambridge University Press, 2012), 69–89; and Maire Vigueur, "Comuni e signorie." Montefiascone and the other sites mentioned here were all on the northern border toward Umbria and Tuscany.

marched out. Giovanni, count of Vallemontone was the captain. He began to ravage the land. He destroyed a third of Viterbo: vineyards, olive groves, and trees. He laid waste to everything. The people blamed the prefect. Raniero de Bussa harassed the prefect. The prefect, doubting his own citizens, like any tyrant, realized he was ill-prepared. *Deliberato consilio saniori*,[13] he draped his cloak over his arm and submitted to the embrace of the Church. He handed over Viterbo, Orvieto, Marta, and Canino. He held onto his own castles firmly. He retained as well Corneto, Civitavecchia, and Respampano.[14] After a short while, Giordano Orsini captured Corneto from him in half a day. The prefect complained to the legate and said that he had been cheated because he was driven out of Viterbo. The legate responded, "Prefect, you were not cheated." He showed him the contract with his sigil. The contract said, "I wish to keep what is mine and restore to others what is theirs." Hearing this, the prefect was silent.

In Viterbo the legate constructed a most beautiful castle compound, furnished with many towers, a palace, and dwellings, which would serve as a foundation and fortress for the church of Rome. That castle stands and flourishes to this very day. It stands at the gate that leads to Montefiascone. It has an abundant water supply and is surrounded by moats.

WITH WORK IN THE PATRIMONY rapidly concluded, the legate lingered for a time in Orvieto. He reformed Orvieto and the surrounding territory, which was very corrupt. Then he did the same in Narni, then Amelia. Then he went on to greater things, rapidly moving to the same ends in the March to bring low the

---

13. "Taking heed of wiser counsel."

14. As with the papal actions behind the scenes before Cola's overthrow in Rome (see Introduction, pp. 40–42), the Anonimo may not have known about Pope Innocent VI's publication of Clement VI's excommunication of the prefect. This was issued on September 15, 1353; and on December 17, Albornoz declared Giovanni de Vico a contumacious enemy of the Church, allowing papal forces to strip the prefect of all his lands and belongings, if he continued to resist. See Musto, *Apocalypse in Rome*, 314–15. Again, the archival record fills out the Anonimo's moral tale.

## CHAPTER TWENTY-SIX

arrogance of the Malatesta. Messer Malatesta was one of the savviest warriors in Romagna.[15] A powerful tyrant, he ruled many cities and castles. He held the better part of the March of Ancona by means of loyalty or force. He had a brother, Messer Galeotto. He constantly sent him out to fight. He held Ancona, that noble city. When Messer Galeotto heard that the legate was approaching the region, he gathered together a great multitude of more than 3,000 knights. He left Ancona. He went to Recanati to confront the legate. With Messer Galeotto was Gentile da Mogliano da Fermo, with many other leading men from the March. He sent messages to the legate declaring that his arrival was in vain, for he could not hope to match the Malatesta or bring them over to his cause.

The legate responded to these words, "From good warriors come good peacemakers, from good peacemakers come good warriors."

Messer Galeotto answered, "Tell the legate that I do not wish to put so many people in danger. I want to fight the legate one-on-one in the field."

The legate responded, "Go say to him, 'Here I am in the field. There I will fight him willingly, man-to-man. He will not walk away.'"

Messer Galeotto replied, "Go tell my lord legate that I do not wish to fight him man-to-man. If I defeat him, I would still come out the loser, for he is an old man, a priest, better suited to fatherhood."[16]

Accompanying the legate was a gentleman from the March by the name of Nicola da Buscareto. This Nicola da Buscareto was present for these exchanges. He said, "Lord legate, do you not realize the Malatesta are broken? Does it not seem to you that, by his very words, Messer Galeotto is broken and lost? He cannot withstand you. We have won. Legate, set upon the Malatesta of Rimini and do

---

15. This is Malatesta II (1299–1364). His brother was Galeotto I (1299–1385). On the Malatesta and others, see Larner, *Lords of Romagna*.

16. Wright renders this as "fit only for the paternal care of souls," which follows logically from the previous dismissal of Albornoz as a mere prelate but ignores the reference to his advanced age. The latter is key here. War was a young man's game; marriage and fatherhood were for older men. Albornoz was, after all, no mere priest but a veteran of the wars in Iberia. The problem wasn't that he was unsuited for war but rather that he was old.

not relent, for Galeotto has already shown that he lacks heart. That is what his words reveal to me."

By the suggestion of Nicola da Buscareto, the legate was inspired to go after the Malatesta. He had with him many good people, many leading men, partisans of the March, Messer Lomo da Esi; Iumentaro dalla Pira, the lord of Cagli; Messer Redolfo de Camerino; Esmeduccio de Santo Severino. He also had German nobles that the emperor had given him. In those days Emperor Charles [IV] was in Rome, of which I will speak later. He had taken the crown. All Tuscany, Lombardy, Romagna, and Germany did him homage. From this emperor the legate requested a subsidy. The emperor sent him the knights he asked for from among those given to him by the communes of Perugia and Florence. Charles also sent him battle-tested German barons. So the legate and his people assembled in the field. Messer Galeotto Malatesta had fallen back to a strong position, a place called Paderno, between Macerata and Ancona, when suddenly from behind him came the noble imperial force, Germans and Tuscans, counts of Germany, battle-tested men with many crests, their horns and drums sounding. They had marched ceaselessly. When Messer Galeotto understood that they had come to reinforce the legate, he lost his mind and his virtue. There was nothing he could do. He declared himself defeated, admitted that he had been captured, and begged mercy of the legate. The legate had taken him with all his people.

In order to recover his brother, Messer Malatesta swore obedience to the legate. He freely handed over to him the city of Ancona and all the lands he held in the March. He handed over what he held in Romagna. So the Church gained the noble city of Ancona, a land rich with ports, with access to the sea, with commerce, and with many other resources. There he built two lovely fortresses that still stand today. Next, he made his nephew lord of the March and sent him to Macerata to govern the region. Then he deliberately and quietly provided for the Malatesta that they might live honorably and nobly of their own. He left for them four good and famous cities: Rimini, Fano, Pesaro, and Fossombrone, four noteworthy and well-resourced lands. Finally, he made them captains of the Church, charged with handling rebels. After these things he moved on to even greater deeds and undertakings.

※

## ✤ CHAPTER TWENTY-SIX

THERE WAS IN ROMAGNA a perfidious Patarine dog, a rebel against the holy Church. He had been excommunicated for thirty years, with all his lands under the interdict so that mass could not be said. He occupied many of the Church's lands: the city of Forlì, the city of Cesena, Forlimpopoli, Castrocaro, Brettonoro, Imola, and Giazolo. All these lands he held and ruled like a tyrant, without the many other castles and communities that belonged to the local people. This Francesco was a desperate man.[17] He had a mad hatred of priests, resenting that he had been ill-treated by the previous legate, Bertrand du Pouget, cardinal of Ostia, as was discussed earlier.[18] *De cetero*,[19] he did not want to live according to the dictates of priests. He was a perfidious, obstinate tyrant. This Francesco, when he heard the bells ringing his excommunication, quickly had the other bells rung and excommunicated the pope and the cardinals. And what was worse, he had effigies of the pope and cardinals stuffed with paper and straw and burned in the piazza. He rationalized this to his noble friends saying, "And so we are excommunicated. Despite that, the bread, meat, and wine that we consume will still taste good and nourish us." When it came to priests and the religious he behaved as follows. Once the excommunication was carried out by the bishop,

---

17. These events took place in 1350. This was Francesco Ordelaffi (1300–1374). He had been excommunicated first for imprisoning the archbishop of Ravenna. Later, he led the Ghibelline forces in the Romagna on behalf of Lewis IV of Bavaria. Ordelaffi set a precedent for Italian humanists by hiring Giovanni Boccaccio as his chancellor in 1347/48. He also joined Lewis of Hungary's invasion of Naples in 1347. See Alma Poloni, "Ordelaffi, Francesco di Sinibaldo di," in *Dizionario Biografico degli Italiani* 79 (2013), online at: https://www.treccani.it/enciclopedia/francesco-di-sinibaldo-ordelaffi_(Dizionario-Biografico). Leardo Mascanzoni notes the Anonimo's contradictory caricature of Ordelaffi. See his "The Italian 'Crusade' against Francesco Ordelaffi (1356-1359), Lord of Forlì, and how it is perceived in the Chronicles," Testo per il Convegno Internazionale Diversity of Crusading, Ninth Quadrennial Conference of the SSCLE (Odense, 27 June–1 July 2016), online at: https://www.academia.edu/34053039; and idem, "La Romagna e Bologna nella *Cronica* di Anonimo Romano," *Atti e Memorie della Deputazione di Storia Patria per le Province di Romagna* n.s. 67 (2017): 119–50.

18. Bertrand's style of governance is described in chapter 5, pp. 75–78.

19. "Among other things."

that same bishop suffered some injury and left the city in disgrace. Then the captain forced the clergy to celebrate the sacraments. Many celebrated despite the interdict, fourteen religious clerics and seven seculars.[20] Eight who would not celebrate received holy martyrdom. Seven were hung by the neck and seven were flayed. He was much beloved by the people of Forlì. He behaved toward them as a man of mercy and charity. He married off orphans, gave dowries to young girls, and succored the poor like a friend.

Now I turn to the war. Don Gilio Conchese of Spain made his base and residence in Ancona. To increase his strength he had a crusade declared. I heard it preached myself. Remission of penance and sin was offered to any who took up the cross or aided the effort in any way. Then the legate descended on that dog, the captain of Forlì, Francesco Ordelaffi. Before taking the field he readied his host with all the necessities. The legate sent bishops and knights and other good people to entreat the captain not to persist in his error. He listened quietly to their words. Come nightfall, he sallied from Forlì and ravaged the lands of the Church. He took plunder and prisoners. He gave no other response. The legate, understanding the obstinate will of Francesco Ordelaffi, set up camp near the city of Cesena. The Malatesta were the head men and leaders of the host. There were 12,000 crusaders and 30,000 other soldiers. They were like two different armies, each one for itself. The host caused great destruction and damage. At the sound of a trumpet 3,000 pillagers bearing banners set to laying waste and then left off again. *Res digna memoratu*.[21] Then the holy father sent letters requesting that Don Gilio return to Provence. The reason for this was that the count of Savoy, with a great company of 3,000 *barbute*,[22] was laying waste to

20. The distinction here is between clergy who were members of religious orders (hence religious) and those who were simply priests. The Anonimo's math does not quite work out here, however.

21. "It was a thing to remember."

22. This was Amadeus VI, the "Green Count" (r. 1343–83), whose military and diplomatic ambitions involved him with the Angevin lands of Queen Giovanna I in Provence, the Hundred Years War, and the expansionist policies of the French crown. See Eugene L. Cox, *The Green Count of Savoy* (Princeton, NJ: Princeton University Press, 1967). A *barbuta* was a kind of helmet, lacking a visor and with a characteristic T-shaped opening that left

## CHAPTER TWENTY-SIX

Provence. He captured lands, robbed, and ransomed people. Before Don Gilio departed, another legate came, a man from France, a Burgundian abbot with many lucrative benefices, a powerful and capable person.[23]

The captain of Forlì had a son named Giovanni and another named Messer Ludovico. The latter approached his father and humbly beseeched him, saying, "Father, by God, please do not be at odds with the Church or with God. Let's carry out the commands. We are obedient. I am sure the legate is a discreet man. He will treat us just as well as he has treated the Malatesta. He will leave us with enough that we are able to live honorably."[24] To these humble words the arrogant father replied, "You must be bastards, or else you were switched at the baptismal font!" Hearing his father's harshness, the son turned his back and walked away from him. Then the father hurled a long knife at his back, a naked blade, and wounded him in the kidneys. Of this wound, his son Ludovico died before midnight.[25]

Even as the legate-abbot was preparing for war, Messer Egidio was not idle. He made war on Cesena fiercely. He made three bastions, each separated from the others by ten miles. The legate returned to Rimini. In Cesena lived Madonna Cia, the wife of the captain of Forlì,[26] with her relatives and with a considerable personal guard inside the fortress. To this Madonna Cia the captain wrote

---

the face, and thus the beard (*barba*) visible. *Barbute* were soldiers wearing such helms, quite likely mercenaries.

23. This was Androin de la Roche, abbot of Cluny. This took place on 1 April 1357 at Faenza. Like Villani, the Anonimo will at times move forward chronologically to complete a narrative. For background to these complex events, still useful is Guillaume Mollat, *The Popes at Avignon, 1305–1378* (London: Thomas Nelson, 1963), 125–46; and Larner, *Lords of Romagna,* 76–98.

24. The legate here is once again Albornoz. De la Roche proved an incapable military commander. Albornoz had been reappointed by Innocent VI in September 1358.

25. The Anonimo once more departs from fact to emphasize moral character. The *Annales Caesenates,* 1183, reports that Ludovico died in battle in 1356.

26. Cia was Marzia degli Ubaldini (1317–81), the wife of Francesco II Ordelaffi. See Sergio Spada, *Gli Ordelaffi: Signori di Forlì e Cesena* (Cesena, Il Ponte Vecchio, 2011); Larner, *Lords of Romagna,* 92–98.

a letter. The letter read as follows: "Cia, take good and solicitous care of the people of Cesena." Madonna Cia replied in this way: "My lord, may it please you to take good care of Forlì, and I will take good care of Cesena." He wrote a follow-up letter. It read this way: "Cia, by our command, see to it that four members of the *popolo* — namely Giovanni Zaganella, Giacomo delli Vastardi, Palazzino, and Vertonuccio — are beheaded. They are Guelfs and we suspect them." The lady received this letter but did not rush to sentencing. Instead, being most measured and diligent, she looked into the condition of the four citizens and found that they were good and faithful people. In particular, the lady sought the advice of two of her husband's most faithful friends, Scaraglino, a nobleman, and Iurio delli Tumberti. She showed them the letter. Their response to her was as follows. "My lady, we see no reason why they should lose their lives. We have no inkling that they plan sedition. If they are killed, there is danger that the people will be upset. So hold off carrying out this judgement for now. Meanwhile, we will monitor their deeds and movements closely. When we see some evil brewing, we will confront them, seize them, and try them in open court." The lady agreed to the plan of her husband's two faithful nobles. They agreed to carry out the plan.

The agreement was secret but also secretly revealed to the four men. These four therefore made a new pact, planning to turn the city upside down. Giovanni Zaganella was the leader among his friends. He rode about the land on his little horse soliciting this person and that. One morning, while the plan was yet young, Giacomo delli Vastardi went with his neighbors to the gate called the Porta della Troia, and they took it. Vertonuccio and Palazzino gathered the people and barred the city. Then they sent two farmers to the Hungarians who were posted in the bastion at Savignano. *Celeriter ille vadunt.*[27] When Madonna Cia heard the noise, she knew that

27. "They went with haste." The Hungarians were most likely mercenaries who remained in Italy after the invasion of Naples by Lewis of Hungary, in which Francesco Ordelaffi participated. Finally defeated by Queen Giovanna and her husband Louis of Taranto by 1352, the Great Company had moved north under the command of Conrad von Landau and Anechin von Bongartz. By the later 1350s the Hungarians were also directly projecting the political alliances of King Lewis. See Matteo Villani, *Cronica*, VIII.84.

## ✸ CHAPTER TWENTY-SIX

the people were rising up. Quickly she armed her personal guard, soldiers both mounted and on foot. She commanded that they take over the city. But they were not able to do so, for the way was barred, the people armed, the gate taken, and the towers fortified. And what was worse, the knights had risen in support of the people. There, in the heat of the sun, eight hundred Hungarian archers, who had been stationed at Savignano in the bastion, came flying, a speedy people, prepared for war. They did not enter Cesena but instead surrounded the city on all sides to give heart to the citizens.

Seeing this, Madonna Cia pulled her guard back and closed herself inside the citadel, where she held out. This citadel was part of the city itself and strongly walled. Within it was the Piazza del Comune, the palace and the tower, and the homes of her followers. It is a rather high place, looking out over the city that spreads out below. Angered by this failure, Madonna Cia turned her rage on the two counselors who were close friends of her husband, Iurio delli Tumberti and Scaraglino, whom she had beheaded.[28] *Quod factum maritus improbavit. Postera die, luce orta*,[29] behold the Malatesta arrived with aid, in full strength.[30] The Porta della Troia was handed over to them, and they entered the city.

Now Madonna Cia was besieged in the citadel. Castle Fiumone was surrendered next. The Malatesta attacked the citadel with great vigor. They attempted to storm it and hurled fire inside. They built trebuchets and hurled many rocks and stones. It was all futile. There was water within the citadel. There was a strong tower that stood over the gate. The legate commanded an undermining operation, wearying work, both onerous and lengthy. They undermined the cistern so that it was broken and the water poured out. Then they undermined the great tower in the piazza. They set fire to the supports.[31] With a great roar and ruin the tower came down. Then

---

28. Matteo Villani (VII.69) believed Cia's anger to be not due to bad advice per se but rather because she suspected the men of colluding with the legate.

29. "Her husband disapproved of this deed. The next day, as the sun rose...."

30. Here the Malatesta of Rimini were allied with Albornoz, and here attempting to regain Cesena, taken by Francesco Ordelaffi in 1334.

31. The technique referred to consisted of undermining a structure, inserting wooden supports to keep it up until the process was finished, then burning the supports inserted and thereby causing the structure to collapse.

they dug under the tower that stood over the gate by which one entered the citadel. Madonna Cia, enraged, did not know what to do. She selected a few citizens who were with her inside the citadel, those about whom she had some doubts, and she put them inside the tower above the gate. She said, "If the tower falls, it falls on you." The tower shook but stayed up.

The legate, Don Gilio, was passing through the area with a large company and came to see the condition of Cesena, the undermining work and the handling of the siege. Then at least five hundred women of Cesena came out, tearing their hair and beating their breasts. They made a tremendous uproar wailing and lamenting. They knelt before the legate and begged for mercy. *Inscius legatus*[32] of the reason for such bitter wailing, asked why they were doing this. The women responded, "Legate, our husbands, brothers, and relatives are shut inside the tower above the gate. The undermining work is prepared. If the tower falls, the men will be lost. So we beg you in the name of God that you delay in setting fire to the supports."

The legate immediately understood that Madonna Cia was riven with doubt and her mind was broken. He parlayed with her and recovered from her the men of Cesena who had been put in the tower. With fire set to the supports, the tower fell along with part of the wall. Then the way was opened for entry. Despite that, no one charged in rashly, instead entering with calm care. The legate captured Madonna Cia with one of her sons and two nephews. Madonna Cia refused to be set free, fearing the anger of her husband, and she begged insistently that the Church should protect her. The masters who engineered the excavations, the trebuchets, and other things cost 3,000 florins a day. The soldiers cost 12,000 florins. The legate entered Cesena and took the land for the Church. That is how the city of Cesena in Romagna was taken.

Now the legate took up a position near the city of Forlì. First, he organized a large and numerous army. Once the imprisonment of Madonna Cia, who was sent to Ancona under guard, became known, one of her daughters, a noble woman married to a great man of the March, came before her father, weeping with her arms crossed. Kneeling, she spoke and said, "My lord and father, may it

---

32. "The legate, unaware..."

# ❋ CHAPTER TWENTY-SIX

please you that the lady, my mother, not be kept in another's hands as a prisoner. I beg you, do the Church's will." To these words the captain gave no reply except to seize his daughter by the hair and cut her head from her body with a knife.[33]

After the fall of Cesena, the legate sent word to the captain, saying "Captain, hand over what does not belong to you. I will give you your wife, son, and nephews."

To these words the captain made the following response: "Tell the legate that I believed him to be a wise man. But now I take him to be an incompetent beast. Say that if I had him in prison, as he does my own people, I would hang him by the neck within three days." With the heart of the perverse Patarine heretic so hardened, Don Gilio, the old legate, departed for Provence. When the [mercenary] company heard that Don Gilio was approaching the region, they melted away like a bit of snow in the hot sun.[34]

THE NEW LEGATE remained, Messer [...], the Burgundian abbot.[35] This legate made brutal war on Forlì.[36] For many years the crusade went on, and the cross was preached throughout Italy. The grain was cut down, the vineyards, orchards, and olive groves were destroyed.

---

33. This was probably Onestina, married to Gentile da Mogliano of Fermo. Again, the Anonimo may be fabricating to emphasize his version of Francesco's moral depravity. See Berardo Pio, "Mogliano, Gentile da," *Dizionario Biografico degli Italiani* 75 (2011), online at: https://www.treccani.it/enciclopedia/gentile-da-mogliano_(Dizionario-Biografico).

34. Here the Anonimo is deploying a narrative technique seen often in trecento historiography, departing from strict sequential chronology and cutting back and forth to various theaters of war. See above, Introduction, pp. 22, 45.

35. The Anonimo omits the abbot's name here, but we are back to the activities of Androin de la Roche, abbot of Cluny.

36. The Anonimo describes the new legate's efforts as *pentolosa*, a word of uncertain meaning. I follow Porta in gleaning from context that the word indicates war without quarter. However, the final capture of Forlì and this phase of the war was headed by Albornoz, not Androin, precisely because the latter was an ineffective commander.

He struck everywhere and at any time. As a result of this fervent attack the captain and his sworn allies the Manfredi lost Faenza. Bertinoro too was lost. Eventually he was boxed within Forlì, in the fortress. In the siege of Forlì crusaders were often captured, those who, to their merit, had come to fight the schismatics. The captured crusaders were taken before Francesco, who said these words to them: "You bear the cross. Your cross is made of cloth. Cloth frays. I want you to carry a cross that will never wear out."[37] Then a hot iron in the form of a cross was prepared. He pressed this iron into the soles of their feet and then, after stripping them, he let them go. He captured many other crusaders, to whom he said these words: "You've come to earn spiritual profit. If I let you go, you might return to your prior sins. It is better that you die in this pious state, while you are contrite. God will receive you into his city." With this said, he had them flayed, hung, decapitated, impaled, torn apart, and martyred by various means.[38] The war lasted many years. To sustain the war the crusade was repeatedly preached. It was preached yet again in the year of our Lord 1358, in January in the city of Tivoli.[39]

*His ferme diebus Iohannes rex Francie captus est a filio regis Anglie bello magis tumultuario quam militari apud villam que dicitur [...] ductusque in Angliam sub custodia annis ferme duobus. Tandem cum magno sui detriment et regni evasit.*[40]

※

37. This refers to the custom by which crusaders wore the sign of the cross sewn onto their clothing.

38. Again, there is little evidence for the Anonimo's portrayal here.

39. This may be a reference to the Anonimo's residence in the city at that time.

40. "Around this time John, the king of France, was captured by the son of the king of England during a battle that was more mob action than military, near a place called [...], and he was taken away to England and kept prisoner for nearly two years. Finally he escaped, much to his own detriment and that of his kingdom." This passage refers to the results of the Battle of Poitiers. This passage has played an important role in efforts to date the chronicle. Campanelli argues that this must have been a late addition to the text, suggesting that in 1360, when French king was liberated, the text was in such a state that new additions were still possible. See his "Gli inserti latini," 13.

# CHAPTER TWENTY-SEVEN
## Messer Cola di Rienzo returns to Rome and reassumes power amid much rejoicing.
## He is cruelly slain by the people of Rome

It was in the year of our Lord 1354, on the first day of August,[1] when Cola di Rienzo returned to Rome and was most solemnly received. In the end, he was killed by the voice of the people. The thing transpired like this.

Once Cola di Rienzo fell from his lordship, he decided to depart and go before the pope. Prior to his departure, he had his party commission a painting on the wall of Sta. Maria Maddalena, in the Piazza de Castello, of an angel girded with the arms of Rome, which held in its hand a cross. On the cross stood a dove. The angel's feet stood over an asp and a basilisk, over the lion and the dragon.[2] Once this was painted the rabble of Rome threw mud on it to obscure it. One evening, Cola di Rienzo came secretly and unrecognized to see the figure prior to his departure. Looking at it he understood how little the rabble had honored him.[3] He therefore ordered that a lamp should burn in that place for a year.

1. August 1 was a sacred day for Rienzo, on which many of the most important events of his life occurred. It was also the feast of the Ara Coeli, when Emperor Augustus was widely believed to have had a miraculous vision of the Virgin.

2. The painting was placed just outside Castel Sant'Angelo on a church now demolished. The image was appropriate, since it was set below the statue of St. Michael atop the castle. The reference here is to Psalm 90:13, which expounds upon the power that lies in taking refuge in God, resulting in angelic protections that allow one to trample on these same beasts. The iconographic program of the painting seems to have derived almost directly from an image in a manuscript (Brussels, Bibliothèque Royale, MS 10168–72) of the *Liber ystoriarum Romanorum*, owned by Cola's patrons, the Savelli. See Musto, *Apocalypse in Rome*, 253; Ernesto Monaci, *Sul* Liber Ystoriarum Romanorum: *Prime ricerche* (Rome: Forzano, 1889), 14–15 [138–39], 45 [169] (for the image); and Internullo, *Ai margini*, , 372–75.

3. The Anonimo records the people's grief at Cola's abdication and departure (chapter 18, p. 242) and the continued presence of his partisans in the city (chapter 23, 249–50), as also reconfirmed in this passage. He was generally a partisan of the upper bourgeoisie in the city. See above, Introduction, pp. 28, 38–42.

He departed by night and spent a long time in search of a patron. This went on for seven years. He set out well disguised for fear of the powerful men of Rome. He lived like one of the Fraticelli residing in the mountains of Maiella with hermits and penitents.[4]

In the end he went to Bohemia, to the court of Emperor Charles, on whose coming I will speak, and found him in a city known as Prague.[5] There, kneeling before his imperial majesty, he spoke without delay. These were his words and eloquent speech before Charles, king of Bohemia, grandson of Emperor Henry, newly elected by the pope.[6]

"Most serene prince, to whom is granted the glory of the whole world. I am that Cola to whom God gave the grace of being able to govern Rome and its district in peace, liberty, and justice. I had the obedience of Tuscany, the Compagna, and Marettima. I reined in the arrogance of the powerful and put an end to many iniquities. I am a worm, a weak man, a weed like all the others. I bore in my hand a rod of steel, which by my humility I converted into a wooden staff, due to the fact that God wished to chastise me.[7] The powerful persecuted me, seeking to take my life. Out of envy and pride they drove me from my domain. They did not wish to be punished. I am of your lineage, a bastard son of the valiant Emperor Henry.[8] With you I seek refuge. Under your wings, I

4. The Anonimo says he lived like a *fraticiello*, the term refers to a marginalized branch of the surviving Spiritual Franciscans, who espoused radical poverty and Joachite prophesy and had been condemned as heretics in the 1310s and 1320s and forced into hiding, with several communities as here in the Abruzzi region of the Regno of Naples. For Cola's time among said hermits, see Musto, *Apocalypse in Rome*, 258–59.

5. Charles IV of Luxemburg's arrival in Italy was to be discussed in the now-lost chapter 28.

6. Charles was the son of the valorous King John of Bohemia, whose death the Anonimo recounted in his description of the Battle of Crécy in chapter 14, 169–71.

7. Here Cola refers to his transformation from one holding the rod of rulership into a penitent hermit like those among whom he dwelt in the mountains.

8. Musto, *Apocalypse in Rome*, 278, notes that if Cola's parentage were as he claimed, it would have made him Charles' illegitimate uncle.

## CHAPTER TWENTY-SEVEN

shelter, beneath your shadow and your shield a man should be safe. I believe that I am safe. I believe that you will defend me. You will not let me die in the hands of tyrants. You will not let me drown in a lake of injustice. And this is as it should be, for you are the emperor. Your sword wards off tyrants. Behold the prophecy of Brother Angelo of Montecielo, in the mountains of Maiella. He says that the eagle will slay the crows."[9]

Once Cola had spoken, Charles extended his hand and received him graciously, saying that no one should doubt him. When Cola arrived in Prague it was the first day of August. He lingered there for some span of time. He debated with masters of theology. He spoke a great deal. He declared marvelous things. His eloquent tongue astonished those Germans, those Bohemians and Slavs. He left everyone gaping. He was not kept in prison but rather under guard with most honorable company. He was given much wine and food. After a time, he asked the grace of the emperor that he might go to Avignon and present himself before the pope and show that he was not a heretic or a Patarine. The emperor was much opposed to this, thinking he ought not to go. In the end he conceded by his own free will. Cola di Rienzo said, "Most serene prince, I go voluntarily before the holy father. Since you are not sending me by force, you have not broken your oath."[10]

As he traveled across the land the people rose up and, gathered together in noisy crowds, they came before him. Taking him, they said that they wanted to save him from the hand of the pope. They did not want him to go. To all of them, he responded, saying "I go voluntarily. I am not being forced." He thanked them, and in this way he went from city to city. All along the way he was treated

9. The Anonimo's text generally agrees with Cola's own account in letters (49, 57) sent to the emperor and others, and probably made public, perhaps seen by many Romans literate in Latin, including the Anonimo. See Burdach and Piur, *Briefwechsel* 2.3. The *Chronicon Estense* (RIS 15.3:150) also records the event with far more detail and drama.

10. The Anonimo is putting a gentle spin on things. Cola does seem to have been a prisoner for at least some of the time he was in Prague. His journey to Avignon came at the pope's demand — which Charles did attempt to resist — rather than by his own free choice. See Musto, *Apocalypse in Rome*, 299–303.

with solemn honor. When the people saw him, they went along with him. And in this way he came to Avignon on the first day of August.[11] Once he reached Avignon, he spoke before the pope. He argued that he was not a Patarine, nor deserving of the sentence passed by the cardinal, Don Bruno.[12] He wished to present himself for examination. In response to this the pope said nothing.

Cola was shut up in a tall and mighty tower. A chain held him, attached to his leg. The chain was connected to the ceiling of the tower. There Cola remained, dressed in shabby clothing. He had lots of books, his Titus Livy, his histories of Rome, the Bible, and many other books too. He never stopped studying. His needs were provided for sufficiently from papal provisions, which were granted him generously. His deeds were examined, and he was found to be a faithful Christian.[13] The judgment and sentence against him by Don Bruno and the cardinal de Ceccano were revoked, and he was absolved. Alongside the legate he traveled through Provence and came to Montefiascone in order to retake the Patrimony, as was said.

Among the first places to turn itself over to the Church was Toscanella, and its fortress was sold for money. Cola de Rienzo was there to take the land for the Church. Then he was present for the siege of Viterbo, and at all the other feats of arms by the knights. He wore garb most honorable and appropriate and had a good horse. Not only when he was with the army but also in Montefiascone, he received so many invitations from Romans that it is astonishing to describe. Every Roman treated him like a ruler. He had a great many visitors. People stretched out behind him like a great tail. Everyone, even the legate, marveled at and noted the many invitations from

---

11. Petrarch wrote an account of Cola's arrival in Avignon to his friend Francesco Nelli (*Familiares* XIII.6), in which he attempted to distance himself from the now disgraced and friendless former tribune. Petrarch may have been in Avignon for these events. He was then residing in nearby Vaucluse. See Cosenza, *Revolution*, 130–38.

12. That is, by the legate Bertrand du Déaulx, cardinal of Embrun, as was described in chapter 18, 242–43.

13. He was freed by the newly elected Innocent VI. Porta identifies his examiners as Bertrand du Déaulx, Gui de Boulogne, and Elia Talleyrand. On this list, see Cosenza, *Revolution*, 122.

the citizens of Rome. They saw it as a marvel. It struck them that he had escaped with his life from among such powerful men.[14]

At the above-mentioned destruction of Viterbo, as was described earlier, there were Romans present. When the army returned a large party of Romans came to see Cola di Rienzo, men of the *popolo*, great of heart and speech, still greater overtures, few results. They said, "Return to your Rome. Cure it of its terrible disease. Be its lord. We will lend you favor and force in support. Do not hesitate. You have never been so desired or so loved as you are now." These empty promises the people of Rome offered him; they did not give him a penny. Cola di Rienzo was moved by these words and by the glory, which naturally he desired, and he pondered how to build up a base in order that he might have the men and support to enter Rome. He spoke of this with the legate, who did not give him a penny. All the same, he ordered that he should have some provisions from the commune of Perugia, so that he might live with honor as was suitable.

These provisions were not enough to recruit soldiers. So Cola rode to Perugia and repeatedly put his requests to the council. He spoke well, gave a good oration, and made still better promises. The councilors listened with attentive ears to the sweetness of the words that they allowed themselves to hear. They allowed themselves to be licked like honey. But because the councilors were answerable to syndics, they were required to guard the commune's assets well. From the commune of Perugia, Cola could not get a single *cortonese* coin. There were in Perugia at the time two young men of Provence, Messer Arimbaldo, doctor of law, and Messer Bettrone, knights of Narbonne in Provence and brothers by blood. These two were also brothers by blood to the douhty Fra Morreale. Fra Morreale fought on behalf of the king of Hungary. Then he led the Great Company. He lay waste to many lands in Puglia, burning and torching many, seizing the property of many communities, and carrying off the women. In Tuscany he held Siena, Florence, Arezzo, and many such places for ransom. He divided the money among his companions. Then he went to the March and consumed the Malatesta. He took by force Montefliaterano and Filino, where

---

14. The Anonimo's description of Rienzo here is at odds with the one several pages below. For these inconsistencies, see Introduction, pp. 41–42, 55–57.

seven hundred countryfolk died. He burned and plundered the land. He held the men for ransom and made off with all the most attractive of the women. He was a Knight of Saint John, a man both zealous and valorous, of whose prowess will be described later. This man had obtained a lot of money by means of robbery and plunder. He had so much money that he could easily have lived an honorable life without needing to fight for pay ever again. He took these two brothers of his to Perugia and had them given provisions by the commune. He gave his money to the merchants and commanded his brothers to keep the peace and not make any trouble, for once he had them situated, he intended to serve his order. Then Fra Morreale departed to tend to his affairs elsewhere.

Once Cola di Rienzo learned that Messer Arimbaldo of Narbonne, a young man and a literate fellow, was residing in Perugia, he went to his inn in order to dine with him. *Sumpto cibo*,[15] Cola di Rienzo began to speak of the power of the Romans. He mixed in the histories of Titus Livy. He cited biblical passages. He let loose the fount of his learning. Oh, how well he spoke! He employed all his virtue in his arguments. He spoke on his subject so that every man was astonished by his speech-making and rose to his feet. Messer Arimbaldo listened silently with a hand to his throat. He marveled at the beautiful speech. He admired the magnificence of the virtuous Romans. *Incalscente vino*,[16] his thoughts ascended to the heights. One dreamer took delight in another. Messer Arimbaldo never took his rest without Cola di Rienzo: he stood with him and went everywhere with him. They ate the same food and slept in the same bed.[17] They contemplated doing great deeds, setting Rome straight and returning it to its pristine state. To do this, they needed money. One can do nothing without soldiers. The final cost came to 3,000 florins. Cola got him to promise the 3,000 florins, and he promised to return them, and for his merits to make Arimbaldo a citizen of Rome and a great and honored captain, despite the reservations of his brother Messer Bettrone. Arimbaldo also took 4,000 florins from the deposit with the merchants and gave them to Cola di Rienzo.

15. "With the meal begun,…"
16. "Growing hot with wine,…"
17. That is, they shared a room at the inn, a common practice in trecento Italy, when rooms and beds were scarce and modern privacy was not yet general.

# ✻ CHAPTER TWENTY-SEVEN

Before he would give these funds to Cola di Rienzo, however, Messer Arimbaldo wanted the permission of his elder brother, Fra Morreale. He sent him a letter. It said this: "Honored brother, I have earned more in one day than you have in all your life. I have acquired the lordship of Rome, which the knight Messer Nicola de Rienzi has promised me, who is the tribune, visited by the Romans, and summoned by the people. I believe our plans will not fail. It seems to me that with the assistance of your talent my state[18] would never fall. We need money to get us started. Whenever it pleases you, my brother, I would take 4,000 florins from our deposit account and proceed to Rome under heavy arms."

Fra Morreale read his brother's letter and wrote back. The gist of his writing was as follows: "I have thought a long while about the undertaking that you intend. What you ask me to provide you with entails a great and significant burden. I don't see how you will do this. My mind simply won't accept it. Reason indicates otherwise. Nevertheless, do what you will and do it well. Above all, take care that the 4,000 florins are not lost. If you encounter any trouble, write me. I will come with aid, with 1,000, or 2,000 men, however many you should need, and I will do magnificent things. Have no doubt. You and your brother are to love and honor one another. Keep this quiet."

Messer Arimbaldo received the letter and was elated. He and the tribune arranged for the journey. Once Cola di Rienzo had the 4,000 florins, he acquired even finer clothes for himself, he dressed himself elaborately as he saw fit: a tunic, overcoat, and cape of fur-trimmed scarlet, decorated with fine gold and with golden hems, a rich sword at his belt, a well accoutered horse, golden spurs, and new attire for his servants.[19] So attired, he returned to Montefiascone and to the legate. He brought for company the brothers Messer Bettrone and Messer Arimbaldo of Narbonne, with their servants and other things. When he

18. The Anonimo here uses the term *"mio stato,"* perhaps a deliberate contrast to the public good of what he termed Rienzo's *buono stato*. Throughout, the Anonimo contrasts the public good with individual gain, a common theme of trecento political thought.

19. For all medieval people, clothing was the most apparent indication of status, wealth and success, and symbolic of political power. Cola here is preparing to present himself to the legate as the man to do the job.

was before the legate, he was like a different person. He puffed himself up with his scarlet hood at his neck and his scarlet fur-lined cape. He cut a haughty figure. He shook his head about. He turned it this way and then the other, as if to say, "Who am I? Who indeed am I?" Then he bobbed on the tips of his toes, first raising himself up and then back down again. The legate marveled at him and gave some credence to his words. Yet he did not give him a single coin. Then Cola spoke and said, "Legate, make me senator of Rome. I will go and prepare the way for you." The legate made him senator and sent him on his way.[20]

In order to go to Rome, he needed men. Messer Malatesta of Rimini had recently dismissed his soldiers, at least sixteen banners, good men, two hundred and fifty mercenaries. They were hanging around Perugia looking for work. Cola di Rienzo had a message sent to them. The message reached the constables and was as follows. "Take two months of pay. You will get one month's pay in advance. You will never again want for coin. Escort Messer Nicola de Rienzi, senator by papal decree, to Rome." The constables discussed these words. The Germans did not want to go. They gave three reasons. The first: "The Romans are bad people, incomparably haughty and arrogant." The second: "This is a man of the people, poor and of ignoble stock. He will not be able to pay us. So, what good does it do us to work for him?" Third: "Rome's powerful do not want this man's governance. They are all his enemies who despise him. That means we will never get this money. This journey to Rome isn't for us." This was truly the response of the Germans, and it was right. There are Germans who come down from Germany simple, pure of heart, and devoid of fraud. As soon as they begin to mix with Italians they become master devils, vicious and accustomed to all manner of malice.[21]

---

20. The Anonimo is eliding events here. Rienzo had actually been named senator while still in Avignon by Innocent VI on September 16, 1353. For the documents, see Musto, *Apocalypse in Rome*, 374 nn. 2–3.

21. The Anonimo specifically says that they become *mastri coduti*, "masters with tails" or "tailed masters," from whence comes the sense of diabolism. It is hard to know whether the Anonimo is being serious about the Germans. These were, after all, the same men who comprised the Great Company, whom the Anonimo condemned repeatedly for their devastation, looting, rapes, and murders throughout Italy.

# CHAPTER TWENTY-SEVEN

A Burgundian constable responded to the Germans, saying, "Let's take this newly offered money for a month. Let's return this good fellow to his home. Let's escort him to Rome. Let's earn absolution.[22] Then whoever wants to leave can leave, and those who want to stay can stay." This argument won the day. The sixteen banners took their pay from Cola di Rienzo. There were mounted fighters among them. There were also a few Perugians, the sons of good men. And there were one hundred Tuscan troops, foot soldiers wearing breast plates, a noble and beautiful company.

With these men Cola descended through Tuscany, traveling through valleys, mountains, and dangerous places. Without stopping he came to Orte.[23] News of his approach was heard in Rome. The Romans happily prepared themselves to receive him. The powerful were on alert. From Orte he arrived at Rome in the year of our Lord 1354. The Roman cavalry came out to meet him at Monte Mario, bearing olive branches in their hands as a symbol of victory and peace.[24] The people followed after him with much happiness, as if he were Scipio Africanus.[25] Triumphal arches were erected. He entered Porta Castel Sant'Angelo gate. The whole piazza, the bridge, and the street were decorated with banners of fine cloth made by women, and with ornaments of gold and silver. It seems like all of Rome had opened itself up with happiness. Great was the pleasure and favor of the people.

---

22. The Anonimo literally has the Burgundian suggest that they would earn *la perdonanza*, a pardon. While this may suggest simply fulfilling the terms of the contract, it seems more likely that, as he saw it, the trip to Rome could conceivably double as a kind of pilgrimage, perhaps to make up for their past sins in Italy. It could also reflect the mercenaries' cynicism: "absolution" here being not spiritual but — as events below demonstrate — material recompense, i.e., Roman loot.

23. About fifty miles north of Rome.

24. Monte Mario, north and west of the medieval city on the Via Triumphalis, was the traditional place where Romans welcomed emperors, popes, and other high dignitaries with gifts, keys to the city, and triumphs. It was also the first place from which pilgrims could view the eternal city. It is now capped by a nature reserve and an observatory.

25. An ancient Roman general famed for his victory over Hannibal at Zama, which ended the Second Punic War. Here again the Anonimo draws on Livy.

With such honor he was led to the palace of the Campidoglio. There he made a beautiful and eloquent speech and said that he had been wandering abroad for seven years, like Nebuchadnezzar, but that by the efficacious power of God he had returned to his senatorial seat by the decree of the pope.[26] It was not so much that he was sufficient for the task but that the pope's voice made him sufficient. He said that he intended to set Rome straight and raise it up again. Then he made Messer Bettrone and Messer Arimbaldo his captains of war and gave them the banner of Rome. He made a certain Cecco da Perugia, who was his counselor, a knight and dressed him in gold. The Romans had a great celebration, as the Jews did for Christ when he entered Jerusalem riding on a donkey. They paid honor to him, waving cloth and olive branches before him and singing, "*Benedictus qui venis!*"[27] In the end they returned home and left him alone among his disciples in the piazza. No one remained who might offer a poor man something to eat.

The next day Cola di Rienzo hosted a certain ambassador from the lands nearby. How masterfully he handled him! He answered inquiries and made promises. He prepared himself to lead energetically. The barons watched on warily to see what would happen. The noise of the triumph was enormous. There were many banners. There had never been so much pomp. Soldiers bearing fancy swords from all over.[28] It seemed clear that Cola wanted to

26. Here Cola alludes to the biblical story of Nebuchadnezzar's dream of a tree, which portended his own seven-year exile, in Daniel 4. Nebuchadnezzar's kingdom is presented as strong and fruitful, but his pride in it results in his downfall and seven years spent living like an animal in the wild. Only when he acknowledges the ultimate power of God, and the triviality of human affairs, is his sanity and station restored.

27. "Blessed are you who comes." This phrase is adapted from one part of the mass, the *sanctus*, in which the phrase is *benedictus qui venit in nomine Domini*, "blessed is he who comes in the name of the Lord." The Romans sing a variation of the liturgical hymn normally sung to Christ. The comparison is made even more explicit in the following reference to his being left alone among his disciples. The Anonimo might also be making a comment on the changed political culture and frustrated hopes of the Romans, who now cynically sought their own advantage: not the *buono stato* but *mio stato*.

28. The Anonimo says specifically that these were *fanti con durindaine*, the last word being the name of the sword of the legendary paladin, Roland.

## ✻ CHAPTER TWENTY-SEVEN

rule tyrannically. Many of the possessions he had lost were restored to him. He sent commandments and letters describing his happy return to power across the land and the district. He wanted everyone to make ready for the *buono stato*.

✻

THE MAN HIMSELF was much changed from his former ways. He had formerly been sober, temperate, and abstinent. Now he had become an excessive drinker, utterly given over to wine. He ate and drank at all hours. He was heedless of the proper order or time. He mixed Greek wine with that of Faiano, Malvasia with Ribolla.[29] He was ready to drink more at any time. He could seem a terrible thing to witness him. He drank too much. He said he had grown accustomed to doing this while he was in prison. He had also grown astonishingly fat. He had a round belly, triumphal like an Asian abbot's.[30] He stuffed himself with fine meats, like peacock. He was flushed and had a long beard. His facial expressions changed rapidly. Suddenly his eyes became inflamed. He changed his mind constantly. His mind flickered from one thing to another like a flame. He had once had white eyes, but bit by bit they became as red as blood.[31]

On the fourth day, as he sat in the highest rooms of the palace of the Campidoglio, he sent for the barons that they might show

---

29. The first two refer to wines from particular regions, the latter two particular varietals. Cola apparently blended his wines rather haphazardly, just as he paid no attention to the proper order or time for eating.

30. One wonders whether this is a literary trope or the Anonimo's interpretation of some statue of Buddha that he had seen.

31. If the Anonimo's description is accurate, this — as he notes — could have been the result of Cola's long exile and imprisonment. Rienzo had also written letters from prison outside Prague referring to his "falling disease." His long beard might reflect his prison years or might also reflect the almost sudden change in fashion in the mid-14th century, when men throughout Europe began to wear long and pointed beards, as shown in many manuscript illustrations and frescoes of the time. The Anonimo himself had criticized such fashion in chapter 9, pp. 107–9. Again, as his reference to an "Asian abbot" indicates, his portrait of Rienzo might reflect an orientalizing critique of an emerging tyrant.

their obedience. Among others, he summoned Stefano Colonna of Palestrina. This little Stefanello had been only a small boy when his father Stefano and brother Giovanni were killed, as I mentioned before. He had taken shelter in the fortifications of Palestrina.[32] To this Stefanello, Cola sent two Roman citizens, Buccio de Iubileo and Ianni Cafariello, as ambassadors to tell him that he must obey the commands of the sacred senate or face his wrath. Stefanello threw one of them into a dark dungeon. From the other he extracted both his teeth and a fine of four hundred florins. The next day he rode through the fields of Rome with his archers and brigands. He seized all the livestock.

A great clamor arose in Rome. Word reached the tribune of Stefanello's plundering of the Romans. The tribune mounted up with his few followers. Alone he exited the gate. The soldiers followed him, some armed and some not as time permitted. They exited the Porta Maggiore and went down Via Prenestina, *per avia*,[33] through savage and deserted regions. The effort was useless and vain. They found neither the man, nor the livestock, nor the archers. The archers and troops of Palestrina, savvy in the ways of war, had many times carried off their plunder and hidden it in a forest called Pantano, which lies between Tivoli and Palestrina. There they hid. At night, they cunningly slipped the plunder out of Pantano and brought it to Palestrina.

The tribune's people searched but found nothing because it was night. They arrived at the city of Tivoli. There he rested. When day came, the news arrived that the livestock of the Romans had been taken from Pantano and led to Palestrina. Enraged at this, the tribune said, "What good is it to ride here and there across trackless lands? I don't want to skirmish with Colonna forces. I want them right in front of me." For four days he remained in Tivoli. He issued his edicts. He summoned the Roman cavalry to come quickly from Rome, all his mounted troops and foot soldiers. He wrote energetically. He posted his standard in Tivoli with his arms: blue

32. The Colonna palace-fortress of Palestrina was built within and on top of the ancient sanctuary of Fortuna Primigenia at Roman Praeneste.

33. "Through wastelands,...". Campanelli points out that this phrase probably originated as an interlinear note that was not intended to be in the main text. See Campanelli, "Benché io aia ià fatta per lettera," 12.

## CHAPTER TWENTY-SEVEN

with a golden sun, stars of silver, and the arms of Rome. Here's a striking fact! That standard was not resplendent as it had been before. It drooped miserably, flaccid, its tail no longer waving proudly in the wind. His troops arrived, with their many banners, horns, and trumpets. Messer Bettrone and Messer Arimbaldo came, whom he had made captains and generals of war. The soldiers murmured, wanting their pay. The German constables demanded money, saying they had been forced to pawn their arms.

Cola made many excuses. There was no point in hiding things any longer. Consider the appalling things he did to his captains! He summoned Messer Bettrone and Messer Arimbaldo and said to them, "I have found it written in the histories of Rome that at one time there was no money in the commune of Rome for the payment of soldiers. The consul brought together the barons of Rome and said, 'Let we who hold offices and dignities be the first to offer whatever each of us can out of good will.' From that collection they gathered up so much money that the militia was justly paid. So you two start the giving. The good people of Rome will see that even foreigners give. They will then be eager to give themselves. We will have money in torrents." So the captains gave him 1,000 florins, five hundred apiece, in two bags. This money the tribune shared out among the soldiers. To the foot soldiers he gave half their pay in the coin of Tivoli. Then he gathered the people in the piazza of San Lorenzo in Tivoli and delivered one of his beautiful speeches. He talked about how he had wandered in poverty for seven years and how he benefitted from the grace of Emperor Charles, whose further aid he expected soon. He talked about how he had been friend of a pope and despised by his enemies the Colonna. Then he had become senator of Rome at the pope's behest, so that the city would not be guided by the tyranny of the Colonna, or by the venomous serpent Stefanello, that bog weed. He therefore intended to destroy the house of Colonna and do worse to it than he had before. A cursed house, due to whose arrogance the land of Rome lived in poverty. Other regions enjoyed wealth. Then he added this, "I want to take my army to Palestrina and lay waste to it. I ask you people of Tivoli that you take heart and accompany me, lend me help in this moment of need, and do not abandon me." He made this speech on the parapet of the Palloni.³⁴

The speech delivered, he supplied his foreign troops, all his cavalry, and the people of Tivoli with foodstuffs and such gear as suited an army and set out for Castiglione di Santa Prassede.³⁵ There he rested for two days. He gathered all this people there. Then, the next day, he descended on Palestrina with all his forces. This was in the year of our Lord, 1354, in the month of [...], on the day [...].³⁶

The tribune lay siege to Palestrina and stationed his army at Santa Maria della Villa, two miles from the city. There were thousands of knights, between the Romans and other soldiers who were from Tivoli and Velletri, as well as the forces mustered in the communities around the abbey of Farfa, and those from the Campagna and from the Montagna. With the place under siege, each person had some task. Only Cola di Rienzo himself kept his eyes fixed on Palestrina. He lifted his head and regarded the high hill and its strong castle and contemplated how he might defeat and destroy the structure. He never shifted his gaze away from it. He said, "I need to flatten this mountain." As he continued to watch, never taking his mind off Palestrina, he often observed that livestock came in from grazing and entered a gate in the upper part in order to drink, before returning to their pastures. He also noted that men with bundles and loaded wagons entered through another gate. He saw a long

---

34. A family name, or perhaps a reference to a playing field, where the pallio is played. This and the reference to San Lorenzo indicates that the Anonimo had some familiarity with Tivoli, and his own comments about his life confirm that he was a resident there, at least later in life.

35. This has not been identified. A place called Castiglione di Santa Perteza had various names over the centuries: Burrano, di Castiglione, di Santa Prassede, di Pantano, and Lacus Gabinus. It is situated near Monte Comprati, east of Frascati. To move an army quickly, Cola would probably have taken the major Roman road from Tivoli, back toward the Roman plain, and then back up to Palestrina, avoiding the mountainous, narrow, and easily defended roads north of Palestrina.

36. The text is blank here but, as Porta notes, the month would have been August.

line of wagoneers bringing supplies to Palestrina. He asked those who stood nearby, "What do you make of those porters?"

They replied, "Senator, those livestock are going out to graze and coming into Palestrina to drink water. The men are carrying grain and foodstuffs to keep the land supplied and prevent it from starving."

Hearing this, Cola responded, "Tell me, might those passes not be blocked, so that the livestock may not go to pasture nor the porters bring supplies with such ease?"

The less loyal of the Romans replied, "The strength of Mount Palestrina is that those upper entrances and exits can scarcely be blocked. The place is so rough that no army can linger there."

But this was not so. In fact, it was the shamelessness of the Roman barons, who were waiting to see how things would turn out and did not want to lift a finger. Then the tribune said, "I will never give up until I have destroyed you, Palestrina. If after the defeat of the Colonna at the Porta San Lorenzo I had ridden out with the people of Rome, I would have entered this land freely and without resistance. It would already be destroyed. I would not have to suffer these current problems. The people of Rome would have lived in peace."

On the second day that the army was there the destruction began and the whole agricultural area of Palestrina was laid waste, the whole plain right up to the town. Nothing remained but the area higher up, less than a third. That little area was not ruined because on the eighth day the army departed. This departure happened for two reasons. The first was that the men of Velletri hated those of Tivoli. The latter abruptly left and took refuge inside Palestrina. As a result of this, there were worries that further trouble within the army would be unavoidable.

*The second reason was that the serving girl of Messer*[37] *Morreale, who had come at the behest of his brothers, heard her master say many that he wanted to kill the Tribune, Cola di Rienzo, by any means possible because he had cast them aside and taken everything they had, because there was no hope of getting anything back, and because, what was worse, he hadn't even tried*

---

[37]. What follows in italics is taken from Ghisalberti's edition of the chronicle, rather than Porta's from which it is absent. See above, p. 58.

*to explain himself. What do you think that good woman did? Because she had suffered many cruel words, outrages, and evil deeds from her master, she went looking for the tribune. She found him and, weeping, revealed to him everything that Messer Morreale had said that he wanted to do.*

*On account of this, the tribune quickly had Morreale summoned and threw him in prison on the Campidoglio, with his feet clapped in irons in the stocks right alongside his brothers, for they had also disparaged the tribune and were of the same mind as their brother, and so bore him ill will. At the same time, the tribune sought some means of breaking Palestrina, and he also contemplated ways of finding money so that he could pay his people, for they were murmuring more and more about how they wanted the money they were to be paid, and for that reason he was troubled.*

*Now, Fra Morreale, seeing that he had been taken due to the work of his serving girl and knowing how much she might have been able to reveal, was extremely worried that this might be his final downfall. But he took heart. Knowing that the tribune was in need of money, he decided to see if in some way he might free himself. And so he led Messer Cola di Rienzo to believe that if he were to let him go he could provide all the money needed, and armed men that were needed too, and that he would give him anything he wanted.*

Fra Morreale, thinking by such means to receive clemency, said to his imprisoned brothers, "Let one or two of us stay here, and let me go. I will bring ten or twenty thousand florins, as much money and as many men as he would like. I will do it by God!" But he could find no one to help him follow up on these words. Night came, around the first bell Fra Morreale was taken to be tortured. When he saw the rope, he scorned it, muttering "I was right to say that you are villainous rustics. You want to put me to torment. Don't you see that I am a knight? How can you be so villainous?"

Next he was hoisted up a little.[38] Then he said, "I was the leader of the Great Company. Since I am a knight, I wanted to live honorably. I held the cities of Tuscany ransom, extorted them, destroyed their lands, and plundered their people."

---

38. It was common to show the prisoner about to be tortured to be shown the implements of torture first. In this case the cord is the implement. The victim's hands would be bound behind their back and then hoisted upward, wrenching their arms in their sockets.

# ❋ CHAPTER TWENTY-SEVEN

Finally, he was taken back to where his brothers were, clapped in irons and returned to confinement with them. He knew that he was going to die. He requested penance and had with him throughout the night a friar to whom he made his confession. So he put his affairs in order. Hearing his brothers murmuring, he turned to them and spoke.[39] These are his words:

Dear brothers, have no doubts. You are young boys and have not yet endured the turbulence of chance. You will not die. I will die, and I have no doubt about that. My life was always marked by tribulations. Living was a burden for me. I never feared death. I am happy to die in the land where the blessed Saint Peter and Saint Paul died, even though our misfortune was your fault, Messer Arimbaldo, for you led me into this labyrinth! But that is not why I now take my leave. Do not mutter or mourn for me, for I die willingly. I am like a man deceived by heaven and betrayed by other men. God will have mercy on me. I was good in this world; I will be good before God, I have no doubt of this, in particular because I acted with good intentions. You are young men. You are afraid because you don't understand what fortune is. I ask you that you love one another and that you live boldly, as I did when I made Puglia, Tuscany, and the March do me homage.

As he continued to speak along these lines, day broke. In the morning he wanted to hear mass, which he stood listening to with his feet and legs bare.[40]

---

39. Musto, *Writing Southern Italy*, 216–22, esp. 219–20, raises some doubts about the veracity of this dialogue, noting that the Anonimo offers no reliable witnesses to these private conversations. If his cellmates did provide a report, they may have intentionally ennobled his words. Musto sees it rather as a genre piece, found in other contemporary histories.

40. One gets the impression that, while hearing mass, Morreale is garbed in a simple, quasi-penitential manner, wearing only a kind of long gown or robe. Similar penitential garb was sometimes worn in Rome during acts of ritual peacemaking, which often incorporated a penitential aspect. See Palmer, "Piety and Social Distinction," 982. Later, when he goes to hear his sentence, Morreale is then dressed in a manner more appropriate to his station.

At the hour of half terce,[41] the bell rang, and the people gathered together. Fra Morreale, conducted to the stairs in front of the lion, knelt before the image of the Virgin Mary. At his neck he wore a dark cloak with gold fringe. Under that he had a jacket of brown velvet, hemmed with gold thread. He lacked any kind of belt. The stockings on his legs were dark in color. His large hands were bound. In them he held a cross. Three friars stood with him.

As he listened to the sentence he spoke and said, "Romans! How is it that you consent to my death? I have never done you harm, but on account of your poverty and my wealth you would have me die." Then he said, "What have I come to? On my faith I have had ten times as many men before me, and now there is no more than this." Then he said, "I am happy to die in the place where Peter and Paul died. My life has not been without tribulation." Then he said, "This evil traitor will be sorry after I am dead!" During sentencing, the gallows were mentioned. He was shocked then and came rapidly to his feet like a person lost. Then those who stood near him comforted him so that he would not be afraid. They assured him that he was condemned to be beheaded. He was calmed by this and stood quietly.[42]

Setting out for the platform, he constantly looked this way and that as he passed down the street. He spoke and said, "Romans, I am dying unjustly. I die for your poverty and my wealth. It was my intention to raise this city up." He said many things. With each step he kissed the cross. He controlled himself as best he could. He was a man of deeds, a conqueror, and a cunning warrior. There had been none better than him since Caesar's day. This is the man who at the stroke of fortune foundered on the Roman coast, as was said earlier when I discussed the galley that ran ashore.[43]

Once he was on the platform, there at the base of the tower, he turned around and knelt on the ground. Then he stood up again

---

41. Approximately 10:30 AM, halfway between terce (9:00 AM) and sext (noon).

42. Unlike Giovanni Pipino, Fra Morreale would die the death of a nobleman, and not of a common thief. See above, p. 243.

43. This story was related in chapter 16, 179–81. Morreale was certainly an accomplished military man, but it is unclear whether the Anonimo is being sincere or sarcastic when he makes this comparison to Caesar.

## CHAPTER TWENTY-SEVEN

and said, "I am not positioned properly." He turned himself toward the east and recommended himself to God. Then he knelt on the ground, kissed his shackles and said, "God save you, holy justice." Over the block he made the sign of the cross with his hand and kissed it. He took off his cloak and cast it aside. When the axe was placed at his throat he spoke and said, "I am not positioned aright." Many good people were around him at the time, among them the doctor that dressed his wounds.[44] This fellow found the proper spot. The blade was placed and at the first blow he fell forward. A few hairs from his beard remained on the block. The Friars Minor took his body into a house and put the head back on his body. It looked like he had a red silk ribbon around his neck.

The excellent man, Morreale, was entombed in Sta. Maria in Aracoeli. The fame of his virtue and glory resounded throughout Italy.[45] In the city of Tivoli there was one of his servants, a man of his lineage, who when he heard of his lord's death died of irremediable grief the very next day.[46]

With this valiant man dead, the Romans were deeply troubled. Then the tribune brought the people together and spoke, saying

Lords, be not troubled by this man's death, for he was the worst man in the world. He plundered cities and castles, slew and kidnapped men and women, and made two thousand women captives. Most recently he came not to raise our condition up but rather to afflict us. He hoped to become an independent ruler. He wanted to control the grain supply. He wanted to plunder the Campagna and the lands of Rome, and the rest of Italy too. We will carry out our campaign well and by the grace of God bring it to a good end. But now let us do what a miller of grain does: cast the chaff and husks to the wind and keep the grain for ourselves. We

---

44. The Anonimo may have been on the scene or may have gotten these details from a fellow medico.

45. As a Hospitaller, Morreale would not automatically have had the benefit of burial in the Franciscan Order's chief church in the city. A tomb of Morreale has not been identified.

46. Again, the Anonimo may be indicating his presence in Tivoli for some time.

have we condemned this false man. His money, horses, and arms we will take to conduct our campaign.

The Romans were quieted by these words.

Before long a letter came from the legate commanding that Messer Arimbaldo be released safe and sound. It was done. His brother, Messer Bettrone, remained in chains. Of Fra Morreale's money the tribune took a great deal, but not all of it, for Messer Giovanni de Castiello took the largest share. Thereafter the Roman nobles considered him a traitor for not keeping faith with his friend.[47] Then Cola di Rienzo quickly paid his soldiers, both the foot soldiers and the cavalry who wanted to remain. The others he allowed to leave freely. He retained a great quantity of archers. He had three hundred mounted men. As captain of the people he named the cunning and wise warrior Liccardo Imprennente delli Annibadli, lord of Monte Compatri,[48] He positioned his host around Palestrina. In Frascati he placed foot soldiers and archers. In Colonna he stationed foot soldiers and archers. In Castiglione de Santa Prassede he stationed foot soldiers. In Tivoli he placed his marshals.

Cola stayed in reserve in Rome, on the Campidoglio, to oversee everything and see what needed to be done. He thought hard about how to obtain money for his soldiers. He was short on money and often in real poverty. He needed any money he could get for their pay. Such a man was never seen. He was the only one who thought about the Romans. He saw more standing on the Campidoglio than his officials did at their posts. He was constantly busy, always writing to his officials. He laid out the manner and order for getting things done expeditiously, closing the routes by which attacks were coming and capturing enemy troops and spies. He worked

---

47. Musto, *Apocalypse in Rome*, 334–35, considers this a cryptic remark that might indicate the barons' disappointment that their arrangement with Morreale to overthrow Rienzo had been upset by Giovanni de Castiello's absconding with the funds to finance it.

48. The Annibaldi were an important baronial family in Rome, though not on the same level as the Colonna or the Orsini. For Monte Comprati and its strategic value, se above, 284 n. 35.

ceaselessly.⁴⁹ But his officials were sluggish and cold. They achieved nothing noteworthy with the exception of the bold warrior Liccardo, who never hesitated. Night and day he⁵⁰ preyed upon the Colonna, pursuing them across all of the Campagna. He gave them no respite even to pause and look up at the sky. He exhausted Stefanello, the Colonna, and the men of Palestrina. A masterful man who understood the byways and places, and who understood the times, he was bringing the war to a good conclusion. He knew how to make himself loved by the soldiers. He was unreluctantly obeyed. The Hungarians said, "Such a valorous captain has never been seen." Unarmed, he raised his hand and said, "The livestock are coming through here." It would happen just as he said. The war was heading to a good conclusion.

NOW I WISH TO RECOUNT the death of the tribune. The tribune had established a tax on wine and other things. He called them a "subsidy." He took six denari for every shipment of wine. He took in a lot of money. The Romans went along with it for the good of their government. He also restricted the salt trade in order to make more money.⁵¹ He restricted his own lifestyle and his household expenses too. He did all this for the soldiers.

*Repente*,⁵² he seized a very noble citizen of Rome, a fellow both well off and well known by the name of Pandalfuccio de Guido.⁵³ A

49. It is at first difficult to reconcile this work ethic with that of a man increasingly described as failing and weak. But if we read his ceaseless labor as that of a man who had already had power slip away from him once and is keen to avoid repeating the experience, but who is also struggling with the weight of that task — and with Fortune — the Anonimo's moral portrait of Cola again becomes more consistent. See above, Introduction, pp. 55–58.

50. It is unclear whether the Anonimo's "he" is referring to Liccardo in the field or to Cola as director of the action.

51. These were all common policies of Italian communes in the trecento. See above, pp. 136–37 n. 9, 192 n. 24, 195, 242.

52. "Abruptly,..."

53. Porta identifies this as Pandolfuccio di Guido Pandolfini de Franchi, a trecento classicist who had served as one of Cola's ambassadors to Florence in 1347, along with several other leading men. This makes Pandolfuccio one

virtuous man, he greatly desired dominion over the people. Cola had him beheaded mercilessly and for no apparent reason. All of Rome was shaken by his death. The Romans stood there like sheep, silent and not daring to say a word. They began to fear the tribune as if he were some kind of demon. *In loco consilii obtinebat omnem suam voluntatem, nullo consiliatore contradicente. Ipso instant ridens plangebat et emittens lacrimas et suspiria ridebat, tanta inerata ei varietas et mobilitas voluntatis.*[54] One moment he wept, the next he seemed unnaturally happy. Then he took to arresting people. He arrested this one and that, holding them for ransom. Ever so quietly, whispers began to ripple across Rome. To fortify himself as a result of this, Cola stationed fifty foot soldiers in each *rione*, ready for any trouble. He did not pay them. He promised to do so every day. He kept them hoping. He promised them a great deal of grain and other things. *Novissime*,[55] he removed Liccardo from the role of captain and made others. This was his undoing. Liccardo stopped his raiding and his war-related endeavors, muttering understandably about how ungrateful the man was.

IT WAS THE MONTH OF SEPTEMBER, on the eighth day. Cola di Rienzo was in his bed that morning. He had just washed the Greek wine from his face.[56] Suddenly, a voice cried out, "Long live the *popolo*!

---

of Cola's earliest and most important political supporters, the sort without whom he would likely never have come to power in the first place. For Pandolfuccio, see Internullo, *Ai margini*, 219–20, 396–97, 407–11 et passim.

54. "In counsels he got his way entirely, with no counselor contradicting him. One moment he was smiling and the next he wept. He would laugh while sighing and shedding tears. Such was his unpredictable changeability and the fickleness of his will." Campanelli, "Benché io l'aia ià fatta per lettera," 21, argues convincingly that this very polished Latin passage, which elaborates on the vernacular lines just before and after it, was probably written by the Anonimo in the margins of his own copy of this work and later incorporated into the text. Had the Anonimo placed it in the text himself, it is possible that it would have replaced the preceding and successive phrases.

55. "Most unusually,…"

56. Here the Anonimo writes *"Avease lavata la facie de grieco."* Rather than assuming special Byzantine ablutions are being described here, I have understood this to refer to Cola's prodigious and indiscriminate taste for wine in his final days.

## ❋ CHAPTER TWENTY-SEVEN

Long live the *popolo*!" People came from all over through the streets, drawn to this cry. The cry grew louder, and so did the crowd. At the upper crossroads of the market armed men came together from Sant'Angelo and Ripa, as well as from Colonna and Trevi.[57] As they gathered together, the cry changed, saying, "Death to the traitor, Cola di Rienzo! Death!" Then the wild youth came, the very ones he had enlisted to help him. Not all the *rioni* were there, only those I have mentioned. They ran to the palace on the Campidoglio.[58] There many people came together: men, women, and young people. They threw stones, made a great outcry and tumult, and surrounded the palace on all sides, front and back, saying, "Death to the traitor who levied the tax! Death!" The noise was terrible.

The tribune had no response to this. He neither sounded the bell nor rallied his people. At first, he said, "They say, 'Long live the *popolo*', and we say the same thing. We are here to raise the *popolo* up. They are my own soldiers. The letter from the pope, confirming my status, has arrived. All that remains is to publish it in the council."[59] Once he finally understood the bad ends to which the cry was aimed, he

---

57. The market stood right at the base of the Campidoglio, more or less were the stairs of the Aracoeli begin today. The armed men were therefore gathering right below the Senate Palace. For recent research on the marketplace, see Bolgia, *Reclaiming the Roman Capitol*, 98–100 et passim. The places named are Roman *rioni*, with the first two being from Cola's own part of Rome. The second two were from the Colonna districts of the city. His own revolution had begun, it will be remembered, in Sant'Angelo.

58. On the trecento Capitoline Palace, see Carlo Pietrangeli, "Il palazzo Senatorio nel Medioevo," *Capitolium* 35 (1960): 3–19; idem, "I palazzi capitolini nel Medioevo," *Capitolium* 39 (1964): 191–94; C. Parisi Presicce, "Dalla *Renovatio Senatus* al Giubileo del 1300: Il Campidoglio nel XII e XIII secolo," in *Carlo I d'Angio: Re di Sicilia e Senatore di Roma. Il monumento onorario nel Campidoglio del Duecento*, E. Di Gioia and C. Parisi Presicce, ed. (Rome: Campisano, 2009), 19–55; and M. Albertoni and M. Dell'Era, "Palazzo Senatorio: Lavori di restauro. Nuovi dati e contributi per una rilettura della storia dell'edificio," *Bollettino dei Musei Comunali di Roma* 25 (2011): 81–120.

59. Since we know from the next paragraph that Cola was not allowed to speak to the crowd outside, he may have said this to himself or to his three remaining companions. But the Anonimo does not specify how he learned this.

was very afraid, especially because he had been abandoned by every living soul on the Campidoglio. The judges, notaries, troops, and every other person there had decided to save their own skins. Only three people remained with him, among them his relative, Locciolo Pellicciaro.[60] And when the tribune saw the tumult of the people growing and that he had been abandoned and left unprepared, he became sorely afraid. He asked the three men what he should do. Wanting to fix things, he steeled himself and said, "I will not go like this, by my faith." He armed himself splendidly with all his arms in the manner of a knight, a helm on his head, breastplate, faulds, and greaves. He took up the banner of the *popolo* and, alone, went out onto the balcony above the great hall. Raising his hand, he gestured as if he wished them to be silent, so that he could speak.

*Sine dubio*,[61] had they listened to Cola they would have been broken and their feelings changed. He would have ended the whole uprising. But the Romans did not want to listen. They acted like pigs. They threw stones and fired crossbows. They rushed in with fire to burn down the door. There were so many crossbow bolts and arrows that Cola could not remain on the balcony. An arrow struck his hand. Then he took the banner and unfurled it with both his hands. He revealed the letters of gold, the arms of the citizens of Rome, as if he was trying to say, "You won't let me speak. See, I am a citizen and one of the *popolo* just like you. I love you, and if you kill me, you kill what is Roman in yourselves." These efforts were in vain. The ignorant people did worse, calling out "Death to the traitor!"

Unable to continue in this manner, Cola contemplated another way to escape. He was afraid to remain in his room up above, for the prison of Messer Bettrone of Narbonne, to whom he had done so much injury, was up there too. He had no doubt that the man would

60. This relative's status is revealed by his second name, which is simply his profession, a tanner. This is the same naming practice used for his uncle Ianni Varvieri (Giovanni the Barber), and for the virtuous Ianni Macellaro (Giovanni the Butcher). The latter makes clear that such names do not necessarily imply a lack of wealth (though they could) but rather a lack of noble status. Surnames were just beginning to take hold in trecento Italy, long before much of the rest of Europe.

61. "Without doubt..."

kill him with his own hands. He saw and recognized that Bettrone was communicating with the *popolo*. He thought he would leave the upper room and get away from Messer Bettrone for his own safety. So, he took the tablecloths from the tables, tied them around his waist, and lowered himself into the courtyard in front of the prison. The prisoners were there inside the prison. They saw everything. He took the keys and brought them with him. He feared the prisoners.

Locciolo Pellicciaro remained in the room above, and every now and again he went to the balcony and gestured with his hands, crying out to the crowd and saying, "He is coming down the back." So they went around behind the palace where he was coming. Then he went to the tribune and comforted him, telling him not to be afraid. Then he went back to the crowd and made similar gestures, "He's in the back! He's down in the back!" He gave them a target and the means of hitting it. Locciolo killed him. Locciolo Pellicciaro destroyed the liberty of the *popolo* who had never found a leader. Only with that man's help could they have achieved liberty. Only Locciolo, if he had helped him, could have prevented Cola's death, for the hall burned and the stairway collapsed only a little while later. No one would have been able to get to him. The day would have gone on and the *rione* Regola and the others would have come, swelling the numbers of the crowd and changing its intentions as they joined. Everyone would have gone home, or there would have been a great battle.[62] But Locciolo took away any hope.

The desperate tribune abandoned himself to the whims of chance. Standing in the courtyard in front of the chancery, the tribune took off his helm and then put it on again. He was of two minds. On one hand, he wanted to die with honor under arms, with sword in hand before people in a magnificent and imperial manner. This he made clear when he put on the helm and took up his arms. On the other hand, he wanted to save himself and not die. Which he made clear by taking his helmet off. These two courses of action made war in his mind. The desire to escape and survive won out. He was a man just like everyone else, afraid of dying. Once he had decided

---

62. Regola was Cola's own *rione*. The clear assumption here is that its people, and those of some of the other *rioni*, would have been opposed to this uprising and could have saved him.

that it was better to try and survive by whatever means he could, he pondered and hit upon a way, a shameful and cowardly way.[63]

The Romans had already set fire to the main door with wood, oil, and pitch. The door was burning. The upper level of the loggia was ablaze. The second door burned and the upper floor collapsed as its timbers fell to pieces. The crashing sounds were horrible. The tribune devised a plan to pass through the fire, mix in with the crowd, and escape. This was his last chance. He could find no other way. He abandoned the signs of baronial status, casting away all his arms. It is painful to contemplate. He cut his beard and blackened his face. Nearby there was a building where the gatekeeper slept. He entered it and picked up a tabard of cheap cloth, made like a rustic shepherd's clothes. This cheap garb he put on. Then he put a bed spread on his head, and so disguised he went out. He passed the burning door, the stairs, and the terror of the collapsed structure. He passed the final gate freely. The fire didn't touch him. He mixed in with the others. Disguised, he also disguised his speech. He spoke like a peasant and yelled, "Up! Up, and at that traitor!" If he had passed the final stairs, he would have escaped. The people were entirely focused on the palace. As he passed the final gate one man saw him and recognized him. Taking him by the hand, he said, "Stop. Where are you going?" He took the cover off of his head, but the thing that really gave him away was the sparkle coming off the bracelets that he wore. They were gold and did not look like cheap stuff.

And so, discovered, the Tribune revealed himself, he made plain who he was. He no longer dared try to flee. There was no option but to hope for mercy and submit to the will of others. Taken by the arm he crossed the stairs without obstruction, to the place where others had heard their sentences and where he had passed sentence on others. Once he had been brought there, silence fell. No one dared touch him. He stood there for less than an hour, his beard shorn, his face as black as a baker's, in an unbelted green tunic with gold straps and blue stockings in the manner of a baron. His arms were crossed. In the silence he looked about, turning his face this

63. The Anonimo could not have known Cola's interior, psychological conflicts. But he may have relied on the account of one of the three left in the palace, who could have narrated what he saw of Cola's external actions. The Anonimo uses the word "*demostrava*," i.e., "he demonstrated" or "he gestured."

## CHAPTER TWENTY-SEVEN

way and that. Then Cecco dello Viecchio took a dagger in his hand and plunged it into his stomach. He was the first.

*Immediate*, he was followed by a fellow from Trevi, a notary, who gave Cola a blow to the head with his sword.[64] Then one after another after another struck him. One struck him and another promised to do so. He did not make a sound. He died with the first blow and felt no pain. A man came with a rope and tied his feet together. They threw him on the ground, dragged him, and flayed his skin. They pierced him like a sieve. Everyone took their turn with him. It was like they were receiving an indulgence. He was dragged in this manner up to San Marcello.[65] There he was hung by the feet like a slaughtered calf. He had no head. Bits of it remained on the road where he had been dragged. He had so many wounds that he looked like a sieve. There was no place on him without wounds. His fat guts hung out. He was horribly fat, white like blood tainted milk. Such was he obesity that he resembled a huge buffalo or a slaughtered cow.[66] He hung there for two days and a night. The little boys threw rocks at him. On the third day, by the command of Iugurta and Sciarretta Colonna, he was taken to the field of Austa.[67] There all the Jews had gathered in a great number, not one was missing. A fire was made there of dry thistles. He was put into that pile of burning thistles. He was fat. Due to his great fatness he burned easily. The Jews were breathless and busy with their sleeves rolled up. They stirred the thistles to make them burn. So the body was burned and reduced to ashot a bit remained.[68]

64. "Immediately,..." Trevi was a *rione* controlled by the Colonna.

65. This church stood directly across from a house of the Colonna family. This was a Colonna church, at the center of their area of control.

66. The Anonimo makes these comparisons often in his descriptions of slain leaders. See for example, his account of the uprising against the duke of Athens in Florence, chapter 12, pp. 144–45. Such comparisons to beasts were common to medieval descriptions of ritualized execution. It reinforces the "otherness" of Rienzo's body.

67. That is, to the Mausoleum of Augustus and its surrounding area in the Campo Marzio. In this way the Colonna may have been deliberately mocking Rienzo's repeated allusions to August and Augustus in his rituals.

68. To medieval minds, the Colonna's forcing the Jews of the city to burn

So, Cola di Rienzo met his end, who had been the "August Tribune" of Rome and wanted to be champion of the Roman people. In his room a mirror of polished steel was found, covered with many characters and figures. In that mirror was bound the spirit of Fiorone.[69] Also found were tablets where he had recorded the names of Romans upon whom he wanted to levy taxes. The first rank contained one hundred people to be charged 500 florins. The second contained one hundred people to be charged 400 florins. The third was those to be charged 100 florins, the fourth 50 florins, and the fifth 10 florins. This man was killed on the eighth day of September, in the year of our Lord 1354, at the hour of terce.[70] Not only was he killed by the fury of the *popolo* but his foreign troops were all robbed of their belongings. They lost their horses and their arms. Those that were found in Rome were stripped naked, as were those stationed in fortresses outside the city.[71]

I WOULD LIKE to say a bit more on this matter.[72] The French entered Rome and attacked the Tarpeian Rock, the hill of the Campidoglio. The Romans had fled there out of fear. Once they saw that there were inadequate provisions at the Tarpeian Rock, they decided to send out the old, since they were useless people, in order to have more to go around and save the young. So it was. The older men, before leaving the Tarpeian Rock, took council. They said, "We go

---

the body reinforced the image of Rienzo's unclean, marginalized corpse, associated with both heresy and witchcraft. It also mocked his early upbringing near the Ghetto and the Jews' support of the tribune. See for example, Dyan Elliott, *Fallen Bodies: Pollution, Sexuality and Demonology in the Middle Ages* (Philadelphia: University of Pennsylvania Press, 1999).

69. Notably, this was the same kind of demonic mirror, and the same demon, cited in chapter 8, pp. 94–95, found after the assassination of the bishop of Verona.

70. Approximately 10:30 AM.

71. This could not have been the work of the disorganized Roman mob but appears to be the coordinated effort of some higher power, perhaps of the barons.

72. Here the Anonimo relates the contents of Livy, *Ab urbe condita libri*, V.41. The French here are the ancient Gauls.

to our houses. Among the French we will be butchered without doubt. It would be better for us to die dressed in virtue rather than wretchedness. Everyone put on your finery." So it was. The old men went home. Each one was garbed in whatever ornaments they had according to the honor of their offices. This one was dressed like a priest, that one a senator, and that one a consul. They arrayed themselves on their adorned thrones, with rods in their hands, and adorned with precious stones and gold. Among them was a man named Papirius. He stood heavily adorned before his house, *cum pretexta, cum trabea indutus*.[73] In the morning, the French marveled at this oddity, rushing to see the novelty. One Frenchman seized the beard of this Papirius and said, "Hey, old man! Old man!" Then Papirius scorned him, for the Frenchman had not spoken with reverence, as his garb required. He raised his rod and smote the Frenchman on the head, not fearing to die in order to preserve the honor of his majesty. A good Roman, therefore, should not die with a blanket on his head like Cola di Rienzo did.

---

73. "Wearing his toga and his mantle of state."

# CHAPTER TWENTY-EIGHT
EMPEROR CHARLES COMES TO ROME.
HIS CORONATION AND HIS DEPARTURE FOR GERMANY

[This chapter is lost.[1]]

❋

1. Failing to urge the papacy to return to Rome, Cola repeatedly called on the emperor to do so, as did Petrarch. Charles did eventually enter Italy and made his way to Rome. But whether Rienzo, Petrarch or any other writers were responsible for this is impossible to determine. Charles was simply following in the footsteps of all his German imperial predecessors who sought both to legitimize their imperial titles and to aid whatever remained of the pro-imperial, Ghibelline alliance in Italy. He had entered Lombardy by the spring of 1355 and then descended to Rome, He was crowned there in St. Peter's on April 5, 1355 and then immediately returned to Germany. His rapid retreat earned Petrarch's condemnation. See Ugo Dotti, *Petrarca civile: Alle origini dell'intellettuale moderno* (Rome: Donzelli, 2001), 199–214.

# BIBLIOGRAPHY

## EDITIONS OF THE ANONIMO ROMANO

Frugoni, Arsenio, ed. *Vita di Cola di Rienzo.* Florence: Le Monnier, 1957.

Ghisalberti, Alberto Maria, ed. *La vita di Cola di Rienzo.* Rome: L.S. Olschki, 1928.

Muratori, Ludovico Antonio, ed. "Historiae Romanae fragmenta ab anno 1327 usque ad 1354." *Antiquitates Italicae Medii Aevi.* 6 vols. Milan: Muratori, 1738–42.

Porta, Giuseppe, ed. *Anonimo romano: Cronica.* Milan: Adelphi, 1979.

Re, Zeferino, ed. *Vita di Cola di Rienzo.* Florence: Le Monnier, 1828.

Toti, Pompilio. *Vita di Cola di Rienzo tribuno del popolo romano.* Rome: Andrea Fei, 1624.

Wright, John, trans. *The Life of Cola di Rienzo.* Toronto: Pontifical Institute of Mediaeval Studies, 1975.

## OTHER PRIMARY SOURCES

Boccaccio, Giovanni. *The Downfall of the Famous.* Louis Brewer Hall, trans. New York: Italica Press, 2018.

Burdach, Konrad and Paul Piur. *Briefwechsel des Cola di Rienzo 2. Kritische Darstellung der Quellen zur geschichte Rienzos.* Berlin: Weidmann, 1928.

Coppi, Antonio. *Discorso sull'agricoltura del'agro romano.* 2nd edition. Rome: Monaldi, 1841.

*Chronicon Estense. Rerum Italicarum Scriptores* 15.3. Bologna: N. Zanichelli, 1908.

Cosenza, Mario E. *The Revolution of Cola di Rienzo.* 3rd. ed. Ronald G. Musto, ed. New York: Italica Press, 1996.

Gabrielli, Annibale, ed. *Epistolario di Cola di Rienzo.* Istituto storico italiano per il medio evo, Fonti per la storia d'Italia 6. Rome: Forzani e Compagnia, 1890.

Kieckhefer, Richard. *Forbidden Rites: A Necromancer's Manual of the Fifteenth Century.* University Park: Pennsylvania State University Press, 1998.

Knox, Lezlie, and Sean L. Field, ed. *Visions of Sainthood in Medieval Rome: The Lives of Margherita Colonna by Giovanni Colonna and Stefania.* Notre Dame, IN: University of Notre Dame Press, 2017.

*The Marvels of Rome: Mirabilia Urbis Romae.* 2nd edition. Francis Morgan Nichols, trans. Eileen Gardiner, ed. New York: Italica Press, 1986.

Noble, Thomas F.X. and Thomas Head, ed. *Soldiers of Christ: Saints and Saints Lives from Late Antiquity and the Early Middle Ages*. University Park: The Pennsylvania State University Press, 1995.

Oppaviensis, Martinus (Martin of Poland). *Chronicon pontificium et imperatorum*. L. Weiland, ed. *Monumenta Germaniae Historica*, SS 22. Berlin: MGH, 1872.

Petrarch, Francesco. *Le familiari: Familiarium rerum libri*. Latin ed. Vittorio Rossi and Umberto Bosco; Italian trans. Ugo Dotti and Felicita Audisio. 5 vols. Turin: N. Aragno, 2004.

—. *Letters on Familiar Matters*. Aldo S. Bernardo, trans. 3 vols. New York: Italica Press, 2005.

—. *Selected Letters*. Elaine Fantham, trans. I Tatti Renaissance Library, 76–77. Cambridge, MA: Harvard University Press, 2017.

Villani, Giovanni. *Cronica nuova*. Giuseppe Porta, ed. 3 vols. Parma: Gianda, 1990–91.

Villani, Matteo and Filippo Villani. *Cronica*. Giuseppe Porta, ed. 2 vols. Parma: Guanda, 1995.

## SECONDARY WORKS

Ait, Ivana, and Anna Esposito, ed. *Vivere la città: Roma nel Rinascimento*. Rome: Viella, 2020.

Albertoni, M. and M. Dell'Era. "Palazzo Senatorio: Lavori di restauro. Nuovi dati e contributi per una rilettura della storia dell'edificio." *Bollettino dei Musei Comunali di Roma* 25 (2011): 81–120.

Allegrezza, Franca. *Organizzazione del potere e dinamiche familiari: Gli Orsini dal Duecento agli inizi del Quattrocento*. Rome: Istituto storico per il Medioevo, 1998.

Andaloro, Maria, and Serena Romano, ed. *Arte e iconografia a Rome: Da Costantino a Cola di Rienzo*. Milan: Jaca Book, 2018.

Anselmi, Gian Mario. "La Cronica dell'Anonimo romano: Problemi di inquadramento culturale e storiografico." *Bullettino dell'Istituto storico Italiano per il Medio Evo e Archivio Muratoriano* 91 (1984): 423–40.

Armellini, Mariano. *Le Chiese di Roma dal secolo IV al XIX*. Rome: Pasquino, 1982.

Atkinson, Niall. *The Noisy Renaissance: Sound, Architecture, and Florentine Urban Life*. University Park: The Pennsylvania State University Press, 2016.

Ayton, Andrew. "Crécy and the Chroniclers." In Ayton and Preston, *The Battle of Crécy*, 287–350.

Ayton, Andrew and Philip Preston, ed. *The Battle of Crécy, 1346*. Woodbridge: Boydell, 2005.

Barash, Moshe. *Giotto and the Language of Gesture*. Cambridge: Cambridge University Press, 1987.

Barber, Malcolm. *The Crusader States*. New Haven: Yale University Press, 2012.

Beneš, Carrie E. "Cola di Rienzo and the *Lex Regia*." *Viator* 30 (1999): 231–51.

Behrman, Carolin. *Images of Shame: Infamy, Defamation and the Ethics of Oeconomia*. Boston: De Gruyter, 2016.

Billanovich, Giuseppe. "Come nacque un capolavoro: La 'Cronica' del non più Anonimo Romano. Il vescovo Ildebrandino Conti, Francesco Petrarca, e Bartolomeo di Iacovo da Valmontone." *Rendiconti. Atti della Accademia Nazionale dei Lincei*. Ser. 9, 6.1 (1995): 195–212.

Birch, Debra J. *Pilgrimage to Rome in the Middle Ages*. Woodbridge, Suffolk: Boydell Press, 2000.

Bisaha, Nancy. "Petrarch's Vision of the Muslim and Byzantine East." *Speculum* 76.2 (2001): 284–314.

Bolgia, Claudia. "The Felici Icon Tabernacle (1372) at S. Maria in Aracoeli, Reconstructed: Lay Patronage, Sculpture, and Marian Devotion in Trecento Rome." *Journal of the Warburg and Courtauld Institutes* 68 (2005): 27–72.

—. *Reclaiming the Roman Capitol: Santa Maria in Aracoeli from the Altar of Augustus to the Franciscans, c.500–1450*. New York: Routledge, 2017.

Bono, James J. "Medical Spirits and the Medieval Language of Life." *Traditio* 40 (1984): 91–130.

Boriaud, J.-Y. "Cola di Rienzo et la mise en scène de la lex Vespasiani." In *La lex de imperio Vespasiani e la Roma dei Flavi: Atti del Convegno (Roma, 20–22 novembre 2008)*. Luigi Capogrossi Colognesi and Elena Tassi Scandone, ed. Rome: L'Erma di Bretschneider, 2009, 115–24

Brilliant, Richard, and Dale Kinney, ed. *Reuse Value: Spolia and Appropriation in Art and Architecture from Constantine to Sherrie Levine*. New York: Routledge, 2016.

Brilliant, Virginia. "Envisaging the Particular Judgement in Late-Medieval Italy." *Speculum* 84.2 (2009): 314–46.

Bruzelius, Caroline. *The Stones of Naples: Church Building in Angevin Italy, 1266–1343*. New Haven: Yale University Press, 2004.

Bueno, Irene, ed. Pope *Benedict XII (1334–1342): The Guardian of Orthodoxy*. Amsterdam: Amsterdam University Press, 2018.

Bullough, Vern L. "Medieval Bologna and the Development of Medical Education." *Bulletin of the History of Medicine* 32.3 (1958): 201–15.

Burckhardt, Jacob. *The Civilization of the Renaissance in Italy*. S.G.C. Middlemore, trans.; Peter Burke, intro.; Peter Murray, notes. London: Penguin, 1990.

Caferro, William. *John Hawkwood: An English Mercenary in Fourteenth-Century Italy*. Baltimore, MD: The Johns Hopkins University Press, 2006.

—. *Mercenary Companies and the Decline of Siena*. Baltimore, MD: The Johns Hopkins University Press, 1998.

Campanelli, Maurizio. "The Anonimo Romano at his Desk: Recounting the Battle of Crécy in Fourteenth-Century Italy." In *The Medieval Chronicle*. Erik Kooper and Sjoerd Levelt, ed. Leiden: Brill, 2014, 33–78.

—. "'Benché io l'aia ià fatta per lettera': Gli inserti Latini nella *Cronica* dell'Anonimo romano." *Filologia & Critica* 37 (2012): 3–29.

—. "The Preface of the Anonimo Romano's *Cronica*: Writing History and Proving Truthfulness in Fourteenth-Century Rome." *The Medieval Journal* 3.1 (2013): 83–101.

Cappelletti, Giuseppe. *Le chiese d'Italia dalla lore origine sino ai nostri giorni*. Venice: Antonelli, 1854.

Carocci, Sandro. *Baroni di Roma: Dominazioni signorili e lignaggi aristocratici nel duecento e trecento*. Rome: Istituto storico per il Medioevo, 1993.

—. "The Papal State." In Gamberini and Lazzarini, *Italian Renaissance State*, 69–89.

Carruthers, Mary. *The Book of Memory: A Study of Memory in Medieval Culture*. Cambridge: Cambridge University Press, 2008.

Castagnetti, A., and G.M. Varanini, ed. *Il Veneto nel medioevo: Dai comuni cittadini al predominio scaligero nella Marca*. Verona: Banca Popolare di Verona, 1991.

Casteen, Elizabeth. *From She-Wolf to Martyr: The Reign and Disputed Reputation of Joanna I of Naples*. Ithaca, NY: Cornell University Press, 2015.

Castellani, A. "Note di lettura: La 'Cronica' dell'Anonimo Romano." *Studi Linguistici Italiani* 13 (1987): 66–84.

Celenza, Christopher S. *The Intellectual World of the Italian Renaissance: Language, Philosophy, and the Search for Meaning.* Cambridge: Cambridge University Press, 2018.

—. *Renaissance Humanism and the Papal Curia: Lapo da Castiglionchio the Younger's* De curiae commodis. Ann Arbor: University of Michigan Press, 1999.

Claussen, Peter Cornelius. "Marmo e splendore: Architettura, arredi liturgici, spoliae." In Andaloro and Romano, *Arte e iconografia,* 193–225.

Cognasso, Francesco. *I Visconti: Storia di una famiglia.* Bologna: Odoya, 2016.

Collins, Amanda. *Greater than Emperor: Cola di Rienzo (ca. 1313–1354) and the World of Fourteenth-Century Rome.* Ann Arbor, MI: University of Michigan Press, 2002.

Contini, Gianfranco. "Invito a un capolavoro." *Letturatura. Rivista trimestrale di letturatura contemporanea* 4.4 (1940): 3–14.

Cossar, Roisin. *Clerical Households in Late Medieval Italy.* Cambridge, MA: Harvard University Press, 2018.

Cox, Eugene L. *The Green Count of Savoy.* Princeton, NJ: Princeton University Press, 1967.

De Angelis, Pietro. *L'ospedale di Santo Spirito in Saxia.* 2 vols. Rome: Tipografia Dario Detti, 1960–62.

D'Onofrio, Cesare. *Visitiamo Roma mille anni fa: La città dei* Mirabilia. Rome: Romana Società Editrice, 1988.

Dotti, Ugo. *Petrarca civile: Alle origini dell'intellettuale moderno.* Rome: Donzelli, 2001.

Doyno, Mary Harvey. *The Lay Saint: Charity and Charismatic Authority in Medieval Italy, 1150–1350.* Ithaca, NY: Cornell University Press, 2019.

Duprè Theseider, Eugenio. *Roma dal commune di popolo alla signoria pontificia, 1252–1377.* Bologna: Cappelli, 1952.

Dykmans, Marc. "Le Cardinal Annibal de Ceccano (c.1282–1350). Étude biographique et testament de 17 Juin 1348." *Bulletin de l'Institut Historique Belge de Rome* 48 (1973): 145–315.

Elliott, Dyan. *Fallen Bodies: Pollution, Sexuality and Demonology in the Middle Ages.* Philadelphia: University of Pennsylvania Press, 1999.

Esposito, Anna. *Un'altra Roma: Minoranze nazionali e comunità ebraiche tra Medioevo e Rinascimento.* Rome: Il Calamo, 1995.

Faini, Enrico. "Alle origini della memoria communale: Prime ricerche." *Quellen und Forschungen aus italienischen Archiven und Bibliotheken* 88 (2008): 61–81.

Falconieri, Tommaso di Carpegna. *Cola di Rienzo.* Rome: Salerno, 2002.

Falkeid, Unn. *The Avignon Papacy Contested: An Intellectual History from Dante to Catherine of Siena.* Cambridge, MA: Harvard University Press, 2017.

Fehl, Philipp. "The Placement of the Equestrian Statue of Marcus Aurelius in the Middle Ages." *Journal of the Warburg and Courtauld Institutes* 37 (1974): 362–67.

Foote, David. "How the Past Becomes a Rumor: The Notarialization of Historical Consciousness in Medieval Orvieto. *Speculum* 75.4 (2000): 794–815.

Formentin, Vittorio. Approssimazioni al testo e alla lingua della 'Cronica' d'Anonimo Romano." *Leggere gli apparati: Testi e testimoni dei classici italiani.* G. Raboni, ed. Milan: Unicopli, 2012, 27–71.

—. "Il volto dell'Anonimo." *Filologia & Critica* 37.1 (2012): 130–49.

—. "Frustoli di romanesco antico in lodi arbitrali dei secoli XIV e XV." *Lingua e Stile* 43 (2008): 21–99.

—. "Nuovi rilievi sul testo della 'Cronica' d'Anonimo romano." *Contributi di filologia dell'Italia mediana* 16 (2002): 23–47.

—. "Proposte di restauro per la 'Cronica' d'Anonimo romano (con una nota etimologica)." *Medioevo romanzo* 14 (1989): 112–25.

—. "Schede lessicali e grammaticali per la 'Cronica' d'Anonimo romano." *La lingua italiana* 4 (2008): 25–43.

—. "Tra storia della lingua e filologia: Note sulla sintassi della 'Cronica' d'Anonimo romano." *Lingua e Stile* 37 (2002): 203–50.

Gamberini, Andrea, and Isabella Lazzarini, ed. *The Italian Renaissance State.* Cambridge: Cambridge University Press, 2012.

Gauvain, Alexis. "Romani e forestieri nelle case di San Pietro in Vaticano nel secondo Quattrocento." In Ait and Esposito, *Vivere la città,* 55–69.

Gennaro, Clara. "Mercanti e bovattieri nella Roma della seconda metà del trecento (Da una ricerca su registri notarili)." *Bullettino dell'Istituto storico italiano per il Medio Evo* 78 (1967): 155–87.

Green, Louis. "The Image of Tyranny in Early Fourteenth-Century Italian Historical Writing." *Renaissance Studies* 7.4 (1993): 335–51.

Guerri dall'Oro, Guido. "Les mercenaires dans les campagnes napolitaines de Louis le Grand, roi de Hongrie, 1347–1350." In *Mercenaries and Paid Men: The Mercenary Identity on the Middle Ages.* John France, ed. Leiden: Brill, 2008, 61–88.

Hankins, James. *Virtue Politics: Soulcraft and Statecraft in Renaissance Italy.* Cambridge, MA: Harvard University Press, 2019.

Harvey, Margaret. *The English in Rome, 1362–1420: Portrait of an Expatriate Community.* Cambridge: Cambridge University Press, 1999.

Holstein, Alizah. "Rome During Avignon: Myth, Memory, and Civic Identity in Fourteenth-Century Roman Politics." Ph.D. diss. Cornell University, 2006.

Housely, Norman. *The Later Crusades, 1274–1580. From Lyons to Alcazar.* Oxford: Oxford University Press, 1992.

Internullo, Dario. *Ai margini dei giganti: La vita intellettuale dei romani nel trecento, 1305–1367.* Rome: Viella, 2016.

Jansen, Katherine L. *Peace and Penance in Late Medieval Italy.* Princeton, NJ: Princeton University Press, 2018.

Jordan, Willian Chester. *The Apple of His Eye: Converts from Islam in the Reign of Louis IX.* Princeton, NJ: Princeton University Press, 2019.

Kelly, Samantha. *The New Solomon: Robert of Naples (1309–1343) and Fourteenth-Century Kingship.* Leiden: Brill, 2003.

Kessler, Herbert L., and Johanna Zacharias. *Rome 1300: The Path of the Pilgrim.* New Haven: Yale University Press, 2000.

Kirshner, Julius. "Hidden in Plain Sight: Citizen Women in Late Medieval Italy." Unpublished paper, 2017.

Kuehn, Thomas. *Law, Family, & Women: Toward a Legal Anthropology of Renaissance Italy.* Chicago: University of Chicago Press, 1991.

—. *Family and Gender in Renaissance Italy, 1300–1600.* Cambridge: Cambridge University Press, 2017.

Krautheimer, Richard. *Rome: Profile of a City, 312–1308.* Princeton, NJ: Princeton University Press, 1980.

Lansing, Carol. *Passion and Order: Restraint of Grief in the Medieval Italian Communes.* Ithaca, NY: Cornell University Press, 2008.

Larner, John. *The Lords of Romagna: Romagnol Society and the Origins if the Signorie.* Ithaca, NY: Cornell University Press, 1965.

Lavin, Irving. *The Art of Commemoration in the Renaissance.* Marilyn Aronberg Lavin, ed. New York: Italica Press, 2020.

Lee, Alexander. *Humanism and Empire: The Imperial Ideal in Fourteenth-Century Italy.* Oxford: Oxford University Press, 2018.

Le Goff, Jacques. *History and Memory.* Steven Rendall and Elizabeth Claman, trans. New York: Columbia University Press, 1992.

Lori Sanfilippo, Isa. *Roma dei Romani: Arti, mestieri, e professioni nella Roma del trecento.* Rome: Istituto Storico per il Medio Evo, 2001.

—. "Un 'luoco famoso' nel medioevo, una chiesa oggi poco nota: Notizie extravaganti su S. Angelo in Pescheria (VI–XX secolo)." *Archivio della Società Romana di Storia Patria* 117 (1994): 231–68.

Maiolo, Francesco. *Medieval Sovereignty: Marsilius of Padua and Bartolus of Saxoferrato.* Delft: Eburon Publishers, 2008.

Maire Vigueur, Jean-Claude. "Comuni e signorie nelle province dello Stato della Chiesa." In *Signorie cittadine nell'Italia comunale.* J.-C. Maire Vigueur, ed. Rome: Viella 2013, 105–72.

—. "La Felice Societas dei Balestrieri e dei Pavesati a Roma: Una società popolare e i suoi ufficiali." In *Scritti per Isa: Raccolta di studi offerti a Isa Lori Sanfilippo.* Antonella Mazzon and Isa Lori Sanfilippo, ed. Rome: Istituto storico italiano per il Medio Evo, 2008, 577–606.

—. *L'altra Roma: Una storia dei romani all'epoca dei comuni (XII-XIV).* Turin: Einaudi, 2011.

Mallett, Michael. *Mercenaries and their Masters: Warfare in Renaissance Italy.* Totowa, NJ: Rowman and Littlefield, 1974.

Marshall, Richard K. *The Local Merchants of Prato: Small Entrepreneurs in the Late Medieval Economy.* Baltimore, MD: The Johns Hopkins University Press, 1999.

Mascanzoni, Leardo. "La Romagna e Bologna nella *Cronica* di Anonimo Romano." *Atti e Memorie della Deputazione di Storia Patria per le Province di Romagna* n.s. 67 (2017): 119–50.

—. "The Italian 'Crusade' against Francesco Ordelaffi (1356-1359), Lord of Forlì, and how it is perceived in the Chronicles." *Testo per il Convegno Internazionale Diversity of Crusading, Ninth Quadrennial Conference of the SSCLE, (Odense, 27 June–1 July 2016).* Online at: https://www.academia.edu/34053039.

McCahill, Elizabeth. *Reviving the Eternal City: Rome and the Papal Court, 1420–1447.* Cambridge, MA: Harvard University Press, 2013.

McKee, Sally. "Domestic Slavery in Renaissance Italy." *Slavery and Abolition* 29.3 (2008): 305–26.

McKitterick, David. *Print, Manuscript, and the Search for Order, 1450–1830*. Cambridge: Cambridge University Press, 2003.

Miglio, Massimo. "Anonimo Romano." In *Il senso della storia nella cultura medievale Italiana (1100–1350): Atti del quattordicesimo Convegno di studi del Centro italiano di studi di storia e d'arte di Pistoia*. Pistoia: Centro italiano di studi di storia e d'arte di Pistoia, 1995, 175–87.

—. "Gruppi sociali e azione politica nella Roma di Cola di Rienzo." *Studi Romani* 23.4 (1975): 443–61.

Mitchell, Russell. "The Longbow–Crossbow Shootout at Crécy (1346): Has the 'Rate of Fire Commonplace' Been Overrated?" In *The Hundred Years War 2. Different Vistas*. L.J. Andrew Villalon and Donald J. Kagay, ed. Leiden: Brill, 2008, 233–57.

Modigliani, Anna. "Antichità e paganesimo nelle feste e nelle ceremonie romane del Rinascimento." In Ait and Esposito, *Vivere la città*, 247–62.

—. "Lo ogliardino de Roma: Il projetto italiano di Cola di Rienzo." *Roma nel Rinascimento* (2014): 241–52.

—. "Signori e tiranni nella *Cronica* dell'Anonimo romano." *Rivista storica italiana* 110 (1998): 357–410.

Mollat, Guillaume. *The Popes at Avignon, 1305–1378*. London: Thomas Nelson, 1963.

Monaci, Ernesto. *Sul* Liber Ystoriarum Romanorum: *Prime ricerche*. Rome: Forzano, 1889.

Morreale, Laura K., and Nicholas Paul, ed. *The French of Outremer: Communities and Communications in the Crusading Mediterranean*. New York: Fordham University Press, 2018.

Muldoon, James. "The Avignon Papacy and the Frontiers of Christendom: The Evidence of Vatican Register 62." *Archivum Historiae Pontificiae* 17 (1979): 125–95.

Musto, Ronald G. *Apocalypse in Rome: Cola di Rienzo and the Politics of the New Age*. Berkeley: University of California Press, 2003.

—. "Cola di Rienzo." Oxford Bibliographies Online. New York: Oxford University Press, 2020. DOI: 10.1093/OBO/9780195399301-0122.

—. *Medieval Naples: A Documentary History, 400–1400*. New York: Italica Press, 2013.

—. *Writing Southern Italy before the Renaissance: Trecento Historians of the Mezzogiorno*. New York: Routledge, 2019.

Najemy, John. *A History of Florence, 1200–1575*. Oxford: Blackwell, 2008.

Necipoğlu, Nevra. *Byzantium Between the Ottomans and the Latins: Politics and Society in the Late Empire*. Cambridge: Cambridge University Press, 2009.

O'Callaghan, Joseph F. *The Gibraltar Crusade: Castile and the Battle for the Strait*. Philadelphia: University of Pennsylvania Press, 2011.

Ortalli, Gherardo. *La pittura infamante: Secoli XIII–XVI*. Rome, Viella, 2015.

Padgett, John F., and Paul D. McLean. "Economic Credit in Renaissance Florence." *Journal of Modern History* 83.1 (2011): 1–47.

Palermo, Luciano. *Il porto di Roma nel XIV e XV secolo: Strutture socio-economiche e statute*. Rome: Istituto di studi romani, 1979.

—. *Mercati di grano a Roma tra Medioevo e Rinascimento*. Rome: Il Centro di Ricerca, 1990.

Palmer, James A. "Medieval and Renaissance Rome: Mending the Divide." *History Compass* 15.11 (2017). DOI: 10.1111/hic3.12424.

—. "Peace Movements: Peace in the Communes." In *A Cultural History of Peace in the Medieval Age (800–1450)*. Walter Simons, ed. London: Bloomsbury Academic, 2020, 101–18.

—. "Piety and Social Distinction in Late Medieval Roman Peacemaking." *Speculum* 89.4 (2014): 974–1004.

—. *The Virtues of Economy: Governance, Power, and Piety in Late Medieval Rome*. Ithaca, NY: Cornell University Press, 2019.

Parisi Presicce, C. "Dalla *Renovatio Senatus* al Giubileo del 1300: Il Campidoglio nel XII e XIII secolo." In *Carlo I d'Angio: Re di Sicilia e Senatore di Roma. Il monumento onorario nel Campidoglio del Duecento*. E. Di Gioia and C. Parisi Presicce, ed. Rome: Campisano, 2009, 19–55.

Partner, Peter. *The Lands of St Peter: The Papal State in the Middle Ages and Early Renaissance*. London: Methuen, 1972.

Peterson, Janine Larmon. *Suspect Saints and Holy Heretics: Disputed Sanctity and Communal Identity in Late Medieval Italy*. Ithaca, NY: Cornell University Press, 2019.

Petrucci, Enzo. "La Chiesa nell'azione del Cardinale Egidio de Albornoz durante la campagna in Italia." *Rivista di Storia della Chiesa in Italia* 1 (2011): 57–99.

Phillips, William D. *Slavery in Medieval and Early Modern Iberia*. Philadelphia: University of Pennsylvania Press, 2014.

Pietrangeli, Carlo. "Il palazzo Senatorio nel Medioevo." *Capitolium* 35 (1960): 3–19.

—. "I palazzi capitolini nel Medioevo." *Capitolium* 39 (1964): 191–94.

Pio, Berardo. "Mogliano, Gentile da." *Dizionario Biografico degli Italiani* 75 (2011). Online at https://www.treccani.it/enciclopedia/gentile-da-mogliano_(Dizionario-Biografico).

Piur, Paul. *Cola di Rienzo: Darstellung seines Lebens und seines Geistes*. Vienna: L.W. Seidel, 1931.

Poloni, Alma. "Ordelaffi, Francesco di Sinibaldo di." In *Dizionario Biografico degli Italiani* 79 (2013). Online at https://www.treccani.it/enciclopedia/francesco-di-sinibaldo-ordelaffi_(Dizionario-Biografico).

Presciutti, Diana Bullen. "Dead Infants, Cruel Mothers, and Heroic Popes: The Visual Rhetoric of Foundling Care at the Hospital of Santo Spirito, Rome." *Renaissance Quarterly* 64.3 (2011): 752–99.

Prestwich, Michael. "The Battle of Crécy." In Ayton and Preston, *The Battle of Crécy*, 139–57.

Rehberg, Andreas. "Gestire l'assistenza: L'ospedale di Santo Spirito e l'ospedale de SS. Salvatore a confronto." In Ait and Esposito, *Vivere la città*, 225–42.

—. "I papi, l'ospedale e l'ordine di S. Spirito nell'età avignonese." *Archivio della Società Romana di Storia Patria* 124 (2001): 35–140.

—. *Kirche un Macht im römischen Trecento: Die Colonna und ihre Klientel auf dem kurialen Pfründenmarkt (1278–1378)*. Tübingen: Neimeyer, 1999.

Reynolds, Susan. *Kingdoms and Communities in Western Europe, 900–1300*. Oxford: Clarendon Press, 1997.

Rollo-Koster, Joëlle. *Avignon and its Papacy, 1309–1417: Popes, Institutions, Society*. Lanham, MD: Rowman and Littlefield, 2015.

Romano, Serena. "L'immagine di Roma, Cola di Rienzo e la fine del Medioevo." In Andaloro and Romano, *Arte e iconografia a Roma*, 227–56.

Rosario, Iva. *Art and Propaganda: Charles IV of Bohemia, 1346–1378*. Woodbridge: Boydell Press, 2000.

Rose, Susan. *Calais: An English Town in France, 1347–1558*. Woodbridge, Suffolk: The Boydell Press, 2008.

Sanders, Lionel Jehuda. *Dionysius I of Syracuse and Greek Tyranny*. New York: Routledge, 1987.

Schmitt, Jean-Claude. *La raison des gestes dans l'occident médiéval*. Paris: Editions Gallimard, 1990.

Seibt, Gustav. *Anonimo romano: Scrivere la storia alle soglie del Rinascimento.* Rome: Viella 2000.

Setton, Kenneth M. *The Papacy and the Levant (1204–1571).* Philadelphia: American Philosophical Society, 1976.

Siraisi, Nancy G. *Medieval and Early Renaissance Medicine: An Introduction to Knowledge and Practice.* Chicago: University of Chicago Press, 1990.

Small, Carola M. "The District of Rome in the Early Fourteenth Century, 1300 to 1347." *Canadian Journal of History/Annales Canadiennes d'Histoire* 16 (1981): 193–213.

Smeets, A. "The Dazzle of Dawn: Visions, Dreams, and Thoughts on Dreams by Gregory the Great." In *Dreams as Divine Communication in Christianity: From Hermas to Aquinas.* B.J. Koet, ed. Leuven: Peeters, 2012, 157–78.

Sordi, Marta. "Cola di Rienzo e le clausole mancanti della 'lex de imperio Vespasiani'." In *Studi in onore di Edoardo Volterra* 2. Università degli Studi (Roma), Facoltà di Giurisprudenza, ed. Milan: A. Giuffrè, 1971, 303–11.

Spada, Sergio. *Gli Ordelaffi: Signori di Forlì e Cesena.* Cesena: Il Ponte Vecchio, 2011.

Spani, Giovanni. "Anonimo Romano." In *Encyclopedia of the Medieval Chronicle.* Graeme Dunphy and Christian Bratu, ed. Leiden: Brill, 2016, at: http://dx.doi.org/10.1163/2213-2219_emc_SIM_00197.

Starn, Randolph. *Contrary Commonwealth: The Theme of Exile in Medieval and Renaissance Italy.* Berkeley: University of California Press, 1982.

Strayer, Joseph. *The Reign of Philip the Fair.* Princeton, NJ: Princeton University Press, 1980.

Stuard, Susan Mosher. *Gilding the Market: Luxury and Fashion in Fourteenth-Century Italy.* Philadelphia: University of Pennsylvania Press, 2006.

Taylor, Rabun, Katherine W. Rinne, and Spiro Kostof. *Rome: An Urban History from Antiquity to the Present.* New York: Cambridge University Press, 2016.

Thompson, Augustine. *Cities of God: The Religion of the Italian Communes, 1125–1325.* University Park: Pennsylvania State University Press, 2005.

Wagner, John A. "Calais, Siege of (1346–1347)." *Encyclopedia of the Hundred Years War.* Woodbridge, Suffolk: Greenwood, 2006, 73–74.

Wickham, Chris. *Medieval Rome: Stability and Crisis of a City, 900–1150.* Oxford: Oxford University Press, 2015.

—. "The Sense of the Past in Italian Communal Narratives." In *The Perception of the Past in Twelfth-Century Europe*. Paul Magdalino, ed. London: Hambledon Press, 1992, 173–90.

—. *Sleepwalking into a New World: The Emergence of the Italian City Communes in the Twelfth Century.* Princeton, NJ: Princeton University Press, 2015.

Witt, Ronald G. *In the Footsteps of the Ancients: The Origins of Humanism from Lovato to Bruni.* Leiden: Brill, 2000.

—. "Medieval 'Ars Dictaminis' and the Beginnings of Humanism: A New Construction of the Problem." *Renaissance Quarterly* 35.1 (1982): 1–35.

—. "What did Giovannino Read and Write? Literacy in Early Renaissance Florence." *I Tatti Studies. Essays in the Renaissance* 6 (1995): 83–114.

Wood, Diana. *Clement VI: The Pontificate and Ideas of an Avignon Pope.* Cambridge: Cambridge University Press, 1989.

Yates, Frances. *The Art of Memory.* Chicago: University of Chicago Press, 1966.

Zabbia, Marino. *I notai e la cronachistica cittadina italiana nel trecento.* Rome: ISIME, 1999.

Zorzi, Andrea. *Conflitti, paci e vendette nell'Italia comunale.* Florence: Firenze University Press, 2009.

—. "Justice." In Gamberini and Lazzarini, *Italian Renaissance State*, 490–514.

—. "The Popolo." In *Italy in the Age of the Renaissance, 1300–1550.* John Najemy, ed. Oxford: Oxford University Press, 2004, 145–64.

Zupko, Edward. *Italian Weights and Measures from the Middle Ages to the Nineteenth Century.* Philadelphia: American Philosophical Society, 1981.

# INDEX

## A
Abbeville 163
Abruzzi 110, 272
Abū al-Hasan. *See* Salim of Benamarin (Bellamarina), king.
Abū al-Hasan ʿAli 117
Abū Mālik ʿAbd al-Wāhid, 117
Academy 148
Achaea 66
Acquapendente 259
Acre 110
Acuto, Fra 114, 208
Aemelius Paulus 18
Agnolo di Tura 71, 143
Aiguillon (Arpiglione) 163
Aito Luoco 146, 147, 148, 151, 152, 158
Albert the Great 26
Albornoz, Giles (Egidio Conchese) 63, 117, 131, 254, 256–69
Alençon, count of 168, 169, 172
Alesahir. *See* Philadelphia (Filadelfia).
Alexander the Great 60, 146
Alfanic, pavillion 126, 128, 129, 130
*alfaqueques* 119
Alfonso IV of Portugal, king 117, 121
Alfonso XI of Castile, king 37, 52, 117–28, 130
Algeciras 62, 117, 131, 133, 258
Alps 237
Altamura 240, 242, 243
Amadeus VI, count of Savoy 264
Amelia 214, 259, 260
*amplificatio* 164
Anagni 230
Anatolia 147
Ancona 63, 157, 158, 256, 261, 262, 264, 268
Andalusians 119

Andreotti, Lorenzo Simone 244
Andrew of Hungary, prince 62, 114, 115, 215, 216, 218–19, 240, 243, 244, 251
Androin de la Roche, abbot 265, 269
Angelo of Montecielo, OFM 273
Annales Caesenates 265
Annibaldi: Bartolomea 71; Cola (Nicola) de Madonna Martomea 37, 71; Liccardo Imprennente delli 290, 291, 292; Pietro 71
Annibaldo da Ceccano 10, 11, 200, 246–50, 274
Anonimo Romano: audience 2, 3, 13, 20, 22, 26, 28, 29, 38, 41, 42, 43, 44, 56, 57, 204; authorship 8, 8–12; Bologna 104; class background 28; Cola di Rienzo 39–41; Continental scholarship 6; cosmology and geography 146, 222; dreams 207–11; history writing 13–26, 16–19; Latin Christendom 27–30; Latin original 3; life and career 9–13; Livy 18, 20; Lucan 18; medical training 15, 21, 26, 98, 134, 201, 252; Milan 43, 104; motives for writing 19; narrative structure & technique 20–26, 44, 61, 265; politics 11; *popolo* 56; preservation, publication, and study 2–8; Roman society and culture 29–31, 42–43; Sallust 18; sources 13–14, 18; themes 44–57; Visconti 21
Anquillara, Bertuollo 218
Anthony, St., of Egypt 153
Antigonus, king 146
Antiochia 206
Antony, Marc 210
Apulia (Puglia) 62, 63, 67, 110, 237, 242, 243, 287

315

Aquileia 209, 210
Aquinas, Thomas 26
Arabs 119
Aragon 112, 121, 122, 163
Arcilasso, knight 126, 127, 129
Arezzo 138, 177, 214, 275
Arimbaldo of Narbonne, mercenary 49, 275, 276, 277, 280, 283, 287, 290
Aristippus, philosopher 107
Aristotle 10, 87, 112, 113, 141, 210, 211
Armagnac, count of 75, 76
*ars dictaminis* 193, 200
Asclepius 257
Astura 85
Athens 46, 47, 62, 135, 136, 137, 145, 148
Attila the Hun 209, 210, 212
Augustus, emperor 271
authority 29, 31, 42, 47, 55, 186, 188, 189, 200; absolute 196; clothing 107; episcopal 79; Roman people 195
Avicenna 10, 21, 23, 85–86, 134
Avignon: Benedict XII 130; Clement VI 247; curia 247; Fra Venturino 81; Giovanna I 219; jubilee of 1350 246; Moors 130; Naples 179; papacy 1, 22, 29, 78; Roman embassy 183; Rome 12, 248; Venice 157. *See also* Cola di Rienzo; Petrarch.
Aydin 148

**B**

Babrius, fabulist 107
Babylon, ancient 186
Baghdad (Cairo) 118, 129
Ballo, Master, architect 84
Bari 243
Bartolo da Sassoferrato 36, 193, 199
Bartolomeo di Iacovo da Valmontone 9

Beatific Vision 74, 81, 247
Beatrice of Taranto 138
Bellamarina. *See* Trebesten (Tlemcen).
Bellovedere, lords of 234
bells 12, 23, 24, 62, 63, 64, 69, 78, 79, 81, 135, 164, 190, 193, 196, 201, 205, 207, 219, 225, 230, 232, 241, 255, 263, 286, 288, 293
Benedict XII, pope 11, 62, 82, 82–83, 121, 130, 131, 135
Benevento 96
Bergamo 79, 102, 103, 104
Bernard of Clairvaux 185
Bertinoro 270
Bertrand du Déaulx, cardinal legate 42, 228, 250, 274
Bertrand du Pouget, papal legate 75, 77, 263
Bettona 63, 254
Bettrone of Narbonne, mercenary 49, 275, 276, 277, 280, 283, 290, 294, 295
bibical references: 1 Kings 16:11 253; Psalms 9:8 216; Psalms 22:1 235; Psalms 90:13 271; Ecclesiastes 1:9-10 60; Ecclesiasticus 20:7 190; Daniel 4 280; 1 Maccabees 8 217; 1 Maccabees 12 216; Matt. 19:29 101; Matt. 26:51 236; Matt. 27:46 235; Mark 10:29–30 101; Mark 14:47 236; Luke 22:50–51 236; John 18:10–11 236; Acts 7–8 256; Apocalypse 147, 185, 187
Billanovich, Giuseppe 8, 12
Bleda the Hun 209
Boccaccio, Giovanni 55, 143, 253, 263
Boethius 112
Bolgia, Claudia 212
Bologna: Anonimo Romano 9, 43; *carroccio* 76; duke of Athens

144; famine 98; Mastino della
   Scala 88; medical school 10,
   10–14, 98; militia 76; natural
   disaster 97; Palazzo della Biada
   77; papacy 46, 62, 75; Piazza
   Maggiore 77; revolts 77
Bolsena 259
Boniface VIII, pope 29, 136, 161,
   220, 230
*bovattieri* 100
Bovolenta 90, 91
Brescia 79, 88, 94, 102, 104
Brettonoro 263
Bruni, Leonardo 18
Bulgaria 209
*buono stato* 47, 185, 190, 191, 192,
   193, 197, 198, 199, 200, 214, 231,
   232, 235, 241, 242, 243, 250, 277,
   280, 281; ordinances 194–95
Burckhardt, Jacob 4
Burgundy, ancient 209
Bussa, Paolo 232
Byzantium 147

## C

Cadmus 59
Caetani (Gaietano, Gaetani):
   Boniface VIII 230; family 212;
   Giovanni 212; Iacovo 200
Cagli 262
Calabria 110
Calais 172–173
Calatrava 258
Camorsino, Manuello, patriarch
   149–56
Campania 110, 237, 246, 247, 251,
   252
Canino 259, 260
cannibalism 144
canon law 78, 188, 250
Cantacuzenus: John VI 147, 148,
   153; Theodora 148
Capranica 218

Carrara, family 93, 215
Carthage 186, 237
Cassino 192
Cassius Parmensis 210
Castelnuovo d'Adda 99
Castelnuovo Scrivia 99
Castiglione delli Alberteschi 99
Castiglione di Santa Prassede
   (Perzeta) 284, 290
Castile 37, 52, 117, 119, 120, 130, 258
Castle Fiumone 267
Castrocaro 263
Cataline 14, 59
Caucassaso 145
Cavallini, Giovanni 14, 258
Ceccano 10, 11, 200, 246, 247, 251
Cecco da Perugia 280
Cere 212
Cerroni, Giovanni 255
Cervia 150
Cesena 263–69
Chalcis. *See* Negroponte.
Charles I, king 111
Charles I of Anjou, king 85, 114
Charles II, king 112, 251
Charles IV, emperor 41, 63, 130,
   170, 171, 242, 262, 272, 283, 300
Charles, king of Hungary 110
Charles of Calabria, prince 111,
   113, 138
Charles of Durazzo, prince 63,
   215, 244
Cherubino 148
Chios 148
*Chronicon Estense* 225, 242, 273
*Chronicon Siculum* 27
*Chronicon Suessanum* 27
Cicero 59, 183, 257
Cistercian Order 82, 102, 131
Città di Castello 218
Civitale 88, 95, 104
Civitavecchia 179, 212, 242, 260
*Clementinae* 78

Clement VI, pope: Alfonso XI 130; Annibaldo da Ceccano 247; Avignon papacy 157; *buono stato* 185; Cola di Rienzo 41, 56; crusades 149, 158; da Vico 260; death 63, 255–56; election 62, 131, 135; Giovanna I 179; jubilee 246; Roman embassy 183; Rome 251; Venice 157

clothing and fashion: Catalan 92, 107; ceremonial 220; extravagance 107–8; Genoese 131; German 188; gift-giving 226; hair 281; Muslim 108; Neapolitan 215; novelties 97; penitential 287; Saracen 107; simplicity 218; Spanish 107; trecento 107; Turkish 151

Çoban Bey 148

coinage: carlini 110, 111, 194; doppie 127; ducats 104, 111; florins 75, 76, 78, 84, 89, 95, 106, 111, 130, 131, 140, 141, 143, 164, 177, 180, 181, 192, 195, 200, 205, 214, 216, 218, 244, 268, 276, 277, 282, 283, 286, 298; gold 127; oncia 111; Roman 65

Cola de Madonna Martomea 37, 71

Cola di Bucio de Braccia 232

Cola di Rienzo: abdication and exile 239–42, 271; Albornoz 259; Annibaldo da Ceccano 250–54; antiquity 7; April 1347 revolution 193–94; Aventine meeting 191; Avignon 40, 56, 184, 200, 214, 242, 246, 259, 273–74; background 183; battle of Porta San Lorenzo 229–36; Boniface VIII 230; Campidoglio image 185–86; character 14, 205, 281; Charles IV 272–73; Clement VI 199, 216, 221, 274; clothing and fashion 107, 188, 198, 203, 204, 221, 224, 239, 281, 296; diplomacy 199–200, 205, 213–17, 280, 291; education 10–14; family 213; Florence 214; Fraticelli 272; Henry VII 272; House of Justice and Peace 198; Ianni da Vico 206; Innocent VI 274; justice 198–99, 200–202, 217–18; knighting 219–23; Knights of the Holy Spirit 231; Lateran speech 187–88; letters 273; Lewis IV 199, 215, 221; life and career 2–3; mercenaries 275–80; Naples 199, 215–19; pan-Italian project 5; peacemaking 226, 242; Perugia 207, 213–17; Philip VI 216; psychology 207; ritual and ceremony 203, 205, 219–22, 279; Roman synod 200; Sant'Angelo in Pescheria painting 189–90; Savelli 271; Scripture 216; second rule and death 271–99; Siena 214; Sta. Maria Maddalena painting 271; titles 197

College of Cardinals 36, 246

Colonna: Andreozzo de Normanno 185; battle of Porta San Lorenzo 54, 229–36; family 227; Giovanni, author 14; Giovanni, benefactor 244; Giovanni, cardinal 184, 200; Giovanni (Gianni), the younger 188, 189, 197, 212, 224, 231, 233, 236, 282; Iugurta 297; Landolfo, author 14; Margherita 236; Oddone, of Genazzano 232; opposition to Rienzo 41; Palestrina 196; Pietro di Agapito 205, 224, 231, 232, 234, 236; Sant'Angelo in Pescheria

189; Sciarra 37, 68, 69, 70, 72, 74; Sciarretta 232, 240, 297; Stefanello 193, 257, 282, 283, 291; Stefano, the Elder 23, 31, 37, 51, 61, 64, 65, 123, 136, 188, 193, 196–97, 205, 207, 224–25, 229, 231, 242; Stefano, the Younger (Stefanuccio) 197, 224, 234, 236, 239, 282
comets 62, 87, 94, 97
Como 79, 101, 102, 103
concord 194, 197; personification 194
Conradin, king 85
Conrad IV, king 85
Constantine, emperor 51, 84, 219, 221, 223
Constantinople 66, 147, 149, 209, 210
Conte, Rienzo's nephew 242
Contini, Gianfranco 5
Cornacervina 117, 120, 122
Corneto 193, 196, 207, 260
Corone 150, 158
Coscia, crier 69
Crécy, battle of 8, 43, 161–72, 272
Crema 88, 104
Crispolto, messer 63
Crispolto, St. 254
Crown of Aragon 112
cruelty 50, 55, 105, 112, 113, 169, 184, 227
Crusader States (Outremer) 146
crusades: fourth 66; Iberia 118; March of Ancona 270

## D

da Buscareto, Nicola 261, 262
da Carrara: Marsilio 90, 93; Ubertiello (Ubertino) 90
Dacians 209
da Esi, Lomo 262
da Fontana, family 75
dalla Pira, Iumentaro 262

da Mogliano: Gentile 261, 269; Onestina 269
Dante 4, 14, 29, 62, 67, 185, 188
da Ponte Carradi, Maffeo 137
da Vico: Francesco 212, 231; Ianni (Giovanni), prefect of Rome 203, 206–8, 212, 232, 239, 259
de Agniletto de Vetralla, Nicola 85
de Alesso, Cecco 204
de Allo, Ianni 203
de Andrea, Giovanni 78
de Antonio, Todino 213
de Belgioia, Fiore 150, 153, 155, 156
de Braio Ianni (Jean de Broy, Gian de Brai) 145
debt 24, 97, 98
de Bussa, Raniero 260
de Camerino, Redolfo 262
de Cenne, Nardo 140
*Decretals* 78
degli Abati di Trapani, Alberto 113
degli Ubaldini, Marzia (Madonna Cia) 265–68
de Guido, Pandalfuccio 291
de Guzmán, Eleanor (Donna Leonora) 52, 120, 134
de Iubileo, Buccio 282
de Lando, Manfredo 99
della Cammora, Poncelletto 205
della Scala: Alberto 53, 87–95; Albuino 94; Bartolomeo 94; Cangrande 87, 91, 95; Cangrande II 89, 94; Mastino 52–54, 62, 87–95, 101, 102, 136, 215
delli Alberteschi, Mascia 201
delli Gozzadini, Brandelisio 77
delli Pepoli, Taddeo 214
delli Tumberti, Iurio 266, 267
delli Vastardi, Giacomo 266
dello Fiesco, Ianni 104
dello Schiavo, Antonio di Pietro 72
dello Viecchio, Cecco 297
de'Medici, Cosimo 35

de Santo Severino, Esmeduccio 262
d'Este: family 75; Niccolò 76;
  Obizzo III 76, 214; origins 75;
  Rinaldo 76
de Treio, Fonneruglia 233
di Buccio di Braccia, Cola 212
di Guccio, Giannino 200
Diodorus 257
Dionisio of Portugal, king 121
Dionysius I of Syracuse 140, 257
Dionysius II of Syracuse 257
Domenico da Gravina 243
Dominican Order 15, 78, 79, 80, 236
Doria, Otto 163, 166, 167
Doves. See Venturino, Fra.
Duchy of Spoleto 214
duke of Athens (Walter of Brienne) 46, 47, 62, 135–45, 297
Durazzo 63, 67

**E**

earthquakes 63, 245
Edward II, king 162
Edward III, king 161–174
Edward, the Black Prince 162–71
Egidio Conchese. See Albornoz, Giles.
Eleanor of Anjou 113
Elisabetta, daugther of Feliciano 115, 116
Elizabeth of Bavaria 89
Elizabeth of Hungary, queen 62, 110, 114, 115, 116
*elucutio* 61
Emilius Paulus, consul 237
Enrico II of Castile, king 120
Ephesus 147
Euboea 149
executions 50, 85, 199, 201, 297

**F**

Fabius, consul 237
Faenza 265, 270
Faiano 281

famine 27, 30, 34, 62, 97, 98, 99, 100, 101, 122, 159, 173, 217, 257, 258
Fano 262
Farfa 284
feasts 54, 67, 69, 92, 129, 142, 144, 153, 203, 219, 220, 221, 223, 238, 271
Federico of Sicily, king 113–14
Fei, Arrigo 141, 145
Feliciano, baron 115, 116
Ferdinand IV, king 117
Ferrara 75, 199; battle of 1333 76; d'Este 76; Mastino della Scala 88
festivals 51, 81, 153
Fiamma, Galvano 101, 105
Fieschi, Giovanni (Ianni dello Fiesco) 103
Filino 275
Fiorone, demon 94, 298
Flaminius, consul 237
floods 27, 62, 124, 175–78
Florence: Anziani 139, 143; Blacks and Whites 72; coinage 65; diplomacy 77; duke of Athens 47, 135–44; floods 178; Fra Venturino 80; Great Company 275; Lucca 141; Mastino della Scala 88–95, 136, 141; Palace of the Priors 141, 142; Palazzo Vecchio (degli Anziani) 139; Pisa 137, 141
Foggia 158
Fogliara Vecchia 148, 150
Forlì 215, 263, 264, 265, 266, 268, 269, 270
Forlimpopoli 263
Fortifocca, Tommaso 8, 185, 205
fortitude 186
Fortuna Primigenia, temple 282
fortune 112, 113, 291
Fossombrone 262
France 1, 43, 175
Franciscans 78, 79, 95, 114, 139, 149, 152, 225; burials 253; Fraticelli 272; Poor Clares 236; Spirituals

11, 74, 272; Sta. Maria in Aracoeli 235, 289
Frangipane, Petruccio 233
Frascati 284, 290
Frederick II, emperor 85
Froissart, Jean 27
Frosinone 192

## G

*gabelle* 137, 141. *See also* taxes.
Gaeta 214
Gaius Terentius Varro 237
Galen 86, 134, 147
Garbo (al-Gharb) 119
Gardiner, Eileen 29, 209
Gascony 163
Gauls 14, 298
Genazzano 224, 232
Genoa: Chios 148; cityscape 132; crossbowmen 163, 166, 167; fleet 132; Naples 179; port 132; slavery 132; Smyrna crusade 148, 150; trade 180; Venice 146, 159
George, St. 194
Germany 63, 67, 85, 159, 170, 215, 222, 262, 278, 300
Ghibellines 11, 62, 67, 72, 73, 138, 159, 263, 300
Ghisalberti, Alberto Maria 8, 58, 285
Giazolo 263
Gibraltar 62, 117, 119, 129, 133
Ginzera. *See* Algeciras.
Giotto 185, 186
Giovanna I, queen 111, 114, 115, 179, 180, 215, 216, 218–19, 240, 251, 264, 266
Giovanni, count of Vallemontone 260
Giovanni da Ceccano 253
Giovanni da Gravina (della Rascione), prince 67
Giovanni de Lucca 248
Giovinale, Paolo 23, 64

*Glossa Ordinaria* 78
Gonzaga, Filippino de 215
governance 39, 40, 42, 45, 46, 47, 50, 54, 55, 56, 57, 246, 263, 278
grain 34, 77, 97, 98, 99, 119, 141, 150, 165, 166, 169, 193, 195, 196, 217, 226, 227, 231, 240, 257, 258, 269, 285, 289, 292
Granada 117, 119, 130
Greece 67, 148, 151, 158, 210
Gregory the Great 14, 208, 209
Grimaldi, Carlo 163, 166
Guarnieri, count 102
Guelfs 11, 62, 67, 72, 73, 138, 159, 266
Guglielmo of Assisi 139, 143, 144
Gui de Boulogne, cardinal legate 246, 251, 274
Gui de Montpellier 100
Guido da Prato, physician 252

## H

Hannibal 18, 237–39, 279
Henry of Asti 149
Henry VII, emperor 111, 170, 272
Hermits of St. Augustine 78
Hippocrates 134
Hohenstaufen 71, 85, 110
Hospitallers of Assisi 208
Hospitallers of St. John in Jerusalem 180, 276, 289
humanism, Renaissance 19
Humbert II of Vienne 158–61
Hundred Years War 264
Hungary, ancient 209
hunger. *See* famine.

## I

Iberia 1, 25, 43
Ilerda (Lérida) 122
Imola 263
Innocent VI, pope 41, 256, 258, 260, 265, 278
Internullo, Dario 10, 18
Isabella of France, queen 161

Ischia 179
Isidore of Seville 14, 24, 59, 147
Iubaltare. *See* Gibraltar.
Izmir. *See* Smyrna crusade.

## J
Jacobus de Voragine 253
James (John) III of Majorca, king 163, 164, 167, 169
Jerusalem 110, 149, 186, 202, 256, 280
John II, king of France 145, 270
John of Bohemia, king 62, 161, 163, 164, 166, 169, 170, 171, 172, 242, 272
John of Normandy, duke 161, 163, 164, 166, 169, 170, 171, 172, 173–74, 242, 272
John the Evangelist, St. 147, 153
John XXII, pope 11, 62, 67, 74, 81, 83, 247
Juan Manuel (Ianni Manuelle) 30, 52, 53, 55, 70, 100, 104, 120–25, 206, 207, 282
jubilee 29, 40, 42, 63, 136, 244, 246–50
Judea 217
Julius Caesar 183, 210
justice: communal 38, 43, 44, 47, 50; cruelty 55; divine 190, 202, 289; harsh 104, 111, 112; liberty 194, 199, 272; mercy 45, 49, 50, 54; orb 215; peace and prosperity 39, 40, 41, 42, 56, 79, 191; personal virtue 55; personifications & symbols 192, 193, 202; retributive 38, 39, 40, 41, 42, 43, 44, 45, 47, 48, 49, 50, 54, 55, 56, 79, 89, 104, 105, 106, 111, 112, 183, 186, 190, 191, 192, 194, 197, 199, 202, 203, 216, 225, 244, 272, 289; Romans 183; tyrannical 49; unequal 49, 50; virtues 186

Justinian I, emperor 78

## K
Knights Hospitaller 159
Knights Templar 161
Koran 133

## L
La Colomma de Chiaravalle 102
Lake Trasimene 237
Languedoc 78
l'Aquila 14
Lavagna 103
Lazio 85, 110, 130, 247
Leo I, pope 210
Leo IV, pope 68
Leonardo de Orvieto 62, 182
Lewis IV, emperor 37, 62, 67, 74, 83–84, 89, 111, 263
Lewis of Hungary, king 63, 114, 215, 217, 218, 243, 244, 246, 251, 263, 266, 275
liberty 36, 106, 194, 199, 238, 272, 295; personification 193
*Liber ystoriarum Romanorum* 14, 271
literacy 258
livestock 30, 46, 100, 174, 177, 227, 282, 284, 285, 291
Livia, Rienzo's wife 213, 220, 241
Livy, Titus 14, 18, 19, 20, 59, 60, 96, 97, 183, 236–38, 274, 276, 279, 298
Locciolo Pellicciaro 49, 294, 295
Lodi 102, 104, 106
Lombardy 62, 75, 79, 80, 87, 97, 104, 175, 199, 214, 237, 246, 262; famine 98; kingdom 89; Mastino della Scala 88; mercenaries 102; tyrants 89; war 101
Lorenzetti, Ambrogio 193
Louis, count of Flanders 163, 164, 166, 168, 172
Louis of Taranto, prince 215, 216, 251, 266
Louis X, king 200

Lovati, Lovato 17
Lubertiello, son of Vertollo. *See* Orsini: Robertello.
Lucan 18, 59
Lucca 88, 136, 137
Lunisciana 88
Luxemburg 170, 272

## M
Maccantregola 228
Macellaro, Ianni 30, 100, 294
Macerata 262
Madonna Cia. *See* degli Ubaldini, Marzia.
Magnacuccia, Stefanello 193
Maharbal 18, 238
Malabranca: Agnilo, chancellor 216, 231; Latino 80; Matteo 231
Malatesta: Galeotto I 77, 137, 215, 261, 262; Malatesta II, of Rimini 77, 137, 215, 261, 262, 265, 267, 275, 278; Rimini 264
Malerva (Malherba, Malerba, Raynald von Giver) 101, 102, 103, 104, 152, 153, 155, 156.
Malieti 213
Mamluks 118
Mancino: Cecco 194, 242; Conte 194
Manfredi lords 270
Manfred of Corneto 207
Mantua 79, 215
manuscripts: Brussels, Bibliothèque Royale, MS 10168–72 271; Venice, Biblioteca Marciana di Venezia, Cod. Cartaceo 4802 58
March of Ancona 63, 256, 260–62
Marcian, emperor 15, 209, 210
Marcuzi, Giuliano di Coluccio 235
Maremma 199
Marie des Baux 158
Marinids 117, 118, 119
Marino 207, 224, 226–29, 238

Marittima 206, 212
Marseille 141, 179, 224, 232, 234
Marsiglio of Padua 11, 74
Marta 259, 260
Martino del Porto 34, 37, 48, 200
Martin of Poland (Martinus Oppaviensis, of Troppau) 14, 15, 209
Martin, St. 230
Massinissa, king 105, 106
Matalena, Rienzo's mother 183
Matteo da Viterbo, physician 252
Medes 118
memory 41
mercenaries: Burgundian 103; Company of San Giorgio 102; French 121; German 103, 121, 278; Great Company 180, 181, 251, 266, 275, 278, 286; Hungarians 266, 291; Malerva 102
mercy: battlefield 171, 233; Christian 45, 95, 99, 101, 264; communal 36, 54, 296; divine 116, 287; foolish 47–53; governance 105, 112, 118, 140; papal 250, 262, 268; royal 113, 127, 173, 174
Merulus, monk 209
Messina 113
Metellina 148
Michelangelo 223
Migliaro, Liello 204
Milan: Fra Venturino 79; Lombardy 102; mercenaries 102; militia 102; Parabiago 101, 103, 104, 152; Patarines 247; Visconti 49, 102, 104, 106, 246
*Mirabilia urbis Romae* 14
Modena 158
Modone 150
Monaco 141, 179
Monsilice 94
monstrosities 37, 62, 75, 199

Montagna 213, 284
Montecassino 237, 251
Monte Comprati 284, 290
Montefiascone 258, 259, 260, 274, 277
Montefliaterano 275
Monte Maiella 272, 273
Monticielli 212
Moors 117, 128, 130, 132
Morbasciano 46, 148–50, 158, 159, 160
Morea 62, 66, 67
Morreale, Fra (Montréal d'Albarno) 49, 58, 180, 275–90
Morocco 117, 119
Mostafa, ameli 152
Muhammad 118, 120, 129, 133
Muhammad IV, king 120
Muratori, Ludovico 4, 5

N
Naples: Angevins 66, 110; kingdom (Regno) 67, 179, 215, 237, 240, 251, 263, 266; royal court 111, 114, 243; Sta. Chiara 110; trade 180
Narbonne 180, 275
Narni 67, 207, 259, 260
Navarre 121, 123
Nebuchadnezzar 280
Negroponte 149, 158
Nelli, Francesco 274
Nepi 227
Nero, emperor 59
Nicholas V, antipope 74
Nicola di Agniletto of Vetralla 10
Nolfo (Arnolfo?), of Cyprus 152, 153, 155, 156
Normandy 162
notaries 9, 10, 12, 35, 40, 42, 135, 183, 184, 187, 191, 193, 194, 198, 200, 203, 218, 222, 242, 294, 297
*Novellae* 78
Novella, Lady 78
Numidia 105, 106

O
Obeda (Úbeda) 127
Octavian (Octavius Caesar) 59, 210
Ordelaffi, Francesco II 11, 215, 263–69
Orhan Gazi, sultan 148
Orlando, count 102
Orsini: Andrea de Campo di Fiori 67, 70; Bertoldo de Francesco de Monte 67, 72, 242, 256–60; Bertoldo (Vertollo) di Napoleone 224, 231; Castel Sant'Angelo 216; Cola del Castel Sant'Angelo 206, 224, 231; family 53, 54, 180, 202; Giordano de Marino 206, 207, 224, 226, 227, 228, 231, 232, 235, 238, 239, 240; Giordano de Monte 224; Giordano 197, 260; Giovanni Gaietano, cardinal 67; Maria 71; Matteuzzo 64; Napoleone 51, 61, 64, 65, 67, 74; Orso del Castel Sant'Angelo 64; Orso of Vicovaro 224; Poncello of Castel Sant'Angelo 23, 64, 65; Raynaldo de Marino 197, 224–28; Robertello (Lubertiello) 224, 231
Orte 279
Orvieto 182, 192, 214, 259, 260
Osman I, sultan 148
Ostia 179, 180, 263

P
Paderno 262
Padua: Anonimo Romano 9; Carrara 215; Cuorvo Bridge 93; della Scala 88, 93, 95; gates 94; Mastino della Scala 89, 90; mercenaries 102; Porta di Santa Croce 93; Scrovegni Chapel 186; Venice 87
Palazzino 266
Palaeologos, John V, emperor 147
Palestrina 58, 64, 196, 229, 282–86, 290, 291

Pamphylia (Pamfilia) 147
Pamplona 121
*Panegyric to Robert of Anjou from the Citizens of Prato* 185
Pannonia 209, 210
Pantano 282, 284
Papal States 76, 214, 258
Papirius 299
Parabiagio, battle of 62, 97, 101–6, 152
Parialoco (Paleologoi) 147, 148
Paris; Crécy 161, 163, 164, 166; royal court 138, 170; Sainte-Chapelle 164; university 135
Parma 88, 104
Parthians 118, 119
Patarines 92, 93, 247, 250, 263, 269, 273, 274
Patmos 147
Patras 150, 158
Patrimony of St. Peter 63, 214, 256, 258, 260, 274
Paul, St. 187, 190, 193, 198, 288
Pavia 237
peace: concord 158, 194, 226; liberty and justice 38–42, 56, 79, 104, 191, 194, 199, 272; inner 250; order and security 38, 48, 110, 189, 198, 219, 242, 276, 285; symbol and personification 80, 194, 279; treaties 95, 208, 217, 237, 242. *See also* Rome: House of Justice and Peace.
peacemaking 22, 141, 189, 198, 203, 261, 287. *See also* Rome: House of Justice and Peace.
Peña del Çiervo 117
Pera 148
Pergamo (Pergamum) 147
Persians 119, 130
Perugia 59, 133, 254, 259, 262, 275, 276, 278; Hannibal 237
Pesaro 262
Peter, St. 80, 187, 190, 194, 253, 288

Petrarch, Francesco: Andrew of Hungary 114; Avignon 274; Charles IV 300; Colonna 184, 240; Cola di Rienzo 5, 7, 274 et passim; crusades 146; earthquake of 1349 245; humanism 4, 5–6, 7, 16, 30–31; letters 27; scholarly research into 4; Roman barons 36, 225, 238; Rome 13, 32, 185, 251
Phaedrus, fabulist 107
Philadelphia (Filadelfia) 107, 146, 147, 150, 158
Philip IV, the Fair, king 161
Philip V, king 74
Philip VI, king 130, 138, 161–74
Phrygia 147
Piacenza 98, 99, 104
Picazzo (Pytazius, Picaço). *See* Abū Mālik 'Abd al-Wāhid.
Piedmont 99, 237
Pietro Rainallucci da Corbara. *See* Nicholas V, antipope.
Piglio 212
Piombino 179
Pipino, Giovanni (Janni), paladin 240–43
Pisa 78, 136, 179; grain supplies 98
Pisciainsanti, butcher 30, 178
Pistoia 138, 214
*pitture infamanti* 227, 242
plague 2, 134, 244, 253; Black Death 244
Plantagenets 161
Pliny 146
Plutarch 257
Poitiers, battle of 145, 270
Ponte della Paglia 192
Ponte di Ceperano 192
Po River 75, 76
Porta, Giuseppe 6, 58
Porta San Lorenzo, battle 54, 229–36, 285

Porto 34, 37, 48, 179, 180, 201, 212
poverty 98, 99, 101, 144, 184, 253, 272, 283, 288, 290
power: authority 29, 47, 118, 120, 187, 195, 248, 249, 276; baronial 36, 39, 68, 196, 229, 231, 298; communal 35, 38, 39; dangers 39; force 88, 111, 162; governance and rule 2, 39, 40, 41, 45, 47, 65, 144, 207, 212, 216, 238, 239, 271, 281, 291, 292; religious 46, 271, 280; social nature of 51–58; symbols of 277
Prague 170, 242, 272, 273, 281
Prato 138
Prefect of Rome. *See* da Vico, Ianni.
proper names 221
Provence 100, 111, 112, 121, 158, 179, 180, 264, 265, 269, 274, 275
prudence 186
Puglia. *See* Naples: kingdom (Regno). *See also* Apulia.
Punic Wars 279
Puortica. *See* Rome: Leonine City.

# R

Ravenna 263
Raymond of Orvieto, papal vicar 214, 222
Reggio Emilia 88
Regno. *See* Naples: kingdom (Regno).
Respampano 206–8, 212, 260
Rhodes 158, 159
Ribolla 281
Ricciaferra (Fatima), queen 118, 125–26, 129
Rienzi (Rienzo). *See* Cola di Rienzo.
Rienzo, Lorenzo 239
Rieti 212, 214
Rimini 59, 77, 215, 261, 262, 265, 267
Rio Salado, battle of 25, 43, 53, 117–33, 258
Robert of Naples (Anjou), king: Beatific Vision 247; death and entombment 62, 110; duke of Athens 138; Giovanna I 114; justice 50, 110–11; last will and testament 114; magic 110, 112; papacy 74; Pipino 240, 243; Rome 37, 64, 66, 67; Sicily 112–13
Romagna 63, 199, 215, 256, 261, 262, 263, 268; lords 75, 76
Romanesco 4, 15
Romania. *See* Byzantium.
Romans, antiquity 96
Rome: Agone Games 80; Anglophone scholarship 6; Arenula 177; authority 222; Aventine Hill 191; Baptistry of San Giovanni 221; barons 36; Borgo Santo Spirito 249; Camera 46, 184, 191, 194; Camigliano 199; Campagna 99, 199, 206, 212, 214, 224, 226, 237, 289, 291; Campidoglio (Capitoline) 23, 53, 61, 64, 65, 69, 72, 80, 184, 185, 194, 196, 197, 198, 201, 202, 205, 207, 208, 212, 223, 224, 227, 238, 239, 240, 242, 256, 280, 281, 286, 290, 293, 294, 298; Campidoglio market 208, 293; Campo de' Fiori 64, 218; Campo Marzio (Campo dell'Austa) 176, 297; Capitoline Museums 187, 201, 223; Castel Sant'Angelo 62, 64, 67, 68, 72, 177, 206, 224, 241, 271; census 206; classical remains 31–32; Colosseum 32; Column of Marcus Aurelius 176; commune 34–35; Constantine's baptismal font 221, 223; Constantine's equestrian statue 222; District 192, 214, 258; economy 33;

## INDEX

Faithful 204; famine 30, 97, 98; Felici chapel 235; *Felix Societas Pavesatorum et Balistrariorum* 203, 248; fish market 64, 189; floods 30, 62, 175–77; Folserace 176; food supply 34; Fra Venturino 80–81; Ghetto 241; governing elite 28, 40, 44; guilds 9, 34, 35; Hospital of Santo Spirito in Sassia 30, 70, 71, 100, 136, 177, 248, 249, 253; Hospital of the Cross (Acuto) 114, 208; House of Justice and Peace 50, 198; Incarcerata 68, 70, 249; Jewish community 33, 176, 241, 297; jubilee of 1350 246–50; Leonine City 68, 99, 177; markets 217–18, 256; Mastino della Scala 88; Mausoleum of Augustus 176, 297; militia 203, 205; mills 177, 183; Milvian Bridge (*See* Rome: Ponte Milvio, Mollo); Montecitorio 176; Monte Mario 279; Monte Testaccio 51, 81, 92; Monument 231; Oppian Hill 177; Palazzo Lalli 241; Palazzo Santacroce 64; Pantheon (Sta. Maria Rotonda) 32, 114, 115, 175; papacy 57; Piazza Colonna 176; Piazza de Castello 70, 271; Piazza del Popolo 176; Piazza di San Pietro 247; Piazza Giudea 176; Piazza Navona 52, 81; Piazza of the Armenians 72; Piazza San Marcello 196; Piazza Santo Spirito 72; pilgrims 29, 114, 249; politics 11, 34–39; *pomerium* 188; Ponte Milvio (Mollo) 114, 115, 208; Ponte San Pietro 69, 204, 229; *popolo* 12, 38; population 33; Porta Arcella (Arzeli) 70; Porta Castel Sant'Angelo (Porta Castello) 67, 279; Porta Cavalleggieri 99; Porta del Popolo 176; Porta Ostiense 177; Porta San Giovanni (Maggiore) 69, 227, 282; Porta San Lorenzo (Porta Tiburtina) 54, 231, 232; Porta San Paolo 177; Porta San Pietro 177; Porta Verdara (Viridaria) 71; Portica of Octavia 32, 72, 176, 189; prefect 203, 206, 207, 208, 212, 231, 239, 259, 260; Puortica (Vatican Borgo) 69, 177, 247; Quirinal Hill 244; religious life 28–30; *rione* Colonna 70, 84, 176, 240, 293; *rione* Monti 70; *rione* Regola 64, 183, 203, 295; *rione* Ripa 190, 293; *rione* Sant'Angelo 189, 193, 240, 293; *rione* Trevi 293, 297; *rioni* 65, 69, 194–95, 292; Ripa Armea (Romea) 201; San Brancacio 177; San Clemente 258; San Crisogono 251; San Giacomo in Settignano (alla Lunghara) 176; San Giorgio in Velabro (della Chiavica) 190, 191; San Giovanni in Laterano 81, 84, 187, 219, 223, 245, 249; San Lorenzo fuori le Mura 196, 231; San Lorenzo in Lucina 247; San Lorenzo in Piscibus 99; San Marcello 196, 297; San Michele (Sant'Angelo de Micinellis) 249; San Paolo fuori le Mura (San Paolo Maggiore) 83, 177, 245, 249; San Salvatore in Pesoli 240; San Silvestro in Capite 176, 236; San Sisto 80; San Stanislao dei Polacchi 240; Sant'Anastasio 198; Sant'Andrea de Colonna 176; Sant'Andrea della Valle 176; Sant'Angelo in Pescheria 32, 72, 176, 189, 193, 240, 241; San Tommaso ai Cenci 183; San Trifone 176; Senate 187;

327

Senate Palace 85, 223, 256, 293; society 12; SS. Celso e Giuliano 229; SS. Michele e Magno (Sant'Angelo delle Scale) 249; SS. Nereo e Achilleo 135; Sta. Maria in Aracoeli 63, 64, 65, 208, 235, 244, 289, 293; Sta. Maria in Publicolis (de Publico) 23, 64; Sta. Maria in Traspontina 68, 72; Sta. Maria Maddalena 271; Sta. Maria Maggiore 248; Sta. Maria Nuova 231; Sta. Maria sopra Minerva 80, 236; St. Peter's 10, 62, 63, 68, 70, 72, 79, 82, 84–85, 135, 185, 203, 204, 249, 253, 255, 300; Synagogue 183; Tarpeian Rock 298; Temple of the Sun 244; Theater of Marcellus 32, 72, 176; Thirteen Good Men 184; Torre dei Conti 245; Twenty-Eight Good Men 65; Vatican 68, 69, 71, 146, 177; Vatican Gardens 71; Via della Scrofa 176; Via Lata (del Corso) 176, 236; Via Trastevere 176; Via Triumphalis 279; Widow 185
Roscio: Ianni 213; Pietro 93, 94
Rouen 135, 162

**S**

Saguntum 237
Saint Denis 164
Saint-Lô (Saluppo) 162
Salim of Benamarin (Bellamarina), king 118, 126
Sallust 14, 18, 59
salt 45, 90, 91, 98, 137, 192, 195, 239, 291. *See also* taxes.
Samnium 96
San Columbano 104
San Germano 251
San Giorgio 190, 191, 252, 253
San Miniato 138

San Severino, count of 72
Sant'Eustachio, family 68
Saracens 77, 118, 122, 124, 125, 126, 127, 130, 131, 132; black 119; Spain 117
Savelli: family 23, 61, 64, 65, 68, 69, 176, 197, 240; Francesco 197; Giacomo 23, 61, 64, 65, 68, 69; Luca 224, 240, 242
Savoy 264
Scaraglino 266, 267
Scarpetta, constable 241
Scipio Africanus 279
Scuotto, Vico 221
Seibt, Gustav 10, 24, 25
Sempronius, consul 237
Seneca 183
Serafin, bodyguard 125
Serchio River 137
Servilius, consul 237
Seville 14, 24, 59, 117, 120, 121, 122, 134
Sicilian Vespers 112
Sicily 65, 110, 112 14, 140, 190, 257
sickness 97
Siena 144, 193, 259, 275
Simone of Casentino 144
slavery 97, 98, 128
Smyrna crusade 37, 43, 46, 62, 146–60
Solomon 60
Spain 175
splendor 31, 37, 51
Spoleto 214, 237
*spolia* 85
Stefaneschi, Giacomo di Pietro 14
Stephen, St. 256
Strabo 146
*studia humanitatis* 7
Sufis 119
Sulpicius Severus 230

## T

Taliffa (Tarifa) 119, 120, 122, 258
Talleyrand, Elia, cardinal 274
Tarlati di Pietramala, Pier Saccone 138
taxes: authority 189; customs 149, 192; excessive 46, 298; fines 46, 111, 192, 195, 204, 205; *gabelle* 137, 141; hearth 45, 191, 195, 206; livestock 192; ports and fortresses 46; salt 91, 192; Seca (Sega) 137; tolls 149, 195; wine 291
Tebaldo Santo Stati 68
Tecino River 237
temperance 186, 201
Terni 214, 259
Terra di Lavoro 110
Tiberius, emperor 189
Tiber River 70, 97, 175–79, 192, 212, 227
Tivoli 130, 212, 214, 270, 282, 283, 284, 285, 289, 290
Todi 177, 207, 214
Tornello, Haundello 171
Tortora, currier 202
torture 140, 143, 286
Toscanella 274
Toulouse 121
Trapani 112
Trebesten (Tlemcen) 118, 119
Trent 102, 103
Treviso 88, 95, 101
Troy 186
Turkey 62, 146, 150, 175
Turks 118, 124, 126, 130, 133, 146, 149, 151, 152, 153, 154, 156, 157, 158, 159; commerce 148
Tuscany 67, 88, 137, 138, 199, 205, 206, 213, 226, 237, 259, 262, 272, 286, 287; Great Company 275
Tusculum 247
tyrants 75, 77, 88, 89, 192, 199, 202, 213, 214, 215, 257, 258, 273

## U

Umbria 259
Umur Bey (Umur Ghazi, Umur Pashi) 147. *See also* Morbasciano.

## V

Vaiani: family 177; Paolo 177
Valentino, count 168
Valerius Maximus 21, 105, 183, 210, 257
Vallati, Cola 193
Valmontone 9
Varvieri, Ianni 213, 294
Vaucluse 274
Velletri 214, 284, 285
Venice: battle standard 94; Camera 90, 91; diplomacy 92, 96, 199; Ferrara 75; fleet 149; Genoa 146; papacy 157; patricians 91; salt works 91, 92; Verona 92, 101
Venturino, Fra 62, 79–81, 92, 157
Verona: comet 87; della Scala 52, 87, 88, 90, 94, 95, 101, 215, 298; Mastino della Scala 88, 95; mercenaries 102; San Salvato 88
Veronica 81
Vertollo, count. *See* Orsini: Bertoldo di Napoleone.
Vertonuccio 266
Vespasian, emperor 187, 188, 189
Vetralla 10, 85, 206, 207, 208
Via Appia 231
Via Prenestina 282
Vicenza 88, 95
Villani, Giovanni 2, 13, 21, 35, 79, 90, 136, 143; Andrew of Hungary 114; chronology 265; Crécy 162, 165; floods 178
Villani, Matteo 13
violence 27, 36, 40, 43, 55, 56, 144
Visconti: Azzo (Azzone) 101, 102, 103, 104; Bruzo 106; family 99; Giovanni, archbishop 104, 246;

329

Isabella 103; Lodrisio 101, 102, 103, 104; Lucchino 49, 50, 101, 103, 104–8, 199, 214
Visdomini, Ceretieri 145
*Vita di Cola di Rienzo tribuno del popolo romano* 3
Viterbo 80, 193, 206, 207, 212, 214, 253, 259, 260, 274, 275
Vitorchiano 204, 212
Volterra 138
Volturno River 237
von Bongartz, Anechin 266
von Giver, Raynald. *See* Malerva.
von Landau, Conrad 266

## W

Waiblingen. *See* Hohenstaufen.
Walter of Brienne. *See* duke of Athens.
weights and measures 41, 51, 97, 124
Welfs. *See* Guelfs.
William of Occam 74

wine 39, 51, 54, 77, 98, 149, 178, 219, 222, 223, 227, 251, 263, 273, 276; casks 159, 201; Faiano 281; Greek 281, 292; Malvasia 104, 150, 158, 281; Ribolla 281; taxes 291
Witt, Ronald G. 17
women 35, 54, 97, 99, 100, 104, 115, 119, 128, 151, 157, 176, 180, 186, 203, 207, 219, 220, 223, 227, 236, 268, 275, 276, 279, 289, 293
Wright, John 8

## Y

Yusuf I, king 117, 119

## Z

Zaccaria, Martino 34, 37, 48, 148, 152, 153, 154, 155, 180, 200, 201, 203
Zaganella, Giovanni 266
Zama, battle of 106, 279
Zeno, Pietro 149, 151, 152, 153, 154, 155
Ziziria 127

*Production of This Book Was Completed on 15 June 2021 at Italica Press, Clifton, Bristol, United Kingdom. It Was Set in Adobe Bembo, Adobe Bembo Expert & Apple Wingdings*

www.ingramcontent.com/pod-product-compliance
Lightning Source LLC
Chambersburg PA
CBHW030101170426
43198CB00009B/453